1 & 2 Thessalonians
Preaching Verse by Verse

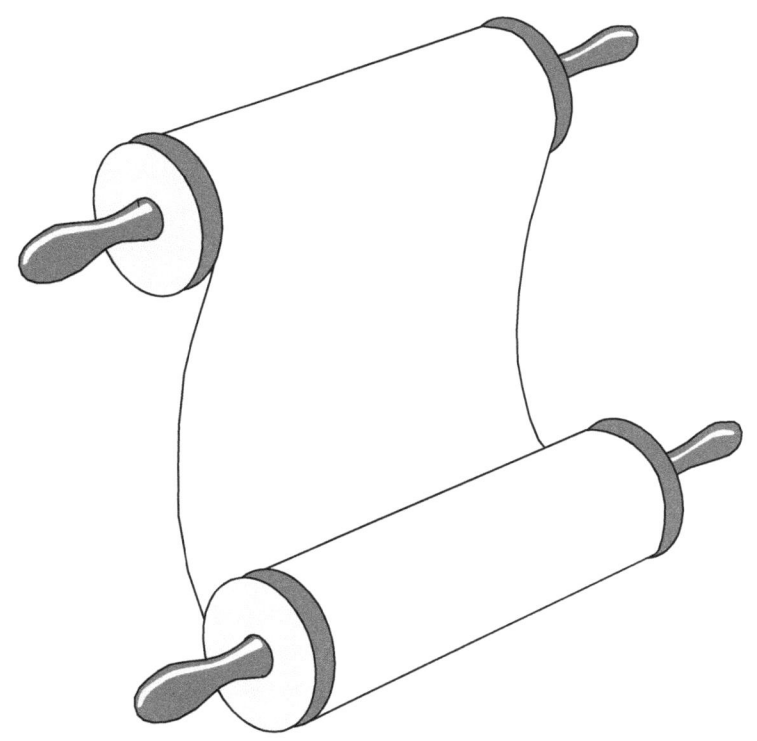

Pastor D. A. Waite, Th.D., Ph.D.

Published by
THE BIBLE FOR TODAY PRESS
900 Park Avenue
Collingswood, New Jersey 08108 U.S.A.
Pastor D. A. Waite, Th.D., Ph.D.
Bible For Today Baptist Church
Church Phone: 856-854-4747
BFT Phone: 856-854-4452
Orders: 1-800-John 10:9
e-mail: BFT@BibleForToday.org
Website: www.BibleForToday.org
FAX: 856-854-2464

We Use and Defend
the King James Bible

Copyright, 2015
All Rights Reserved
December, 2015

BFT #4137

ISBN #978-1-56848-102-9

Acknowledgments

I wish to thank and to acknowledge the assistance of the following people:

- **The Congregation** of the **Bible For Today Baptist Church**—for whom these messages were prepared, to whom they were delivered, and by whom they were published. They listened attentively and encouraged their Pastor.
- **Yvonne Sanborn Waite**—my wife, who encouraged the publication of these sermons, read the manuscript, developed the various boxes, suggested sentences to underline, and gave other helpful suggestions and comments. The boxes help the reader to see some of the more important topics that are covered in the various chapters.
- **Patricia Canter**—a friend of Mrs. Waite who volunteered to take the cassette tapes of the verse by verse exposition of the book of Hebrews and put these words into digital format to be used for this book.
- **Tamara A. Waite**—one of our daughters-in-law, who attends our church services regularly, is a helper in many of our church projects, and has devoted many hours to her very detailed verse verifications, and other detailed proofreading of the book before its publication.
- **Dr. Kirk DiVietro**—a friend for many years, one of our Dean Burgon Society Vice Presidents, who is an expert on the use of computers. He has helped in various ways to make the computer work easier when performing the needed tasks.

Foreword

- **The Beginning.** This book is the **eleventh** in a series of books based on my expository preaching from various books of the Bible. It is an attempt to bring to the minds of the readers two things: (1) the **meaning** of the words in the verses and (2) the practical **application** of those words to the lives of both saved and unsaved.
- **Preached Sermons.** These were messages that I preached to our **Bible For Today Baptist Church** in Collingswood, New Jersey. They were broadcast over the radio, and over the Internet by computer streaming around the world. They are now eventually all placed on the following LINK #1 for further use for people. http://www.sermonaudio.com/search.asp?speakeronly=true&currsection=sermonsspeaker&keyword=D._A._Waite,_Th.D.,_Ph.D. As the messages were preached, I took half a chapter each Sunday.
- **Other Verses.** In connection with both the **meaning** and **application** of the verses in this book, there are many verses from other places in the Bible that have been quoted for further elaboration on the teachings in this book. All the verses of Scripture that were used to illustrate further truth are written out in full for easy reference.
- **A Transcription.** This entire book was typed into computer format by Patricia Canter from the tape recordings of the messages as they were preached. Click the LINK #2 below to see and hear these. In addition to the words used as I preached these sermons, I have added other words for clarification as needed.
  http://biblefortoday.org/AudioBibleSermons/1thessalonians.htm
  http://biblefortoday.org/AudioBibleSermons/2thessalonians.htm
- **The Audience.** The intended audience for this book is the same as the audience that listened to the messages in the first place. These studies are not meant to be overly scholarly, though there are some references to various Greek Words used. My aim and burden is to try to help genuine Christians to understand the Words of God. It is also my hope that my children, grandchildren, great grandchildren, and many others might profit from this study of 1&2 Thessalonians. The INDEX takes you to any word or topic.

Yours For God's Words,

D. A. Waite

Pastor D. A. Waite, Th.D., Ph.D.
Bible For Today Baptist Church

Table of Contents

Publisher's Data.. i
Acknowledgments..................................... ii
Foreword... iii
Table of Contents..................................... iv
1 Thessalonians Chapter One......................... 1
1 Thessalonians Chapter Two........................ 37
1 Thessalonians Chapter Three...................... 71
1 Thessalonians Chapter Four....................... 103
1 Thessalonians Chapter Five....................... 143
2 Thessalonians Chapter One........................ 197
2 Thessalonians Chapter Two........................ 231
2 Thessalonians Chapter Three...................... 267
Index of Words and Phrases........................ 309
About the Author.................................... 339
Order Blank Pages................................... 341
Defined King James Bible Orders................... 347

1 Thessalonians Chapter One

The Background Of 1 Thessalonians

This book was written by Paul on his second missionary journey. In Acts 15, he stood up with Barnabas and chose Silas to go with him. In Acts 16, he found Timothy who also went with him. These three made up a team. They were writing to the church which was located in the city of Thessalonica.

Verses That Mention Thessalonica or The Thessalonians

- **Acts 17:1**
"Now when they passed through Amphipolis and Apollonia, they came to Thessalonica, where was a synagogue of the Jews."

In this verse, we see that there was a synagogue in the city of Thessalonica.

- **Acts 17:11**
"These were more noble than those in Thessalonica, in that they received the word with all readiness of mind, and searched the scriptures daily, whether those things were so."

I like this verse, because it is talking about those in Berea. My home for many years was in Berea, Ohio. Mrs. Waite and I both graduated from the Berea High School. According to this verse, those who lived in Berea of Asia Minor were *"more noble"* than those in Thessalonica because of the way they received the Words of God *"with all readiness of mind, and searched the scriptures daily."*

- **Acts 17:13**
"But when the Jews of Thessalonica had knowledge that the word of God was preached of Paul at Berea, they came thither also, and stirred up the people."

THE JEWS' HATRED OF PAUL

The Thessalonian Jews hated that Paul preached the gospel to those at Berea. So they went to Berea and *"stirred up the people."*

- **Acts 20:4**

"And there accompanied him into Asia Sopater of Berea; and of the Thessalonians, Aristarchus and Secundus; and Gaius of Derbe, and Timotheus; and of Asia, Tychicus and Trophimus."

This verse shows that there were two men from Thessalonica who accompanied him on his missionary journeys to Asia.

- **Acts 27:2**

"And entering into a ship of Adramyttium, we launched, meaning to sail by the coasts of Asia; *one* Aristarchus, a Macedonian of Thessalonica, being with us."

Aristarchus, of Thessalonica, was with Paul on that journey to Rome where the ship was wrecked in the storm.

- **Philippians 4:16**

"For even in Thessalonica ye sent once and again unto my necessity."

The Thessalonian Christians, on various occasions, gave to Paul to meet his needs.

- **1 Thessalonians 1a**

"Paul, and Silvanus, and Timotheus, unto the church of the Thessalonians which is in God the Father and *in* the Lord Jesus Christ: . . ."

THE CHURCH HAD SAVED MEMBERS IN IT

This church in Thessalonica had members in it who were genuinely born-again and saved.

- **2 Timothy 4:10**

"For Demas hath forsaken me, having loved this present world, and is departed unto Thessalonica; Crescens to Galatia, Titus unto Dalmatia.

After Demas forsook Paul, "having loved this present world," he went to Thessalonica.

The Background Of The Church At Thessalonica

- **Acts 17:1-2**

"Now when they had passed through Amphiplis and Apollponia, they came to Thessalonica, where was a synagogue of the Jews: And Paul, as his manner was, went in unto them, and three sabbath days reasoned with them out of the scriptures,"

PAUL WAS THERE FOR THREE WEEKS

Paul spent three weeks in Thessalonica, reasoning with them from the Words of God.

- Acts 17:3-4

"Opening and alleging, that Christ must needs have suffered, and risen again from the dead; and that this Jesus, whom I preach unto you, is Christ. And some of them believed, and consorted with Paul and Silas; and of the devout Greeks a great multitude, and of the chief women not a few."

A GREAT MULTITUDE WERE SAVED

The Lord used Paul to win to a saving faith in the Lord Jesus Christ *"a great multitude"* of the men and women in Thessalonica.

- Acts 17:5-6

"But the Jews which believed not, moved with envy, took unto them certain lewd fellows of the baser sort, and gathered a company, and set all the city on an uproar, and assaulted the house of Jason, and sought to bring them out to the people. And when they found them not, they drew Jason and certain brethren unto the rulers of the city, crying, These that have turned the world upside down are come hither also;"

The *"baser sort"* of unbelievers who were in Thessalonica rose up against those who were Christians.

- Acts 17:7-10a

"Whom Jason hath received: [they came to Jason's house which might have been a house church] and these all do contrary to the decrees of Caesar, saying that there is another king, one Jesus. And they troubled the people and the rulers of the city, when they heard these things. When they had taken security of Jason, and of the other, they let them go. And the brethren immediately sent away Paul and Silas by night unto Berea: . . ."

PAUL LEFT THESSALONICA AND WENT TO BEREA

Paul and his company had to leave Thessalonica because of the Jews that did not believe. These Jews stirred up the people so much that Paul had to leave. They then went to Berea.

- Acts 17:11-12

"These were more noble than those in Thessalonica, in that they received the word with all readiness of mind, and searched the scriptures daily, whether those things were so. Therefore many of them believed; also of honorable women which were Greeks, and of men, not a few."

> **MANY WERE SAVED AT BEREA**
> Paul had good results for the Lord Jesus Christ there in Berea. Many–both men and women--genuinely believed on the Lord Jesus Christ and were saved.

- Acts 17:13

"But when the Jews of Thessalonica had knowledge that the word of God was preached of Paul at Berea, they came thither also, and stirred up the people."

> **LOST JEWS STIRRED UP THE PEOPLE**
> When the unbelieving Jews of Thessalonica heard that the gospel of Christ was being preached in Berea, they came over there and stirred up the people as they had done in their town.

- Acts 17:14-15

"And then immediately the brethren sent away Paul to go as it were to the sea: but Silas and Timotheus abode there still. And they that conducted Paul brought him unto Athens: [they either wrote this letter from Corinth or Athens, we are not certain which city it was] and receiving a commandment unto Silas and Timotheus for to come to him with all speed, they departed."

1 Thessalonians 1:1

"Paul, and Silvanus, and Timotheus, unto the church of the Thessalonians which is in God the Father and in the Lord Jesus Christ: Grace be unto you, and peace, from God our Father, and the Lord Jesus Christ."

Those Who Greeted This Church. Notice also the three men who greeted the church at Thessalonica--*"Paul, and Silvanus* [Silas], *and Timotheus* [Timothy]."

> **THE THESSALONIAN CHURCH WAS SOUND**
> The church at Thessalonica was a sound and Biblical church for it was *"in God the Father and in the Lord Jesus Christ."* It was not an apostate church like many churches in our day.

The Greeting. "Grace be unto you, and peace, from God the Father, and the Lord Jesus Christ." Paul is addressing the Greek Christians with their main greeting (CHARIS *"grace"*) as well as the Hebrew Christians with their main greeting (EIREINE *"peace"*).

> **THE DEITY OF THE LORD JESUS CHRIST**
> The Lord Jesus Christ is <u>not</u> just another human being. He is joined as co-equal with God the Father because He is God the Son.

Other References To Paul, Silas, and Timothy In The New Testament

- **2 Corinthians 1:19**

"For the Son of God, Jesus Christ, who was preached among you by us, *even* by me and Silvanus and Timotheus, was not yea and nay, but in him was yea."

This verse shows that Silvanus and Timotheus were both with Paul in Corinth.

- **2 Thessalonians 1:1**

"Paul, and Silvanus, and Timotheus, unto the church of the Thessalonians in God our Father and the Lord Jesus Christ:

They were together as he wrote this letter. This greeting is similar to the one in 1 Thessalonians where all three men were present at the writing of both letters.

- **1 Peter 5:12**

"By Silvanus, a faithful brother unto you, as I suppose, I have written briefly, exhorting, and testifying that this is the true grace of God wherein ye stand."

Silas is mentioned by the Apostle Peter as being a "faithful brother."

- **Acts 15:22**

"Then pleased it the apostles and elders, with the whole church, to send chosen men of their own company to Antioch with Paul and Barnabas; *namely*, Judas surnamed Barsabas, and Silas, chief men among the brethren:"

Silas was sent to Corinth along with others. He was one of the "*chief men among the brethren.*"

- **Acts 15:40**

"And Paul chose Silas, and departed, being recommended by the brethren unto the grace of God."

Paul chose Silas to go with him on his missionary journeys after John Mark had forsaken him and gone back home.

- **Acts 16:25**

"And at midnight Paul and Silas prayed, and sang praises unto God: and the prisoners heard them."

> **PAUL AND SILAS WERE JAILED AT PHILIPPI**
> Paul and Silas were both put in jail at Philippi because they led a demon-possessed woman to Christ and cast out her demon.

- Acts 17:14

"And then immediately the brethren sent away Paul to go as it were to the sea: but Silas and Timotheus abode there still."

Both Silas and Timothy stayed in Thessalonica after Paul had left the city.

- Acts 18:5

"And when Silas and Timotheus were come from Macedonia, Paul was pressed in the spirit, and testified to the Jews *that* Jesus *was* Christ."

On this occasion, Paul was at Corinth. Silas and Timothy came from Macedonia and joined him at Corinth.

- 1 Corinthians 4:17

"For this cause have I sent unto you Timotheus, who is my beloved son, and faithful in the Lord, who shall bring you into remembrance of my ways which be in Christ, as I teach every where in every church."

> **THREE CHARACTERISTICS ABOUT TIMOTHY**
> Paul sent Timothy to Corinth. He mentioned three things about him:

1. Timothy was Paul's "*beloved son.*" Not that Timothy was Paul's physical son, but was his spiritual son because Paul had led him to genuine faith in the Lord Jesus Christ.
2. Timothy was "*faithful in the Lord.*" Timothy did not waiver in his love and service for the Lord Jesus Christ as some did then and as some do today as well. He was steadfast for His Saviour.
3. Timothy would teach Paul's Doctrines. Timothy would bring to the "*remembrance*" of those in Thessalonica all of Paul's ways and doctrines which he taught "everywhere in every church."

1 Thessalonians 1:2

"We give thanks to God always for you all, making mention of you in our prayers;"

> **THANKFUL FOR THE THESSALONIAN BELIEVERS**
> Paul thanked God for all of true Christians in the church at Thessalonica. He not only thanked God for them, but he

made mention of them in his prayers. We know that there are various kinds of Christians. Some are walking closely with the Lord, and others are not walking in fellowship with the Lord. If they are genuinely saved and born-again, we must pray for the weak ones as well for the strong ones. That's what Paul said he was doing for all those believers in Thessalonica. They had been through a lot of persecution and trouble. They needed Paul's fervent prayers. We today must follow Paul's example and thank God for and pray for our fellow Christian believers.

Verses On Thanksgiving

Here are some of the many verses on thanksgiving that I'd like to share with you:

- **John 6:11**

"And Jesus took the loaves; and when he had given thanks, he distributed to the disciples, and the disciples to them that were set down; and likewise of the fishes as much as they would."

At the feeding of the 5,000 men (plus women and children), the Lord Jesus Christ gave thanks before he distributed the loaves of bread to them.

- **Acts 27:35**

"And when he had thus spoken, he took bread, and gave thanks to God in presence of them all: and when he had broken *it*, he began to eat."

Paul was in a ship as a Roman prisoner. There was a terrific storm on the Mediterranean sea. The ship was about to be sunk in the storm. Paul urged those other prisoners on board to eat some food. They had not eaten anything for fourteen days. Before he ate, Paul gave thanks to the Lord even in this serious storm.

- **1 Corinthians 11:24**

"And when he had given thanks, he brake *it*, and said, Take, eat: this is my body, which is broken for you: this do in remembrance of me."

This speaks of the Lord Jesus Christ Who was with his disciples at the last supper before He suffered for the sins of the world on Calvary's cross. As our Saviour did, so do we before partaking each month of the Lord's Supper in remembrance of His death for us.

- **Ephesians 1:16**

"Cease not to give thanks for you, making mention of you in my prayers;"

Paul is speaking about his giving thanks for these genuine Christians at Ephesus even though he himself was in prison in Rome.

- **Ephesians 5:3-4**
"But fornication, and all uncleanness, or covetousness, let it not be once named among you, as becometh saints; Neither filthiness, nor foolish talking, nor jesting, which are not convenient: but rather giving of thanks."

He told the Ephesian Christians not to get involved in any of these sins that he mentioned. Rather than to be involved with these wicked things, they were to be giving thanks to the Lord for all He had done for them.

- **Colossians 1:3**
"We give thanks to God and the Father of our Lord Jesus Christ, praying always for you,"

This is another letter Paul wrote from his first Roman imprisonment. Even in prison, Paul gave thanks for the Colossian Christians and prayer for them.

- **Colossians 3:17**
"And whatsoever ye do in word or deed, *do* all in the name of the Lord Jesus, giving thanks to God and the Father by him."

Again Paul urged these Christians, whether in their words or in their deeds, to give thanks to God the Father by the Lord Jesus Christ.

- **1 Thessalonians 5:18**
"In every thing give thanks: for this is the will of God in Christ Jesus concerning you."

Paul commands true Christians to give thanks "*in every thing*." This is God's will for them.

- **2 Thessalonians 2:13**
"But we are bound to give thanks alway to God for you, brethren beloved of the Lord, because God hath from the beginning chosen you to salvation through sanctification of the Spirit and belief of the truth:"

Paul gave thanks for these Thessalonian Christians who were "*beloved of the Lord.*"

- **Hebrews 13:15**
"By him therefore let us offer the sacrifice of praise to God continually, that is, the fruit of *our* lips giving thanks to his name."

THE FRUIT OF THANKS TO GOD

The fruit of genuine Christians lips should be "*giving thanks*" to the Name of God the Father and the Lord Jesus Christ. This is an acceptable New Testament "sacrifice." The Old Testament sacrifices of animals was not to be practiced in the New Testament. The Lord Jesus Christ died once for all the world on the cross. That sacrifice was never to be repeated. The mass of the Roman Catholic Church is a pagan, satanic, unBiblical and blasphemous alleged "sacrifice." In this verse (Hebrews 13:15) we have an acceptable *"sacrifice of praise to God continually."* This means *"the fruit of our lips giving thanks to His Name."* That's the sacrifice that God wants every saved born-again Christian to give to Him.

1 Thessalonians 1:3

"Remembering without ceasing your work of faith, and labour of love, and patience of hope in our Lord Jesus Christ, in the sight of God and our Father;

Paul remembers three commendable things about the Thessalonians:
        (1) their *"work of faith"*
        (2) their *"labour of love"* and
        (3) their *"patience of hope."*

PAUL DID NOT FORGET THE CHRISTIANS

The words, *"remembering without ceasing,"* shows that Paul did not forget these genuine Christians in Thessalonica. He was mindful of their troubles and problems with the Jews who wanted to imprison or slay the Christians.

Their *"work of faith"* speaks of a work that is motivated by faith. If you are genuinely saved and have true faith in the Lord Jesus Christ as your Saviour, that faith should motivate you to get busy and work for the Lord. That's the thing that motivates us instead of doing nothing and sitting down and doing nothing,. We should be motivated by faith.

Verses About the Work of Faith

- **John 6:28-29**

"Then said they unto him, What shall we do, that we might work the works of God? Jesus answered and said unto them, This is the work of God, that ye believe on him whom he hath sent."

The only *"work"* that is acceptable to God is that which is motivated by believing or having faith in the Lord Jesus Christ whom God sent into this world to die for our sins.

- **Acts 14:26**

"And thence sailed to Antioch, from whence they had been recommended to the grace of God for the work which they fulfilled."

> **RECOMMENDED BY GOD'S GRACE**
>
> Paul and Barnabas were recommended by God's grace for the work which they fulfilled. It was a work motivated by their faith in the Lord Jesus Christ.

- **Acts 15:38**

"But Paul thought not good to take him [John Mark] with them, who departed from them from Pamphylia, and went not with them to the work."

Apparently, <u>John Mark did not have the faith that motivated him to continue in the work with Paul for the Lord Jesus Christ</u>. Therefore, Paul dismissed John Mark and took Silas with him instead of him.

- **1 Corinthians 3:13**

"Every man's work shall be made manifest: for the day shall declare it, because it shall be revealed by fire; and the fire shall try [or test] every man's work of what sort it is."

> **THE JUDGMENT SEAT OF CHRIST**
>
> This section of 1 Corinthians 3 describes the Judgment Seat of Christ for all genuine Christians. If their works for the Lord Jesus Christ are motivated by faith, they will be sound works which are built up upon that Foundation, the Lord Jesus Christ. Godly works will be works likened to the value of gold and silver and precious stones. Selfish works are pictured as wood, hay, and stubble.

- **1 Corinthians 15:58**

"Therefore, my beloved brethren, be ye stedfast, unmoveable, always abounding in the work of the Lord, forasmuch as ye know that your labour is not in vain in the Lord."

<u>Genuine faith should motivate all the work that true Christians do for the Lord</u>. This faith motivates us to do the work of the Lord.

- **Ephesians 4:11-12**

"And he gave some, apostles; and some, prophets; and some, evangelists, and some, pastors and teachers; For the perfecting of the saints, for the work of the ministry, for the edifying of the body of Christ:"

This *"work of the ministry"* should be motivated by genuine faith.

- **Philippians 2:30**

"Because for the work of Christ he was nigh unto death, not regarding his life, to supply your lack of service toward me."

<u>Paul's *"work of Christ"* was motivated by true faith</u>.

- **2 Timothy 4:5**
"But watch thou in all things, endure afflictions, do the work of an evangelist, make full proof of thy ministry."
The "*work of an evangelist*" can only be done based on genuine faith.
- **Hebrews 13:21**
"Make you perfect in every good work to do his will, working in you that which is wellpleasing in his sight, through Jesus Christ; to whom *be* glory for ever and ever. Amen."

GOOD WORK TO GLORIFY CHRIST
The "*good work*" mentioned here, if motivated by real faith, will produce a solid work for the Lord Jesus Christ.

Verses About the Labor of Love

The Greek Word used for "*labour*" is KOPOU. This involves "*intense labor and toil.*" For it to be acceptable to the Lord, this labour must be motivated by love.
- **Romans 16:6**
"Greet Mary, who bestowed much labour on us."

LABOR MOTIVATED BY LOVE
For her love of Christ, Mary expended much "*labour*" for Paul and his companions.

- **Romans 16:12**
"Salute Tryphena and Tryphosa, who labour in the Lord. Salute the beloved Persis, which labored much in the Lord."
That "*labour*" expended by Tryphena and Tryphosa would have been motivated by their love for the Lord Jesus Christ.
- **1 Corinthians 4:11-12**
"Even unto this present hour we both hunger, and thirst, and are naked, and are buffeted, and have no certain dwellingplace; And labour, working with our own hands: being reviled, we bless; being persecuted, we suffer it:"
Paul didn't have it easy as many pastors do today. This missionary was laboring while hungry, thirsty, and with few clothes. He didn't have a large wardrobe. He was buffeted. He had no certain dwellingplace or home that he could call his own. Paul' labour was strong labour. What was the motivation for that labour? It was the love that he had for the Lord Jesus Christ.
- **Galatians 4:11**
"I am afraid of you, lest I have bestowed upon you labour in vain."

> **PAUL'S HARD WORK AT GALATIA**
> Paul worked very hard for the Galatian church. He labored strenuously, motivated by the love of the Lord Jesus Christ. He didn't know if they would go back into Judaism. That's what he was wondering about. Was his labour *"in vain"*?

- 1 Thessalonians 2:9

"For ye remember, brethren, our labour and travail: for laboring night and day, because we would not be chargeable unto any of you, we preached unto you the gospel of God."

> **PAUL'S LABOR NIGHT AND DAY**
> Paul was laboring very hard, making tents. He didn't have churches supporting him. It was strong labour and travail, working both by night and by day. He worked hard because he didn't want to be *"chargeable"* or dependent on any of them. He didn't want to take their money. He labored on his own, motivated by love for His Saviour.

- 1 Thessalonians 3:5

"For this cause, when I could no longer forbear, I sent to know your faith, lest by some means the tempter have tempted you, and our labour be in vain."

> **NOT LABORING IN VAIN**
> Paul labored strenuously, motivated by love for the Thessalonian church to start. He hoped they hadn't had some Satanic person come in to destroy his work. Otherwise his labour would have been *"in vain."*

- 2 Thessalonians 3:8

"Neither did we eat any man's bread for nought; but wrought with labour and travail night and day, that we might not be chargeable to any of you:"

Once again, Paul mentioned his strong, hard, and strenuous labour. He didn't want to take funds from the Christians.

- 1 Timothy 4:10

"For therefore we both labour and suffer reproach, because we trust in the living God, who is the Saviour of all men, specially of those that believe."

> **PAUL'S LABOR OF FOR THE LORD JESUS CHRIST**
> Paul's labour because of the love he had for the Lord Jesus Christ, sometimes caused reproach.

Verses About the Patience of Hope

The third thing Paul remembered without ceasing was their patience which was motivated by hope.

The Greek Word for *"patience"* is HYPOMONE. Some of the meanings of this Greek Word are

"endurance, perseverance, stedfastness, or patience" (Lk 8:15; 21:19; Ro 2:7; 5:3; 8:25; 15:4; 2Co 6:4; 1Ti 6:11; 2Ti 3:10; Heb 12:1; Jas 1:3; 5:11; 2Pe 1:6; Rev 2:2, 19; Gal 5:23)

IN THE NEW TESTAMENT, "PATIENCE" IS:
"the characteristic of a man who is not swerved from his deliberate purpose and his loyalty to faith and piety by even the greatest trials and sufferings."

There can be patience because a true Christian knows that there is something far better ahead of them in Heaven.
- **Romans 8:25**

"But if we hope for that we see not, *then* do we with patience wait for *it*."

Here is *patience, motivated by hope of what lies ahead.* Some day that hope will be fulfilled.
- **Romans 15:4**

"For whatsoever things were written aforetime were written for our learning, that we through patience and comfort of the scriptures might have hope."

THE OLD TESTAMENT TEACHES PATIENCE & HOPE

The Old Testament was preserved for the genuine Christians today so that they might give them patience motivated by hope which has been proved by God's past faithfulness.

- **2 Corinthians 6:4a**

"But in all *things* approving ourselves as the ministers of God, in much patience,"

Paul did not have everything instantaneously. Just like our church goes to the fast food place after the church service. It's not always fast. But we must be patient motivated by hope that we will be served eventually. Paul was patient as an apostle.
- **Colossians 1:11**

"Strengthened with all might, according to his glorious power, unto all patience and longsuffering with joyfulness;"

STRENGTHENED TO PATIENCE & HOPE

In this verse, Paul was strengthened unto *"all patience"* motivated by hope. He knew that at the end of his life the hope in the Lord Jesus Christ to go Home to Heaven would be fulfilled. This made him patient in all that he did. Genuine Christians should be the same.

- **2 Thessalonians 1:4**

"So that we ourselves glory in you in the churches of God for your patience and faith in all your persecutions and tribulations that ye endure:"

The Thessalonian Christians had many persecutions and tribulations, yet remained patient motivated by hope in the Lord Jesus Christ.

- **Titus 2:2**

"That the aged men be sober, grave, temperate, sound in faith, in charity, in patience."

Why did Paul limit patience only to the older men? What about the older women, younger men, and younger women? I believe he addressed the older men here, and the others in other places. There is a great need for older men who are genuine Christians to have patience motivated by hope as they live their lives.

- **Hebrews 6:12**

"That ye be not slothful, but followers of them who through faith and patience inherit the promises."

The leading Old Testament saints had patience motivated by hope in God's promises that would one day come to pass exactly.

- **Hebrews 10:36**

"For ye have need of patience, that, after ye have done the will of God, ye might receive the promise."

This is a very important need for patience that is motivated by hope. The hope is in God's unfailing promises for doing His will. Usually these promises are not fulfilled immediately.

- **Hebrews 12:1**

"Wherefore seeing we also are compassed about with so great a cloud of witnesses, let us lay aside every weight, and the sin which doth so easily beset *us*, and let us run with patience the race that is set before us,"

RUNNING LIFE'S RACE WITH PATIENCE

Running the Biblical race that is set before them with patience, motivated by hope, should be the goal of all genuine Christians in our day. God is honored by such an activity. Every true Christian has a different race to run but each must be faithful in running it to please the Lord Jesus Christ. One day our race will be over, and the Lord Jesus Christ will have to replace us with someone else to run in our place.

- **James 5:7**
"Be patient therefore, brethren, unto the coming of the Lord. Behold, the husbandman waiteth for the precious fruit of the earth, and hath long patience for it, until he receive the early and latter rain."

THE FARMER'S PATIENCE FOR HIS CROP
The farmer can't immediately get the crop that he has just sown. He plants the seed and then must wait with patience motivated by hope that the full grown plant will one day come forth. Every genuine Christian must wait for the coming of the Lord Jesus Christ with patience motivated by hope.

- **James 5:11**
"Behold, we count them happy which endure. Ye have heard of the patience of Job, and have seen the end of the Lord; that the Lord is very pitiful, and of tender mercy."

Though Job lost his goods, his property, his family, his children, his health and many other things, he had patience motivated by hope because he knew that the Lord would somehow work things out. And He did, in a wonderful and miraculous way!

1 Thessalonians 1:4

"Knowing, brethren beloved, your election of God."

This word "election," is a biblical, as well as a theological word. I believe in it, provided it is defined properly. My definition of "election," as regarding salvation, is that it is a "corporate" election. Just like the nation of Israel was a corporate body, chosen or elected by God, so those that He saves make up a corporate body.

- **Isaiah 45:4**
"For Jacob my servant's sake, and **Israel mine elect**, I have even called thee by thy name: I have surnamed thee, though thou hast not known me."

That corporate body of the true Church--which is Christ's Body--was chosen as a Body before the foundation of the world. It is a corporate body consisting of all those who will be genuinely saved by true faith in the Lord Jesus Christ.

> **THE BODY OF CHRIST–CORPORATE ELECTION**
>
> When people truly and genuinely believe on and receive the Lord Jesus Christ as their Saviour, they become members of the previously chosen or elected Body of Christ. That is my definition of election. I believe it is a corporate election. I know other people see it differently, but that is my understanding of it. When a person chooses to receive the Lord Jesus Christ as their Saviour, they become a member of *"the Church which is His Body"* which was chosen as a corporate body by God from all eternity past. When a person genuinely trust the Lord Jesus Christ as their Saviour, he or she is saved and becomes a member of the eternally chosen *"Church which is His body."*
>
> *"And hath put all things under his feet, and gave him to be the head over all things to <u>the church, Which is his body</u>, the fulness of him that filleth all in all."* (Ephesians 1:22-23)

1 Thessalonians 1:5

"For our gospel came not unto you in word only, but also in power, and in the Holy Ghost, and in much assurance; as ye know what manner of men we were among you for your sake."

It's interesting when Paul preached the gospel of the Lord Jesus Christ unto the Thessalonian Christians, he wanted to remind them how it was delivered. I trust that the gospel message as I preach from our church is the same clear message that Paul preached. Paul said that it is not in word only, but we have to use words. Words must be given in order to explain the gospel of God's grace.

> **PREACHING IN WORD AND POWER**
>
> Paul preached not *"in word only,"* but also in the power of the Holy Ghost. For gospel of the Lord Jesus Christ to have any power to convert the lost, God the Holy Spirit must lead the preacher in that proclamation. A final need of gospel preaching is that it must be done *"in much assurance."*

There are some groups such the holiness groups, who believe in the heresy that once people are genuinely saved, they can lose their salvation when they commit sin. They lack the gospel *"in much assurance."* They just preach that a person genuinely believe on and receive the Lord Jesus Christ as their Saviour, but they must hang on, and not sin. If they sin, their salvation is lost! What "*assurance*" is that? Everyone of us sins.

ETERNAL LIFE CAN NEVER BE WITHDRAWN
The Bible is clear that once genuine eternal life has been granted to a believing sinner, it can never be withdrawn. If a genuine Christians sins, they must follow 1 John 1:9 and get back into fellowship with the Saviour. The Lord Jesus Christ is very clear about never perishing once a person is genuinely born-again and saved.

"*My sheep hear my voice, and I know them, and they follow me: And I give unto them eternal life; and **they shall never perish**, neither shall any man pluck them out of my hand. My Father, which gave them me, is greater than all; and no man is able to pluck them out of my Father's hand.*" (John 10:27-29)

The Greek Word for "*never*" is OU ME. That is the strongest negative in the Greek language. It means **never, never, never** "*perish*"!

Notice what Paul said about the Thessalonian true Christians and himself. "*Ye know what manner of men we were among you.*" What does he mean? I believe he was saying that when he, Silas, and Timothy were there among the Thessalonians, these Thessalonians looked at all three of these Christian leaders and studied them. They knew them well. These Christian leaders didn't hide under some bushel and come out once a week and preach. They met with the Thessalonians who could see what manner of men all three of them were.

TRUE CHRISTIANS ARE LIKE GOD'S EPISTLES
Genuine Christians as epistles are "*known and read of all men*" (2 Corinthians 3:2). All men see and look at them. They know them. They should be known as proper, Christian men and women. These three Christian leaders were gospel preachers who lived to please the Lord Jesus Christ.

Verses On The Gospel And Faith In It
- Mark 16:15

"And he said unto them, Go ye into all the world, and preach the gospel to every creature."

THE VALIDITY OF MARK 16:9-20
This verse, along with the entire section of Mark 16:9-20, is wrongly left out of the Gnostic Critical Greek Texts. **It is also omitted from the main text of almost all of the modern English and other language versions.** It is either eliminated completely, or put into brackets or footnotes causing doubt on

the words. The gospel's good news must be preached to every creature. The Lord Jesus Christ believed in evangelizing the entire world with the true Biblical gospel of God's grace through His Son, the Lord Jesus Christ.

- Romans 10:17

"So then faith *cometh* by hearing, and hearing by the word of God."

SAVING FAITH COMES FROM RECEIVING GOD'S WORDS

The Words of God give us what we need to know about the Lord Jesus Christ and His substitutionary death on the cross of Calvary so we can have saving faith in Him.

Verses On The Gospel Preached In The Power Of God

Not only was the gospel of Christ preached in word. It was also preached in the power of the Holy Spirit of God.

- Romans 1:16

"For I am not ashamed of the gospel of Christ: for it is the power of God unto salvation to every one that believeth; to the Jew first, and also to the Greek."

CHRIST'S GOSPEL--THE POWER OF GOD TO SALVATION

The accurate *"gospel of Christ"* is *"the power of God unto salvation to every one that believeth."* This gospel is not simply words, it is powerful through God.

- 1 Corinthians 2:4

"And my speech and my preaching was not with enticing words of man's wisdom, but in demonstration of the Spirit and of power:"

Many preachers use enticing words, philosophy, and foolish deceit. Paul preached with the power of God the Holy Spirit.

- 1 Corinthians 2:5

"That your faith should not stand in the wisdom of men, but in the power of God."

Paul wanted the believers in Corinth to have their faith stand in the *"power of God."* That's where genuine Christians' faith today should stand rather than in the *"wisdom of men."*

When Paul prayed three times for the Lord to remove his thorn in the flesh, the Lord said "No!" Notice God's reply and Paul's reaction in the following verse.

- 2 Corinthians 12:9

"And he said unto me, My grace is sufficient for thee: for my strength is made perfect in weakness. Most gladly therefore will I rather glory in my infirmities, that the power of Christ may rest upon me."

Paul wanted the "power of Christ" to rest on him and control him.
- **Ephesians 6:10**
"Finally, my brethren, be strong in the Lord, and in the power of his might."
True Christians today must also be strong in the *"power of his might."*

Verses On The Gospel Preached Depending On The Holy Spirit Of God

The third thing that Paul did when he preached the gospel was not only in word and in power, but also in the Holy Spirit. Pastors who preach and who do not have God the Holy Spirit indwelling them, would be unable to preach the gospel in the power of the Holy Spirit.
- **Acts 1:8**
"But ye shall receive power, after that the Holy Ghost is come upon you: and ye shall be witnesses unto me both in Jerusalem, and in all Judaea, and in Samaria, and unto the uttermost part of the earth."

The Lord Jesus Christ promised the disciples power after the descent of God the Holy Spirit. He would give them power to witness for Him.
- **Acts 13:2**
"As they ministered to the Lord, and fasted, the Holy Ghost said, Separate me Barnabas and Saul for the work whereunto I have called them."

The Holy Spirit of God is the One Who put His hand upon Paul and Barnabas and sent them forth to His missionary work. Unfortunately Barnabas lasted only for one of Paul's missionary journeys. Silas accompanied Paul on his second and third journeys.
- **Acts 13:52**
"And the disciples were filled with joy, and with the Holy Ghost."
The Holy Spirit of God filled the disciples with joy and power to preach the gospel.
- **Acts 16:6**
"Now when they had gone throughout Phyrygia and the region of Galatia, and were forbidden of the Holy Ghost to preach the word in Asia,"

The Holy Spirit of God sometimes forbade the apostles to go to certain places.
- **Romans 15:13**
"Now the God of hope fill you with all joy and peace in believing, that ye may abound in hope, through the power of the Holy Ghost."

ABOUNDING IN HOPE THROUGH GOD'S SPIRIT
The Spirit of God permits true Christians to *"abound in hope"* rather than to be discouraged.

- Ephesians 5:18
"And be not drunk with wine, wherein is excess; but be filled with the Spirit;"

CONTROLLED BY THE SPIRIT FOR GOD'S POWER
Genuine Christians should be filled or controlled by the Holy Spirit for maximum power and influence for the Lord.

Verses On The Gospel Preached With Assurance
The fourth thing that characterized Paul's preaching was that it was in *"much assurance."*
- Isaiah 32:17
"And the work of righteousness shall be peace; and the effect of righteousness quietness and assurance for ever."

SHALL NEVER PERISH--ASSURANCE FOREVER
The effect of having God's imputed righteousness is *"assurance for ever."* The Lord Jesus Christ said clearly that the genuine Christians who have been born-again by faith in him *"shall never perish"*:

- John 10:28
"And I give unto them eternal life; and **they shall never perish**, neither shall any man pluck them out of my hand."

That is *"much insurance"* indeed right from the Saviour's own mouth.
- Hebrews 6:11
"And we desire that every one of you do shew the same diligence to the full assurance of hope unto the end:"

Paul preached with full assurance. He was assured of eternal salvation.
- Hebrews 10:22
"Let us draw near with a true heart in full assurance of faith, having our hearts sprinkled from an evil conscience, and our bodies washed with pure water."
- 1 John 5:13
"These things have I written unto you that believe on the name of the Son of God; that ye may know that ye have eternal life, and that ye may believe on the name of the Son of God."

The knowledge that persons have eternal life gives them assurance.

1 Thessalonians 1:6

"And ye became followers of us, and of the Lord, having received the word in much affliction, with joy of the Holy Ghost:"

Now there are four things about the Thessalonian Christians that Paul mentioned in this verse.
(1) They were followers of Paul, Silas, and Timotheus.
(2) They followed the Lord.
(3) They received God's Word in much affliction.
(4) They had joy from God the Holy Spirit, despite their troubles.

Verses On Following The Proper Leaders

- **1 Corinthians 11:1**

"Be ye followers of me, even as I also am of Christ."
Paul was to be followed only as he followed the Lord Jesus Christ.

- **Philippians 3:17**

"Brethren, be followers together of me, and mark them which walk so as ye have us for an ensample."
He was an "example man"-- an example apostle.

- **Hebrews 6:12**

"That ye be not slothful, but followers of them who through faith and patience inherit the promises."
Christians should be followers of those that are following the Lord Jesus Christ Himself. Many verses teach the true Christians to follow their Saviour.

Verses On Following The Lord Jesus Christ Himself

- **Matthew 4:19**

"And he saith unto them, Follow me, and I will make you fishers of men."

- **Matthew 9:9**

"And as Jesus passed forth from thence, he saw a man, named Matthew, sitting at the receipt of custom: and he saith unto him, Follow me. And he arose, and followed him."
He was a tax collector. Yet, he followed the Lord Jesus Christ.

- **Matthew 16:24**

"Then said Jesus unto his disciples, If any man will come after me, let him deny himself, and take up his cross, and follow me."

- **John 1:43**

"The day following Jesus would go forth into Galilee, and findeth Philip, and saith unto him, Follow me."

FOLLOWING CHRIST AND HIS WORDS

Genuine Christians must follow the Lord Jesus Christ. He has given them His words in the New Testament and His Words in the Old Testament. They are to follow Him, and His Words that He gave to them.

- **John 10:27-30**

"My sheep hear my voice, and I know them, and they follow me: And I give unto them eternal life; and they shall never perish, neither shall any man pluck them out of my hand. My Father, which gave *them* me, is greater than all; and no man is able to luck them out of my Father's hand. I and *my* Father are one."

- **John 12:26**

"If any man serve me, let him follow me; and where I am, there shall also my servant be: if any man serve me, him will *my* Father honour."

Service is measured by following the Lord Jesus Christ.

- **John 16:12-13**

"I have yet many things to say unto you, but ye cannot bear them now. Howbeit when he, the Spirit of truth, is come, he will guide you into all truth: for he shall not speak of himself; but whatsoever he shall hear, that shall he speak: and he will shew you things to come."

The Words of the entire New Testament (and the Words of the Old Testament as well, by implication), are the Words given by the Lord Jesus Christ to God the Holy Spirit Who then gave them to the writers of the various Bible books. If we want to follow Him, we must obey His Words.

THE BIBLE–CHRIST'S LOVE LETTER TO US

The Bible is a love letter, Christ gave the words to the Holy Spirit, then to the writers of the Old and New Testaments. Truly saved people must follow those Words of the Lord Jesus Christ.

- **John 21:19**

"This spake he, signifying by what death he should glorify God. And when he had spoken this, he saith unto him, Follow me."

FOLLOWING THE LORD BY FOLLOWING THE BIBLE

The Lord Jesus Christ said to Peter, (who, if you remember, denied him three times), *"Follow me."* Those who are true Christians are to follow the Lord Jesus Christ. He is in Heaven now. They can't follow Him literally, step by step, but they can follow His Words which He gave them in the Bible.

Verses On Receiving The Scriptures In Afflictions
These true Thessalonian Christians received the scriptures in much affliction. It wasn't an easy thing to do. Here are a few more verses on "*affliction.*"
- Mark 4:17

"And these are they likewise which are sown on stony ground; who, when they have heard the word, immediately receive it with gladness;"

DON'T RECEIVE GOD'S WORDS ON STONY GROUND!
Remember, there are four types of ground. One type of ground is stony ground. Those receiving God's Words on stony ground had no root in themselves, and so endure but for a short time. Afterward, when affliction or persecution arises for the Word's sake, immediately these people are offended. It's not good ground at all to receive the Words of God.

- 2 Corinthians 4:17

"For our light affliction, which is but for a moment, worketh for us a far more exceeding *and* eternal weight of glory;"

LIGHT AFFLICTION VERSUS ETERNAL GLORY
Future glory is permanent. The "*light affliction*" is momentary.

- 2 Corinthians 8:2

"How that in a great trial of affliction the abundance of their joy and their deep poverty abounded unto the riches of their liberality."
Paul is talking about the churches in Macedonia. As they, so genuine Christians today, should have joy in any of their afflictions. Even though they didn't have much money, they gave so others could be helped.
- 1 Thessalonians 3:3a

"That no man should be moved by these afflictions:"
Paul did not want these Christians in Thessalonica to be moved or shaken up by their afflictions.
- 1 Thessalonians 3:3b

". . . for yourselves know that we are appointed thereunto."

APPOINTED TO AFFLICTIONS
Every true Christian is appointed to afflictions of some kind or another. You might say that this not why you became a genuine Christian. The life of a true Christian is not a bed of

> roses. But there are afflictions that they have been appointed to. They must be endured with joy from God the Holy Spirit.

- **2 Timothy 1:8**

"Be not thou therefore ashamed of the testimony of our Lord, nor of me his prisoner: but be thou partaker of the afflictions of the gospel according to the power of God;"

When the gospel of the Lord Jesus Christ is preached straight, it must include that God considers all people as sinners. The self-righteous don't admit they are sinners and bring affliction and conflict to those who are preaching soundly. The true Christian life is not always a smooth trail. Timothy was a partaker *"of the afflictions of the gospel according to the power of God."*

2 Timothy 4:5

"But watch thou in all things, endure afflictions, do the work of an evangelist, make full proof of thy ministry."

Pastor Timothy was to *"endure afflictions."* He was not to be submerged by them. He was to put up with them in a satisfactory manner.

- **Hebrews 11:25**

"Choosing rather to suffer affliction with the people of God, than to enjoy the pleasures of sin for a season;"

Moses was the adopted son of the Pharaoh in Egypt. As such, he had all the riches of Egypt at his disposal. He was trained in Egypt. He had all the luxuries of Egypt, but *chose "to suffer affliction with the people of God"* rather than *"to enjoy the pleasures of sin"* for just a little while.

- **James 5:10**

"Take, my brethren, the prophets, who have spoken in the name of the Lord, for an example of suffering affliction, and of patience."

The Old Testament prophets give us a twofold example, suffering affliction and being patient. This included Isaiah, Jeremiah, Daniel, Ezekiel, and all the other prophets. True Christians today should also be patient in all their affliction.

Verses On Having Joy In God The Holy Spirit

> **SPIRITUAL JOY AMIDST AFFLICTIONS**
>
> Notice, the Thessalonian Christians received the Words of God, not only with affliction, but also with joy in the Holy Spirit. Affliction does not have to rule out spiritual joy. The joy of the Lord can still be the strength of genuine Christians today regardless of problems, troubles, difficulties, sicknesses, and weakness that might attend them.

- **Acts 13:52**

"And the disciples were filled with joy, and with the Holy Ghost.

- **Acts 20:24**

"But none of these things move me, neither count I my life dear unto myself, so that I might finish my course with joy, and the ministry, which I have received of the Lord Jesus, to testify the gospel of the grace of God."

Paul was writing about the dangers of going to Jerusalem. He knew that in Jerusalem afflictions would come to him. He was warned about these dangers by other people who told him not to go to Jerusalem. But Paul wanted to fulfill the course that the Lord Jesus Christ laid out for him when He saved him on the road to Damascus. He hadn't finished that course yet. In order to finish that course with joy, he felt that he had to go to Jerusalem and tell the Jews there about His wonderful Saviour, no matter what it might cost him.

- **Galatians 5:22-23**

"But the fruit of the Spirit is love, joy, peace, longsuffering, gentleness, goodness, faith, Meekness, temperance: against such there is no law."

JOY FROM GOD THE HOLY SPIRIT

Even in affliction, these Thessalonian Christians had joy in the Spirit of God. Joy is one of the parts of the fruit or control of God the Holy Spirit.

- **Hebrews 12:2**

"Looking unto Jesus the author and finisher of our faith; who for the joy that was set before him endured the cross, despising the shame, and is set down at the right hand of the throne of God."

As the Lord Jesus Christ faced the cruel cross at Calvary, He "*endured the cross*" because of the "*joy that was set before him.*" He knew that because of His dying on the cross and shedding His blood as an atonement for the sins of the entire world, it would bring into existence a whole host of born-again and saved Christians who would truly trust Him for their salvation. That thought brought our Saviour true joy even in the midst of such a painful and lonely death.

- **1 Peter 4:13**

"But rejoice, inasmuch as ye are partakers of Christ's sufferings, that, when his glory shall be revealed, ye may be glad also with exceeding joy."

The glories of Heaven for the genuine Christians will bring them "*exceeding joy*" for all eternity.

1 Thessalonians 1:7

"**So that ye were ensamples to all that believe in Macedonia and Achaia.**"

Because of all of these preceding qualities, these Thessalonian Christians were "*ensamples*" or examples to all the other true believers in the areas of Macedonia and Achaia. May the genuine Christians in our day be good examples to others. Here are some other verses on being ensamples and examples for others.

- **John 13:15**
"For I have given you an example, that ye should do as I have done to you."

THE LORD JESUS CHRIST GAVE US AN EXAMPLE
The Lord Jesus Christ gave His apostles and other followers an example for them to follow. He wanted them to do as he did and do what He said to them. These apostles were with him for 3 ½ years. It was clear to them how He lived, what He did, and what He didn't do. They were to follow His example.

- **1 Corinthians 10:11**
"Now all these things happened unto them for ensamples: and they are written for our admonition, upon whom the ends of the world are come."

The entire Old Testament happened unto those who lived then as examples. They were written for the admonition of the true Christians living in New Testament times. This is why I encourage true Christians to read the entire Bible, 85-verses each day, not only from the New Testament, but also from the Old Testament so as to learn from these examples, both good and bad.

- **2 Thessalonians 3:9**
"Not because we have not power, but to make ourselves an ensample unto you to follow us."

Paul wanted to make himself a good ensample or example unto these genuine Christians.

- **1 Timothy 4:12**
"Let no man despise thy youth; but be thou an example of the believers, in word, in conversation, in charity, in spirit, in faith, in purity."

Paul wanted Timothy, pastor of the church at Ephesus, to be an "*example of the believers*" in the areas of charity, spirit, faith, and purity. Every true Christian should be such an example as well.

- 1 Peter 2:21
"For even hereunto were ye called: because Christ also suffered for us, leaving us an example, that ye should follow his steps:"

> **CHRIST GAVE US AN EXAMPLE OF SUFFERING**
> The Lord Jesus Christ left every true Christian an example through His suffering for them. They should follow His steps.

- 1 Peter 5:3
"Neither as being lords over God's heritage, but being ensamples to the flock."

Pastors-bishops-elders should not be lords or masters over the local church members, but rather should be *"ensamples to the flock."* Unfortunately, some pastors act like big bosses over their members and crack the whips over them. That is not their purpose.

1 Thessalonians 1:8

" For from you sounded out the word of the Lord not only in Macedonia and Achaia, but also in every place your faith to God-ward is spread abroad; so that we need not to speak any thing."

The Greek Word for *"sounded out"* (EXECHETAI) is in the perfect tense. So is the Greek Word for *"spread abroad"* (EXELELUTHEN). The Greek perfect tense indicates an action that happened in the past, continues into the present, and continues on into the future. This action was true of these Thessalonian Christians both as to the *"Word of the Lord"* and as to their *"faith to God-ward."* These actions occurred not only in the areas of Macedonia and Achaia, but *"in every place."*

Our **Bible For Today Baptist Church** seeks to do this as well. This is done through our sending out DVD's, books, CD's, and tape recordings. It is also done by our Internet ministry which was set up and operated by our assistant Pastor Daniel Waite. Through the means of our video cameras, we are notified of monthly downloads of our services from each of our 50 states as well as from 60 to 70 foreign countries.

Verses On Preaching The Gospel

- Mark 16:15
"And he said unto them, go ye into all the world, and preach the gospel to every creature."

The Lord Jesus Christ, before He ascended bodily back into Heaven, commanded His apostles to preach His gospel *"to every creature."* That means sounding it out worldwide.

- Luke 20:1

"And it came to pass, *that* on one of those days, as he taught the people in the temple, and preached the gospel, the chief priests and the scribes came upon *him* with the elders,"

The Lord Jesus Christ Himself "*preached the gospel*" in the temple.

- Acts 5:40

"And to him they agreed: and when they had called the apostles, and beaten them, they commanded that they should not speak in the name of Jesus, and let them go."

THE COMMAND NOT TO PREACH THE GOSPEL
The unbelieving Jews didn't like the apostles. They commanded them not to preach the gospel or speak about anything in the Name of the Lord Jesus Christ.

- Acts 5:41-42

"And they departed from the presence of the council, rejoicing that they were counted worthy to suffer shame for his name. And daily in the temple, and in every house, they ceased not to teach and preach Jesus Christ."

UNBIBLICAL GOVERNMENT ORDERS DISOBEYED
The apostles disobeyed the unBiblical orders of the Jewish unbelievers and they continued teaching and preaching the Lord Jesus Christ regardless of the suffering that might come because of it. They sounded out the truth of God.

- Acts 8:4

"Therefore they that were scattered abroad went every where preaching the word."

The true Christians who were scattered out of Jerusalem went everywhere sounding forth and preaching God's Words.

- Acts 8:25

"And they, when they had testified and preached the word of the Lord, returned to Jerusalem, and preached the gospel in many villages of the Samaritans."

The preaching of the gospel was not limited to Jerusalem, but it was given also to many Samaritan villages as well.

- Acts 8:40

"But Philip was found at Azotus: and passing through he preached in all the cities, till he came to Caesarea."

Philip was an evangelistic preacher who sounded out the Words of God in city after city.

- **Acts 10:42**
"And he commanded us to preach unto the people, and to testify that it is he which was ordained of God *to be* the Judge of quick and dead."
This refers to the command of the Lord Jesus Christ to preach and testify to the people about His being the Judge of the quick and the dead.
- **Acts 15:35**
"Paul also and Barnabas continued in Antioch, teaching and preaching the word of the Lord, with many others also."
Paul and Barnabas were faithful in sounding out the Words of God by preaching and teaching.
- **Romans 1:15**
"So, as much as in me is, I am ready to preach the gospel to you that are at Rome also."
Paul was willing to go to Rome to preach the gospel. He did this as a prisoner of the Roman government and sounded out God's Words even in prison.
- **1 Corinthians 1:18**
"For the preaching of the cross is to them that perish foolishness; but unto us which are saved it is the power of God."

THE GOSPEL IS GOD'S POWER
Though to those that perish, the preaching of the cross is foolishness, it is God's power to those who are saved.

- **Ephesians 3:8**
"Unto me, who am less than the least of all saints, is this grace given, that I should preach among the Gentiles the unsearchable riches of Christ;"

PAUL WAS EDUCATED, BUT NOT ARROGANT
Though Paul was well educated and of an important religious background, he was not proud or arrogant in his attitude. He was humble. The Lord Jesus Christ called him to preach the *"unsearchable riches of Christ"* unto the Gentiles wherever they were. He was called to do this.

- **2 Timothy 4:2**
"Preach the word; be instant in season, out of season; reprove, rebuke, exhort with all longsuffering and doctrine."
This was Paul's last letter. He told Pastor Timothy to *"preach the Word,"* not only in season, but also out of season. He was to use those Words of God in reproof, in rebuke, and in exhortation. His attitude was to be with *"longsuffering."* The content of his preaching was with all *"doctrine."*

1 Thessalonians 1:9

"For they themselves shew of us what manner of entering in we had unto you, and how ye turned to God from idols to serve the living and true God;"

Those who lived in the areas of Macedonia and Achaia told Paul, Silas, and Timothy about what happened in Thessalonica. They knew that these heathen people after their sound conversion to the Lord Jesus Christ, *"turned to God"* and away from their *"idols."* They continued to *"serve the living and true God."* The Greek Word for *"serve"* (DOULEUEIN) is in the Greek present tense. It means a continuous service for the Lord, not just on Sundays, or once year (as some seem to do today), but day by day, hour by hour, and moment by moment.

Notice the order here. It was *"to God"* first and then *"from idols."* It was not the reverse. There would have been no reason to turn from idols if they had not first turned *"to God"* through the Lord Jesus Christ as their Saviour.

MACARTHUR'S HERESY OF LORDSHIP SALVATION

There are many, such as John MacArthur and his followers, who teach what they call *"lordship salvation."* This heretical teaching says that a person must make the Lord Jesus Christ the "Lord" of their lives before they can be saved. This involves giving up various works and sins. This is like giving up "idols" before they turn to God. The Thessalonian Christians had it right. The turned to God first and then they were motivated to turn from their idols.

Many verses speak about coming out of something and going into something else. These are two sides of the doctrine of separation, a positive aspect and a negative aspect.
- Exodus 3:17

"And I have said, I will bring you up out of the affliction of Egypt unto the land of the Canaanites, and the Hittites, and the Amorites, and the Perizzites, and the Hivites, and the Jebusites, unto a land flowing with milk and honey."

God brought Israel out of Egypt and into the land of Canaan.
- Exodus 13:5

"And it shall be when the LORD shall bring thee into the land of the Canaanites, and the Hittities, and the Amorites, and the Hivites, and the Jebusites, which he sware unto thy fathers to give thee, a land flowing with milk and honey, that thou shalt keep this service in this month."

As in the previous verse, God took His people out of Egypt, and then brought them into Canaan.
- **Romans 12:1-2**
"I beseech you therefore, brethren, by the mercies of God, that ye present your bodies a living sacrifice, holy, acceptable unto God, *which is* your reasonable service. And be not conformed to this world: but be ye transformed by the renewing of your mind, that ye may prove what *is* that good, and acceptable, and perfect, will of God."

GOD'S WILL IS PERFECT, THOUGH OFTEN DIFFICULT
The will of God is perfect. God wants genuine Christians to present their bodies to Him as holy and living sacrifices. After this is done, He then wants them to stop being conformed to this world. This is what the Thessalonian Christians did. They turned to God from idols to serve the true God.

- **Galatians 5:16**
"*This* I say then, Walk in the Spirit, and ye shall not fulfil the lust of the flesh."

Here is God's New Testament order once again. True Christians should walk moment by moment in dependance on God the Holy Spirit. When this is done, they will not fulfill the lusts of their flesh. If they walk in the Spirit, the lust of the flesh will disappear. This is the order followed by the Thessalonian Christians.

1 Thessalonians 1:10

"And to wait for his Son from heaven, whom he raised from the dead, even Jesus, which delivered us from the wrath to come."

Not only did these Thessalonian Christians turn to God from their idols, and continuously served the Lord, but they also were waiting for God's Son from Heaven. The Lord Jesus Christ did not come in their lifetime. He has not come yet in our lifetime. But God has commanded true Christians to wait for the Lord Jesus Christ to come in the air at the Rapture of the saved ones. The Greek Word for "*wait*" (ANAMENEIN) is in the Greek present tense. It implies a continuous non-stop waiting for the Saviour.

THE LORD JESUS CHRIST'S BODILY RESURRECTION
God's Son, Who is now in Heaven is there because God raised Him bodily from the dead after three days and three

> nights in the grave. There is not any other religious group that ever existed whose founder or leader was raised bodily from the dead. The Lord Jesus Christ is unique in this miracle.

Through His substitutionary death on the cross, shedding His blood for the forgiveness of the sins of the world, He is able to "*deliver*" from the "*wrath to come*" those who truly trust and believe on Him as their Saviour.

Verses On Patient Waiting For God

There are many verses to encourage those who trust in the Lord to wait for Him patiently.

- Psalm 27:14

"Wait on the LORD: be of good courage, and he shall strengthen thine heart: wait, I say, on the LORD."

> **PATIENCE IS DIFFICULT BUT NECESSARY**
>
> It's very difficult to be patient and wait for things. Even true Christians often want the Lord to rush things for them, but the Lord says that they are to "*Wait on the LORD.*" The Lord repeats it twice in this verse to be sure the readers understand it clearly.

- Isaiah 40:31

"But they that wait upon the LORD shall renew *their* strength; they shall mount up with wings as eagles; they shall run, and not be weary; and they shall walk, and not faint."

If people "*wait upon the Lord,*" all these other wonderful things will happen.

- John 14:1-3

"Let not your heart be troubled: ye believe in God, believe also in me. In my Father's house are many mansions: if it *were* not *so*, I would have told you. I go to prepare a place for you. And if I go and prepare a place for you, I will come again, and receive you unto myself; that where I am, *there* ye may be also."

> **PATIENT WAITING FOR OUR HEAVENLY HOME**
>
> Before genuine Christians go Home to be with the Lord Jesus Christ, their Saviour, (either by death or by the Rapture of the Church to Heaven), there must be a time of patient waiting to see Him. This verse teaches clearly that the Lord Jesus Christ is preparing a place for those who are truly saved Christians.

- **Hebrews 10:36**
"For ye have need of patience, that, after ye have done the will of God, ye might receive the promise."
God's promises for those who do His will do not necessarily come instantaneously. They must wait for Him to fulfill His promise in His own proper time.
- **Hebrews 10:37**
"For yet a little while, and he that shall come will come, and will not tarry."

Verses On Christ Delivering From Wrath To Come

DELIVERED FROM HELL & THE TRIBULATION
The last part of verse ten talks about *"Jesus, which delivered us from the wrath to come."* The Lord Jesus Christ is the Deliverer. He is the only One Who can deliver the genuinely saved ones from the penalty of sin and the wrath of Hell.

There is the wrath of the Tribulation which will last for seven years. It's called Daniel's seventieth week. The Lord Jesus Christ will deliver all the genuine Christians from any part of that Tribulation period.
- **2 Corinthians 1:10**
"Who delivered us from so great a death, and doth deliver: in whom we trust that he will yet deliver us;"

The Lord Jesus Christ will deliver truly born-again Christians from spiritual death and being eternally separated from God in the fires of Hell for ever. God's deliverance has three tenses:
(1) **PAST deliverance**–from the penalty of sin;
(2) **PRESENT deliverance**–from the power of sin; and
(3) **FUTURE deliverance**–from the presence of sin.

As God delivered Daniel, Shadrach, Meshach, and Abednego from the wrath of their governmental authorities who despised them and the God of Heaven, so, may he deliver genuine Christians from the wrath of the present government of the United States of America whose Department of Homeland Security (DHS), under Janet Napolitano, named *"evangelical Christians"* as #72 of the 72 *"Potential terrorists"* in our country. **[If you want a copy of all 72 of those who were named as alleged *"potential terrorists,"* I'll send you a copy.]** If our government attacks these true Christians, may the Lord Jesus Christ be their Deliverer as well.
- **Galatians 1:4**
"Who gave himself for our sins, that he might deliver us from this present evil world, according to the will of God and our Father;"
This is speaking of the Lord Jesus Christ and the deliverance He made

possible for the entire world. But it is only realized by those who genuinely trust Him as their Saviour Who died for them.

> **DELIVERANCE FROM THIS PRESENT EVIL WORLD**
> The purpose for the Lord Jesus Christ's deliverance in this verse is *"from this present evil world."* Evil is all around genuine Christians. There are the evils of homosexuality, adultery, drugs, and many other things in this present evil world. They must be separated from these sins (and many, many more) and from those who practice them.

- John 3:16

"For God so loved the world, that he gave his only begotten Son, that whosoever believeth in him should not perish, but have everlasting life."

True faith in the Lord Jesus Christ will deliver that person from *"perishing"* in the Lake of Fire for all eternity.

- Colossians 1:13

"Who hath delivered us from the power of darkness, and hath translated *us* into the kingdom of his dear Son:"

> **DELIVERED FROM WORLD DARKNESS & FROM HELL**
> The Lord Jesus Christ has delivered every one who genuinely trusts Him as Saviour from the power of the darkness of this world and from the darkness of Hell. At the same moment in time, He has translated them into His eternal kingdom.

- 2 Timothy 3:11

"Persecutions, afflictions, which came unto me at Antioch, at Iconium, at Lystra; what persecutions I endured: but out of *them* all the Lord delivered me."

The Lord Jesus Christ delivered Paul out many persecutions and afflictions.

- 2 Timothy 4:17

"Notwithstanding the Lord stood with me, and strengthened me; that by me the preaching might be fully known, and *that* all the Gentiles might hear: and I was delivered out of the mouth of the lion."

PAUL'S SAVIOUR STOOD WITH HIM NEAR DEATH

Paul knew that His Saviour stood near him in his many persecutions. He strengthened him and delivered him out of the *"mouth of the lion,"* either literally from the stadium where Christians were killed by lions, or figuratively about the lions of adversity and terror.

- **2 Timothy 4:18**

"And the Lord shall deliver me from every evil work, and will preserve *me* unto his heavenly kingdom: to whom *be* glory for ever and ever. Amen."

Paul was confident of the Lord's deliverance of him from every evil work and would preserve him for Heaven.

- **Hebrews 2:14-15**

"Forasmuch then as the children are partakers of flesh and blood, he also himself likewise took part of the same; that through death he might destroy him that had the power of death, that is, the devil; And deliver them who through fear of death were all their lifetime subject to bondage."

DELIVERED FROM SATAN'S BONDAGE

The Lord Jesus Christ delivers those who genuinely trust Him from Satan's power and bondage. They are no longer in the family of the Devil, but in the family of God.

- **2 Peter 2:9**

"The Lord knoweth how to deliver the godly out of temptations, and to reserve the unjust unto the day of judgment to be punished:"

If the genuinely saved Christian depends on the Divine power of God the Holy Spirit in their lives, God can deliver them from all the temptations that surround them in this world.

1 Thessalonians Chapter Two

1 Thessalonians 2:1

"For yourselves, brethren, know our entrance in unto you, that it was not in vain:"

When Paul first came to Thessalonica, it was not *"in vain."* The Greek Word for *"vain"* is KENOS. Some of the meanings for this Word are:

"1) empty, vain, devoid of truth; 1a) of places, vessels, etc. which contain nothing; 1b) of men; 1b1) empty handed; 1b2) without a gift; 1c) metaph. destitute of spiritual wealth, of one who boasts of his faith as a transcendent possession, yet is without the fruits of faith; 1d) metaph. of endeavours, labours, acts, which result in nothing, vain, fruitless, without effect; 1d1) vain of no purpose"

Paul didn't waste any time, but began preaching the gospel of the Lord Jesus Christ and teaching the Bible clearly.

- **Psalm 127:1**
"Except the LORD build the house, they labour in vain that build it: except the LORD keep the city, the watchman waketh *but* in vain."

IS THE LORD JESUS CHRIST YOUR BUILDER?
The Lord must be the Builder of any spiritual house of any genuine Christian. Otherwise, the builder labors in vain. So with the watchmen, unless the Lord is guarding a city.

- **1 Corinthians 15:10**
"But by the grace of God I am what I am: and his grace which *was* bestowed upon me was not in vain; but I labored more abundantly than they all: yet not I, but the grace of God which was with me."
God's grace to Paul was not in vain. Paul labored abundantly because of it.

- **1 Corinthians 15:58**
"Therefore, my beloved brethren, be ye stedfast, unmoveable, always abounding in the work of the Lord, forasmuch as <u>ye know that your labour is not in vain in the Lord</u>."
If true Christians really labor for the Lord according to His Words, that labor is never in vain.
- **Galatians 2:2c**
"lest by any means I should run, or had run, in vain."
Paul didn't want to run in vain in the Galatian church either. They were mixing the law of Moses with the grace of the Lord Jesus Christ.
- **Philippians 2:16**
"Holding forth the word of life; that I may rejoice in the day of Christ, that I have not run in vain, neither labored in vain."

> **PAUL DIDN'T WANT TO LABOR IN VAIN**
> Paul wanted many souls to be truly saved so his labor and race would not have been in vain.

1 Thessalonians 2:2

"But even after that we had suffered before, and were shamefully entreated, as ye know, at Philippi, we were bold in our God to speak unto you the gospel of God with much contention."

Paul preached the *"gospel of God"* while in their city, even though there was much contention. He was doing that even after his poor reception by many at Philippi. Nothing stopped Paul in his preaching about the Lord Jesus Christ.

The Greek Word for *"shamefully entreated"* is HUBRIZO. Some of the meanings for this Word are:

1) to be insolent, to behave insolently, wantonly, outrageously; 2) <u>to act insolently and shamefully towards one</u>, to treat shamefully; 3) of one who injures another by speaking evil of him"

- **Acts 16:20-24**
"And brought them to the magistrates, saying, These men, being Jews, do exceedingly trouble our city, And teach customs, which are not lawful for us to receive, neither to observe, being Romans. And the multitude rose up together against them: and the magistrates rent off their clothes, and commanded to beat *them*. And when they had laid many stripes upon them, they cast *them* into prison, charging the jailor to keep them safely: Who, having received such a charge, thrust them into the inner prison, and made their feet fast

in the stocks."
This explains how shamefully Paul and Silas were treated in Philippi. They were beaten, cast into prison, and put into the stocks. In spite of all this, Paul was faithful in preaching the gospel of the Lord Jesus Christ. The prisoners heard Paul and Silas praying and singing praises as did the jailor who then received the Saviour as his own.
- **Acts 16:30-32**
"And brought them out, and said, Sirs, what must I do to be saved? And they said, Believe on the Lord Jesus Christ, and thou shalt be saved, and thy house. And they spake unto him the word of the Lord, and to all that were in his house."

SALVATION MUST BE PERSONAL, NOT FAMILIAL
Paul answered the jailor's question, *"Sirs, what must I do to be saved?"* He said, *"Believe on the Lord Jesus Christ, and thou shalt be saved, and thy house."* The jailor truly believed and was saved. Those in his house also genuinely believed and were saved. This verse does not teach, as some believe, automatic *"household salvation."* Just by being born in a house where both parents are genuine Christians does not make the children Christians. They must truly believe in the Saviour themselves before they can be saved.

- **Proverbs 28:4**
"They that forsake the law praise the wicked: but such as keep the law contend with them."

Genuinely saved people must not give in to wicked people, they must contend with them. Contention and disagreement with sin and evil is part of their ministry.
- **Jude 3**
"Beloved, when I gave all diligence to write unto you of the common salvation, it was needful for me to write unto you, and exhort *you* that ye should earnestly contend for the faith which was once delivered unto the saints."

Jude urged his readers to *"earnestly contend for the faith which was once delivered unto the saints."* We seek to do this at our Bible For Today Baptist Church. *"The faith,"* when it's with the Greek article, refers to that body of doctrine and teachings found in the Bible.

We contend in our church for many things. We contend about Bible versions, standing for the King James Bible and the underlying Hebrew, Aramaic, and Greek Words. We contend about the preservation of the Hebrew, Aramaic, and Greek Words. We contend for sound, traditional music, rather than the contemporary Christian music which is so popular today in many fundamental churches and growing more popular each day. Pretty soon it will be completely rock music. We contend also for Biblical morals and standards. We stand against fornication, adultery, and the homosexual lifestyle, and against many other things. As Paul preached boldly, without fear or favor, and with much contention, so we strive to do the same.

1 Thessalonians 2:3
"For our exhortation was not of deceit, nor of uncleanness, nor in guile:"

The Greek Word for *"exhortation"* is PARAKLESIS. Some of the meanings of the Word are:

"1) a calling near, summons, (esp. for help); 2) importation, supplication, entreaty; 3) exhortation, admonition, encouragement; 4) consolation, comfort, solace; that which affords comfort or refreshment; 4a) thus of the Messianic salvation (so the Rabbis call the Messiah the consoler, the comforter); 5) persuasive discourse, stirring address; 5a) instructive, admonitory, conciliatory, powerful hortatory discourse"

PAUL USED PERSUASIVE SPEAKING
When Paul spoke to the Thessalonians, he encouraged them with persuasive discourse and a stirring address.

There were three characteristics about Paul's exhortation.

1. Exhortation Not Of Deceit
Paul did not exhort by using *"deceit."* The Greek Word for *"deceit"* is PLANE. Some of the meanings of this Word are:

"1) a wandering, a straying about; 1a) one led astray from the right way, roams hither and thither; 2) metaph.; 2a) mental straying; 2a1) error, wrong opinion relative to morals or religion; 2b) error which shows itself in action, a wrong mode of acting; 2c) error, that which leads into error, deceit or fraud."

Paul was not deceitful in any of these above senses or meanings.

2. Exhortation Not Of Uncleanness
The second thing about Paul's exhortation was that it was not of *"uncleanness."* The Greek Word for *"uncleanness"* is AKATHARSIA. Some of the meanings of this Word are:

"*1) uncleanness; 1a) physical; 1b) in a moral sense: the impurity of lustful, luxurious, profligate living; 1b1) of impure motives*"

PAUL WAS CLEAN AND PURE FOR CHRIST
Paul's lifestyle did not exhibit any uncleanness whatsoever. He kept himself clean and pure for the Lord Jesus Christ.

3. Exhortation Not In Guile

PAUL DID NOT USE GUILE
The third thing about Paul's exhortation was that it was not *"in guile."* The Greek Word for *"guile"* is DOLOS. Some of the meanings of this Word are: *"1) craft, deceit, guile."* The root of that Word is probably DELLO which means *"to decoy."* Paul did not use this as he preached and taught.

- Mark 7:21-22

"For from within, out of the heart of men, proceed evil thoughts, adulteries, fornications, murders, thefts, covetousness, wickedness, deceit, lasciviousness, an evil eye, blasphemy, pride, foolishness:" Among the thirteen things listed that from the heart of men is *"deceit."* Paul did not use *"deceit"* when he preached and taught.

1 Thessalonians 2:4

"But as we were allowed of God to be put in trust with the gospel, even so we speak; not as pleasing men, but God, which trieth our hearts."

By God's grace, Paul was allowed of Him to be *"in trust with the gospel"* of the Lord Jesus Christ. Before the Lord Jesus Christ saved Paul, he was going to imprison and kill Christians, but God stopped him. The Lord Jesus Christ met him on the road to Damascus, straightened him out, and saved his soul. He blinded Paul for awhile so he wouldn't be able to find his way. Paul went into the city and someone told him what to do. The Lord Jesus Christ said that He would show him how many things he would suffer for His sake (Acts 9:16).

He was allowed of God to be *"put in trust"* with the gospel. The Greek Word for *"put in trust"* is PISTEUO. Some of the meanings of this Word are:

"1) to think to be true, to be persuaded of, to credit, place confidence in 1a) of the thing believed; 1a1) to credit, have confidence; 1b) in a moral or religious reference; 1b1) used in the NT of the conviction and

trust to which a man is impelled by a certain inner and higher prerogative and law of soul; 1b2) to trust in Jesus or God as able to aid either in obtaining or in doing something: saving faith; 1bc) mere acknowledgment of some fact or event: intellectual faith; 2) to entrust a thing to one, i.e. his fidelity; 2a) to be intrusted with a thing."

BEWARE OF FALSE TEACHERS AND PREACHERS

Paul was *put in trust* with the gospel of the Lord Jesus Christ. There are some pastors and evangelists today who proclaim false and unbiblical gospels. These people should not be *"put in trust"* with these false gospels. They are false teachers and false preachers. When the Lord Jesus Christ saved Paul's soul, He entrusted him with His gospel message.

PAUL WANTED TO PLEASE GOD, NOT HIMSELF

As Paul preached the true gospel of the Lord Jesus Christ, he did not do so with the primary object of *"pleasing men."* Rather, Paul preached with the purpose of pleasing God Who looks at the hearts.

The Greek Word for *"pleasing"* is ARESKO. Some of the meanings of this Word are:

"1) to please; 2) to strive to please; 2a) to accommodate one's self to the opinions desires and interests of others."

Paul was not that kind of a preacher. However, many preachers today, in pulpits all over the land, are pleasing men. If they can't please men, they have to leave that church. They must get a big crowd in order to pay their bills and stay in their buildings. To do this, they can't speak about various sins. They can't speak about how to be saved according to the Bible too much. That might cause many to leave their churches. This the practice of preachers in these huge, mammoth churches, with two thousand, five thousand, or ten thousand people who meet in stadiums. Some of them have fourteen thousand in attendance. In this case, there must be a *"pleasing of men"* or these thousands of people would leave their churches.

Paul did not do this. He was put in trust with the Biblical gospel which says that all men and women--apart from being saved by genuine faith in the Lord Jesus Christ--are sinners who are lost and bound for the everlasting fires of Hell. Unless a person changes their mind about their sinfulness, and changes their mind about the Lord Jesus Christ Who died for their sins and can save them, they are lost. Paul sought to please God in all of his preaching. That should be the goal of every preacher today.

Notice what this verse says about what God is doing in regard to these preachers. It says that God *"trieth our hearts."* The Greek Word for *"trieth"* is DOKIMAZO. Some of the meanings of this Word are:

"1) to test, examine, prove, <u>scrutinise</u> (to see whether a thing is genuine or not), as metals; 2) to recognise as genuine after examination, to approve, deem worthy."

GOD TESTS HEARTS

God scrutinizes the hearts of these preachers hearts. He tests their hearts as though a person were testing metals to see if they are genuine, or fake. <u>God tests the *"hearts"* here, not the minds, although the minds are also important.</u>

The Greek Word for *"heart"* is KARDIA. Some of the meanings for this Word are:

"1) the heart; 1a) that organ in the animal body which is the centre of the circulation of the blood, and hence was regarded as the seat of physical life; 1b) denotes the centre of all physical and spiritual life; 2a) the vigour and sense of physical life; 2b) the centre and seat of spiritual life; 2b1) <u>the soul or mind, as it is the fountain and seat of the thoughts, passions, desires, appetites, affections, purposes, endeavours;</u> 2b2) of the understanding, the faculty and seat of the intelligence; 2b3) of the will and character; 2b4) of the soul so far as it is affected and stirred in a bad way or good, or of the soul as the seat of the sensibilities, affections, emotions, desires, appetites, passions; 1c) of the middle or central or inmost part of anything, even though inanimate."

THE HEART IS THE CENTER OF OUR BEING

The *"heart"* is the fountain and seat of the thoughts, passions and desires, appetites, affections, purposes and endeavors. It is the center of our being.

1 Thessalonians 2:5

"For neither at any time used we flattering words, as ye know, nor a cloke of covetousness; God is witness:"

Paul mentioned that *God is witness* as he preaches the gospel and teaches the Bible. There are two more things that he does not use in his preaching: (1) *"flattering words"* and (2) *"a cloke of covetousness."*

1. No Flattering Words

In his preaching, Paul never flattered anyone with the words that he used. The Greek Word for *"flattering"* is KOLAKEIA. Some of the meanings of this Word are:

"1) flattery, flattering discourse"

This is a very brief meaning of the Greek Words.

English dictionaries give a more detailed meaning of *"flattery"*:
"Flattery is defined as praise or compliments, usually exaggerated or false; excessive, untrue, or insincere praise; exaggerated compliment or attention"

Though many preachers today use flattering words to some of the more wealthy supporters in order to get a raise in their salaries or for other reasons, Paul refused to use such *"flattering words."*

Verses On Flattery

- Psalm 12:2-3

"They speak vanity every one with his neighbor: *with* flattering lips *and* with a double heart do they speak. The LORD shall cut off all flattering lips, *and* the tongue that speaketh proud things:"

FLATTERY SOUNDS SWEET, BUT IS REALLY SOUR

When you say something true about a person, that's one thing, but when you say something false, that might sound good to the ears of the listener who might think it to be true, that's the use of flattering. God said that He cuts off all *"flattering lips."*

- Proverbs 7:5

"That they may keep thee from the strange woman, from the stranger *which* flattereth with her words."

The prostitutes and harlots make use of flattery to convince men to commit sin with them.

- Proverbs 28:23

"He that rebuketh a man afterwards shall find more favour than he that flattereth with the tongue."
Honest rebuke has more favor than speaking lies in order to please or gain favor with someone.
Paul did not use any *"flattering words"* as he preached and taught the gospel of the Lord Jesus Christ.

2. No Cloke Of Covetousness

The second thing that was absent from Paul's preaching was that he did not use any *"cloke of covetousness."* The Greek Word for *"cloke"* is PROPHASIS. Some of the meanings of this Word are:

"1) a pretext (alleged reason, pretended cause); 2) show; 2a) under colour as though they would do something; 2b) in pretence, ostensibly"

The Greek Word for *"covetousness"* is PLEONEXIA. Some of the meanings of that Word are:

"1) greedy desire to have more, covetousness, avarice"

PAUL DID NOT USE A CLOKE OR A PRETEXT

A *"cloke"* is a covering or garment that hides something from others. Since Paul was not *"covetous,"* he did not a cloke, either large or small, to cover something that didn't exist.

Verses On Cloke Or Covetousness

- **John 15:22**

"If I had not come and spoken unto them, they had not had sin: but now they have no cloke for their sin."

As I said before, a *"cloke"* covers something up. In this case, they had no "cloke" to cover their sin.

- **1 Peter 2:16**

"As free, and not using your liberty for a cloke of maliciousness, but as the servants of God."

Peter didn't want the church to use a *"cloke"* to cover-up *"maliciousness"* and evil of all kinds.

- **Jeremiah 6:13**

"For from the least of them even unto the greatest of them every one *is* given to covetousness, and from the prophet even unto the priest every one dealeth falsely."

"Covetousness" is the sin of many pastors in big churches. They love taking in millions of dollars for their own homes, planes, and other expenses. It seems like they will stop at nothing in order to get more money and what money can buy.

- Mark 7:21-22

"For from within, out of the heart of men, proceed evil thoughts, adulteries, fornications, murders, thefts, covetousness, wickedness, deceit, lasciviousness, an evil eye, blasphemy, pride, foolishness:"

COVETOUSNESS–THE ITCH FOR MORE

"*Covetousness*" is one of the thirteen sins that proceed from the hearts of people. "*Covetousness*" can be described as "*the itch for more*," especially of what other people have. Paul was not a covetous man. He didn't use a cloke to cover anything up. He gave up all of his former status and prestige to follow the Lord Jesus Christ. He didn't even ask people to support his ministry. He was a tent maker. He worked hard and long hours.

---

1 Thessalonians 2:6

"**Nor of men sought we glory, neither of you, nor yet of others, when we might have been burdensome, as the apostles of Christ.**"

Paul did not seek glory from people. He sought how to please God. He could have been "*burdensome*" since he was an apostle, but chose not to be.

The Greek Word for "*burdensome*" is BAROS. Some of the meanings of that Word are:

"*1) heaviness, weight, burden, trouble*"

The Word usually has to do with giving of money. "*Burdensome*" is usually understood in this context as seeking funds that would be a burden to the poor people that Paul ministered to.

- 2 Corinthians 11:9

"And when I was present with you, and wanted, I was chargeable to no man: for that which was lacking to me the brethren which came from Macedonia supplied: and in all *things I* have kept *myself* from being burdensome unto you, and so will I keep myself."

PAUL DIDN'T BURDEN PEOPLE

Paul didn't want to burden the people of Corinth or any other churches for his personal needs. That's why he worked hard as a tent maker.

- **2 Corinthians 12:14**

"Behold, the third time I am ready to come to you; and I will not be burdensome to you: for I seek not yours, but you: for the children ought not to lay up for the parents, but the parents for the children."

When the Lord gave the gospel of the Lord Jesus Christ to Corinth through Paul and they were genuinely saved, he was their spiritual father. They were his spiritual children. The children shouldn't support the parents, but parents should support the children.

1 Thessalonians 2:7

"But we were gentle among you, even as a nurse cherisheth her children:"

Paul was *"gentle"* among those in Thessalonica. The Greek Word for *"gentle"* is EPIOS. Some of the meanings for that Word are:

"1) affable; 2) mild, gentle"

This is the opposite of being "burdensome" or pleasing men rather than God. There is a simile that Paul used. He was gentle *"as a nurse cherisheth her children."* When newborn babies arrive in hospitals, they must be under the gentle care of the nurses in the children's ward. These newly born-again people in Thessalonica were Paul's spiritual children. He cared for them just like a nurse would care for a newborn baby. He *"cherished"* them. The Greek Word for *"cherish"* is THALPO. Some of the meanings of this Word are:

"1) to warm, keep warm; 2) to cherish with tender love, to foster with tender care."

That term describes what Paul's ministry was to these people at Thessalonica and other churches as well. He was as gentle and as cherishing as a nurse who is caring for her little children.

Verses On Being Gentle

Here are some verses that speak of being gentle, nursing and cherishing little babies and others as well.

- **2 Timothy 2:24**

"And the servant of the Lord must not strive; but be gentle unto all *men*, apt to teach, patient,"

SERVANTS OF THE LORD MUST BE GENTLE

Any servant of the Lord, especially a pastor of a local church, must be *"gentle"* in his service for the Lord Jesus Christ. Yet, in this gentleness, there must also be a firm standing for principles of the Words of God.

- **Titus 3:2**

"To speak evil of no man, to be no brawlers, *but* gentle, shewing all meekness unto all men."

Pastor Titus was to be gentle as a pastor personally, and in his preaching and teaching of the Words of God.

- **Exodus 2:7-8**

"Then said his sister to Pharaoh's daughter, Shall I go and call to thee a nurse of the Hebrew women, that she may nurse the child for thee? And Pharaoh's daughter said to her, Go. And the maid went and called the child's mother."

Moses' own mother was able to nurse him and nourish him up for many years before giving him to Pharaoh's daughter.

- **Exodus 2:9**

"And Pharaoh's daughter said unto her, Take this child away, and nurse it for me, and I will give *thee* thy wages. And the woman took the child, and nursed it."

Moses' own mother was paid by Pharaoh's daughter to be the nurse for her own baby.

- **Ephesians 5:29**

"For no man ever yet hated his own flesh; but nourisheth and cherisheth it, even as the Lord the church:"

HUSBANDS TO LOVE THEIR WIVES AS THEMSELVES

Paul is talking about a husband who is to love his wife even as he loves his own body. That is the task which is commanded even though it is practically impossible for any man, no matter how godly he may be, to ever fulfil. This is a picture of how the Lord Jesus Christ loves those who are genuinely saved in the Church which is His body.

1 Thessalonians 2:8

"**So being affectionately desirous of you, we were willing to have imparted unto you, not the gospel of God only, but also our own souls, because ye were dear unto us.**"

THE THESSALONIANS WERE DEAR TO PAUL

Though this could be the editorial "we" used by Paul alone, on the other hand, the "we," "our," and "us" in this verse could include not only Paul, but also Silas and Timothy. All three of these servants of the Lord were motivated by an affectionate desire for these Thessalonian Christians.

The Greek Word for "*affectionately desirous*" is HIMEIROMAI. Some of the meanings of this Word are:
"*1) to desire, long for, esp. the longing of love*"

THESE SERVANTS LOVED THE THESSALONIANS

These servants longed for the Thessalonian Christians and loved them in the Lord Jesus Christ. They wanted the best possible things for this church. Because of this love for the Thessalonian Christians, these men were willing not only to give them the Gospel of God, but also to give them their own "*souls*" in endearment.

The Greek Word for "*soul*" is PSUCHE. Some of the many meanings of that Word are:
"*1) breath; 1a) the breath of life; 1a1) the vital force which animates the body and shows itself in breathing; 1a1a) of animals; 1a12) of men; 1b) life; 1c) that in which there is life; 1c1) a living being, a living soul; 2) the soul; 2a) the seat of the feelings, desires, affections, aversions (our heart, soul etc.); 2b) the (human) soul in so far as it is constituted that by the right use of the aids offered it by God it can attain its highest end and secure eternal blessedness, the soul regarded as a moral being designed for everlasting life; 2c) the soul as an essence which differs from the body and is not dissolved by death (distinguished from other parts of the body).*"

The reason that these three servants of the Lord Jesus Christ were willing to give their own soul to the Thessalonians was because they were dear unto them. The Greek Word for "*dear*" is AGAPETOS. Some of the meanings of this Word are:
"*1) beloved, esteemed, dear, favourite, worthy of love*"

- **Luke 7:2**

"And a certain centurion's servant, who was dear unto him, was sick, and ready to die."

This servant was ready to die, but because he was dear unto his centurion master, the centurion came to the Lord Jesus Christ in behalf of his servant.

- **Colossians 1:13**

"Who hath delivered us from the power of darkness, and hath translated us into the kingdom of his dear Son:"

The Lord Jesus Christ was God's dear Son. Those of us who are true Christians should walk with the Lord following His Words as His dear children.

1 Thessalonians 2:9

"For ye remember, brethren, our labour and travail: for labouring night and day, because we would not be chargeable unto any of you, we preached unto you the gospel of God."

If this is an editorial *"our"* referring to Paul himself, he wants the Thessalonians to remember his labour and his travail laboring both night and day. The Greek Word for *"labour"* is KOPOS. Some of the meanings of that Word are:

"1) a beating; 2) a beating of the breast with grief, sorrow; 3) labour; 3a) trouble; 3a1) to cause one trouble, make work for him; 3b) intense labour united with trouble and toil."

TENT-MAKING WAS HARD LABOR

Tent-making was not easy. I understand it is a very difficult, serious task. The Greek Word for *"labour"* indicates intense labor. It was a night and day labor. He didn't want to be *"chargeable"* to the Thessalonians.

The Greek Word for *"chargeable"* this word is EPIBAREO. Some of the meanings for this Word are:

"1) to put a burden upon, to load 2) to be burdensome"

Paul didn't want to be a burden to this church. That is why he labored so intensely and then preached the gospel of God to them. The Greek Word for *"preached"* is KERUSSO. Some of the meanings of this Word are:

"1) to be a herald, to officiate as a herald; 1a) to proclaim after the manner of a herald; 1b) always with the suggestion of formality, gravity and an authority which must be listened to and obeyed; 2) to publish, proclaim openly: something which has been done; 3) used of the public proclamation of the gospel and matters pertaining to it, made by John the Baptist, by Jesus, by the apostles and other Christian teachers."

A herald is one who represented a lofty official, a king or some other important person. Those words that were given by the king, were to be given exactly to the people who were to receive them. A preacher of the Words of God, must be a "*herald.*" As such, he is to take the Words of God that God has given in the Scriptures and preach them faithfully unto the people.

HERALDS MUST HAVE PROPER BIBLE WORDS
He must be sure that he had these proper Hebrew, Aramaic, and Greek Words that have been accurately translated into his own language--like the King James Bible translators have done in English. Paul was a herald and a preacher of the gospel of the Lord Jesus Christ.

1 Thessalonians 2:10
"Ye are witnesses, and God also, how holily and justly and unblameably we behaved ourselves among you that believe:"

PAUL LIVED A GODLY LIFE
The Thessalonian Christians were witnesses as to how "*holily and justly and unblameably*" Paul was among them. For many months he was there in their city. They saw him and heard him.

GOD KNOW EVERYTHING ABOUT US
Even though people might not see us, God sees us. He's omniscient. He knows everything. He knows our thoughts, and our words, even before we say them. Everywhere we go, God is a witness as well as people who observe us.

Paul said that the Thessalonians were his witnesses as well as God Himself. There were three things that they witnessed concerning Paul. They saw that he behaved himself (1) holily, (2) justly, and (3) unblameably.

1. Behaving Holily.
The Greek Word for "*holily*" is HOSIOS. Some of the meanings of the Word are:
"*1) piously, holily*"
In his life and comportment he agreed with the ways of God in every way.

2. Behaving Justly.
The Greek Word for "*justly*" DIKAIOS. Some of the meanings of this Word are:

"*1) just, agreeably to right; 2) properly, as is right; 3) uprightly, agreeable to the law of rectitude.*"
As such, Paul's life was agreeable to that which was right in the sight of the Lord.

3. Behaving Unblameably.

The Greek Word for "**unblameably**" is AMEMPTOS. Some of the meanings of that Word are:

"*1) blameless, so that there is no cause for censure*"

PAUL LIVED A BLAMELESS LIFE

Paul's life was lived so that he was "*blameless*" giving people no just cause for them to censure him. These were traits that Paul mirrored and showed to the Thessalonian Christians and to His God.

Verses On True Christian Character Traits
- Ephesians 1:4

"According as he hath chosen us in him before the foundation of the world, that we should be holy and without blame before him in love:"

EVERY CHRISTIAN SHOULD BE HOLY

God's purpose is that every genuine Christian should be "*holy*" not unholy.

- Ephesians 5:27

"That he might present it to himself a glorious church, not having spot, or wrinkle, or any such thing; but that it should be holy and without blemish."

Those that are truly saved are members of the "*Church which is His body*" (Ephesians 1:22-23). As such, their lives should be holy and without blemish.

- Colossians 1:22

"In the body of his flesh through death, to present you holy and unblameable and unreproveable in his sight."

SALVATION IS ONLY FOR THOSE WHO TRUST CHRIST

Through the death of the Lord Jesus Christ and the shedding of His blood, He truly saves those who put their genuine trust in Him. After this salvation, God expects them to be holy, unblameable, and unreproveable in His sight. That's quite a challenge and goal, but it is Biblical.

- Titus 1:8

"But a lover of hospitality, a lover of good men, sober, just, holy, temperate;"
A holy life is what is expected of those who are Biblically qualified to be Pastors of local churches. It is scandalous to have such wickedness as has been seen in the wicked and unholy life of Pastor Jack Schaapp formerly of the First Baptist Church of Hammond, Indiana. He was sentenced to 12 years in prison for having repeated sex with a 17-year old member of his church across state lines. He was unholy like his former pastor, Jack Hyles, was, in many areas.
- **1 Peter 1:15-16**
"But as he which hath called you is holy, so be ye holy in all manner of conversation; Because it is written, Be ye holy; for I am holy."
The goal of every genuine Christian, even if they can't achieve it perfectly, is to be holy, just as their God and their Saviour is holy.
- **Mark 6:20**
"For Herod feared John, knowing that he was a just man and an holy, and observed him; and when he heard him, he did many things, and heard him gladly."

JOHN THE BAPTIST WAS JUST AND HOLY
Herod knew that John the Baptist was both just and holy. He had a good testimony before this ungodly ruler. His godly reproof of Herod's adultery caused his execution.

- **1 Thessalonians 3:13**
"To the end he may stablish your hearts unblameable in holiness before God, even our Father, at the coming of our Lord Jesus Christ with all his saints."
Notice that God wants to establish the hearts, not the heads, unblameable in holiness. If the heart is holy, the head and the rest of the body will also participate in holiness.

1 Thessalonians 2:11

"**As ye know how we exhorted and comforted and charged every one of you, as a father doth his children,**"
Paul, as a spiritual father, led these Christians to Christ at Thessalonica. He was there "*three sabbath days*" (`:2) preaching to them and teaching them about the Lord Jesus Christ.
As their spiritual father, Paul did three things for them:
(1) he exhorted them;
(2) he comforted them; and
(3) he charged them--as a father to his children.
There is a need for all three of these things today among true Christians.

1. The Need To Be Exhorted
- **Acts 14:22**

"Confirming the souls of the disciples, and exhorting them to continue in the faith, and that we must through much tribulation enter into the kingdom of God."

Genuine Christians must be exhorted to continue in the doctrines of the faith as taught in the Bible.

- **1 Timothy 4:13**

"Till I come, give attendance to reading, to exhortation, to doctrine."

Part of Pastor Timothy's ministry at Ephesus was exhortation.

- **2 Timothy 4:2**

"Preach the word; be instant in season, out of season; reprove, rebuke, exhort with all longsuffering and doctrine."

Paul repeated the need for exhortation in the preaching of God's Words.

- **Titus 2:15**

"These things speak, and exhort, and rebuke with all authority. Let no man despise thee."

Pastor Titus was also told to exhort the true Christians in Crete where he was ministering for the Saviour.

- **Hebrews 10:25**

"Not forsaking the assembling of ourselves together, as the manner of some is; but exhorting *one another*: and so much the more, as ye see the day approaching."

Paul spoke to the Jews who came to know the Lord Jesus Christ that they were to exhort one another in the faith.

2. The Need To Be Comforted
- **Psalm 23:4c**

"Thy rod and thy staff they comfort me."

The shepherd's staff gave comfort to the sheep as it was used to pull the sheep out various pits and dangers. So God's staff can give comfort to those who are true Christians who might get into various pits from which His staff can lift them out.

- **Romans 15:4**

"For whatsoever things were written aforetime were written for our learning, that we through patience and comfort of the scriptures might have hope."

The Scriptures give true Christians comfort as they show God's power, protection, and leadership of His own people.

- **2 Corinthians 1:3-4**

"Blessed *be* God, even the Father of our Lord Jesus Christ, the Father of mercies, and the God of all comfort; Who comforteth us in all our tribulations, that we may be able to comfort them which are in any trouble, by the comfort wherewith we ourselves are comforted of God."

THE BIBLE'S GOD IS THE "GOD OF ALL COMFORT"
One of God's titles is *"the God of all comfort."* He comforts the true Christians in all their trouble and enables them to comfort others.

- **1 Thessalonians 4:18**

"Wherefore comfort one another with these words."
The Rapture by the Lord Jesus Christ of all the genuine Christians will bring comfort to them. They will one day be gathered together to meet Him in the air at the Rapture. These are comforting words.

3. The Need To Be Charged

THE NEED TO BE GIVEN ORDERS
One of the meanings of *"charge"* is *"implore"* which is like a command or an order. God has orders to give to His true born-again children so they don't go astray.

- **Acts 23:22**

"So the chief captain *then* let the young man depart, and charged *him, See thou* tell no man that thou hast shewed these things to me."
The chief captain charged the man not to show these matters to anyone.

- **1 Thessalonians 5:27**

"I charge you by the Lord that this epistle be read unto all the holy brethren."
Paul wanted this letter of 1 Thessalonians to be read to all the genuine Christians.

- **1 Timothy 1:3b**

". . . that thou mightiest charge some that they teach no other doctrine,"

TEACH ONLY BIBLICAL DOCTRINE
This is a command to teach no other doctrine than that clearly taught in the Bible.

- **1 Timothy 1:18**

"This charge I commit unto thee, son Timothy, according to prophecies which went before on thee, that thou by them mightest war a good warfare;"

WE MUST WAR A GOOD WARFARE
The charge to Pastor Timothy is to be sure to war a good warfare for the Lord Jesus Christ.

- 1 Timothy 5:21

"I charge *thee* before God, and the Lord Jesus Christ, and the elect angels, that thou observe these things without preferring one before another, doing nothing by partiality."

The command here is for Pastor Timothy to do nothing by any partiality, but treat everyone alike.

- 1 Timothy 6:13a

"I give thee charge in the sight of God,"

The charge was to fight the good fight of faith from the previous verse.

- 1 Timothy 6:17a

"Charge them that are rich in this world, that they be not highminded, nor trust in uncertain riches,"

Certainly riches in these days are uncertain indeed. Don't trust in them. As of the writing of this part of the book, there are about sixty-five billion paper dollars printed every month in the USA. This is worthless paper money without backing of any kind which is spiraling run away inflation. Paper dollars are worthless. They are backed by nothing. Those of us who are genuine Christians should not put our trust such "*uncertain riches,*" but in the living God and His Son, the Lord Jesus Christ.

- 2 Timothy 4:1

"I charge thee therefore before God, and the Lord Jesus Christ, who shall judge the quick and the dead at his appearing and his kingdom;"

This charge, completed in the next verse, is for Pastor Timothy to "*preach the Word*" of God faithfully.

4. The Need To Be As A Father

- Psalm 103:13

"Like as a father pitieth *his* children, *so* the LORD pitieth them that fear him:"

True Christians must pity those to whom they minister. The Lord pities those who trust Him.

- Proverbs 3:12

"For whom the LORD loveth he correcteth; even as a father the son *in whom* he delighteth."

GOD CORRECTS AS FATHERS SHOULD
Part of a father's obligation is correcting his children when they need correction. Children without needed correction do

not make good adults, parents, or future fathers. God corrects those in whom He delights. This should be the reason for fathers to give needed correction to their children in whom they delight and love.

- **1 Timothy 5:1**
"Rebuke not an elder, but intreat *him* as a father; and the younger men *as* brethren;"

TREAT ELDERS AS YOU SHOULD TREAT FATHERS
We must respect those that who are our elders and treat them we would our own father.

1 Thessalonians 2:12
"That ye would walk worthy of God, who hath called you unto his kingdom and glory."

CHRISTIANS MUST WALK WORTHY OF THE LORD
The reason Paul wanted to charge every one of these Christians at Thessalonica is that they would walk worthy of God. That means some of them were not walking worthy of the Lord.

The Greek Word for *"worthy"* is AXIOS. Some of the meanings of that Word are:
"1) *suitably, worthily, in a manner worthy of*"

Verses On The Word, Worthy

- **Ephesians 4:1**
"I therefore, the prisoner of the Lord, beseech you that ye walk worthy of the vocation wherewith ye are called,"

None of those who are genuine Christians are worthy of the Lord Jesus Christ and His salvation, yet they should seek to "walk worthy" of the Lord Jesus Christ Who has called them.

- **Colossians 1:10**
"That ye might walk worthy of the Lord unto all pleasing, being fruitful in every good work, and increasing in the knowledge of God;"

Paul again urges the true Christians at Colosse to *"walk worthy"* of their Saviour.

- **James 2:7**
"Do not they blaspheme that worthy name by the which ye are called?"

Another thing that is "worthy" is the name of the Lord Jesus Christ.

- **Revelation 4:11**

"Thou art worthy, O Lord, to receive glory and honour and power: for thou hast created all things, and for thy pleasure they are and were created."

The Lord Jesus Christ as well as God the Father and God the Holy Spirit are all "*worthy*" to receive all glory, honor, and power.

- **Revelation 5:12**

"Saying with a loud voice, Worthy is the Lamb that was slain to receive power, and riches, and wisdom, and strength, and honour, and glory, and blessing."

Those who are genuinely saved are not worthy. Jacob, in the Old Testament would say of himself, "*I am not worthy*" (Genesis 32:10).

ONLY THE LORD JESUS CHRIST IS WORTHY

The Lamb, the Lord Jesus Christ, is the only One Who is genuinely worthy. True Christians should walk worthy of that Lamb Who has called them into His kingdom and glory.

1 Thessalonians 2:13

"For this cause also thank we God without ceasing, because, when ye received the word of God which ye heard of us, ye received it not as the word of men, but as it is in truth, the word of God, which effectually worketh also in you that believe."

Paul was continuously thankful that the Thessalonians received the Word of God as it is in truth. These Words of God work "*effectually*" in those who truly believe in the Lord Jesus Christ as their Saviour.

THE RIGHT WORDS OF GOD ARE VITAL

We must know the right Words of God in order to make God's Words work effectively. That's why we use the King James Bible which is an accurate English translation based upon the proper inspired and preserved Hebrew, Aramaic, and Greek Words.

Verses On Characteristics Of The Bible

1. **The Words Of God Are Right.**
   - **Psalm 33:4a**

"For the word of the LORD *is* right;"

We don't learn from papers, magazines, television, the Internet or any other source what is right and wrong. We find that only in the Bible.

2. **The Words Of God Can Cleanse.**
   - Psalm 119:9
   "Wherewithal shall a young man cleanse his way? By taking heed *thereto* according to thy word."
3. **The Words Of God Can Prevent From Sinning.**
   - Psalm 119:11
   "Thy word have I hid in mine heart, that I might not sin against thee."
4. **The Words Of God Can Give Life.**
   - Psalm 119:25
   "My soul cleaveth unto the dust: quicken thou me according to thy word."
   - Philippians 2:16
   "Holding forth the word of life; that I may rejoice in the day of Christ, that I have not run in vain, neither labored in vain."
5. **The Words Of God Can Strengthen.**
   - Psalm 119:28
   "My soul melteth for heaveiness: strengthen thou me according unto thy word."
6. **The Words Of God Can Give Hope.**
   - Psalm 119:49
   "Remember the word unto thy servant, upon which thou hast caused me to hope."
7. **The Words Of God Can Comfort.**
   - Psalm 119:50
   "This *is* my comfort in my affliction: for thy word hath quickened me."
8. **The Words Of God Can Keep From Straying.**
   - Psalm 119:67
   "Before I was afflicted I went astray: but now have I kept thy word."
9. **The Words Of God Can Keep From Evil Ways.**
   - Psalm 119:101
   "I have refrained my feet from every evil way, that I might keep thy word."
10. **The Words Of God Can Light Our Feet And Path.**
    - Psalm 119:105
    "Thy word *is* a lamp unto my feet, and a light unto my path."
11. **The Words Of God Can Keep From Iniquity.**
    - Psalm 119:133
    "Order my steps in thy word: and let not any iniquity have dominion over me."

12. The Words Of God Can Keep From Transgression.
- Psalm 119:158

"I beheld the transgressors, and was grieved; because they kept not thy word."

13. The Words Of God Can Bring Rejoicing.
- Psalm 119:162

"I rejoice at thy word, as one that findeth great spoil."

14. The Words Of God Can Give Understanding.
- Psalm 119:169

"Let my cry come near before thee, O LORD: give me understanding according to thy word."

15. The Words Of God Can Sanctify And Cleanse.
- John 17:17

"Sanctify them through thy truth: thy word is truth."
- Ephesians 5:26

"That he might sanctify and cleanse it with the washing of water by the word,"

16. The Words Of God Can Build Up.
- Acts 20:32

"And now, brethren, I commend you to God, and to the word of his grace, which is able to build you up, and to give you an inheritance among all them which are sanctified."

17. The Words Of God Can Give Faith.
- Romans 10:17

"So then faith *cometh* by hearing, and hearing by the word of God."

18. The Words Of God Can Give Reconciliation.
- 2 Corinthians 5:19

"To wit, that God was in Christ, reconciling the world unto himself, not imputing their trespasses unto them; and hath committed unto us the word of reconciliation."

19. The Words Of God Are The Sword Of The Spirit.
- Ephesians 6:17

"And take the helmet of salvation, and the sword of the Spirit, which is the word of God:"

20. The Words Of God Can Give Nourishment.
- 1 Timothy 4:6b

"nourished up in the words of faith and of good doctrine"

21. The Words Of God Are Something To Preach.
- 2 Timothy 4:2

"Preach the word; be instant in season, out of season; reprove, rebuke, exhort with all longsuffering and doctrine."

22. The Words Of God Can Convince The Unbelievers.
- Titus 1:9

"Holding fast the faithful word as he hath been taught, that he may be able by sound doctrine both to exhort and to convince the gainsayers."

23. The Words Of God Are Powerful.
- Hebrews 4:12

"For the word of God is quick, and powerful, and sharper than any twoedged sword, piercing even to the dividing asunder of soul and spirit, and of the joints and marrow, and is a discerner of the thoughts and intents of the heart."

24. The Words Of God Are Righteous.
- Hebrews 5:13

"For every one that useth milk is unskillful in the word of righteousness: for he is a babe."

25. The Words Of God Can Bring New Birth.
- James 1:18

"Of his own will begat he us with the word of truth, that we should be a kind of firstfruits of his creatures."

- James 1:21

"Wherefore lay apart all filthiness and superfluity of naughtiness, and receive with meekness the engrafted word, which is able to save your souls."

- 1 Peter 1:23

"Being born again, not of corruptible seed, but of incorruptible, by the word of God, which liveth and abideth for ever."

26. The Words Of God Give The Gospel.
- 1 Peter 1:25

"But the word of the Lord endureth for ever. And this is the word which by the gospel is preached unto you."

27. The Words Of God Can Give Growth.
- 1 Peter 2:2

"As newborn babes, desire the sincere milk of the word, that ye may grow thereby:"

28. The Words Of God Can Give Accurate Prophecy.
- 2 Peter 1:19

"We have also a more sure word of prophecy; whereunto ye do well that ye take heed, as unto a light that shineth in a dark place, until the day dawn, and the day star arise in your hearts:"

> **CORRECT TRANSLATIONS ARE ESSENTIAL**
> The Words of God, as found in the correct translations of the inspired and preserved Hebrew, Aramaic, and Greek Words, can yield all twenty-eight of these effects and purposes. These Words work effectually in those who are genuinely born-again and saved.

1 Thessalonians 2:14

"For ye, brethren, became followers of the churches of God which in Judaea are in Christ Jesus: for ye also have suffered like things of your own countrymen, even as they have of the Jews:"

> **SUFFERING FROM UNBELIEVING JEWS**
> It is clear that genuine Christians in Paul's day suffered many things from the Jews who despised the gospel of the Lord Jesus Christ.

Verses On Paul's Persecution

Here are some of the verses that show the Jewish hatred for the Saviour and for those who truly trusted Him.

- Acts 9:23

"And after that many days were fulfilled, the Jews took counsel to kill him."

The Jews wanted to kill Paul because he was preaching about salvation that was found in truly trusting the Lord Jesus Christ.

- Acts 13:50

"But the Jews stirred up the devout and honourable women, and the chief men of the city, and raised persecution against Paul and Barnabas, and expelled them out of their coasts."

> **THE APOSTLES REMOVED FROM SOME CITIES**
> The Jews stirred up many to persecute Paul and Barnabas and removed them from their cities.

- Acts 14:2

"But the unbelieving Jews stirred up the Gentiles, and made their minds evil affected against the brethren."

The Jews stirred up the Gentiles to have mental hatred against the genuine Christians.

1 & 2 Thessalonians–Preaching Verse by Verse

- **Acts 14:5**
"And when there was an assault made both of the Gentiles, and also of the Jews with their rulers, to use *them* despitefully, and to stone them,"

Both Jews and Gentiles tried to stone the true Christians.

- **Acts 14:19**
"And there came thither *certain* Jews from Antioch and Iconium, who persuaded the people, and, having stoned Paul, drew *him* out of the city, supposing he had been dead."

PAUL WAS STONED AT ANTIOCH
These Jews from Antioch and Iconium stoned Paul and thought he was dead. Later, we learn that though he died and went to Heaven, the Lord Jesus Christ brought him back to life again to continue serving Him.

- **Acts 17:5**
"But the Jews which believed not, moved with envy, took unto them certain lewd fellows of the baser sort, and gathered a company, and set all the city on an uproar, and assaulted the house of Jason, and sought to bring them out to the people."

These Jews despised the gospel of the Lord Jesus Christ and the true Christians who believed it. They were filled with envy and evil.

- **Acts 18:12**
"And when Gallio was the deputy of Achaia, the Jews made insurrection with one accord against Paul, and brought him to the judgment seat,"

Here the Jews made insurrection against Paul and took him to court.

- **Acts 20:19**
"Serving the Lord with all humility of mind, and with many tears, and temptations, which befell me by the lying in wait of the Jews:"

The Jews wanted to kill Paul because of their hatred of him and the gospel of Christ that He preached to them.

- **Acts 21:27**
"And when the seven days were almost ended, the Jews which were of Asia, when they saw him in the temple, stirred up all the people, and laid hands on him,"

These Jews laid hands on Paul to take him.

- **Acts 23:12**
"And when it was day, certain of the Jews banded together, and bound themselves under a curse, saying that they would neither eat nor drink till they had killed Paul."

Though these Jews didn't kill Paul, they wanted to very badly.

- Acts 26:21

"For these causes the Jews caught me in the temple, and went about to kill *me*."

Again, these Jews wanted to kill Paul. When Paul talks about the persecution by the Jews, these verses demonstrate that he knows it well. These Thessalonians also had persecution from their own countrymen who were probably mostly Gentiles.

1 Thessalonians 2:15

"Who both killed the Lord Jesus, and their own prophets, and have persecuted us; and they please not God, and are contrary to all men:"

In this verse, Paul lays down a fivefold indictment of the unbelieving Jews:

(1) They killed the Lord Jesus Christ;
(2) They killed their own prophets;
(3) They persecuted Paul and his friends;
(4) They don't please God; and
5) They are contrary to all men.

PAUL–A JEW BY BIRTH, A CHRISTIAN BY NEW BIRTH

Paul was a Jew by race, but Christian by his new birth. He tells the truth about these things, regardless of the consequences.

Verses On Paul's Fivefold Indictment

Here are some of the verses that illustrate what Paul is talking about.

- Matthew 27:20

"But the chief priests and elders persuaded the multitude that they should ask Barabbas, and destroy Jesus."

The Jewish chief priests and elders persuaded Pilate to release Barabbas, a murderer, and to crucify the Lord Jesus Christ Who had done nothing amiss.

- Matthew 27:21

"The governor answered and said unto them, Whether of the twain will ye that I release unto you? They said, Barabbas."

These Jews wanted the Lord Jesus Christ to be murdered by crucifixion.

- 1 Kings 18:13

"Was it not told my lord what I did when Jezebel slew the prophets of the LORD, how I hid an hundred men of the LORD'S prophets by fifty in a cave, and fed them with bread and water?"

Jezebel, the Jewish wife of wicked King Ahab, slew many Old Testament prophets.

- **Acts 7:52**
"Which of the prophets have not your fathers persecuted? And they have slain them which shewed before of the coming of the Just One; of whom ye have been now the betrayers and murderers:"
The Jewish fathers slew the faithful prophets as they did the Just Lord Jesus Christ by betrayal and murder.
- **Acts 9:22, 23**
"But Saul increased the more in strength, and confounded the Jews which dwelt at Damascus, proving that this is very Christ. And after many days were fulfilled, the Jews took counsel to kill him."
Once again, the Jews took counsel to kill Paul.
- **2 Corinthians 11:24**
"Of the Jews five times received I forty *stripes* save one."
Paul wrote about these beatings with whips on five different occasions. Thirty-nine lashes each time were given to Paul.

1 Thessalonians 2:16

"Forbidding us to speak to the Gentiles that they might be saved, to fill up their sins alway: for the wrath is come upon them to the uttermost."

Here are three more things against the unbelieving Jews:
(6) They forbade Paul to preach to the Gentiles;
(7) They fill up their sins always; and
(8) They have God's wrath upon them.
- **2 Peter 3:9b**
"Not willing that any should perish, but that all should come to repentance."

GOD IS NOT WILLING THAT ANY PERISH IN HELL

God does not want anyone to perish and go to the Lake of Fire for all eternity. God is willing that all people should come to Him through true faith in the Lord Jesus Christ, but each person must put his or her trust in Him in order to be saved. It doesn't come automatically.

1 Thessalonians 2:17

"But we, brethren, being taken from you for a short time in presence, not in heart, endeavoured the more abundantly to see your face with great desire."

Paul said he was taken from them for a short while, not in heart, but in presence only.

The Greek Word for *"taken"* here is: APORPHANIZO. Some of the meanings of this Word are:
"1) to <u>bereave of a parent</u> or parents"
We get our English word, *"orphaned"* from this Greek term.

WHEN FATHERS LEAVE, THE CHILDREN ARE ORPHANS

The picture is that of a father (Paul) leaving his spiritual children (the Thessalonians) without him, thus leaving them as *"orphans."* Though Paul left them in presence, he did not in his heart. He wrote to them again in 2 Thessalonians and no doubt visited them again as well. Paul wanted to be with them, but he had other duties to undertake for the Lord Jesus Christ.

1 Thessalonians 2:18

"Wherefore we would have come unto you, even I Paul, once and again; but Satan hindered us."

THE HINDRANCES OF SATAN

Paul wanted to come to them at different times, but Satan hindered him in some way. Satan is not just a force, as many unbelievers teach. Satan is a person. He was created by God as one of His leading angels, but he sinned and fell from that exalted status. He said *"I will"* to God five different times in Isaiah 14:12-15. He was cast out of Heaven and became the enemy of all true Christians.

- Romans 15:22

"For which cause also I have been much hindered from coming to you."

Perhaps it was Satan who hindered Paul from coming to Rome as well. We are not told. But it is clearly stated that it was Satan who hindered Paul from coming to those true Christians in Thessalonica.

EIGHT CHARACTERISTICS OF SATAN

Satan does a number of things, as the Scripture says. Let me list some of the things that he does:

1. Satan is an adversary who opposes true Christians.
2. Satan is the prince or leader of evil spirits.
3. Satan is the adversary of God and the Lord Jesus Christ.
4. Satan incites apostasy from God into sin,

5. Satan circumvents men by his wiles and clever schemes.
6. Satan controls those who worship idols.
7. Satan, by his demons, takes possession of men and sometimes inflicts them with diseases.
8. Satan is overcome by the power of God.
Genuine Christians are to resist the Devil by being steadfast in the faith (James 4:7 and 1 Peter 5:8-9).

When the Lord Jesus Christ returns, in the second phase of His return, after the Tribulation period, He will set up His earthly reign for one thousand years.

SATAN WILL BE BOUND 1,000 YEARS

During all those years, Satan will be bound (Revelation 20:2). After these thousand years of his imprisonment, Satan will be loosed (Revelation 20:7) to walk the earth with great power. In the end, Satan will be "cast into the lake of fire and brimstone" (Revelation 20:10) and shall be *"tormented day and night for ever and ever."* The Lake of Fire was originally prepared for the Devil and his angels (Matthew 25:41).

1 Thessalonians 2:19

"For what is our hope, or joy, or crown of rejoicing? Are not even ye in the presence of our Lord Jesus Christ at his coming?"

Paul talks in this verse about the genuine Christians of Thessalonica as being his hope, his joy, and his crown of rejoicing. Because he led them to a saving knowledge of the Lord Jesus Christ as their Saviour, he speaks about a *"crown."*

THE SOUL-WINNER'S CROWN

Of the five crowns mentioned in the New Testament, this is apparently the soul-winners crown. Paul says that they will be in the presence of the Lord Jesus Christ when He returns. They were to be in Christ's presence, either: if He were to come in the Rapture, or when they died, whichever came first.

I know what Paul was talking about when he thought about how these true Christians would be with the Saviour because he led them to Christ. I am reminded of my early ministry as a Navy Chaplain on active duty for five years. I remember a married lady whose husband died. She came into my office shocked and in tears. I told her the simple gospel of the Lord Jesus Christ and she received Him as her Saviour. After these many years since that time, she has been faithful each month in her support for our Bible For Today ministries. I am so grateful for her faithfulness, and that she will be in the presence of her Saviour when she dies or when He returns in the Rapture.

Verses On True Christians' Future In Heaven
- **John 14:2**

"In my Father's house are many mansions: if *it were* not so, I would have told you. I go to prepare a place for you."

The Lord Jesus Christ was speaking these words to his believing apostles who were trusting Him as their Saviour.

- **John 14:3**

"And if I go and prepare a place for you, I will come again, and receive you unto myself; that where I am, *there* ye may be also."

That's a promise from the Lord Jesus Christ for true Christians to be with Him in Heaven for all eternity.

- **John 17:24**

"Father, I will that they also, whom thou hast given me, be with me where I am; that they may behold my glory, which thou hast given me: for thou lovedst me before the foundation of the world."

This was the high priestly prayer of the Lord Jesus Christ. He prayed to His Father that those who are His true followers will be with Him in Heaven when they die.

- **2 Corinthians 5:8**

"We are confident, *I say*, and willing rather to be absent from the body, and to be present with the Lord."

If you are truly saved, born-again and redeemed, unless the Lord should come in the Rapture, you will be absent from this body one day and you will be present with the Lord.

I remember one of the ladies in our Bible study that we had on Thursday nights for many years. She was a Roman Catholic who had been taught that there was a purgatory that people had to go to when they died. I used this verse to show her that for those who were genuinely saved and born-again, would go directly to Heaven to be with the Lord Jesus Christ without any stop in a purgatory which is not in the Bible. I don't know if she ever believed it, but I used this verse and other verses to tell her the truth about Heaven and against purgatory.

- **Philippians 1:23**

"For I am in a strait betwixt two, having a desire to depart, and to be with Christ, which is far better."

PURGATORY IS FALSE--NOT IN THE BIBLE

It is very clear that there is no in-between place of purgatory. Everyone who is a genuine Christian, upon their death, will depart and be with Christ instantaneously. This is crystal clear.

- Colossians 3:4

"When Christ, who is our life, shall appear, then shall ye also appear with him in glory."

AT THE RAPTURE, ALL CHRISTIANS ARE WITH CHRIST

At the Rapture, when the Lord Jesus Christ returns in the air, every true Christian then living will appear with Him in glory.

- 1 Thessalonians 4:16-17

For the Lord himself shall descend from heaven with a shout, with the voice of the archangel, and with the trump of God: and the dead in Christ shall rise first: Then we which are alive *and* remain shall be caught up together with them in the clouds, to meet the Lord in the air: and so shall we ever be with the Lord."

This is depicting what will happen at the Rapture of the true Christians. It is very simple, they will meet the Lord Jesus Christ in the air and be with Him for all eternity to come.

1 Thessalonians 2:20

"For ye are our glory and joy."

The Thessalonian genuine Christians who Paul led to the Lord Jesus Christ are his glory and his joy.

1 Thessalonians Chapter Three

1 Thessalonians 3:1

"Wherefore when we could no longer forbear, we thought it good to be left at Athens alone;"

Paul wanted to be in Athens alone. Athens was an important Grecian city many miles south of Thessalonica. He was happy with the Thessalonians, but really felt that he had to remain in Athens. Paul sent Timothy to the Thessalonian church to minister to them in his absence.

1 Thessalonians 3:2

"And sent Timotheus, our brother, and minister of God, and our fellowlabourer in the gospel of Christ, to establish you, and to comfort you concerning your faith:"

Notice the three qualifications that Paul mentions concerning Timothy.

TIMOTHY INTRODUCED

1. **Timothy Was A Brother In Christ.** First, Timothy was a genuine Christian and brother in the Lord Jesus Christ. Paul probably led him to the Lord during the time he knew him as recorded in the book of Acts.

2. **Timothy Was A Minister Of God.** Secondly, Timothy was a minister or servant of God. He was not working on his own, but had God Himself as his Director and Guide. He served the Lord, rather than just himself or Paul.

3. **Timothy Was A Fellowlabourer In The Gospel.** Thirdly, Timothy was a fellowlabourer with the Apostle Paul in the gospel of the Lord Jesus Christ. He was Paul's right hand man. Timothy was there during the book of Acts. He was also part of Paul's various missionary journeys. Timothy labored with Paul in Paul's ministry in various places.

Because Paul trusted Timothy, he sent him to the Thessalonian Christians to help them.

Timothy was to do two things for the Thessalonian true Christians: (1) Timothy was to establish them, and (2) Timothy was to comfort them.

1. Timothy Was To Establish Them In The Faith

The Greek Word for *"establish"* is STERIZO. Some of the meanings of this Word are:

"1) to make stable, place firmly, set fast, fix; 2) to strengthen, make firm; 3) to render constant, confirm, one's mind."

It is interesting that the word, *"faith"* occurs in this chapter three in verses 2, 5, 6, and 7. In each case the Word for *"faith"* (PISTIS) is preceded by the Greek article. This indicates that it refers to the objective body of doctrine and teachings found in the Bible. Paul sent Timothy to make firm and establish the doctrines of the faith as taught in the Bible. There should be no wavering from Bible teachings and doctrines.

Verses On Being Established In The Faith

- **Acts 16:5**

"And so were the churches established in the faith, and increased in number daily."

Churches today should be *"established in the faith"* just as here in the book of Acts. It is sad that this is not true today in many instances.

- **Romans 1:11**

"For I long to see you, that I may impart unto you some spiritual gift, to the end ye may be established;"

Paul wanted the true Christians in Rome to be established in the doctrines of the faith.

- **Romans 16:25**

"Now to him that is of power to stablish you according to my gospel, and the preaching of Jesus Christ, according to the revelation of the mystery, which was kept secret since the world began,"

The God of the genuine Christian is able to establish them in His Bible doctrines so they do not change them. Our church is established in the things of Bible doctrine. We're in our 17th year at this writing. We haven't altered our doctrines and things that we believe. Our doctrines are established, fixed, and firm. That's what God wants of all the churches in the world, but, sad to say, this is far from what most churches are.

- **2 Thessalonians 2:17**

"Comfort your hearts, and stablish you in every good word and work."

Paul's prayer is that God would establish these genuine Christians in Thessalonica in every good word and work.

- **2 Thessalonians 3:3**
"But the Lord is faithful, who shall stablish you, and keep *you* from evil."

GOD CAN ESTABLISH TRUE CHRISTIANS
The Lord is able and willing to establish the true Christians even today and keep them from evil.

- **1 Peter 5:10**
"But the God of all grace, who hath called us unto his eternal glory by Christ Jesus, after that ye have suffered a while, make you perfect, stablish, strengthen, settle *you*."

The apostle Peter wanted these true Christians to be established, strengthened, and settled.

- **2 Peter 1:12**
"Wherefore I will not be negligent to put you always in remembrance of these things, though ye know *them*, and be established in the present truth."

Peter repeats to his readers that he wants them to be established in the doctrines of the Bible and not to drift from them.

2. Timothy Was To Comfort Them In The Faith
Verses On Comfort

- **Romans 1:12**
"That is, that I may be comforted together with you by the mutual faith both of you and me."

GENUINE CHRISTIANS NEED GOD'S COMFORT
All true Christians need God's comfort. The Lord doesn't want any Christian to be distressed. They need the comfort of God. Timothy was to comfort those Thessalonian Christians who were appointed to afflictions and trouble.

- **2 Corinthians 7:6**
"Nevertheless God, that comforteth those that are cast down, comforted us by the coming of Titus;"

Paul was comforted by the coming of Titus to visit him. Even the apostle Paul needed comfort from his fellow leader, Pastor Titus.

- **2 Corinthians 7:13**
"Therefore we were comforted in your comfort: yea, and exceedingly the more joyed we for the joy of Titus, because his spirit was refreshed by you all."

Here Paul himself was comforted by the comfort that the Corinthians found with the Lord's help.

- **Ephesians 6:22**
"Whom I have sent unto you for the same purpose, that ye might know our affairs, and *that* he might comfort your hearts."
Genuine Christians need to have their hearts comforted by the Lord Jesus Christ.
- **1 Thessalonians 4:18**
"Wherefore comfort one another with these words."

TRUE CHRISTIANS CAN COMFORT ONE ANOTHER
This verse refers back to the preceding verses and speaks of the comfort that can be possessed by those Christians who have lost their loved ones in death.

When the Lord Jesus Christ returns in the Rapture, those who have died will be caught up from their graves with glorified bodies and will be reunited in the air with those true Christians who were still living.

1 Thessalonians 3:3
"That no man should be moved by these afflictions: for yourselves know that we are appointed thereunto."

These genuine Christians at Thessalonica were appointed to afflictions. This appointment to afflictions is very clear to this church. But they were not to be "*moved*" by these afflictions. The Greek Word for "*moved*" is SAINO. Some of the meanings of that Word are:

"*1) to wag the tail; 1a) of dogs; 2) metaph. 2a) to flatter, fawn upon; 2b) to move (the mind of one); 2b1) agreeably; 2b2) to agitate, disturb, trouble.*"

They were not to be agitated, disturbed or troubled by these afflictions that they were experiencing. The Greek Word for "*afflictions*" is THLIPSIS. Some of the meanings of that Word are:

"*1) a pressing, pressing together, pressure; 2) metaph. oppression, affliction, tribulation, distress, straits.*"

CHRISTIANS--APPOINTED TO AFFLICTIONS
These Thessalonian Christians are not the only ones with afflictions. Every true believer today (whether they are in Communist Russia, Communist China, Communist Cuba, or in any other nation of the world) must realize that oppression awaits them. They are appointed to affliction and they must realize it.

Verses About Affliction
- **Psalm 34:19**

"Many are the afflictions of the righteous: but the LORD delivereth him out of them all."

Praise the Lord for His deliverance in these afflictions.
- **Mark 4:17**

"And have no root in themselves, and so endure but for a time: afterward, when affliction or persecution ariseth for the word's sake, immediately they are offended."

STONY GROUND SEED AND AFFLICTION

The Words of God that fall on stony ground are received only for a time, but when affliction comes these people are offended.

- **Acts 7:34**

"I have seen, I have seen the affliction of my people which is in Egypt, and I have heard their groaning, and am come down to deliver them. And now come, I will send thee into Egypt."

GOD DELIVERED ISRAEL FROM AFFLICTIONS

God was well aware of the affliction of the people of Israel in Egypt and made plans to deliver them.

- **2 Corinthians 2:4**

"For out of much affliction and anguish of heart I wrote unto you with many tears; not that ye should be grieved, but that ye might know the love which I have more abundantly unto you."

Paul was afflicted greatly as he wrote to the Corinthian church. He wanted them to know of his abundant love for them.
- **2 Corinthians 4:17**

"For our light affliction, which is but for a moment, worketh for us a far more exceeding *and* eternal weight of glory,"

LIGHT AFFLICTION VERSUS HEAVEN'S GLORY

Paul considered his beatings, his shipwreck, and all the other sufferings that came to him as being but a *"light affliction"* when compared to the glories of Heaven.

- **2 Corinthians 8:2**

"How that in a great trial of affliction the abundance of their joy and their deep poverty abounded unto the riches of their liberality."

Paul was referring to the churches of Macedonia. They gave to the Lord's work despite their afflictions and problems.

- **1 Thessalonians 1:6**

"And ye became followers of us, and of the Lord, having received the word in much affliction, with joy of the Holy Ghost."

Though the Thessalonian Christians had much affliction, they also had the joy of God the Holy Spirit.

- **1 Thessalonians 3:7**

"Therefore, brethren, we were comforted over you in all our affliction and distress by your faith."

Even though Paul had affliction and distress, he was comforted by the faith that the Thessalonian church had.

- **2 Timothy 1:8**

"Be not thou therefore ashamed of the testimony of our Lord, nor of me his prisoner: but be thou partaker of the afflictions of the gospel according to the power of God;"

In Paul's last letter before his execution by the Romans, he reminded Pastor Timothy that he would have to be a partaker of the afflictions of the gospel.

- **2 Timothy 4:5**

"But watch thou in all things, endure afflictions, do the work of an evangelist, make full proof of thy ministry."

Pastor Timothy, as he ministered to the church at Ephesus, was told by Paul to endure the afflictions that would come to him.

- **Hebrews 11:25**

"Choosing rather to suffer affliction with the people of God, than to enjoy the pleasures of sin for a season;"

Moses chose the affliction with his people Israel rather than the transitory pleasure of sin in Pharaoh's palace.

- **James 5:10**

"Take, my brethren, the prophets, who have spoken in the name of the Lord, for an example of suffering affliction, and of patience."

The Old Testament prophets were to be an example for those in James' day who were suffering affliction.

- **1 Peter 5:9**

"Whom resist stedfast in the faith, knowing that the same afflictions are accomplished in your brethren that are in the world."

The genuine Christians were to resist the Devil knowing that other Christians were afflicted by him as well.

1 Thessalonians 3:4

"For verily, when we were with you, we told you before that we should suffer tribulation; even as it came to pass, and ye know."

Paul predicted that they would have tribulation and the prediction came true.

Verses About Tribulation

- **Matthew 13:21**

"Yet hath he not root in himself, but dureth for a while: for when tribulation or persecution ariseth because of the word, by and by he is offended."

These are those who received the Words of God on stony ground. When tribulation came because of the Word, they were offended. That soil was not productive soil.

- **John 16:33**

"These things I have spoken unto you, that in me ye might have peace. In the world ye shall have tribulation: but be of good cheer; I have overcome the world."

CHRISTIANS PROMISED TRIBULATION

The Lord Jesus Christ did not want to deceive his disciples about the cost of becoming a true Christian. In the world, they were promised tribulation.

- **Acts 14:22**

"Confirming the souls of the disciples, *and* exhorting them to continue in the faith, and that we must through much tribulation enter into the kingdom of God."

Trouble and tribulation is a part of being saved and being a true Christian today.

- **Romans 8:35-37**

"Who shall separate us from the love of Christ? *shall* tribulation, or distress, or persecution, or famine, or nakedness, or peril, or sword? As it is written, for thy sake we are killed all the day long; we are accounted as sheep for the slaughter. Nay, in all these things we are more than conquerors through him that loved us."

TRIBULATION CAN'T SEPARATE FROM CHRIST'S LOVE

This tribulation that comes upon genuine Christians today cannot separate them from the love of the Lord Jesus Christ.

- **Romans 12:12**

"Rejoicing in hope, patient in tribulation; continuing instant in prayer;"

When tribulation comes, God tells us who are true Christians to be patient in all of it, praying throughout the ordeals.

- **2 Corinthians 1:4**

"Who comforteth us in all our tribulation, that we may be able to comfort them which are in any trouble, by the comfort wherewith we ourselves are comforted of God."

God Himself is the Comforter to those who have been redeemed by genuine faith in His Son, the Lord Jesus Christ. He is the God of all comfort.

- **2 Corinthians 7:4**

"Great *is* my boldness of speech toward you, great *is* my glorying of you: I am filled with comfort, I am exceeding joyful in all our tribulation."

Tribulation did not make Paul sour. It shouldn't sour true Christians either. He was "*exceeding joyful*" in all of his many tribulations. May sound Christians today also have the joy of the Lord even in trouble.

1 Thessalonians 3:5

"For this cause, when I could no longer forbear, I sent to know your faith, lest by some means the tempter have tempted you, and our labour be in vain."

The "*tempter*" is none other than the Devil and Satan. He seeks to harm and destroy the testimony of genuine Christians.

THE FAITH REFERS TO THE BIBLE'S DOCTRINES

As mentioned earlier, "*your faith*" has the Greek article (HE). Because of this, it refers to the doctrines and teachings of the Bible. Paul was so concerned about having the Thessalonians have sound and Biblical doctrines that he sent Timothy to them to ascertain whether or not they had not deviated in any way from Bible doctrines.

Paul wanted to know whether or not they were still holding to the doctrines that he taught them. He wanted to know if they were still stable in those doctrines. Satan the "*tempter*" wants, more than anything else, to get genuine Christians to depart from the Words of God. Slowly drifting, and then apostate heresy, are the results of leaving God's Words. Satan is very happy when this happens and the Lord Jesus Christ is very sad.

The most important thing that Satan wants to do is to get true Christians away from their faith, away from the doctrines, away from the Bible's teachings, and away from God's Words. Satan would move Heaven and earth to make Biblical Christians to move, to falter, and to drift for God's Words in the Bible. He has done this successfully in church after church, church movement after church movement, denomination after denomination, college after college, theological seminary after theological seminary, and news media after news media in the past history of our country and the entire world.

Paul did not want his labor in founding the church in Thessalonica to be in vain. If they had departed from the doctrines and teachings he had received from the Lord Jesus Christ and taught to them, his labor would have been in vain and wasted.

Verses About Satan

Here are a few verses about Satan and his desires to destroy the doctrines of God and His born-again Christians.

- **Matthew 4:3**

"And when the tempter came to him, he said, If thou be the Son of God, command that these stones be made bread."

SATAN IS A TEMPTER AND TESTER

Satan is a tempter and a tester as he was of the Lord Jesus Christ on this occasion. The Lord Jesus Christ was tested in three different ways by Satan and He resisted everyone. Adam just had one test by Satan and didn't resist it. Because of this, he caused every human being to be sinners in the sight of God.

- **Ephesians 4:27**

"Neither give place to the devil."

DON'T GIVE THE DEVIL ANY ROOM

When the Devil wants true Christians to move from their Biblical doctrines, they should not give any place or room to him, or any of his agents, regarding his errors regarding the Bible and its truths.

- **Ephesians 6:11**

"Put on the whole armour of God, that ye may be able to stand against the wiles of the devil."

GOD'S WHOLE ARMOR DEFEATS SATAN'S TRICKS

The whole armor of God is the only thing that will enable true Christians to stand against the Devil's wiles and tricky devices.

- **1 Timothy 3:7**
"Moreover he must have a good report of them which are without; lest he fall into reproach and the snare of the devil."
The Devil has all kinds of snares and traps for sinners as well as for pastors and all genuine Christians as well.
- **James 4:7**
"Submit yourselves therefore to God. Resist the devil, and he will flee from you."
When a genuine Christians submit to God, they are then able to resist the Devil. When he is resisted, he will flee.
- **1 Peter 5:8**
"Be sober, be vigilant; because your adversary the devil, as a roaring lion, walketh about, seeking whom he may devour:"

THE DEVIL'S REAL CHARACTER–A ROARING LION
The Devil wants to devour and destroy everyone in his path. The Devil is not only a roaring lion, but he is also an angel of light. That is a very subtle form in which to come. It is very deceptive. A roaring lion is something you can see and hear. He shows himself as being dangerous. You know to flee from such a lion. But when he comes as an angel of light, he is very deceptive and more dangerous than ever because of his beguiling secrecy and artifice.

1 Thessalonians 3:6
"But now when Timotheus came from you unto us, and brought us good tidings of your faith and charity, and that ye have good remembrance of us always, desiring greatly to see us, as we also to see you:"

Paul had sent Timothy to the Thessalonian church in order to know about their faith. As mentioned before, the word for "*faith*" (PISTIS) has the article before it. It refers to the doctrines and teachings of the faith. Paul wanted to know if they were still firm in these doctrines that he had taught them.

TIMOTHY BROUGHT GOOD NEWS ABOUT THEM
Timothy brought Paul good news about their doctrinal stand, their love, their good remembrance of Paul, and their great desire to see Paul once again. These true Christian people loved Paul. Paul had led them to the Lord Jesus Christ as their Saviour. I am sure that Paul was very happy at the report that Timothy brought back to him.

1 Thessalonians 3:7

"Therefore, brethren, we were comforted over you in all our affliction and distress by your faith:"

Paul was comforted by the Thessalonians, in his affliction and distress because of their strong adherence to Biblical doctrines and teachings that Paul had given them. As I have mentioned before, this word for *"faith"* (PISTIS) in verses 2, 5, 6, and 7 has the Greek article before it, indicating that it refers to the body of doctrine and teaching of the Bible. Paul was comforted concerning these people in Thessalonica. Here are a few other verses about the comfort that God can bring to those who are truly saved.

Verses On Comfort

- **Psalm 23:4**

"Yea, thought I walk through the valley of the shadow of death, I will fear no evil: for thou *art* with me; they rod and thy staff they comfort me."

GOD'S ROD AND STAFF COMFORTED DAVID

David was comforted by God's rod and staff. The rod was for correction, when needed. The staff was for pulling him out of various traps and difficulties. David found comfort in the Lord protective Hands.

- **Psalm 69:20**

"Reproach hath broken my heart; and I am full of heaviness: and I looked *for some* to take pity, but *there was* none; and for comforters, but I found none."

KING DAVID FOUND NO COMFORTERS

David needed comfort, but found none to comfort him. Paul also needed comfort and found it because the Thessalonian Christians adhered to the doctrines and teachings Paul had given them.

- **John 11:19**

"And many of the Jews came to Martha and Mary, to comfort them concerning their brother."

Mary and Martha needed comfort because of the death of their brother, Lazarus. The Lord went to raise Lazarus from the dead, but Mary and Martha did not know this was going to happen. Many of the Jews came to comfort Mary and Martha.

- **Romans 1:12**

"That is, that I may be comforted together with you by the mutual faith both of you and me."

> **TRUE CHRISTIANS CAN COMFORT ONE ANOTHER**
> If people have the same like precious faith and doctrines, they can be a comfort to one another.

- **Romans 15:4**

"For whatsoever things were written aforetime were written for our learning, that we through patience and comfort of the scriptures might have hope."

This verse refers to the Old Testament Scriptures. These Words of God give the genuine Christians in Paul's day and today comfort because of God's faithfulness in the Old Testament in all His ways. Those Old Testament Scriptures were written for learning so that all true Christians might have both patience and comfort.

> **FOR COMFORT, SCRIPTURES MUST BE KNOWN**
> If genuine Christians do not read the Scriptures, they don't know anything about the comfort that these Words of God give. Though all of the Bible is not written to the true Christians in the age of grace, it was written for us and for our comfort.

> **HYPER-DISPENSATIONALISTS ARE IN SERIOUS ERROR**
> Some people who are known as hyper-dispensationalists maintain that only the books written by the apostle Paul are for the genuine Christians today. They say that all the Gospels, as well as Acts, James, 1 Peter, 2 Peter, 1 John, 2 John, 3 John, Jude, and Revelation are not for the true Christians today. Some even throw out Hebrews as well while others leave it in. This is a false and heretical view of the Bible.

In this verse 7 above, Paul states that it is the mutual faith shared by true Christians that comforts them. The shared doctrines of the faith bring comfort and encouragement to those who hold them.

Verses About Faith

- **Matthew 8:10**

"When Jesus heard it, he marveled, and said to them that followed, Verily I say unto you, I have not found so great faith, no, not in Israel."

This verse is talking about the centurion. This centurion had great faith in the Lord Jesus Christ to heal his servant. The Saviour answered that faith by healing this servant.

1 & 2 Thessalonians–Preaching Verse by Verse

- **Matthew 9:2**

"And, behold, they brought to him a man sick of the palsy, lying on a bed: and Jesus seeing their faith said unto the sick of the palsy; Son, be of good cheer; thy sins be forgiven thee."

These people brought this palsied man to the Lord Jesus Christ. When He saw their faith, He healed this man of his palsy.

- **Matthew 9:22**

"But Jesus turned him about, and when he saw her, he said, Daughter, be of good comfort; thy faith hath made thee whole. And the woman was made whole from that hour."

The Lord Jesus Christ saw this woman's faith and healed her of this serious malady.

- **Matthew 15:28**

"Then Jesus answered and said unto her, O woman, great *is* thy faith: be it unto thee even as thou wilt. And her daughter was made whole from that very hour."

Another miracle by the Lord Jesus Christ was made possible when He saw the strong faith of the mother. Because of her faith, her daughter was healed by the Lord.

- **Romans 1:8**

"First, I thank my God through Jesus Christ for you all, that your faith is spoken of throughout the whole world."

THEIR GENUINE FAITH WAS KNOWN WORLDWIDE
Those genuine Christians at Rome had such strong faith in their Saviour that it was noted all over the world of their day.

- **Romans 1:12**

"That is, that I may be comforted together with you by the mutual faith both of you and me."

PAUL'S AND TRUE CHRISTIANS' MUTUAL FAITH
Here is mutual faith between Paul and the true Christians at Rome that gives both parties comfort.

- **1 Corinthians 16:13**

"Watch ye, stand fast in the faith, quit you like men, be strong."

STAND FAST IN BIBLE DOCTRINES
True Christians are to stand fast in their faith. This *"faith"* has the Greek article and therefore refers to the doctrines and teachings of the Bible. Paul is commanding the Corinthian Christians to stand true and fast to the doctrines of the Bible and not deviate from them in any way.

- **Ephesians 1:15-16**
"Wherefore I also, after I heard of your faith in the Lord Jesus, and love unto all the saints. Cease not to give thanks for you, making mention of you in my prayers;"
Paul gave thanks to the Lord when he heard of the Ephesians faith and love for all the saints.
- **Colossians 1:3-4**
"We give thanks to God and the Father of our Lord Jesus Christ, praying always for you, Since we heard of your faith in Christ Jesus, and of the love *which ye have* to all the saints,"
The faith of the Colossians in the Lord Jesus Christ made Paul thankful as well.
- **Colossians 2:5**
"For though I be absent in the flesh, yet am I with you in the spirit, joying and beholding your order, and the stedfastness of your faith in Christ."

STEADFAST IN DOCTRINES–NOT DRIFTING
Our faith and the doctrines of that faith must be stedfast, rather than moveable, drifting, and shaking as the faith of many is today.

- **Thessalonians 1:8**
"For from you sounded out the word of the Lord not only in Macedonia and Achaia, but also in every place your faith to Godward is spread abroad; so that we need not to speak any thing."

TRUE CHRISTIAN FAITH WAS SPREAD ABROAD
The faith to God of the Thessalonian Christians was spread all around the area. These Christians were genuine. Their faith shined out from them.

- **2 Thessalonians 1:4**
"So that we ourselves glory in you in the churches of God for your patience and faith in all your persecutions and tribulations that ye endure:"
These Christians had not only patience in their persecutions but continued faith in the Lord Jesus Christ and God the Father.

1 Thessalonians 3:8
"For now we live, if ye stand fast in the Lord."

THE NEED TO STAND FAST IN THE LORD
Paul said he has a full life if the Thessalonian Christians stand fast in the faith and doctrines of the Lord Jesus Christ. They are to stand fast, not in their own selves, not in their own ideas, but in the Lord Jesus Christ.

The Greek Word for "*stand fast*" is STEKO. Some of the meanings of this Word are:
"*1) to stand firm; 2) to persevere, to persist; 3) to keep one's standing*"
Every genuine Christian believer should stand fast in the Lord without any drift from the clear Bible doctrines.
- **1 Corinthians 16:13**
"Watch ye, stand fast in the faith, quit you like men, be strong."

VARIOUS GROUPS ARE DRIFTING BADLY TODAY
Paul again commands that true Christians "stand fast" in the doctrines of the Biblical faith. Today, there are many drifters among us in many so-called Christian churches, Christian groups, Christian colleges, and Christian theological seminaries. These organizations have been drifting badly for many centuries. Paul did not want the church that he founded in Thessalonica to be drifters. He wanted them to stand fast-- permanently--in the doctrines of the Biblical faith.

1 Thessalonians 3:9
"For what thanks can we render to God again for you, for all the joy wherewith we joy for your sakes before our God;"

Paul was both a thankful and a joyful Christian because of all that God had done for Him. Here are some other verses on thanks and on *joy* and *rejoicing*.

Verses On Thanks
- **Psalm 18:49**
"Therefore will I give thanks unto thee; O LORD, among the heathen, and sing praises unto thy name."

THANKSGIVING IN ALL CIRCUMSTANCES
True Christians must give thanks to the Lord no matter what happens to them. Even in their misery, troubles, and trials they should give thanks to the Lord Jesus Christ Who saved them.

- Psalm 118:1

"O give thanks unto the LORD; for *he is* good: because his mercy *endureth* for ever."
Thanks should be given to the Lord for His goodness and enduring mercy.

- Acts 27:35

"And when he had thus spoken, he took bread, and gave thanks to God in presence of them all: and when he had broken *it*, he began to eat."
Paul is giving thanks in this verse while in the midst of a stormy sea that lead to a shipwreck.

- 1 Corinthians 15:57

"But thanks *be* to God, which giveth us the victory through our Lord Jesus Christ."

THANKSGIVING FOR VICTORY IN CHRIST
Thanks should be given to God by genuine Christians because He has given them victory and salvation through the Lord Jesus Christ.

- 2 Corinthians 2:14

"Now thanks *be* unto God, which always causeth us to triumph in Christ, and maketh manifest the savour of his knowledge by us in every place."
<u>Real Christians might not triumph in this wicked world</u>, or in their business, or in their lives, but <u>God causes them to triumph</u> through the Lord Jesus Christ.

- 2 Corinthians 9:15

"Thanks *be* unto God for his unspeakable gift."

CHRIST IS GOD'S UNSPEAKABLE GIFT
Such a gift of redeeming faith in the Lord Jesus Christ is unspeakable. Words fail in describing such a wonderful, bountiful, and eternal gift of eternal life in Heaven.

- Ephesians 5:20

"Giving thanks always for all things unto God and the Father in the name of our Lord Jesus Christ."

This is a command for true Christians to be thankful to God the Father in the Name of the Lord Jesus Christ for all things, even the difficult circumstances of life. This is very difficult, but it is a command.
- **Colossians 3:17**
"And whatsoever ye do in word or deed, *do* all in the name of the Lord Jesus, giving thanks to God and the Father by him."
Truly saved Christians should give thanks to God through the Lord Jesus Christ in the midst of all their words as well as their deeds.
- **Hebrews 13:15**
"By him therefore let us offer the sacrifice of praise to God continually, that is, the fruit of *our* lips giving thanks to his name."
For the true Christian to give thanks to the Saviour's Name is a proper New Testament sacrifice.

Verses On Joy And Rejoicing

In 1 Thessalonians 3:9, Paul was joyful because of what the Lord Jesus Christ did for him.
- **Psalm 16:11b**
". . in thy presence *is* fullness of joy; at thy right hand *there are* pleasures for evermore."

FULLNESS OF JOY IN GOD'S PRESENCE

In the presence of the Lord is fullness of joy. This old world here is filled with sadness, not joy. The drunks think they are joyful, but they aren't joyful at all. One of the fruits of God the Holy Spirit is joy. This is evidenced when true Christians are filled and controlled by God the Holy Spirit (Galatians 5:22-23).

- **John 15:11**
"These things have I spoken unto you, *that* my joy might remain in you, and that your joy might be full."
The Lord Jesus himself spoke to His disciples that they might have fullness of joy. He wants true Christians today to have this full joy as well.
- **Acts 20:24**
"But none of these things move me, neither count I my life dear unto myself, so that I might finish my course with joy, and the ministry, which I have received of the Lord Jesus, to testify the gospel of the grace of God."
People told Paul not to go to Jerusalem, because he would be killed there. But Paul felt that it was his duty to finish with joy the course that the Lord Jesus Christ had laid out for him. Part of that course was to go to Jerusalem, come what may.

- Galatians 5:22

"But the fruit of the Spirit is love, joy, peace, longsuffering, gentleness, goodness, faith,"

JOY-- ONE OF THE FRUITS OF THE HOLY SPIRIT
As I wrote earlier, one of the fruits of God the Holy Spirit in the genuine Christian who is filled and controlled by Him is joy.

- 1 Thessalonians 2:20

"For ye are our glory and joy."

These Christians were saved through the ministry of Paul. Because of this, Paul considered them to be his glory and joy.

- 2 John 1:4a

"I rejoiced greatly that I found of thy children walking in truth,"

JOY BY WALKING IN THE WORDS OF GOD
The Apostle John rejoiced greatly when those to whom he ministered walked in accord with the truth of the Words of God.

1 Thessalonians 3:10

"Night and day praying exceedingly that we might see your face, and might perfect that which is lacking in your faith?"

PERFECTING WHAT IS LACKING
Paul wanted to see these saved Christians at Thessalonica. He prayed for them night and day for this to come to pass. He wanted to visit this church that he founded at Thessalonica. The purpose of his visit was that he might *"perfect that which is lacking"* in their "faith." The Greek Word for *"faith"* is PISTIS. There is a Greek article before it making the meaning be the doctrines and teachings of *"the faith."*

Paul wanted their knowledge and practice of these doctrines to be *"perfect."* The Greek Word for this is KATARTIZO. Some of the meanings for this Word are:

"1) to render, i.e. to fit, sound, complete; 1a) <u>to mend</u> (what has been broken or rent), <u>to repair</u>; 1a1) to complete; 1b) to fit out, equip, put in order, arrange, adjust; 1b1) to fit or frame for one's self, prepare; 1c) ethically: to strengthen, perfect, complete, make one what he ought to be."

THE IMPORTANCE OF BIBLE DOCTRINES

Paul wanted to repair and complete whatever was lacking in this local church. This emphasizes the importance of Bible doctrine which is described as *"the faith."* Jude argued that this "faith" or Bible doctrines and teachings should be something about which genuine Christians should contend earnestly.

"Beloved, when I gave all diligence to write unto you of the common salvation, it was needful for me to write unto you, and exhort you that ye should earnestly contend for the faith which was once delivered unto the saints." (Jude 1:3)

THE NEED TO CONTEND FOR BIBLE DOCTRINES

When a person is first truly saved, they have a great lack of understanding about the doctrines of the faith. They must grow in that understanding and knowledge and the willingness to abide by all these doctrines without wavering.

Verses On Concepts of Perfect

- **Psalm 138:8a**

"The LORD will perfect *that which* concerneth me:"

The Lord promised the Psalmist to make perfect, mature, and complete the things that concerned him

- **Romans 12:2**

"And be not conformed to this world: but be ye transformed by the renewing of your mind, that ye may prove what *is* that good, and acceptable, and perfect, will of God."

God's will is good, acceptable, and perfect. His will is found in His Words which every genuine Christian should have daily access to.

- **2 Corinthians 12:9**

"And he said unto me, My grace is sufficient for thee: for my strength is made perfect in weakness. Most gladly therefore will I rather glory in my infirmities, that the power of Christ may rest upon me."

GOD'S STRENGTH MADE PERFECT IN OUR WEAKNESS

In this verse, we see that God's strength is made perfect in our own weakness. There is a great contrast between His strength and our weakness.

- **2 Corinthians 13:11**

"Finally, brethren, farewell. Be perfect, be of good comfort, be of one mind, live in peace; and the God of love and peace shall be with you."

MATURITY AND GROWN-UPNESS NEEDED
Though no one can be *"perfect"* in the absolute sense, but true Christians can be made more mature and grown up in the things of the Lord by diligent study of His Words and doctrines.

- **Philippians 3:12**

"Not as though I had already attained, either were already perfect: but I follow after, if that I may apprehend that for which also I am apprehended of Christ Jesus."

Paul was writing from a prison in Rome. Even Paul the apostle was not completely perfect or mature. He followed after and pursued maturity in the things of the Lord as all true Christians should do. There is always room for growth in the things of the Lord Jesus Christ.

- **Colossians 1:28**

"Whom we preach, warning every man, and teaching every man in all wisdom; that we may present every man perfect in Christ Jesus:"

The goal that Paul wanted for every true Christian was for them to be perfect, mature, grown up, and of a full age in the things that concerned the Lord Jesus Christ.

- **Colossians 4:12**

"Epaphras, who is *one* of you, a servant of Christ, saluteth you, always laboring fervently for you in prayers, that ye may stand perfect and complete in all the will of God."

This was a noble goal that Epaphras had for the Colossian Christians. He wanted them perfect, complete, and mature in God's Will as found in God's Words.

- **2 Timothy 3:17**

"That the man of God may be perfect, throughly furnished unto all good works:"

New Testament preachers must be mature, firm, and grown up in things of the Lord Jesus Christ do that they can properly teach their people.

- **Hebrews 13:20-21**

"Now the God of peace, that brought again from the dead our Lord Jesus, that great shepherd of the sheep, through the blood of the everlasting covenant, Make you perfect in every good work to do his will, working in you that which is wellpleasing in his sight, through Jesus Christ; to whom *be* glory for ever and ever. Amen."

Part of maturity is doing the will of God. Before His will can be followed, it must first be known. It can be known by diligent study of His Words in the proper and accurate Bibles like the King James Bible.
- **James 1:4**
"But let patience have *her* perfect work, that ye may be perfect and entire, wanting nothing."

PATIENCE MUST MATURE AND FULLY GROWN
Patience is very difficult to possess. It must mature and grow to a full growth to enable a true Christian to be entire and have want or need of nothing.

- **James 2:22**
"Seest thou how faith wrought with his works, and by works was faith made perfect?"

WORKS AS A PROOF OF TRUE FAITH
Abraham had solid faith in the Lord. That faith was made mature and perfect when people could see his works. The Lord that proved that his faith was there.

- **James 3:2**
"For in many things we offend all. If any man offend not in word, the same *is* a perfect man, and able also to bridle the whole body."

The test in this verse of a perfect or mature person is whether or not they are able <u>not</u> to offend in their words. If this is true, they can bridle their entire body. If mature true Christians can bridle their tongues, and can not offend in their words, they would be able to bridle the whole body. He won't offend in the body, won't be out of touch in his body as well.

Verses On Things "Lacking"

- **1 Corinthians 16:17**
"I am glad of the coming of Stephanas and Fortunatus and Achaicus: for that which was lacking on your part they have supplied."

In this case, these three men supplied whatever the Corinthians lacked.

- **2 Corinthians 11:9**
"And when I was present with you, and wanted, I was chargeable to no man: for that which was lacking to me the brethren which came from Macedonia supplied: and in all *things* I have kept myself from being burdensome unto you, and *so* will I keep *myself*."

Paul had all of his needs supplied here by the Macedonian brethren so he didn't have to burden the people of Corinth. <u>The Christians at Macedonia helped Paul by giving him gifts as he was working for the Lord Jesus Christ, in addition to his tent-making work to supply his needs</u>.

1 Thessalonians 3:11

"Now God himself and our Father, and our Lord Jesus Christ, direct our way unto you."

Paul was praying that the both God the Father and God the Son, and the Lord Jesus Christ might direct his way so that he could visit this church at Thessalonica. He wanted to see them and wanted God to *"direct"* his way to them. The Greek Word for *"direct"* is KATEUTHUNO. Some of the meanings of this Word are:

"1) to make straight, guide, direct; 1a) of the removal of the hindrances to coming to one"

PAUL WANTED THE GUIDANCE OF THE LORD

Paul wanted his way to be guided and made straight without any hindrances to his coming to visit them. As Paul prayed to be directed by God the Father and God the Son (the Lord Jesus Christ). Genuine Christians should pray this prayer as well. They should not want to be out of line in anything they do.

Verses On Direction

These verses have to do with *"direction"* for those who wish to do the will of God.

- **Genesis 24:27**

"And he said, Blessed *be* the LORD God of my master Abraham, who hath not left destitute my master of his mercy and his truth: I *being* in the way, the LORD led me to the house of my master's brethren."

GOD CAN DIRECT US WHEN WE'RE MOVING

Abraham's servant was looking for a bride for Isaac. He was *in the way*. That is where the Lord directed or led him to the proper destination. True Christians should move in the general direction of the will of God and while in that way, they should ask the Lord to direct them specifically.

- **Genesis 46:28**

"And he sent Judah before him unto Joseph, to direct his face unto Goshen; and they came into the land of Goshen."

When Jacob came to Egypt during the famine in Israel, he asked his son, Judah, to go ahead to Joseph, so that Joseph could direct their way to Goshen for their cattle. Egypt was a huge land. It would be the proper place for all Jacob's cattle, there needed to be accurate direction.

- **Proverbs 3:6**
"In all thy ways acknowledge him, and he shall direct thy paths." When the genuine Christian acknowledges the Lord in all their ways, as found in His Words, God promises to direct their paths.
- **Proverbs 11:5**
"The righteousness of the perfect shall direct his way: but the wicked shall fall by his own wickedness." Righteousness, as found in the Bible, can direct the way of those who believe it and follow it.
- **Jeremiah 10:23**
"O LORD, I know that the way of man *is* not in himself: *it is* not in man that walketh to direct his steps." Without the clear teachings and directives of God's Words in the Bible, we are left without proper direction. The world should not direct the steps of the true child of God–God's Words should direct them.
- **2 Thessalonians 3:5**
"And the Lord direct your hearts into the love of God, and into the patient waiting for Christ."

IN GOD'S LOVE AND WAITING FOR CHRIST
The prayer is that the genuine Christians' hearts might be directed in two areas–the love of God and the patient waiting for the Lord Jesus Christ Who will return one day in the Rapture of the true Church. No one knows the day or the hour of that reunion, but saved people must be patient and waiting for Him.

1 Thessalonians 3:12

"And the Lord make you to increase and abound in love one toward another, and toward all men, even as we do toward you:"

Paul's desire for the Thessalonian genuine Christians was twofold. He desired them to have:
(1) abounding love for one another; and
(2) abounding love for all people.

Verses On True Christian Love

- **John 13:34-35**
"A new commandment I give unto you, That ye love one another; as I have loved you, that ye also love one another. By this shall all *men* know that ye are my disciples, if ye have love one to another."

> **LOVING TRUE CHRISTIANS–A MARK OF DISCIPLESHIP**
> Loving true fellow Christians is a mark of discipleship. We don't have to necessarily agree with one another in our doctrines. For example, we don't have to agree with those that tear apart our King James Bible and/or the Hebrew, Aramaic, and Greek Words that underlie it. But if they are genuinely saved, we can love them as believers without necessarily agreeing with some of their doctrines.

- John 15:12

"This is my commandment, That ye love one another, as I have loved you."

That's a good goal to aim at, even though absolutely impossible to attain.

- John 3:16

"For God so loved the world, that he gave his only begotten Son, that whosoever believeth in him should not perish, but have everlasting life."

> **THE WORLD'S GREATEST LOVE**
> The greatest love of the entire world was God's love that sent His only begotten Son into this world to pay the penalty for their sins, so that they who genuinely believe in that Son might have everlasting life. There is no greater love than this.

- John 15:17

"These things I command you, that ye love one another."

> **THE POWER BEHIND TRUE CHRISTIAN LOVE**
> Some true Christians are not always easier to love than others. But by the power of God the Holy Spirit, Who indwells genuine Christians, it can be possible. "*Love*" is one of the fruits of God the Holy Spirit which is manifested when these believers are filled and controlled by Him.

- Romans 12:10

"*Be* kindly affectioned one to another with brotherly love; in honour preferring one another;"

Brotherly love and kind affection is commanded for the true Christians here.

- Romans 13:8

"Owe no man any thing, but to love one another: for he that loveth another hath fulfilled the law."

Loving fellow Christians fulfills the law.

- **Galatians 5:14**

"For all the law is fulfilled in one word, *even* in this; Thou shalt love thy neighbor as thyself."

The law is fulfilled in loving one's neighbors as themselves.

- **Ephesians 1:15**

"Wherefore I also, after I heard of your faith in the Lord Jesus, and love unto all the saints,"

The Ephesian Christians loved all the saints or fellow Christians, not just certain ones. This is sometimes very difficult.

- **Colossians 1:4**

"Since we heard of your faith in Christ Jesus, and of the love *which ye have* to all the saints,"

Even in Colosse, the true Christians loved all the saints or fellow Christians rather than just certain ones.

- **1 Thessalonians 4:9**

"But as touching brotherly love ye need not that I write unto you: for ye yourselves are taught of God to love one another."

True Christians are taught of God to love one another.

- **Philemon 1:5**

"Hearing of thy love and faith, which thou hast toward the Lord Jesus, and toward all saints;"

Philemon had love toward all the saints or fellow Christians.

- **Hebrews 13:1**

"Let brotherly love continue."

Paul told the Hebrew Christians to continue their brotherly love. They were not to stop it.

- **1 Peter 1:22**

"Seeing ye have purified your souls in obeying the truth through the Spirit unto unfeigned love of the brethren, *see that ye* love one another with a pure heart fervently:"

GOD WANTS NON-HYPOCRITICAL LOVE

Unfeigned or non-hypocritical love for the brethren must be with a pure heart and it should be fervent rather than lukewarm. There should be no sexual sins involved in this pure and fervent love.

- **1 Peter 2:17**

"Honour all *men*. Love the brotherhood. Fear God. Honour the king:"

True Christians are to love those who are saved and born-again.

- **1 Peter 3:8**

"Finally, *be ye* all of one mind, having compassion one of another, love as brethren, *be* pitiful, be courteous:"

Genuine Christians are to love as brethren (brothers and sisters.)
- **1 John 3:11**

"For this is the message that ye heard from the beginning, that we should love one another."

The Lord Jesus Christ told this to all of His followers many times in the Gospel of John.
- **1 John 3:14**

"We know that we have passed from death unto life, because we love the brethren. He that loveth not his brother abideth in death."

Love for fellow true Christians is one proof that a person has passed from death unto life.
- **1 John 3:23**

"And this is his commandment, That we should believe on the name of his Son Jesus Christ, and love one another, as he gave us commandment."

Genuine belief in the Lord Jesus Christ and love for fellow Christians are two commands in this verse.
- **1 John 4:7**

"Beloved, let us love one another: for love is of God; and every one that loveth is born of God, and knoweth God."

Genuine love is from God Himself.
- **1 John 4:11, 12**

"Beloved, if God so loved us, we ought also to love one another. No man has seen God at any time. If we love one another, God dwelleth in us, and his love is perfected in us."

True Christians should love one another (even if they differ on some doctrines) in the same manner as God Himself has loved them.
- **1 John 4:20**

"If a man say, I love God, and hateth his brother, he is a liar: for he that loveth not his brother whom he hath seen, how can he love God whom he hath not seen?"

LOVE FOR GOD BRINGS LOVE FOR TRUE CHRISTIANS

Genuine love for God should bring with it genuine love for those who are true Christians.

- **1 John 4:21**

"And this commandment have we from him, That he who loveth God love his brother also."

True love for God should also bring love for true Christians.

1 Thessalonians 3:13

"To the end he may stablish your hearts unblameable in holiness before God, even our Father, at the coming of our Lord Jesus Christ with all his saints."

HEARTS ESTABLISHED UNBLAMEABLE
The goal that Paul had for these Thessalonian Christians was that the Lord might establish their hearts unblameable in holiness when the Lord Jesus Christ returns with all His saved ones.

The Greek Word for "*establish*" is STERIZO. Some of the meanings of that Word are:

"*1) to make stable, place firmly, set fast, fix; 2) to strengthen, make firm; 3) to render constant, confirm, one's mind*"

Now notice God wants to make the hearts of the genuine Christians to be strengthened, made strong, and fixed, not merely their heads.

CHRIST'S RETURN WITH ALL HIS SAINTS
The "*coming of our Lord Jesus Christ*" mentioned here is "*with His saints.*" His coming for his saints will precede this by seven years during which time the Tribulation will take place on this earth. The true Christians will be with the Lord Jesus Christ in Heaven for these seven years and return with Him as He destroys His enemies at the battle of Armageddon and then sets up His millennial kingdom.

Verses On Being Established
Here are some other verses that relate to true believers being established in their hearts with joy and with sound Biblical doctrine.
- **Acts 16:5**
"And so were the churches established in the faith, and increased in number daily."

Paul went back, after he had preached to these different churches, and established and grounded them in the doctrines of the Bible. This is very important for churches even today.
- **Romans 1:11**
"For I long to see you, that I may impart unto you some spiritual gift, to the end ye may be established;"

Paul wanted the church at Rome to be grounded, firm, unwavering and not drifting as many churches and schools are drifting in the days in which we live.

- **Romans 16:25**
"Now to him that is of power to stablish you according to my gospel, and the preaching of Jesus Christ, according to the revelation of the mystery, which was kept secret since the world began,"

ONLY GOD CAN ESTABLISH TRUE CHRISTIANS
God is the One Who can make true Christians established, firm, solid, and unmoveable. It's a sad thing when many groups of churches, schools, and other organizations have apostatized from the Words of God.

- **1 Thessalonians 3:2**
"And sent Timotheus, our brother, and minister of God, and our fellowlabourer in the gospel of Christ, to establish you, and to comfort you concerning your faith."

Timothy was to establish and ground these Christians at Thessalonica in the doctrines of the faith as taught in the Words of God.

- **2 Thessalonians 2:17**
"Comfort your hearts, and stablish you in every good word and work."

Saved people should be established in their words as well as in their works.

- **2 Thessalonians 3:3**
"But the Lord is faithful, who shall stablish you, and keep *you* from evil."

GENERATION GAPS ARE NOT NECESSARY
God is the only One Who can establish and keep firm true Christians. I do not believe there needs to be any generation gap, but, sad to say, there often is such a gap. I would love to see, not only our generation of genuine Christians to be established but also the generation of our sons and daughters, grandchildren, and great grandchildren. Why not? Should they not be?

- **2 Peter 1:12**
"Wherefore I will not be negligent to put you always in remembrance of these things, though ye know *them*, and be established in the present truth."

True Christians must be established in the truth of God's Words by studying these Words and seeking to follow them.

- **1 Peter 5:10**
"But the God of all grace, who hath called us unto his eternal glory by Christ Jesus, after that ye have suffered a while, make you perfect, stablish, strengthen, settle *you*."

Even after suffering, God wants His genuine believers to be perfect and mature as well as being established, strengthened, and settled.

Verses On Being Holy And Righteous

- **Romans 6:13**

"Neither yield ye your members *as* instruments of unrighteousness unto sin: but yield yourselves unto God, as those that are alive from the dead, and your members as instruments of righteousness unto God."

THE NEED TO YIELD OUR BODIES TO GOD

Genuine believers in Christ are told to stop yielding their members to unrighteousness and sin, but instead yield them unto God and to the righteousness as taught in the Bible. Some have illustrated the members of our body as ten special members: two hands, two feet, two eyes, two ears, one mouth, and one heart. These should all be yielded to the Lord Jesus Christ at all times.

- **Romans 6:22**

"But now being made free from sin, and become servants to God, ye have your fruit unto holiness, and the end everlasting life."

Biblical Christians should have their fruit unto holiness as servants of the Lord.

- **2 Corinthians 7:1**

"Having therefore these promises, dearly beloved, let us cleanse ourselves from all filthiness of the flesh and spirit, perfecting holiness in the fear of God."

Saved people should separate from wickedness and evil. They should aim at perfecting holiness according to the Bible.

- **2 Corinthians 6:14**

"Be ye not unequally yoked together with unbelievers: for what fellowship hath righteousness with unrighteousness? and what communion hath light with darkness?"

True Christians are to stand for righteousness and against unrighteousness in all areas of their lives.

- **1 Thessalonians 3:12, 13**

"And the Lord make you to increase and abound in love one toward another, and toward all *men*, even as we *do* toward you: To the end he may stablish your hearts unblameable in holiness before God, even our Father, at the coming of our Lord Jesus Christ with all his saints."

The hearts of true Christians should be in holiness rather than unholiness as they live in this world.

- **1 Thessalonians 4:7**
"For God hath not called us unto uncleanness, but unto holiness." God has called genuine Christians unto holiness not uncleanness. God the Holy Spirit, can enable them to be holy. They cannot be holy in the flesh, but only by the power of the Spirit of God.
- **Titus 2:3**
"The aged women likewise, that *they be* in behavior as becometh holiness, not false accusers, not given to much wine, teachers of good things;"
Older true Christian women were not to forget to have holiness in their lives.
- **Hebrews 12:10**
"For they verily for a few days chastened *us* after their own pleasure; but he for *our* profit, that *we* might be partakers of his holiness."
God chastens true Christians in order that they might partake of God's holiness.
- **Hebrews 12:14**
"Follow peace with all *men*, and holiness, without which no man shall see the Lord:"
Genuine Christians must follow holiness. That does not mean that the Bible teaches the errors of the "holy rollers," of the holiness cults, or "isms" of either some Methodist denominations, or other holiness churches. The Bible does not teach that true Christians can ever reach sinless perfection in this world. The sinful flesh is always with them. They will never be perfected until they get their new bodies, but God still wants them to be holy and separated unto Himself and separated from sin.

Verses On The Coming Of The Lord For All Genuine Christians

TWO PHASES OF CHRIST'S COMING

The coming of the Lord Jesus Christ is in two phases: The first phase is when He comes for His saints--genuine Christians. The second phase is when He comes with His saints to bring victory at the battle of Armageddon and set up His thousand year millennial reign upon this earth.

These verses speak about the coming of the Lord Jesus Christ **for** all of His true Christians. This is in contrast to His coming back to this earth **with** all those genuine Christians.

- **1 Corinthians 1:7**
"So that ye come behind in no gift; waiting for the coming of our Lord Jesus Christ:"

TRUE CHRISTIANS' BODIES TRANSFORMED
True Christians should wait for the coming of their Saviour to transform their mortal bodies into immortal bodies like unto His glorified body. No one knows when this Rapture will take place, but they should be ready, willing and waiting for it.

- **1 Corinthians 15:23**
"But every man in his own order: Christ the firstfruits; afterward they that are Christ's at his coming."

The genuine Christians will be Raptured when the Lord Jesus Christ returns in the clouds of Heaven.

- **1 Thessalonians 2:19**
"For what *is* our hope, or joy, or crown of rejoicing? *Are* not even ye in the presence of our Lord Jesus Christ at his coming?"

This is the first phrase of the Lord Jesus Christ's return at the Rapture when true Christians will be caught up to meet Him in the air."

- **1 Thessalonians 4:15**
"For this we say unto you by the word of the Lord, that we which are alive *and* remain unto the coming of the Lord shall not prevent them which are asleep."

At the Rapture of all genuine Christians, those who have died will precede those who are alive at the time.

- **1 Thessalonians 4:16**
"For the Lord himself shall descend from heaven with a shout, with the voice of the archangel, and with the trump of God: and the dead in Christ shall rise first:"

As mentioned previously, the "*dead in Christ shall rise first*" and immediately afterwards the then living true Christians will be caught up.

- **1 Thessalonians 5:23**
"And the very God of peace sanctify you wholly; and *I pray God* your whole spirit and soul and body be preserved blameless unto the coming of our Lord Jesus Christ."

THE RAPTURE OF ALL TRUE CHRISTIANS
This verse is again referring to the first phrase of the Saviour's return. It will be a meeting in the air of all true Christians. They should prepare their spirit, soul, and body to meet Him at that time.

- **2 Thessalonians 2:1**
"Now we beseech you, brethren, by the coming of our Lord Jesus Christ, and *by* our gathering together unto him,"
This is another picture of the Rapture of all true Christians.
- **James 5:7**
"Be patient therefore, brethren, unto the coming of the Lord. Behold, the husbandman waiteth for the precious fruit of the earth, and hath long patience for it, until he receive the early and latter rain."

GENUINE CHRISTIANS NEED MUCH PATIENCE
Genuine Christians must be patient rather than anxious in anticipation of the coming of the Lord Jesus Christ in the Rapture.

- **James 5:8**
"Be ye also patient; stablish your hearts: for the coming of the Lord draweth nigh."

THE COMING OF CHRIST MUCH NEARER NOW
If the coming of the Lord Jesus Christ was drawing "nigh" in 60 A.D. in James' day, how much nearer is it today in 2015 when this book is being written?

- **2 Peter 3:3-4**
"Knowing this first, that there shall come in the last days scoffers, walking after their own lusts, And saying, Where is the promise of his coming? for since the fathers fell asleep, all things continue as *they were* from the beginning of the creation."
Many scoffers even today deny the promise of the coming of the Lord Jesus Christ. But He will come as it has been promised in the Bible.
- **1 John 2:28**
"And now, little children, abide in him; that, when he shall appear, we may have confidence, and not be ashamed before him at his coming."

NOT ASHAMED BEFORE CHRIST
Only if true Christians are abiding in the Lord Jesus Christ will they have confidence and not be ashamed before Him when He returns. They should not be ashamed for what they are either thinking, saying, or doing, or where they are going.

1 Thessalonians Chapter Four

1 Thessalonians 4:1

"**Furthermore then we beseech you, brethren, and exhort you by the Lord Jesus, that as ye have received of us how ye ought to walk and to please God, so ye would abound more and more.**"

Paul is talking about the brethren in Thessalonica. This is the earliest epistle of the New Testament. He is exhorting the true Christians at Thessalonica that they have received the Words of God that told them how they *"ought to walk"* in order to *"please God."*

THE MEANING OF "WALK" TO PLEASE GOD

The Greek Word for *"walk"* is PERIPATEO. Some of the meanings of that Word are:

"1) to walk; 1a) to make one's way, progress; to make due use of opportunities; 1b) Hebrew for, to live; 1b1) to regulate one's life; 1b2 to conduct one's self; 1b3) to pass one's life"

The Greek verb is in the present tense which implies a continuous action without any interruption. The Greek verb for *"please"* is also in the Greek present tense which also implies continuous and uninterrupted attempt to please God.

Verses On The Christians' Walk

- **Romans 6:4b**

". . . like as Christ was raised up from the dead by the glory of the Father, even so we also should walk in newness of life."

True Christians should walk in newness of life, not as the life of being unsaved.

- **Romans 8:1**

"There is therefore now no condemnation to them which are in Christ Jesus, who walk not after the flesh, but after the Spirit."

Genuine Christians should not walk after their old flesh, which is sinful, but in the power of God the Holy Spirit Who resides within them.
- **Romans 13:13**
"Let us walk honestly, as in the day; not in rioting and drunkenness, not in chambering and wantonness, not in strife and envying."

Another way for true Christians to walk is to walk honestly rather than in rioting, drunkenness, strife and envying.
- **1 Corinthians 3:3**
"For ye are yet carnal: for whereas *there is* among you envying, and strife, and divisions, are ye not carnal, and walk as men?"

Sad to say, the Christians at Corinth were walking after their flesh like the other human beings in their city. This should not have been. Nor should genuine Christians today walk after their old nature and flesh.
- **Galatians 5:16**
"*This* I say then, Walk in the Spirit, and ye shall not fulfil the lust of the flesh."

THE POWER OF GOD THE HOLY SPIRIT
The true Christians must walk in the power of the Holy Spirit Who indwells them by allowing Him to control and fill them. Only then will the lust of their flesh be controlled.

- **Ephesians 2:10**
"For we are his workmanship, created in Christ Jesus unto good works, which God hath before ordained that we should walk in them."

GOOD WORKS SHOULD FOLLOW SALVATION
Though it is true that no one can be genuinely saved by good works, after being truly saved, God wants these people to walk in good works as measured by the Bible's standards.

- **Ephesians 4:17**
"This I say therefore, and testify in the Lord, that ye henceforth walk not as other Gentiles walk, in the vanity of their mind,"

DON'T WALK AS THE HEATHEN WALK
True Christians should not walk as the unsaved heathen walk in the vanity of their mind.

- **1 John 1:6-7**
"If we say that we have fellowship with him, and walk in darkness, we lie, and do not the truth. But if we walk in the light, as he is in the light, we have fellowship one with another, and the blood of Jesus Christ his Son cleanseth us from all sin."

The genuine Christian has the choice of walking in darkness or walking in the light of God's Words. They should always walk in the light and renounce the darkness.

Verses On Pleasing God

The walk of genuine Christians is very important, especially if they wish to please God.

- **John 8:29**

"And he that sent me is with me: the Father hath not left me alone; for I do always those things that please him."

Even in view of the horrible events that transpired leading up to and including the cross of Calvary, the Lord Jesus Christ pleased God the Father.

- **2 Timothy 2:4**

"No man that warreth entangleth himself with the affairs of *this* life; that he may please him who hath chosen him to be a soldier."

> **SOLDIERS SHOULD PLEASE HIM WHO CHOSE THEM**
>
> Pleasing the Lord Jesus Christ Who has chosen true Christians to be soldiers is paramount and primary.

- **Hebrews 11:6**

"But without faith *it is* impossible to please *him*: for he that cometh to God must believe that he is, and *that* he is a rewarder of them that diligently seek him."

> **THE ONLY ONES WHO CAN PLEASE GOD**
>
> No one on earth can please the God of the Bible unless they believe He exists, and unless they have personal and genuine faith in the Lord Jesus Christ His Son.

1 Thessalonians 4:2

"For ye know what commandments we gave you by the Lord Jesus."

These commandments are orders and imperative statements in the New Testament. This does not refer to the ten commandments of the Old Testament. Someone has compiled 1,050 commands, orders, or imperatives for true Christians to obey today. Write us if you are interested in ordering a copy of these 1,050 New Testament commandments.

1 Thessalonians 4:3

"For this is the will of God, even your sanctification, that ye should abstain from fornication:"

THE WILL OF GOD–ABSTAIN FROM FORNICATION

The will of God is for every genuine Christian to be sanctified and never to be involved with fornication.

Verses On The Will Of God

There are many references in the Bible to the will of God. Here are a few of them.

- **Mark 3:35**

"For whosoever shall do the will of God, the same is my brother, and my sister, and mother."

The Lord Jesus Christ told His followers that there is a family relationship for those who know and do the will of God as He has revealed it in His Words.

- **Acts 13:36**

"For David, after he had served his own generation by the will of God, fell on sleep, and was laid unto his fathers, and saw corruption:"

King David died and was buried at the time and season which was in conformity to the will of God.

- **Romans 1:10**

"Making request, if by any means now at length I might have a prosperous journey by the will of God to come unto you."

PAUL WANTED TO SEE THE ROMANS

Paul wanted to see, and have a prosperous journey to visit, the genuine Christians at Rome. He wanted it to be in the will of God for him to come to see them. As you might remember, Paul came to Rome as a Roman prisoner. This, too, was by the will of God.

- **Romans 12:2**

"And be not conformed to this world: but be ye transformed by the renewing of your mind, that ye may prove what is that good, and acceptable, and perfect, will of God."

God does not want true Christians to be conformed to this world, but He wants them to prove or test out His perfect and acceptable will as it is found in His Words.

- **Romans 15:32**
"That I may come unto you with joy by the will of God, and may with you be refreshed."
Paul wanted to see the Christians at Rome by God's will and with joy so they could be refreshed.
- **1 Corinthians 1:1**
"Paul, called *to be* an apostle of Jesus Christ through the will of God, and Sosthenes *our* brother,"
The Lord Jesus Christ called Paul to be an apostle by the will of God. I believe it was he who took the place of Matthias whom the apostles called to be an apostle in Acts chapter 1.
- **Galatians 1:4**
"Who gave himself for our sins, that he might deliver us from this present evil world, according to the will of God and our Father:"

DELIVERED FROM THIS WICKED WORLD
It is God's will that genuine Christians might be delivered from this wicked world.

- **Ephesians 6:6**
"Not with eyeservice, as menpleasers; but as the servants of Christ, doing the will of God from the heart;"

DOING GOD'S WILL FROM THE HEART
True Christians should do God's will from their hearts, not only by going through the motions with their heads and outer actions.

- **Colossians 4:12**
"Epaphras, who is *one* of you, a servant of Christ, saluteth you, always laboring fervently for you in prayers, that ye may stand perfect and complete in all the will of God."

STANDING COMPLETE IN THE WILL OF GOD
Epaphras was praying that the Ephesian Christians could stand perfect and complete in all the will of God. You won't find the will of God in newspapers, comic books, or on television, radio, or the Internet. The will of God is found in the Bible, the Words of the living God. This is why we must have the proper Hebrew, Aramaic, and Greek Words and the accurate translation of those Words as we have in our King James Bible.

- **1 Thessalonians 5:18**
"In every thing give thanks: for this is the will of God in Christ Jesus concerning you."
Giving thanks is also the will of God, for true Christians around the world.

- **Hebrews 10:36**
"For ye have need of patience, that, after ye have done the will of God, ye might receive the promise."
After genuine Christians have done the will of God, they must be patient and wait for God's promise to be fulfilled. Often this promise takes a long time—maybe, days, months, years, or even decades. But God's promise will be fulfilled.
- **1 Peter 3:17**
"For *it is* better, if the will of God be so, that ye suffer for well doing, than for evil doing."
Sometimes suffering is part of the will of God for true Christians, but, if it comes, it should be for well doing, not evil doing.
- **1 Peter 4:2**
"That he no longer should live the rest of *his* time in the flesh to the lusts of men, but to the will of God."
After people are truly born-again and saved, they should no longer live in the lusts of men, but should live in the will of God.
- **1 Peter 4:19**
"Wherefore let them that suffer according to the will of God commit the keeping of their souls *to him* in well doing, as unto a faithful Creator."
Genuine Christians who suffer must commit themselves to the care of their faithful Creator.
- **1 John 2:17**
"And the world passeth away, and the lust thereof: but he that doeth the will of God abideth for ever."
The true Christian who does God's will as revealed in His Words abides forever in Heaven and receives God's rewards.

Verses On Departing From Sin And Evil

In 1 Thessalonians 4:3, Paul says that "*sanctification*" and holiness is the will of God for these Christians.

THE MEANING OF THE GREEK WORD, "HAGIASMOS"

The Greek Word For "*sanctification*" is HAGIASMOS. Some of the meanings of this Word are:

"*1) consecration, purification; 2) the effect of consecration; 2a) sanctification of heart and life.*"

Part of the genuine Christians' lives is for them "*to abstain from fornication*" and from all other kinds of evil and sin.

- **1 Thessalonians 5:22**
"Abstain from all appearance of evil."

This includes not only the evil itself, but even if something appears to be evil.
- **1 Peter 2:11**
"Dearly beloved, I beseech *you* as strangers and pilgrims, abstain from fleshly lusts, which war against the soul,"
Peter urges these true Christians to abstain from all fleshly lusts, because they are strangers and pilgrims on this earth.

Verses On The Sin Of Fornication

In this verse (1 Thessalonians 4:3) there is a specific command that genuine Christians should abstain from the sin of fornication.

THE MEANING OF THE GREEK WORD, "PORNEIA"
The Greek Word for *"fornication"* PORNEIA. Some of the various meanings for this Word are:
"1) illicit sexual intercourse; 1a) adultery, fornication, homosexuality, lesbianism, intercourse with animals etc.; 1b) sexual intercourse with close relatives; Lev. 18; 1c) sexual intercourse with a divorced man or woman; Mk. 10:11,12."

Normally, we think of fornication as sexual relations on the part of an unmarried person. As you see, there are a few other meanings for that word.
- **Matthew 15:19**
"For out of the heart proceed evil thoughts, murders, adulteries, fornications, thefts, false witness, blasphemies:"
Fornication, along with many other evil sins, originates in the heart of people.
- **Acts 15:20**
"But that we write unto them, that they abstain from pollutions of idols, and *from* fornication, and *from* things strangled, and *from* blood."
Among the four things prohibited under the law of Moses is the sin of fornication.
- **Romans 1:28-29**
"And even as they did not like to retain God in *their* knowledge, God gave them over to a reprobate mind, to do those things which are not convenient; Being filled with all unrighteousness, fornication, wickedness, covetousness, maliciousness; full of envy, murder, debate, deceit, malignity; whisperers,"
Fornication was one of the wicked sins of the pagan world mentioned in Romans Chapter 1.

> **HOMOSEXUALITY IS INCLUDED IN "PORNEIA"**
> In that case, homosexuality–both male and female–was included in the definition.

- 1 Corinthians 5:1

"It is reported commonly *that there is* fornication among you, and such fornication as is not so much as named among the Gentiles, that one should have his father's wife."

Incest was reported at Corinth.

- 1 Corinthians 5:9-11

"I wrote unto you in an epistle not to company with fornicators: Yet not altogether with the fornicators of this world, or with the covetous, or extortioners, or with idolators; for then must ye needs go out of the world. But now I have written unto you not to keep company, if any man that is called a brother be a fornicator, or covetous, or an idolater, or a railer, or a drunkard, or an extortioner; with such an one no not to eat."

> **SEPARATE FROM CHRISTIAN FORNICATORS**
> If any one who is a genuine Christian should be a fornicator, other Christians should not have close fellowship with them. They should separate from them.

- 1 Corinthians 6:13b

"Now the body *is* not for fornication, but for the Lord; and the Lord for the body."

God did not create human bodies for fornication but to be used for the Lord.

- 1 Corinthians 6:18

"Flee fornication. Every sin that a man doeth is without the body; but he that committeth fornication sinneth against his own body."

Paul told the true Christians at Corinth to flee fornication which is a sin against their own bodies.

- 1 Corinthians 7:2

"Nevertheless, *to avoid* fornication, let every man have his own wife, and let every woman have her own husband."

One of the reasons for marriage is to avoid the sin of fornication.

- 1 Corinthians 10:8

"Neither let us commit fornication, as some of them committed, and fell in one day three and twenty thousand."

> **GOD KILLED 23,000 BECAUSE OF FORNICATION**
> In the Old Testament, God punished more than 23,000 by killing them for committing whoredom and fornication with the daughters of Moab (Numbers 25:1, 9).

- 2 Corinthians 12:21

"*And* lest, when I come again, my God will humble me among you, and *that* I shall bewail many which have sinned already, and have not repented of the uncleanness and fornication and lasciviousness which they have committed."

> **FORNICATION NOT REPENTED OF**
> Paul refers to the fornication that some in the church at Corinth had committed and had not repented of.

- Galatians 5:19-21

"Now the works of the flesh are manifest, which are *these*, Adultery, fornication, uncleanness, lasciviousness, Idolatry, witchcraft, hatred, variance, emulations, wrath, strife, seditions, heresies, Envyings, murders, drunkenness, revellings, and such like: of the which I tell you before, as I have also told *you* in time past, that they which do such things shall not inherit the kingdom of God."

The second of these seventeen specific "*works of the flesh*" is fornication. This sin, as the other sixteen, has its source in the fallen Adamic flesh of every man, woman, and child, whether truly saved or lost.

- Ephesians 5:3

"But fornication, and all uncleanness, or covetousness, let it not be once named among you, as becometh saints;"

> **BIBLE "SAINTS" ARE GENUINE CHRISTIANS**
> The "*saints*" here are those who are genuine Christians. They are commanded not to have fornication named among them.

- Colossians 3:5

"Mortify therefore your members which are upon the earth; fornication, uncleanness, inordinate affection, evil concupiscence, and covetousness, which is idolatry:"

> **HOW TO AVOID FORNICATION**
> True Christians are to spiritually put to death the members of their body which allures them into the sin of fornication.

- **Jude 7**
"Even as Sodom and Gomorrha, and the cities about them in like manner, giving themselves over to fornication, and going after strange flesh, are set forth for an example, suffering the vengeance of eternal fire."

> **THE GREEK WORD, PORNEIA=MANY SINS**
> In the case of the use of the Greek Word PORNEIA regarding Sodom and Gomorrha, the meaning of homosexuality or Sodomy would apply. Here are some of the meanings of that Word as mentioned before:
> *"1) illicit sexual intercourse; 1a) adultery, fornication, homosexuality, lesbianism, intercourse with animals etc. 1b) sexual intercourse with close relatives; Lev. 18; 1c) sexual intercourse with a divorced man or woman; Mk. 10:11,12; 2) metaph. the worship of idols; 2a) of the defilement of idolatry, as incurred by eating the sacrifices offered to idols."*

The penalty for this sin is for the perpetrators to suffer *"the vengeance of eternal fire."* Some statistics report that there is a sexual assault of some kind every 90 seconds in our country. A few years back there were 10,700 men raped in the military since President Obama's pro-homosexual leaders approved homosexuals to be in the military and practice their sin on other men. This number is increasing every year now.

The Boy Scouts Of America have ordered the ban against Boy Scouts who are homosexuals not to pass. At the present time, Sodomite homosexuals are welcomed into the Boy Scouts groups. Because of this unBiblical decision, there will be, without a doubt, an increase of wicked and sinful homosexual activity among the Scout troops. As a former active EAGLE SCOUT, I object to this decision practice strongly! I don't know how this is progressing, but some people have urged the Boy Scouts Of America to have homosexual and Sodomite Scout Masters to lead the homosexual Sodomite scouts and others in the troop.

1 Thessalonians 4:4

"That every one of you should know how to possess his vessel in sanctification and honour;"

"VESSEL" REFERS TO THE BODY

Paul's reference to the "*vessel*" here is a reference to the bodies of the genuine Christians in Thessalonica. Their bodies were to be for sanctification and honor, not for wickedness and sin.

Verses On Vessels

- **Acts 9:15**

"But the Lord said unto him, Go thy way: for he is a chosen vessel unto me, to bear my name before the Gentiles, and kings, and the children of Israel:"

The Lord Jesus Christ told Ananias that Paul was a chosen vessel unto Himself to go to the Gentiles, kings and the children of Israel as well.

- **Romans 9:21**

"Hath not the potter power over the clay, of the same lump to make one vessel unto honour, and another unto dishonour?"

Human bodies are called vessels. Some people's bodies are to honor and some are to dishonor.

- **2 Corinthians 4:7**

"But we have this treasure in earthen vessels, that the excellency of the power may be of God, and not of us."

THE HOLY SPIRIT WITHIN VESSELS OF CLAY

The true Christians have the treasure of God the Holy Spirit and salvation in their earthen vessels of clay so that the excellent power might be of God and not of them.

- **2 Timothy 2:20**

"But in a great house there are not only vessels of gold and of silver, but also of wood and of earth; and some to honour, and some to dishonor."

VESSELS OF HONOR OR DISHONOR

In people's houses, they have some expensive and honorable vessels and some less expensive vessels of less honor. So among genuine Christians, some of their lives are more honorable and spiritual than the lives of others who might be carnal Christians and thus possessing dishonor.

> Both kinds of vessels are in the redeemed family of God, regardless of the difference in their different honor.

- 1 Peter 3:7

"Likewise, ye husbands, dwell with *them* according to knowledge, giving honour unto the wife, as unto the weaker vessel, and as being heirs together of the grace of life; that your prayers be not hindered."

Genuine Christian husbands should give honor to their wives since they are weaker vessels. They should not run roughshod over them.

Verses On Sanctification

> **BODIES UNTO SANCTIFICATION AND HONOR**
>
> So true Christians should know how to manage their bodies in both sanctification and honor.

- John 17:17

"Sanctify them through thy truth: thy word is truth."

> **GOD'S WORDS SANCTIFY**
>
> The Lord Jesus Christ, in His high priestly prayer, prayed for the genuine Christians to be sanctified through God's Words which are truth.

- John 17:19

"And for their sakes I sanctify myself, that they also might be sanctified through the truth."

> **GOD'S WORDS MUST BE STUDIED AND BELIEVED**
>
> The only thing that is going to set apart and sanctify true Christians is the truth of God's Words. These Words must be read, studied, believed, and followed.

- Acts 20:32

"And now, brethren, I commend you to God, and to the word of his grace, which is able to build you up, and to give you an inheritance among all them which are sanctified."

> **USE THE PROPER BIBLE VERSION**
>
> The only thing on this earth that can build up and edify genuine Christians are the Words of God. That is why it so important to have an accurate translation of the original Hebrew, Aramaic, and Greek Words. In English, the only accurate translation of those original, inspired, and preserved Words is the King James Bible. All others have great and serious defects.

- **Acts 26:18**
"To open their eyes, *and* to turn *them* from darkness to light, and *from* the power of Satan unto God, that they may receive forgiveness of sins, and inheritance among them which are sanctified by faith that is in me."

The true Christians are ones who have been sanctified or set apart to God by genuine faith in the Lord Jesus Christ.

- **Romans 15:16**
"That I should be the minister of Jesus Christ to the Gentiles, ministering the gospel of God, that the offering up of the Gentiles might be acceptable, being sanctified by the Holy Ghost."

God the Holy Spirit is the Divine Person Who indwells every genuine Christian. He alone can set them apart and sanctify them--making them to live holy lives.

- **1 Corinthians 6:11**
"And such were some of you: but ye are washed, but ye are sanctified, but ye are justified in the name of the Lord Jesus, and by the Spirit of our God."

AFTER SALVATION GOD CAN SANCTIFY

Paul mentions that before these true Christians were saved, they lived very unholy lives. But now they are both sanctified and justified in the Name of the Lord Jesus Christ and by God the Holy Spirit.

- **Ephesians 5:25-26**
"Husbands, love your wives, even as Christ also loved the church, and gave himself for it; That he might sanctify and cleanse it with the washing of water by the word,"

CHRIST WANTS HIS OWN TO BE CLEAN

The Lord Jesus Christ wants to sanctify and cleanse every genuine Christian who is a member of His true Church and Body. The means that He has to perform this cleansing and washing is by the Words of God.

- **1 Thessalonians 5:23**
"And the very God of peace sanctify you wholly; and *I pray God* your whole spirit and soul and body be preserved blameless unto the coming of our Lord Jesus Christ."

SANCTIFIED IN SPIRIT, SOUL, AND BODY

Paul prayed that the true Christians in Thessalonica might be sanctified in every part of their persons–their spirits, their souls, and their bodies.

- **2 Timothy 2:21**
  "If a man therefore purge himself from these, he shall be a vessel unto honour, sanctified, and meet for the master's use, *and* prepared unto every good work."

Genuine Christians should separate themselves from evil and evil people in order to be sanctified and fit for the use of the Lord Jesus Christ.

1 Thessalonians 4:5

"Not in the lust of concupiscence, even as the Gentiles which know not God:"

THE MEANING OF THE GREEK WORD, "EPITHUMIA"
The Greek Word for *"concupiscence"* is EPITHUMIA. Some of the meanings of this Word are:
"1) desire, craving, longing, desire for what is forbidden, lust"

There are various verses that speak of lust.
- **Proverbs 6:23-29**
  "For the commandment *is* a lamp; and the law *is* light, and reproofs of instruction *are* the way of life: To keep thee from the evil woman, from the flattery of the tongue of a strange woman. Lust not after her beauty in thine heart; neither let her take thee with her eyelids. For by means of a whorish woman *a man is brought* to a piece of bread: and the adulteress will hunt for the precious life. Can a man take fire in his bosom, and his clothes not be burned? Can one go upon hot coals, and his feet not be burned? So he that goeth in to his neighbour's wife; whosoever toucheth her shall not be innocent."

Good and decent men in the Old Testament were not to lust after prostitutes or any other woman to whom they are not married.
- **Matthew 5:27-29**
  "Ye have heard that it was said by them of old time, Thou shalt not commit adultery: But I say unto you, That whosoever looketh on a woman to lust after her hath committed adultery with her already in his heart. And if thy right eye offend thee, pluck it out, and cast *it* from thee: for it is profitable for thee that one of thy members should perish, and not *that* thy whole body should be cast into hell."

SPIRITUAL ADULTERY–LOOKING WITH LUST
The Lord Jesus Christ is not speaking of men who merely look at women; but if his look includes this *"lust after her,"* He calls it adultery of the heart.

- Romans 1:24
"Wherefore God also gave them up to uncleanness through the lusts of their own hearts, to dishonor their own bodies between themselves:"

THE SINS OF THE PAGAN WORLD
This verse relates to the sins of the pagan Gentile world. This is why the lusts of homosexual men and lesbian women are specifically listed in Romans 1. These wicked sinners followed the lusts of their own hearts.

- Romans 1:27
"And likewise also the men, leaving the natural use of the woman, burned in their lust one toward another; men with men working that which is unseemly, and receiving in themselves that recompence of their error which was meet."

THE BIBLE CONDEMNS SODOMY
This burning lust in the ancient heathen world led to both Sodomy and lesbianism. That same lust is present today and is being more publicly accepted, and yet contrary to the standards of God and the Bible. Homosexual intermarriages are being pushed and accepted in many states. Even though some say homosexuals number only 1% or 2% of our nation, the homosexual lobby is ruling what the other 98% or 99% of us must do for them!

According to recent statistics, not many male homosexuals live beyond forty five. Not many female lesbians live too much beyond that because of this wickedness and sin. The serious disease of AIDS comes most frequently from the homosexual lifestyle. This verse states that these homosexuals receive a *"recompence of their error"* which is fitting.

- Romans 6:12
"Let not sin therefore reign in your mortal body, that ye should obey it in the lusts thereof:"

The sin nature of the true Christian should not rule and be obeyed in its lusts.

- Romans 13:14
"But put ye on the Lord Jesus Christ, and make not provision for the flesh, to *fulfil* the lusts *thereof.*"

MAKE NO PROVISIONS FOR FLESHLY LUST
Genuine Christians can avail themselves of the power of their Saviour, the Lord Jesus Christ, and should not make provision for the lusts of their fleshly nature.

- **Galatians 5:16**
"*This* I say then, Walk in the Spirit, and ye shall not fulfil the lust of the flesh."
True Christians are indwelt by the Holy Spirit. If they walk in His power, they will not fulfil the lust of their flesh.
- **Ephesians 2:3**
"Among whom we all had our conversation in times past in the lusts of our flesh, fulfilling the desires of the flesh and of the mind; and were by nature the children of wrath, even as others."
This is a picture of the former lives of genuine Christians when they lived in the lusts of their flesh.
- **2 Timothy 2:22**
"Flee also youthful lusts: but follow righteousness, faith, charity, peace, with them that call on the Lord out of a pure heart."

ALL ARE TO FLEE THE LUSTS OF YOUTH
Paul ordered Timothy who was the pastor of the church at Ephesus to flee the lusts that are prominent during youth. These same lusts must be avoided regardless of the age of the person, whether in their fifties, sixties, seventies, eighties, or even nineties. The lusts of youth should be discarded and be replaced with righteousness.

- **1 Peter 2:11**
"Dearly beloved, I beseech *you* as strangers and pilgrims, abstain from fleshly lusts, which war against the soul;"
All fleshly lusts war against the soul and should not be pursued.
- **1 Peter 4:3**
"For the time past of *our* life may suffice us to have wrought the will of the Gentiles, when we walked in lasciviousness, lusts, excess of wine, revellings, banqueting, and abominable idolatries:"
Yielding to the past lusts of true Christians should no longer be a part of them now that they have been born-again and saved.

1 Thessalonians 4:6
"That no man go beyond and defraud his brother in any matter: because that the Lord is the avenger of all such, as we also have forewarned you and testified."

THE MEANING OF THE GREEK WORD, "HUPERBAINO"
The Greek Word for "*go beyond*" is HUPERBAINO. Some of the meanings of this Word are:

> *"1) to step over, beyond; 2) metaph. 2a) to transgress; 2b) <u>to overstep the proper limits</u>; 2c) trespass, do wrong, sin; 2c1) of one who defrauds another in business; 2d) overreaches"*

Paul told these genuine Christians that they should do this.

1 Thessalonians 4:7
"For God hath not called us unto uncleanness, but unto holiness."

<u>God has called true Christians to holiness</u>. He wants them to have nothing to do any longer with uncleanness.

Verses On Uncleanness
- **Romans 1:24**

"Wherefore God also gave them up to uncleanness through the lusts of their own hearts, to dishonor their own bodies between themselves."

> **GOD GAVE UP THE HEATHEN WORLD**
> God gave up the heathen world as mentioned in Romans 1 because of their uncleanness and sin.

- **Romans 6:19**

"I speak after the manner of men because of the infirmity of your flesh: for as ye have yielded your members servants to uncleanness and to iniquity unto iniquity; even so now yield your members servants to righteousness unto holiness."

> **BEFORE SALVATION LIVES ARE UNCLEAN**
> Before people are genuine Christians, their lives are unclean in the eyes of God. This should all stop once they become born-again by true faith in the Lord Jesus Christ. Righteousness and holiness should then prevail.

- **Galatians 5:19-21**

"Now the works of the flesh are manifest, which are *these*; Adultery, fornication, <u>uncleanness</u>, lasciviousness, Idolatry, witchcraft, hatred, variance, emulations, wrath, strife, seditions, heresies, Envyings, murders, drunkenness, revellings, and such like: of the which I tell you before, as I have also told *you* in time past, that they which do such things shall not inherit the kingdom of God."

Of the seventeen works of the flesh mentioned in these verse, the sin of <u>uncleanness is mentioned third</u>.

- **Ephesians 4:19**
"Who being past feeling have given themselves over unto lasciviousness, to work all uncleanness with greediness."
Many of the unsaved non-Christian world have given themselves over to uncleanness as a way of life.
- **Ephesians 5:3**
"But fornication, and all uncleanness, or covetousness, let it not be once named among you, as becometh saints."
Uncleanness is not in any way appropriate for genuine Christians. It is by no means becoming or fitting.
- **Colossians 3:5**
"Mortify therefore your members which are upon the earth; fornication, uncleanness, inordinate affection, evil concupiscence, and covetousness, which is idolatry:"

MORTIFY ANY UNCLEANNESS
The true Christians at Colosse were to mortify or put to death any uncleanness.

Verses On Holiness
- **Exodus 15:11**
"Who *is* like unto thee, O LORD, among the gods? Who *is* like thee, glorious in holiness, fearful *in* praises, doing wonders?"

GOD IS SINLESS AND HOLY
The God of the Bible is glorious in holiness. He is without sin of any kind. He is perfect in all His ways even if we do not always understand them.

- **Psalm 96:9**
"O worship the LORD in the beauty of holiness: fear before him, all the earth."
Genuine Christians are to worship the Lord in the beauty of holiness.
- **Romans 6:19c**
"... even so now yield your members servants to righteousness unto holiness."

BODIES YIELDED TO HOLINESS
The members of the Christians' bodies are to be yielded to holiness once the Lord Jesus Christ has saved them by His grace. Among all their other bodily members, this includes their eyes, their ears, their hands, their feet, their mouth, and their heart.

- 2 Corinthians 7:1

"Having therefore these promises, dearly beloved, let us cleanse ourselves from all filthiness of the flesh and spirit, perfecting holiness in the fear of God."

After Paul exhorts the genuine Christians at Corinth in the areas of Biblical separation with all of its promises, he urges them be mature in holiness in the fear of God.

- 1 Thessalonians 3:13

"To the end he may stablish your hearts unblameable in holiness before God, even our Father, at the coming of our Lord Jesus Christ with all his saints."

God will establish true Christians in all holiness by giving them new and resurrected bodies like to that of the Lord Jesus Christ. They will return to this earth with Him to reign with Him a thousand years in the Millennium.

- Titus 2:3

"The aged women likewise, that *they be* in behavior as becometh holiness, not false accusers, not given to much wine, teachers of good things;"

THE BEHAVIOR OF THE AGED WOMEN

Pastor Titus of the church at Crete reminded the aged women to have a behavior that went along with holiness.

1 Thessalonians 4:8

"He therefore that despiseth, despiseth not man, but God, who hath also given unto us his holy Spirit."

True Christians have the Holy Spirit indwelling them.

THE MEANING OF THE GREEK WORD, "ATHETEO"

The Greek Word for *"despiseth"* is ATHETEO. Some of the meanings of this Word are:

"1) to do away with, to set aside, disregard; 2) to thwart the efficacy of anything, nullify, make void, frustrate; 3) to reject, to refuse, to slight"

No one should disregard or reject God or the Words of God that tell us that genuine Christians should abstain from all kinds of wickedness.

1 Thessalonians 4:9

"But as touching brotherly love ye need not that I write unto you: for ye yourselves are taught of God to love one another."

Love that genuine Christians should have for one another is mentioned many times in the New Testament.

Verses On True Christian Love

- John 13:34

"A new commandment I give unto you, That ye love one another; as I have loved you, that ye also love one another."

Now no other true Christian can love another true Christian as the Lord Jesus Christ loved them, but that's the goal that He laid down for them. The Lord Jesus Christ said genuine Christians were to love one another even if those believers don't love them back.

- John 13:35

"By this shall all *men* know that ye are my disciples, if ye have love one to another."

CHRISTIAN LOVE FOR OTHER TRUE CHRISTIANS

True Christian discipleship is detected by true Christian love for the brethren. Genuine Christians are to love one another even though they might differ on some doctrines or teachings. They do not have to agree on all the doctrines of the Bible for them to exemplify genuine Christian love. Admittedly, this is a very difficult thing to do.

- Ephesians 1:15

"Wherefore I also, after I heard of your faith in the Lord Jesus, and love unto all the saints,"

The Christians at Ephesus had love for **all** (not just some) of the genuine Christians who are called "*saints*" in this verse.

- 1 Peter 1:22

"Seeing ye have purified your souls in obeying the truth through the Spirit unto unfeigned love of the brethren, *see that ye* love one another with a pure heart fervently:"

"*Unfeigned*" love means love that is not hypocritical, false, or phony. Some people give a big outward smile, but their inward heart is frowning and sad. The heart should be smiling so that it shows on the face. I have said many times that there are many important differences that we have with other genuine Christians.

SEVEN DOCTRINES WHERE PEOPLE DISAGREE

Some of these differences with other true Christians include our stand for the following:

(1) for the Masoretic Hebrew, Aramaic, and Greek Words underlying the King James Bible;

(2) for the superiority and accuracy of the King James Bible rather than for any other English translation;

(3) <u>for our using the term, *"inspiration"* (2 Timothy 3:16-17) only for the original Hebrew, Aramaic, and Greek Words but not for any translation of those Words</u>;

(4) for every true born-again Christian being in the "Church which is His Body" rather than only a small group of special Baptist churches;

(5) for the death of the Lord Jesus Christ for the sins of the entire world, not just for the sins of a small group called the "elect";

(6) for salvation being open to *"whosoever* [truly] *believeth"* on the Lord Jesus Christ, not just for a small group called the "elect";

(7) for eternal salvation that can never be lost for those who have put their genuine faith in the Lord Jesus Christ as their Saviour and are truly born-again; and many other doctrines that we hold dear.

LOVE TRUE CHRISTIANS

However, just because we do not agree on some or all of the above distinctions (and many others) does not mean that we are not commanded to love other genuine Christians who differ with us on these (and many other) doctrines. We must follow the doctrines and teachings that we find in the Words of God, no matter what other true Christians believe contrary to those doctrines and teachings.

1 Thessalonians 4:10

"And indeed ye do it toward all the brethren which are in all Macedonia: but we beseech you, brethren, that ye increase more and more;"

Paul is referring back to verse 9, where he says the Thessalonian Christians have love for the brethren--the saved, born-again Christians-- and do this. <u>They were examples to all of Macedonia</u>. Thessalonica is a large province north of Greece. Their love of the brethren was a testimony to all that region.

> **TEACHINGS BEFORE TALKING ABOUT THE RAPTURE**
> There are some things that Paul mentions before he talks about the Rapture of the Church, taking them home to Heaven: (1) increasing the love for the brethren; (2) being quiet (v. 11); (3) doing their own business (v. 11); (4) working with your own hands (v. 11); (5) being honest (v 12); (6) lacking nothing (v. 12); (7) sorrowing not (v. 13).

Verses On Increasing Genuine Christian Love
- Ephesians 4:16

"From whom the whole body fitly joined together and compacted by that which every joint supplieth, according to the effectual working in the measure of every part, maketh increase of the body unto the edifying of itself in love."

Those who are saved are to love the brethren. True Christians don't have to agree with the doctrines of the brethren but love the brethren themselves.

- 1 Thessalonians 3:12

"And the Lord make you to increase and abound in love one toward another, and toward all men, even as we do toward you:"

This is one of those things that Paul mentions before he talks about the Rapture of the Church.

1 Thessalonians 4:11

"And that ye study to be quiet, and to do your own business, and to work with your own hands, as we commanded you;"

In this verse there are three more things that Paul talks about before he tells them about the Rapture of all genuine Christians: being quiet; doing their own business; and working with their own hands.

Here are a few thoughts on studying to be quiet.

> **THE GREEK WORD, "PHILOTIMEOMAI"**
> The Greek Word for *"study"* is PHILO-TIMEOMAI. Some of the meanings of this Word are:
> *"1) to be fond of honour; 1a) to be actuated by love of honour; 1b) from a love of honour to strive to bring something to pass; 2) to be ambitious 2a) to strive earnestly, make it one's aim"*

THE GREEK WORD, "HESUCHAZO," MEANING

The Greek Word for *"be quiet"* is HESUCHAZO. Some of the meanings of this Word are:

"1) to keep quiet; 1a) to rest, cease from labour; 1b) to lead a quiet life, said of those who are not running hither and thither, but stay at home and mind their business; 1c) to be silent, i.e. to say nothing, hold one's peace"

Verses On Being Quiet

- **Psalms 107:30**

"Then are they glad because they be quiet; so he bringeth them unto their desired haven."

The Israelites were glad because they were quiet and without wars.

- **Proverbs 17:1**

"Better *is* a dry morsel, and quietness therewith, than an house full of sacrifices *with* strife."

Even though the food is meager, if there is quietness when eating it, it is better than much food with much bickering and fighting.

- **Ecclesiastes 4:6**

"Better *is* an handful *with* quietness, than both the hands full *with* travail and vexation of spirit."

Like the preceding verse, little with quietness is better than much in the midst of trouble.

- **Ecclesiastes 9:17**

"The words of wise *men are* heard in quiet more than the cry of him that ruleth among fools.

Wise words in quietness outweigh loud cries of fools.

- **Isaiah 30:15b**

". . . in quietness and in confidence shall be your strength: and ye would not."

Strength comes with quietness and confidence.

- **Isaiah 32:17**

"And the work of righteousness shall be peace; and the effect of righteousness quietness and assurance for ever."

BIBLICAL RIGHTEOUSNESS BRINGS ASSURANCE

Biblical righteousness has the effect of bringing quietness and assurance forever.

- **2 Thessalonians 3:12**

"Now them that are such we command and exhort by our Lord Jesus Christ, that with quietness they work, and eat their own bread."

True Christians are exhorted to work with quietness and without tumult.
- **1 Timothy 2:2**

"For kings, and *for* all that are in authority; that we may lead a quiet and peaceable life in all godliness and honesty."

PRAY THAT RULERS BRING US PEACEABLE LIVES

That's why genuine Christians should pray for our rulers, so that that these Christians might lead quiet and peaceable lives.

- **1 Peter 3:4**

"But *let it be* the hidden man of the heart, in that which is not corruptible, *even the ornament* of a meek and quiet spirit, which is in the sight of God of great price."

MEEK AND QUIET SPIRITS NEEDED

God is pleased when genuine Christians have meek and quiet spirits.

Verses On Doing Business

The third command relates genuine Christians doing their own business, taking charge of their own affairs.

- **Proverbs 22:29**

"Seest thou a man diligent in his business? he shall stand before kings; he shall not stand before mean *men*."

Diligence in business will bring great rewards and privileges.

- **Luke 2:49**

"And he said unto them, How is it that ye sought me? wist ye not that I must be about my Father's business?"

The Lord Jesus Christ, when He was in the temple, His mother and Joseph wondered where He was. He needed to be about the business affairs of His Father Who had sent Him into this world. True Christians should never neglect the business of God. They should follow God's Words and seek to please Him throughout their lives until He calls them Home.

Verses On Working--Good And Bad

The fourth command tells the true Christians to work with their own hands. They are not to be lazy. Here are some verses that deal with this theme.

- **Psalms 9:16**
"The LORD is known *by* the judgment *which* he executeth: the wicked is snared in the work of his own hands. Higgaion. Selah."
Idols are the work of men's hands. They are a wicked snare.
- **Psalms 28:4**
"Give them according to their deeds, and according to the wickedness of their endeavours: give them after the work of their hands; render to them their desert."
I believe this is another reference to the work of making idols.
- **Psalms 90:17**
"And let the beauty of the LORD our God be upon us: and establish thou the work of our hands upon us; yea, the work of our hands establish thou it."
These are works of hands that are proper and for the beauty of the LORD.
- **Psalms 102:25**
"Of old hast thou laid the foundation of the earth: and the heavens *are* the work of thy hands."
The creation of the earth, the heavens and all that is contained in them is the work of God's own hands. This mighty works did not come about by any form of evolution or chance.
- **Psalms 115:4**
"Their idols *are* silver and gold, the work of men's hands."
Idols are the evil work of man's hands.
- **Proverbs 18:9**
"He also that is slothful in his work is brother to him that is a great waster."
True Christians must be diligent in their work, not slothful.
- **Isaiah 2:8**
"Their land also is full of idols; they worship the work of their own hands, that which their own fingers have made:"
Again, idols are the evil work of men's hands.
- **Luke 13:14**
"And the ruler of the synagogue answered with indignation, because that Jesus had healed on the sabbath day, and said unto the people, There are six days in which men ought to work: in them therefore come and be healed, and not on the sabbath day."

In the Old Testament, the weekly sabbath was to be kept without any physical work. Work was to be done only on the other six days.
- **2 Thessalonians 2:17**
"Comfort your hearts, and stablish you in every good word and work."

> **ESTABLISHED IN GOOD WORDS AND WORKS**
> God wants every true Christian to be established in good words and good works.

- 2 Thessalonians 3:10

"For even when we were with you, this we commanded you, that if any would not work, neither should he eat."

> **IF UNWILLING TO WORK, NO EATING**
> This is a clear command for those genuine Christians who are not willing to work—"*neither should he eat.*" The verse is not speaking of those who might be sick or incapacitated and are unable to work. It speaks only of those who are able to work, but not willing to work. This at first sounds hard and cold, but God expects His people to have a desire to work and be active in providing for themselves and their families. Our present federal government feeds and helps who are able, but unwilling to work. This is contrary to this verse.

- 2 Thessalonians 3:12

"Now them that are such we command and exhort by our Lord Jesus Christ, that with quietness they work, and eat their own bread."

> **WORK QUIETLY WITHOUT COMPLAINING**
> Paul wanted the genuine Christians in Thessalonica to work in quietness and without complaining about things.

1 Thessalonians 4:12

"**That ye may walk honestly toward them that are without, and that ye may have lack of nothing.**"

In this verse, Paul speaks of two other things that true Christians should do in preparation for their Rapture when they will meet their Saviour in the air. This is at a future time unknown to the Thessalonian Christians, or anyone else.

Verses On Being Honest

Here is the fifth thing that genuine Christians should do. They should walk honestly, especially before those who are not Christians. They should not be cheating people or stealing from people. They should be righteous in all that they do. Here are some verses that deal with being honest.

- **Luke 8:15**

"But that on the good ground are they, which in an honest and good heart, having heard the word, keep *it*, and bring forth fruit with patience."

One of the four grounds on which the seed fell was the good ground which brought forth fruit because it was received by those who had honest and good hearts.

- **Acts 6:3**

"Wherefore, brethren, look ye out among you seven men of honest report, full of the Holy Ghost and wisdom, whom we may appoint over this business."

Before the appointing those who were to be helpers in the church--deacons and other workers--honesty was essential.

- **Romans 12:17**

"Recompense to no man evil for evil. Provide things honest in the sight of all men."

True Christians were to be honest before all people so that the testimony of the Lord Jesus Christ would not be tarnished.

- **Romans 13:13**

"Let us walk honestly, as in the day; not in rioting and drunkenness, not in chambering and wantonness, not in strife and envying."

The walk and lifestyle of genuine Christians should be honest as well. None of these things mentioned should be a part of their lives.

- **2 Corinthians 8:21**

"Providing for honest things, not only in the sight of the Lord, but also in the sight of men."

True Christians must provide for honest things in the sight of the Lord and men.

A FALSE CHARGE OF STEALING FUNDS

One of the false charges a few years ago that was written against me by former leaders in the Dean Burgon Society was that I, as the President of that Society, was somehow misappropriating some of the funds from the Society's income. These men thought that this was the reason why, for a short time, the IRS took away the tax exemption of the Society.

That was totally untrue. The tax exempt status of the Society has been restored for many years now. The real reason (which was not believed by these DBS leaders) was as follows. For more than 35 years of the life of the Dean Burgon Society, the IRS rules stated that it was under no obligation to file any tax reports because it received less than $30,000 a year in contributions.

> However, recently, the IRS changed their rules. They now require every tax exempt organization to file yearly reports, no matter how much their contributions are. We were not properly informed of this change so did not file any annual reports. So DBS was removed from tax exemption for a short time. It has now been restored to tax exempt status as before.
> <u>These leaders were not willing to listen to the facts of the case</u>, but jumped to the conclusion that their DBS President had somehow not been honest in dealing with the funds of the Society. For many years now, our church has given $100.00 every month to the Dean Burgon Society. There has not been any dishonesty in me as Pastor of our church or as President of the Society. <u>I have worked for no salary for all 37 years as President of the Dean Burgon Society and have never misappropriated any of its funds.</u> These leaders have all left the DBS despite the exoneration of its President and the full restoration of the former tax exempt status of the Dean Burgon Society.

- 2 Corinthians 13:7

"Now I pray to God that ye do no evil; not that we should appear approved, but that ye should do that which is honest, though we be as reprobates."

> **DO HONEST THINGS NOT EVIL THINGS**
> Paul exhorted the true Christians not to do evil things, but do things that are honest.

- Philippians 4:8

"Finally, brethren, whatsoever things are true, <u>whatsoever things are honest</u>, whatsoever things *are* just, whatsoever things *are* pure, whatsoever things *are* lovely, whatsoever things *are* of good report; if *there be* any virtue, and if *there be* any praise, think on these things."

Genuine Christians are to think on many things. One of them involves thinking on *"whatsoever things are honest."*

- 1 Timothy 2:2

"For kings, and *for* all that are in authority; that we may lead a quiet and peaceable life in all godliness and honesty."

One of the important prayers for true Christians is for those in authority over them. They should pray <u>that they can live their lives in godliness and honesty</u>.

- **Hebrews 13:18**
"Pray for us: for we trust we have a good conscience, in all things willing to live honestly."
- **1 Peter 2:12**
"Having your conversation honest among the Gentiles: that, whereas they speak against you as evildoers, they may by *your* good works, which they shall behold, glorify God in the day of visitation."

Verses On Lacking Nothing

Here is the sixth thing that Paul wants these true Christians to do. He wants them to *"have lack of nothing."*
- **Acts 4:34**
"Neither was there any among them that lacked: for as many as were possessors of lands or houses sold them, and brought the prices of the things that were sold."

They all had things that they needed and they were supplied.

VOLUNTARY SHARING IS NOT COMMUNISM

The early church of genuine Christians had no lack because they acted like a private family and voluntarily shared with one another. This was not communism which is involuntary sharing. There is quite a difference in the two types of sharing.

- **2 Corinthians 8:15**
"As it is written, He that *had gathered* much had nothing over; and he that *had gathered* little had no lack."

This is a reference to when God supplied the Israelites in the Sinai wilderness with manna from Heaven. There was no lack of food for them throughout the forty years of wandering.
- **1 Thessalonians 3:10**
"Night and day praying exceedingly that we might see your face, and might perfect that which is lacking in your faith?"

THE NEED TO PERFECT WHAT IS LACKING

Paul didn't want anything lacking in the faith of those true Christians at Thessalonica. He was to perfect anything that was lacking in that faith and doctrine.

1 Thessalonians 4:13

"But I would not have you to be ignorant, brethren, concerning them which are asleep, that ye sorrow not, even as others which have no hope."

Paul begins in this verse to prepare his readers for the Rapture of the genuine Christians who would meet the Lord Jesus Christ in the air before any part of the seven year Tribulation would take place. He does not want them to be ignorant of this prophetic truth as many are today. Nor does he want them to be ignorant of the state of those true Christians who have died.

"ASLEEP" HERE REFERS TO DEATH

The word here for *"sleep"* is a reference to their death. There is no teaching in the Bible concerning soul sleep as some false cults teach. Those genuine Christians who had died were right then present with the Lord Jesus Christ in Heaven. Paul didn't want those true Christians at Thessalonica to be in sorrow about them as other non-Christians without hope.

It is very clear in the New Testament that the only people who will be in Heaven are those who have exercised genuine faith in the Lord Jesus Christ as their Saviour. Those who have not exercised that faith in the Saviour have *"no hope."* Phony religious people falsely teach that everyone in the world is going to Heaven. These (whether Roman Catholics, Protestants, or any others) are contradicting the clear teachings of the Lord Jesus Christ Himself when He said to the Apostle Thomas:

> *"Jesus saith unto him, I am the way, the truth, and the life: no man cometh unto the Father, but by me."* (John 14:6)

The Lord Jesus Christ alone is the only Way to God the Father and to Heaven.

SORROW NOT FOR CHRISTIANS WHO DIE

Paul did not want true Christians to have sorrow for those who were genuinely saved and had died. They were immediately with the Lord Jesus Christ in Heaven. Other true Christians would be joined with them at the Rapture.

Verses On Sorrow

Not sorrowing is the seventh thing mentioned by Paul. This is Not only is *"sorrow"* mentioned here, but there are many other verses about this emotion.

- **Psalms 32:10**

"Many sorrows *shall be* to the wicked: but he that trusteth in the LORD, mercy shall compass him about."

Though many wicked don't think they have sorrows, God says that their sorrows are many.

- **Psalms 90:10**

"The days of our years *are* threescore years and ten; and if by reason of strength *they be* fourscore years, yet *is* their strength labour and sorrow; for it is soon cut off, and we fly away."

THE SORROWS OF OLD AGE

Even if people live 80 years, God says there is sorrow connected with these years.

- **Proverbs 10:22**

"The blessing of the LORD, it maketh rich, and he addeth no sorrow with it."

GOD'S BLESSINGS WITHOUT SORROW

When God's blessings from the Lord are present, no sorrow is present with them.

- **Proverbs 14:13**

"Even in laughter the heart is sorrowful; and the end of that mirth *is* heaviness."

NON-CHRISTIANS HAVE SORROWFUL HEARTS

Those who have never truly trusted the Lord Jesus Christ as their Saviour have sorrowful and heavy hearts. This is sad!

- **Proverbs 23:29-30**

"Who hath woe? who hath sorrow? who hath contentions? who hath babbling? who hath wounds without cause? who hath redness of eyes?"

This is a very accurate description by the Lord of the drinkers of this world. They have sorrow, wounds, contentions, and much babbling.

- **1 Timothy 6:10**

"For the love of money is the root of all evil: which while some coveted after, they have erred from the faith, and pierced themselves through with many sorrows."

STRAYING FROM THE FAITH BRINGS MANY SORROWS

When people covet money, they stray away from the doctrines of the Bible and get pierced with many sorrows.

- Revelation 21:4

"And <u>God shall wipe away all tears from their eyes</u>; and there shall be no more death, neither sorrow, nor crying, neither shall there be any more pain: for the former things are passed away."

Among the many important things absent in the Bible's Heaven is the sorrow that we know in this life.

1 Thessalonians 4:14

"For if we believe that Jesus died and rose again, even so them also which sleep in Jesus will God bring with him."

GOD WILL BRING CHRISTIANS WITH CHRIST It is a fact that the Lord Jesus Christ died for all sinners. He also rose bodily from the dead. This verse declares that <u>God will bring with the Lord Jesus Christ those genuine Christians who have died.</u> The details will follow.

Verses On The Meaning Of Sleep As Death

- John 11:11-13

"These things said he: and after that he saith unto them, Our friend Lazarus sleepeth; but I go, that I may awake him out of sleep. Then said his disciples, Lord, if he sleep, he shall do well. Howbeit Jesus spake of his death: but they thought that he had spoken of taking of rest in sleep."

<u>In this context</u>, the Lord Jesus Christ used the word, <u>"sleep" clearly as meaning physical death</u>.

- 1 Corinthians 11:30

"For this cause many *are* weak and sickly among you, and many sleep."

Because of misbehavior and drunkenness at the Lord's table, the Lord slew some of <u>these true Christians who were out of order. It was a sleep of death</u>.

- 1 Corinthians 15:51

"Behold, I shew you a mystery; We shall not all sleep, but we shall all be changed,"

> **SOME CHRISTIANS WILL NOT DIE PHYSICALLY**
> He was saying that the genuine Christians would not all die. All of them will be changed and receive resurrected bodies like to that of the Lord Jesus Christ. <u>Those true Christians who live until the Rapture of the Lord Jesus Christ will be transformed instantly and not die.</u> Their mortal bodies will be changed to immortal bodies.

- **1 Thessalonians 5:10**

"Who died for us, that, whether we wake or sleep, we should live together with him."

The Lord Jesus Christ died for the sins of the whole world.

Verses On The Coming Of Christ To Judge

- **Revelation 19:11**

"And I saw heaven opened, and behold a white horse; and he that sat upon him *was* called Faithful and True, and in righteousness he doth judge and make war."

<u>This speaks of the Lord Jesus Christ returning at the end of the Tribulation to defeat Satan and his followers.</u>

- **Revelation 19:12-13**

"His eyes *were* as a flame of fire, and on his head *were* many crowns; and he had a name written, that no man knew, but he himself. And he *was* clothed with a vesture dipped in blood: and his name is called The Word of God."

<u>Again, this is speaking of the Lord Jesus Christ's defeat of Satan's forces at the end of the Tribulation.</u>

- **Revelation 19:14**

"And the armies *which were* in heaven followed him upon white horses, clothed in fine linen, white and clean."

Now notice, those saved, born-again Christians will be with the Lord Jesus Christ at the judgement of the heathen nations at the battle of Armageddon.

- **Revelation 20:4**

"And I saw thrones, and they sat upon them, and judgment was given unto them: and *I saw* the souls of them that were beheaded for the witness of Jesus, and for the word of God, and which had not worshipped the beast, neither his image, neither had received *his* mark upon their foreheads, or in their hands; and they lived and reigned with Christ a thousand years."

The Tribulation saints that are saved and all the other true Christians will reign with the Lord Jesus Christ for one thousand years in the Millennium.

Verses On Heaven

- Psalms 23:6

"Surely goodness and mercy shall follow me all the days of my life: and I will dwell in the house of the LORD for ever."

HEAVEN IS FOREVER FOR TRUE CHRISTIANS
For true Christians, they will be in God's House in Heaven forever.

- John 14:1-3

"Let not your heart be troubled: ye believe in God, believe also in me. In my Father's house are many mansions: if *it were* not *so*, I would have told you. I go to prepare a place for you. And if I go and prepare a place for you, I will come again, and receive you unto myself; that where I am, *there* ye may be also."

This is a promise from the Lord Jesus Christ that genuine Christians will be with Him in Heaven that He has prepared for them.

- John 17:24

"Father, I will that they also, whom thou hast given me, be with me where I am; that they may behold my glory, which thou hast given me: for thou lovedst me before the foundation of the world."

One of the petitions the Lord Jesus Christ made to God the Father was that the true Christians would be with Him in Heaven.

- Philippians 1:23-24

"For I am in a strait betwixt two, having a desire to depart, and to be with Christ; which is far better: Nevertheless to abide in the flesh *is* more needful for you."

AT DEATH, TRUE CHRISTIANS GO TO HEAVEN
For those who are true Christians, departure at their death brings them directly to be with the Lord Jesus Christ in Heaven. There is no purgatory or limbo that Roman Catholicism has invented.

1 Thessalonians 4:15

"For this we say unto you by the word of the Lord, that we which are alive and remain unto the coming of the Lord shall not prevent them which are asleep."

NO PROPHECY NEEDED BEFORE THE RAPTURE
Notice that there is not a single prophecy that must be fulfilled before this first phase of the *"coming of the Lord"* in

the air occurs. This is speaking of the Rapture of all genuine Christians which will take place before any part of the Tribulation. All true Christians will meet the Lord Jesus Christ in the air. The true Christians who are living at the time of the Rapture will be caught up after those genuine Christians who have already died.

1 Thessalonians 4:16

"For the Lord himself shall descend from heaven with a shout, with the voice of the archangel, and with the trump of God: and the dead in Christ shall rise first:"

This is the description of the first phase of the return of the Lord Jesus Christ. It is called the Rapture of all true Christians.

(1) This first phase of His coming is in the air.

(2) The second phase of His coming is when He returns to earth to set up His thousand year reign called the Millennium.

THE RAPTURE FOR TRUE CHRISTIANS AT ANY MOMENT

In this first phase of the second coming of the Lord Jesus Christ, there are no prophecies that must be fulfilled. It can occur at any moment.

SIX DIFFERENT VIEWS ABOUT THE RAPTURE

There are at least six different views regarding the Rapture of the genuine Christians.

1. The Pre-Tribulation Rapture Position. This is the Biblical view. It states that the Lord Jesus Christ will come in the clouds of the heavens to take up all the genuine Christians before any part of the seven year Tribulation period.

2. The Mid-Tribulation Rapture Position. This is a false view of the Rapture. It states that the Rapture will occur in the middle of the seven year Tribulation period.

3. The Post-Tribulation Rapture Position. This is a false view of the Rapture. It states that the Rapture will occur at the end of the seven year Tribulation period.

4. The Pre-Wrath Rapture Position. This is a false view of the Rapture. It states that the Rapture will occur some time during the seven year Tribulation period just before God's special wrath is about to fall upon the world. This is a fairly recent false position.

> 5. **The Partial Rapture Position.** This position wrongly teaches that only certain kind of genuine Christians will be included in the Rapture. Those who, though saved, are not living for the Lord will be left behind. This is in error. The Pre-Tribulation Rapture will be for all true Christians.
> 6. **The No Rapture Of Any Kind Position.** This is the position of many theologians living today. Though contrary to clear Biblical teachings, those who hold this position do not believe there will be any kind of Rapture at all.

> **WHAT HAPPENS AT THE RAPTURE?**
> This present verse sixteen explains exactly what will happen at the Rapture of the genuine Christians.
> (1) The Lord Jesus Christ Who is in Heaven now, at the right hand of God the Father, will descend from Heaven.
> (2) There will be a shout.
> (3) There will be the voice of the archangel.
> (4) There will be the sound of the trumpet of God.
> (5) The dead in Christ, who have died before the Rapture, will be raised up from their graves first.

Verses On "Shout"

- **Joshua 6:5**

"And it shall come to pass, that when they make a long *blast* with the ram's horn, *and* when ye hear the sound of the trumpet, all the people shall shout with a great shout; and the wall of the city shall fall down flat, and the people shall ascend up every man straight before him."

God used "*shouts*" in the Bible, at different times. Here, it was in Joshua's day and the fall of the wall of Jericho. In the future, it will be in the pre-Tribulation Rapture of all the genuine Christians.

- **Joshua 6:16**

"And it came to pass at the seventh time, when the priests blew with the trumpets, Joshua said unto the people, Shout; for the LORD hath given you the city."

Again, this is at the fall of the wall of Jericho.

- **Joshua 6:20**

"So the people shouted when *the priests* blew with the trumpets: and it came to pass, when the people heard the sound of the trumpet, and the people shouted with a great shout, that the wall fell down flat, so that the people went up into the city, every man straight before him, and they took the city."

JERICHO'S WALLS REALLY FELL DOWN FLAT

At one of our former Thursday night Bible studies, we discussed the fall of the wall of Jericho. One of the ladies who attended the class said she didn't believe this could happen. She never returned to the classes. Many people today do not believe that this miracle could happen. But God did exactly what is recorded in this verse of Scripture. God and His Word never lie.

- **2 Samuel 6:15**

"So David and all the house of Israel brought up the ark of the LORD with shouting, and with the sound of the trumpet."

When the ark of the Lord was brought to the city of David, there was shouting.

- **2 Chronicles 15:13-14**

"That whosoever would not seek the LORD God of Israel should be put to death, whether small or great, whether man or woman. And they sware unto the LORD with a loud voice, and with shouting, and with trumpets, and with cornets."

There was shouting on this occasion as well.

"God is gone up with a shout, the LORD with the sound of a trumpet."

A shout is found here where God has gone up.

One Verse On The "Archangel"

Now this word, referring to the archangel, for instance in,

- **Jude 1:9**

"Yet Michael the archangel, when contending with the devil he disputed about the body of Moses, durst not bring against him a railing accusation, but said, The Lord rebuke thee."

Other than Jude 1:9, 1 Thessalonians 4:16 is the only other place where the word "*archangel*" occurs in the Bible. Michael is named as the lead angel, or the "*archangel.*" At the Rapture, this present verse states that "*the voice of the archangel*" will be heard as well as the "*shout*" and the "*trump of God.*"

Verses On A "Trumpet"

There are a number of verses that speak of trumpets in addition to 1 Thessalonians 4:16 which speaks of "*the trump of God.*"

- **Numbers 10:2**

"Make thee two trumpets of silver; of a whole piece shalt thou make them: that thou mayest use them for the calling of the assembly, and for the journeying of the camps."

THE SPECIAL USES FOR TRUMPETS

The Old Testament had several special uses of the trumpets. The calling of the assembly and the journeys of their camps were two of the uses.

- 1 Corinthians 14:8

"For if the trumpet give an uncertain sound, who shall prepare himself to the battle?"

The trumpet sound must not be phony or insincere. So true Christians should be clear in what they believe and how they live. While in a boys camp as a young person, I was one of the buglers. As such, I learned all the special bugle calls that were used at camp. The call to battle should not be mistaken for reveille or taps. It must be a certain sound, not an uncertain sound.

- 1 Corinthians 15:52

"In a moment, in the twinkling of an eye, at the last trump: for the trumpet shall sound, and the dead shall be raised incorruptible, and we shall be changed."

THE RAPTURE TRUMPET FOR ALL TRUE CHRISTIANS

In this verse, the trumpet will sound at the Rapture when every genuine Christian will be caught up to meet the Lord Jesus Christ in the air. Those true Christians who have died will have their corruptible bodies raised to incorruptible bodies like the resurrected body of the Lord Jesus Christ.

1 Thessalonians 4:17

"Then we which are alive and remain shall be caught up together with them in the clouds, to meet the Lord in the air: and so shall we ever be with the Lord."

In this verse, Paul talks about those genuine Christians who are still living at the time of the Rapture. Their mortal bodies will be immediately changed into immortal bodies by the Lord Jesus Christ. They will be caught up together with the saved Christians who have previously died. Both groups will be caught up into the clouds and will meet the Lord Jesus Christ in the air. They will be with Him forever.

There is no such thing in the Bible as a *"partial"* Rapture of just some of the real Christians. It will be for all of them. In other words, when this happens, those who have been saved and born-again who have died will be raptured to Heaven to be forever with the Lord Jesus Christ and God the Father. Heaven is forever. It is everlasting

- **John 3:16**

"For God so loved the world, that he gave his only begotten Son, that whosoever believeth in him should not perish, but have everlasting life."

There is no end to *"everlasting life."* Heaven is forever.
- **Psalms 23:6**

"Surely goodness and mercy shall follow me all the days of my life: and I will dwell in the house of the LORD for ever."

Even the Old Testament testifies to the eternality of Heaven.
- **Psalms 16:11**

"Thou wilt shew me the path of life: in thy presence *is* fulness of joy; at thy right hand *there are* pleasures for evermore.

Heaven for those who are genuine Christians is a place with pleasures that last *"for evermore."*

Mrs. Waite's mother, Gertrude Grace Sanborn, has written an excellent poem about the Pre-Tribulation Rapture of the Church. It's called:

"It May Be Today"

"One day, may be today,
We shall hear
His great command
And commanding shout.

He will come to take us out
With wondrous joy.
We shall hear His voice
Which bids the dead to rise

Our dear, dear dead
That we have missed so long.
They rise in beauty
To meet us in the clouds

Fulfill His promise
We arise.
And leave behind
those tears and fears

The things we could not understand
Or comprehend.
We'll be together with Him
Eternal years"

This will be true of those who are genuine Christians.

1 Thessalonians 4:18

"Wherefore comfort one another with these words."
Paul wanted the true Christians in Thessalonica to be comforted with these words about the Rapture of those who have been saved by the Lord Jesus Christ. Evidently, the people were concerned about their genuine Christian friends who had died. What was going to become of them? Paul comforted them with the preceding verses by telling them that all who have died who were true Christians would be caught up in the clouds to meet the Lord Jesus Christ in the air in a pre-Tribulation Rapture. These *"dead in Christ"* will also be joined by those genuine Christians who are still living when the Lord Jesus Christ returns in the Rapture before any part of the Tribulation begins.

COMFORT OF TRUE CHRISTIANS GOING TO HEAVEN
Christians at Thessalonica were to comfort one another with these truths. Genuine Christians today should also be comforted by these truths concerning those saved persons who have died. They will be reunited with them in Heaven one day. Here are some other verses that speak of comfort.

- Romans 15:4

"For whatsoever things were written aforetime were written for our learning, that we through patience and comfort of the scriptures might have hope."
Even the Scriptures of the Old Testament, not just those of the New Testament, give true Christians comfort as well as hope.

- 2 Corinthians 1:3

"Blessed *be* God, even the Father of our Lord Jesus Christ, the Father of mercies, and the God of all comfort;"

ONE OF GOD'S TITLES--"THE GOD OF ALL COMFORT"
The God of the Bible is called the *"God of all comfort."* He alone can give the comfort that is real and genuine to those of His own who have lost loved ones who were true Christians.

1 Thessalonians Chapter Five

1 Thessalonians 5:1

"But of the times and the seasons, brethren, ye have no need that I write unto you."

> **NEED FOR A PRE-TRIBULATION RAPTURE LIFESTYLE**
> Since truly saved people should believe in the Pre-Tribulation Rapture of the Church (although many are denying this today), they should have a lifestyle to go along with this joyous event.

The word, *"rapture"* does not appear in the Scriptures. Nor does the word, "Trinity" appear in the Scriptures. But both words are good and useful words to explain truth. As far as the "Trinity" is concerned, it means that God is a Tri-Unity or three Persons (God the Father, God the Son, and God the Holy Spirit) and yet one God.

This word for *"rapture"* means to be *"snatched up"* or *"caught away."* Last week, in 1 Thessalonians 4, I talked about how every genuinely saved Christian will be caught up, snatched away, or raptured before any part of Daniel's 70th week called the Tribulation.

> **MEANING OF THE GREEK WORD "HARPAZO"**
> The Greek Word for *"rapture"* or *"caught up"* (1 Thessalonians 4:17) is HARPAZO. Some of the meanings of this Greek Word are:
> *"1) to seize, carry off by force; 2) to seize on, claim for one's self eagerly; 3) to snatch out or away"*
> Even the English word, *"rapture"* comes from the Latin *"rapere."* One of meanings of this word is: *"The act of seizing and carrying off as prey or plunder. Obs."*

Verses On Times And Seasons

- Acts 1:6

"When they therefore were come together, they asked of him, saying, Lord, wilt thou at this time restore again the kingdom to Israel?"

KINGDOM OF HEAVEN NOT "AT THIS TIME"

The apostles wondered whether or not "*at this time*" would Israel be restored and would the Kingdom of Heaven on earth be set up.

- Acts 1:7

"And he said unto them, It is not for you to know the times or the seasons, which the Father hath put in his own power."

The Lord Jesus Christ told His apostles that it is not for them to know these times or seasons that God alone has determined. They were not to set dates, and true Christians today are not to set dates, either.

NO PROPHETIC EVENTS BEFORE THE RAPTURE

The Rapture, of all those who are saved, may occur at any time. There are no prophetic events that must precede this event, whether a series of what some are calling "*Blood Moons*," or any other event that seeks to set a date for the Rapture of all true Christians.

- Acts 24:25

"And as he reasoned of righteousness, temperance, and judgment to come, Felix trembled, and answered, Go thy way for this time; when I have a convenient season, I will call for thee."

Felix wanted a more convenient season to accept the Lord Jesus Christ as his Saviour. I don't know if that "*season*" ever came. Salvation should not be put off or set for a later season. It should be accepted immediately.

- 2 Timothy 4:2

"Preach the word; be instant in season, out of season; reprove, rebuke, exhort with all longsuffering and doctrine."

The faithful preaching of the Words of God by pastors, missionaries, and teachers should always be "in season." It should be done all the time.

1 Thessalonians 5:2

"For yourselves know perfectly that the day of the Lord so cometh as a thief in the night."

"DAY OF THE LORD" DURING TRIBULATION PERIOD

The day of the Lord is spoken of in many places in the Bible. It is a time of judgment. It speaks of the time of Jacob's trouble or of Daniel's 70th week. It is the seven-year Tribulation upon this earth. Those who are truly saved will be caught up to be with the Lord Jesus Christ before any part of this Tribulation period.

3½ YEARS OF PHONY ANTICHRIST PEACE

It will come upon this world *"as a thief in the night."* It will be unexpected. The first 3½ years of the seven will be relatively peaceful with the Antichrist pretending to be a wonderful person. But during the last 3½ years of the Tribulation, he will show his true evil colors and will destroy many.

Verses On The Day Of The Lord

- **Isaiah 13:6**

"Howl ye; for the day of the LORD *is* at hand; it shall come as a destruction from the Almighty."

It is a day of destruction from God.

- **Isaiah 13:9**

"Behold, the day of the LORD cometh, cruel both with wrath and fierce anger, to lay the land desolate: and he shall destroy the sinners thereof out of it."

It will be a day of wrath and fierce anger.

- **Jeremiah 46:10**

"For this *is* the day of the Lord GOD of hosts, a day of vengeance, that he may avenge him of his adversaries: and the sword shall devour, and it shall be satiate and made drunk with their blood: for the Lord GOD of hosts hath a sacrifice in the north country by the river Euphrates."

It will be a day of vengeance by the Lord.

- **Joel 1:15**

"Alas for the day! for the day of the LORD *is* at hand, and as a destruction from the Almighty shall it come."

Here again shows that it is a day of destruction from God.

- **Joel 2:31**
  "The sun shall be turned into darkness, and the moon into blood, before the great and the terrible day of the LORD come."

This physical phenomenon will occur during the Tribulation, not before as the "blood moon" people are falsely saying. These false teachers leave out that the "*sun shall be turned into darkness*" before this can be fulfilled. If the sun is dark, the "blood moons" as are being falsely portrayed could not happen.

- **Amos 5:18**
  "Woe unto you that desire the day of the LORD! to what end *is* it for you? the day of the LORD *is* darkness, and not light."

It is a day of darkness rather than light.

- **Zechariah 14:1-2**
  "Behold, the day of the LORD cometh, and thy spoil shall be divided in the midst of thee. For I will gather all nations against Jerusalem to battle; and the city shall be taken, and the houses rifled, and the women ravished; and half of the city shall go forth into captivity, and the residue of the people shall not be cut off from the city."

VICTORY AT THE BATTLE OF ARMAGEDDON

All nations shall battle Jerusalem. The battle of Armageddon will be won by the Lord Jesus Christ when He returns at the end of the Tribulation to set up His 1,000-year millennial kingdom.

- **Acts 2:20**
  "The sun shall be turned into darkness, and the moon into blood, before that great and notable day of the Lord come:"

Once again, it is affirmed that the sun will be turned to darkness. This would make the present false "blood moon" teachings impossible. With the sun darkened, there could be no "blood moons" as they speak of them today.

Verses On Christ's Return
As A Thief In The Night

- **2 Peter 3:10**
  "But the day of the Lord will come as a thief in the night; in the which the heavens shall pass away with a great noise, and the elements shall melt with fervent heat, the earth also and the works that are therein shall be burned up."

THE UNEXPECTED "DAY OF THE LORD"

We don't know when a thief plans to enter your home and steal from you. He just comes when you're not looking for him. We

> know that the Tribulation day of the Lord will occur during the seven-year Tribulation which will be preceded by the Rapture of all true Christians. We don't know when they will happen, so the entire chronology of events is unknown.

- **Matthew 24:43**
"But know this, that if the goodman of the house had known in what watch the thief would come, he would have watched, and would not have suffered his house to be broken up."

THE RAPTURE PRECEDES THE DAY OF THE LORD
This day of the Lord is going to come like a thief, you don't know when. The genuine Christians will be raptured to Heaven before any of it happens.

- **2 Peter 3:10**
"But the day of the Lord will come as a thief in the night; in the which the heavens shall pass away with a great noise, and the elements shall melt with fervent heat, the earth also and the works that are therein shall be burned up."

These are some of the events that will occur during the Tribulation period which is the day of the Lord.

- **Revelation 3:3**
"Remember therefore how thou hast received and heard, and hold fast, and repent. If therefore thou shalt not watch, I will come on thee as a thief, and thou shalt not know what hour I will come upon thee."

Every true Christian should be prepared to meet their Lord Jesus Christ by living dedicated Christian lives.

- **Revelation 16:15**
"Behold, I come as a thief. Blessed *is* he that watcheth, and keepeth his garments, lest he walk naked, and they see his shame."

Again, there must be preparation and watching in anticipation of the coming of the Lord Jesus Christ.

1 Thessalonians 5:3
"For when they shall say, Peace and safety; then sudden destruction cometh upon them, as travail upon a woman with child; and they shall not escape."

Merely talking about peace and safety will not bring it. Destruction will come instead during this Tribulation.

- **Proverbs 21:31**
"The horse *is* prepared against the day of battle: but safety *is* of the LORD."

Certainly true safety is found in the Lord Jesus Christ.
- **Daniel 11:27**
"And both these kings' hearts *shall be* to do mischief, and they shall speak lies at one table; but it shall not prosper: for yet the end *shall be* at the time appointed.

PEACE IN THE MOUTH, BUT WAR IN THE HEART
During this Tribulation period, even as is today, there will talk of peace, but lies will be told rather than truth. The promises of the Antichrist during the first 3½ years of the Tribulation will be revealed as lies during the last 3½ years.

- **Daniel 9:27**
"And he shall confirm the covenant with many for one week: and in the midst of the week he shall cause the sacrifice and the oblation to cease, and for the overspreading of abominations he shall make *it* desolate, even until the consummation, and that determined shall be poured upon the desolate."

THE ANTICHRIST BREAKS HIS PROMISES
This prophecy of Daniel shows that in the middle of the seven years of the Tribulation, the Antichrist will break his promises with the religious leaders and everyone else.

1 Thessalonians 5:4
"But ye, brethren, are not in darkness, that that day should overtake you as a thief."

NO LONGER IN DARKNESS
Those who are *"brethren"* are genuinely saved people. They are no longer in the darkness of sin. The day of the Lord will not overtake them because they will be raptured to Heaven before it occurs.

- **2 Corinthians 4:6**
"For God, who commanded the light to shine out of darkness, hath shined in our hearts, to *give* the light of the knowledge of the glory of God in the face of Jesus Christ."

True Christians have been called out of the darkness of sin.
- **Ephesians 5:8**
"For ye were sometimes darkness, but now *are ye* light in the Lord: walk as children of light:"

Before being saved, God considers genuine Christians as being in the darkness. Now, they are light and should walk that way.

- **1 Peter 2:9**
"But ye *are* a chosen generation, a royal priesthood, an holy nation, a peculiar people; that ye should shew forth the praises of him who hath called you out of darkness into his marvellous light:"
Saved people are out of darkness and into light.

1 Thessalonians 5:5

"Ye are all the children of light, and the children of the day: we are not of the night, nor of darkness."
True Christians are children of light and are no longer in the darkness of sin.
- **Acts 26:16-18**
"But rise, and stand upon thy feet: for I have appeared unto thee for this purpose, to make thee a minister and a witness both of these things which thou hast seen, and of those things in the which I will appear unto thee; Delivering thee from the people, and *from* the Gentiles, unto whom now I send thee, To open their eyes, and to turn them from darkness to light, and *from* the power of Satan unto God, that they may receive forgiveness of sins, and inheritance among them which are sanctified by faith that is in me."
When the Lord Jesus Christ saved Paul, He gave him a mission to turn those to whom he preached from darkness to light and from Satan's power to God's power.
- **2 Corinthians 4:6**
"For God, who commanded the light to shine out of darkness, hath shined in our hearts, to *give* the light of the knowledge of the glory of God in the face of Jesus Christ."
Genuine Christians have had the Lord Jesus Christ, God's Light, shine in their hearts.
- **Ephesians 5:8**
"For ye were sometimes darkness, but now *are ye* light in the Lord: walk as children of light:
Once true Christians are saved, they should be light in the Lord and should walk in the light of God's Words.
- **1 Peter 2:9**
"But ye *are* a chosen generation, a royal priesthood, an holy nation, a peculiar people; that ye should shew forth the praises of him who hath called you out of darkness into his marvellous light:"
Genuine Christians have been called out of the darkness of this old world into God's marvellous light. What a miraculous change that is!

1 Thessalonians 5:6

"Therefore let us not sleep, as do others; but let us watch and be sober."

True Christians should not sleep as those who are lost, but they should watch and be sober.

> **THE MEANING OF THE GREEK WORD, "NEPHO"**
> The Greek Word for *"sober"* is NEPHO. Some of the meanings of that Greek Word are:
> *"1) to be sober, to be calm and collected in spirit; 2) to be temperate, dispassionate, circumspect"*

Because these genuine Christians are of the light and will be called Home to Heaven by the Lord Jesus Christ before any part of the Tribulation takes place, they are to watch in a sober, calm, and circumspect manner.

Since the Greek Word for *"sleep"* is in the Greek present tense, it is a very specific construction. It is a negative prohibition. As such, it means to stop an action already in progress. These true Christians are to stop sleeping as those who are lost and unsaved. Their lifestyle of sleeping should be ended now that they have been redeemed by genuine faith in the Lord Jesus Christ.

Another meaning of NEPHO and NEPHALIOS refers to those who do not use alcohol in any form. Genuine Christians should abstain from this as those who are no longer asleep.

Verses On NEPHO Or NEPHALEOS
Meaning Abstaining From Alcohol

There are five other verses in the New Testament that use either NEPHO or NEPHALEOS for various groups of true Christians, telling them that they should abstain from alcoholic beverages. Some of the meanings of the Greek Word, (NEPHALEOS) used here for *"sober"* are:

"1) sober, temperate; 1a) __abstaining from wine, either entirely__ or at least from its immoderate use; 1b) __of things free from all wine__, as vessels, offerings."

- 1 Timothy 3:2

"A bishop then must be blameless, the husband of one wife, vigilant, sober, of good behaviour, given to hospitality, apt to teach;"

> **STANDARD FOR PASTORS-BISHOPS-ELDERS**
> This refers to the one office with three titles, pastor-bishop-elder. The Greek Word for *"vigilant"* is NEPHALIOS

which means that pastors-bishops-elders should abstain from alcoholic beverages.

- **1 Timothy 3:11**

"Even so *must their* wives *be* grave, not slanderers, sober, faithful in all things."

It important for the local church's deacons' wives also to be "*sober*" (NEPHALIOS) and thus be without the use of alcoholic beverages.

- **2 Timothy 4:5**

"But watch thou in all things, endure afflictions, do the work of an evangelist, make full proof of thy ministry."

Paul, in his last letter before being killed by the Roman government, told Pastor Timothy to do a number of things. The first thing in this verse was for him to "*watch.*" The Greek Word for this is NEPHO. Paul is telling Timothy to keep away from alcoholic beverages.

- **Titus 2:2**

"That the aged men be sober, grave, temperate, sound in faith, in charity, in patience."

In this verse, Paul is telling Pastor Titus that older men should also be "*sober*" (NEPHALIOS) and thus abstain from alcoholic beverages.

- **1 Peter 1:13**

"Wherefore gird up the loins of your mind, be sober, and hope to the end for the grace that is to be brought unto you at the revelation of Jesus Christ;"

Peter is telling his readers to be "*sober*" (NEPHO) and to stay away from alcoholic beverages.

Verses On Not Sleeping

- **Psalms 121:4**

"Behold, he that keepeth Israel shall neither slumber nor sleep."

The Lord doesn't sleep. He is always on duty to survey the happenings of the entire world.

- **Romans 13:11-12**

"And that, knowing the time, that now *it is* high time to awake out of sleep: for now *is* our salvation nearer than when we believed. The night is far spent, the day is at hand: let us therefore cast off the works of darkness, and let us put on the armour of light."

CAST OFF THE WORKS OF DARKNESS

Once people become genuine Christians by true faith in the Lord Jesus Christ, they should awake out of the sleep of the sins of their past life and live for their Saviour. They should cast off the works of their former darkness and live in the light of the Bible to be ready for the return of their Saviour.

Verses On Watching

- **Matthew 24:42**

"Watch therefore: for ye know not what hour your Lord doth come."

> **THE MEANING OF THE GREEK WORD, "GREGOREUO"**
> The Greek Word for *"watch"* is GREGOREUO. Some of the meanings of this Greek Word are:
> *"1) to watch; 2) metaph. give strict attention to, be cautious, active; 2a) to take heed lest through remission and indolence some destructive calamity suddenly overtake one."*

The Lord Jesus Christ told His followers to watch and look out in order to be ready for the return of the Lord Jesus Christ.

- **Matthew 25:13**

"Watch therefore, for ye know neither the day nor the hour wherein the Son of man cometh."

The Saviour repeats this command to watch again because of not knowing when He will return.

- **Matthew 26:41**

"Watch and pray, that ye enter not into temptation: the spirit indeed *is* willing, but the flesh *is* weak."

Peter, James, and John were commanded by the Lord Jesus Christ to watch as He was praying in the garden of Gethsemane. They failed to watch, but fell asleep.

- **Acts 20:27-28**

"For I have not shunned to declare unto you all the counsel of God. Take heed therefore unto yourselves, and to all the flock, over the which the Holy Ghost hath made you overseers, to feed the church of God, which he hath purchased with his own blood."

In this verse Paul gives the three ministries of the church leaders who are pastors-bishops-elders. The Greek Word for *"overseers"* is EPISCOPOS. The meaning of this word implies that pastors are to watch what things are happening in their churches and in the world in general to prepare true Christians for any eventualities.

- **Acts 20:29-32**

"For I know this, that after my departing shall grievous wolves enter in among you, not sparing the flock. Also of your own selves shall men arise, speaking perverse things, to draw away disciples after them. Therefore watch, and remember, that by the space of three years I ceased not to warn every one night and day with tears. And now, brethren, I commend you to God, and to the word of his grace,

which is able to build you up, and to give you an inheritance among all them which are sanctified."
Paul preached three years to the church at Ephesus and now he is leaving the church. He charged the pastors-bishops-elders to watch for the apostasy that he warned them about. This is one reason why I, as a pastor, seek to be a watchman for things happening in both the church and the state which are concerns for genuine Christians today. These pastors were to watch and not to allow anything that would cause their churches to fall down flat, dwindle away, and leave their firm Biblical stand.

- **1 Corinthians 16:13**

"Watch ye, stand fast in the faith, quit you like men, be strong."
Paul is commanding all true Christians at Corinth to watch for anything that might come into their lives to hinder them from following their Saviour, or might endanger them.

- **2 Timothy 4:5**

"But watch thou in all things, endure afflictions, do the work of an evangelist, make full proof of thy ministry."
Pastor Timothy was told to **watch in all things**. As a pastor, I try to do this. Each Sunday morning I comment on various events that I have been watching in the church world and in the secular world that might have an effect on true Christians in our church. In the second church that I pastored, Faith Baptist Church, in Newton, Massachusetts, I used to call this part of the service C.C.C.C. This stood for Current Comments For Concerned Christians. Genuine Christians should be watchful for what is going on around in the world around them and in the church world as well.

- **Hebrews 13:17**

"Obey them that have the rule over you, and submit yourselves: for they watch for your souls, as they that must give account, that they may do it with joy, and not with grief: for that *is* unprofitable for you."

ACCOUNTABILITY OF THOSE WHO WATCH FOR SOULS

This refers to careful and true Bible-believing pastors who minister to their churches. They watch for the souls of those who attend their services. They must give an account to the Lord as to how well they have watched for the souls of those who are a part of their churches.

1 Thessalonians 5:7

"For they that sleep sleep in the night; and they that be drunken are drunken in the night."

This verse is speaking again about how genuine Christians are not to be. They should not be sleeping as if it is in the darkness of the night. On the contrary, they are to walk in the light of the Words of God and abstain from the sins of drunkenness or other sins that are often practiced quite often in the night.

THE MEANING OF THE GREEK WORD "METHUSKO"

The Greek Word for *"drunken"* is METHUSKO. Some of the meanings of this Word are:

"1) to intoxicate, make drunk; to get drunk, become intoxicated"

It is especially in the night that the sin of drunkenness and other sins occur. I remember one time that one of my daughter asked me to help one of her children find the various evils that are committed at night so she could put it in a paper she was writing.

Verses On Sins Practiced In The Night
- **Proverbs 7:8-10**

"Passing through the street near her corner; and he went the way to her house, In the twilight, in the evening, in the black and dark night: And, behold, there met him a woman *with* the attire of an harlot, and subtil of heart."

Prostitution is often practiced in the darkness of the night.

- **Isaiah 29:15**

"Woe unto them that seek deep to hide their counsel from the LORD, and their works are in the dark, and they say, Who seeth us? and who knoweth us?"

Here there is mention of those who do their works in the darkness of the night so no one will see them. God can see all that people do whether it is day or night.

- **Acts 2:13-15**

"Others mocking said, These men are full of new wine. But Peter, standing up with the eleven, lifted up his voice, and said unto them, ye men of Judaea, and all *ye* that dwell at Jerusalem, be this known unto you, and hearken to my words: For these are not drunken, as ye suppose, seeing it is *but* the third hour of the day."

The explanation for the actions of those who were there on that occasion was that they couldn't be drunk because it was still daylight and drunkenness was usually not done until the night came.

- **Romans 13:13**
"Let us walk honestly, as in the day; not in rioting and drunkenness, not in chambering and wantonness, not in strife and envying."
It seems to contrast what was done in the day rather than sins done in the night, such as rioting and the other sins listed in this verse.

1 Thessalonians 5:8

"But let us, who are of the day, be sober, putting on the breastplate of faith and love; and for an helmet, the hope of salvation."

Those who are of the day are true Christians who have been born-again by genuine faith in the Lord Jesus Christ. They are to be "***sober***." This is the Greek Word NEPHO once again, meaning to abstain from alcohol rather than being drunken. They are also to put on the breastplate and helmet to get ready for the battles of this world.

THE CHRISTIAN'S BREASTPLATE AND HELMET

The breastplate which goes from the neck to the center part of our body. For the genuine Christians, it should be connected with both faith and love. They also have a helmet which is their hope of a future salvation in Heaven. It guards their heads and brains while they are awaiting the Rapture of the Lord Jesus Christ.

Verses On The Breastplate

- **Exodus 28:4**
"And these *are* the garments which they shall make; a breastplate, and an ephod, and a robe, and a broidered coat, a mitre, and a girdle: and they shall make holy garments for Aaron thy brother, and his sons, that he may minister unto me in the priest's office."
One of the garments worn by the Old Testament priests was a breastplate.
- **Isaiah 59:17**
"For he put on righteousness as a breastplate, and an helmet of salvation upon his head; and he put on the garments of vengeance *for* clothing, and was clad with zeal as a cloke."
True Christians have the righteousness of the Lord Jesus Christ. That righteousness is like a breastplate that protects them.
- **Ephesians 6:14**
"Stand therefore, having your loins girt about with truth, and having on the breastplate of righteousness;"

> **GOD'S RIGHTEOUSNESS IS LIKE A BREASTPLATE**
> Again, the genuine Christians are reminded that they have the righteousness of the Lord Jesus Christ as a breastplate of protection.

Verses On The Helmet

This helmet, referred to by Paul here, protects the heads of true Christians. For the riders' protection, helmets are now required in most states when riding scooters, motor bikes, motorcycles, or bicycles.

- **1 Samuel 17:5**

"And *he had* an helmet of brass upon his head, and he *was* armed with a coat of mail; and the weight of the coat *was* five thousand shekels of brass.

Goliath, the 9 foot-9 inch Philistine giant, had a helmet of brass on his head. But God used a little shepherd named David to defeat him. David found Goliath's one vulnerable spot.

- **1 Samuel 17:38**

"And Saul armed David with his armour, and he put an helmet of brass upon his head; also he armed him with a coat of mail."

Little David was given a helmet of brass by king Saul, but David rejected it and still defeated Goliath.

- **Isaiah 59:17**

"For he put on righteousness as a breastplate, and an helmet of salvation upon his head; and he put on the garments of vengeance *for* clothing, and was clad with zeal as a cloke."

Here God describes His salvation as a helmet of protection.

- **Ephesians 6:17**

"And take the helmet of salvation, and the sword of the Spirit, which is the word of God:"

> **GENUINE FAITH AS A HELMET OF PROTECTION**
> Paul also talks about God's salvation through genuine faith in the Lord Jesus Christ as a helmet of protection. His salvation seeks to protect true Christians from their own flesh, the world, and the Devil.

1 Thessalonians 5:9
"For God hath not appointed us to wrath, but to obtain salvation by our Lord Jesus Christ,"

NO FUTURE WRATH FOR TRUE CHRISTIANS
The "*us*" in this verse refers to all genuine Christians from the day of Pentecost until the Rapture by the Lord Jesus Christ. I believe very strongly that they are not appointed to the "wrath" of God–which includes both the "*wrath*" of the Lake of Hell-fire, and also the "*wrath*" of the seven-year Tribulation. The Tribulation is also called Daniel's seventieth week and the day of Jacob's trouble. This is a very clear proof verse for the pre-Tribulation Rapture of all the true Christians living at that time. They will not experience a single day, week, month, or any part of the Tribulation.

Verses On Wrath
- Luke 3:7

"Then said he to the multitude that came forth to be baptized of him, O generation of vipers, who hath warned you to flee from the wrath to come?"

This is the wrath of Hell from which genuine Christians have been delivered.

- John 3:36

"He that believeth on the Son hath everlasting life: and he that believeth not the Son shall not see life; but the wrath of God abideth on him."

ESCAPING THE WRATH OF GOD AND HELL
This is a very clear gospel verse which teaches that every person who exercises genuine faith in the Lord Jesus Christ receives everlasting life immediately. It also clearly teaches that a person who does not exercise genuine faith in the Lord Jesus Christ has God's wrath abiding on them continually. If this person abides in this state of unbelief in the Lord Jesus Christ, that person will experience the wrath of God in the Lake of Fire which is Hell.

- Romans 1:18

"For the wrath of God is revealed from heaven against all ungodliness and unrighteousness of men, who hold the truth in unrighteousness;"

This verse in Romans is speaking in reference to the heathen all around the world. God's wrath is revealed against three things: (1) ungodliness; (2) unrighteousness; and (3) holding back the truth in unrighteousness.
- Romans 5:9
"Much more then, being now justified by his blood, we shall be saved from wrath through him."

SAVED FROM ALL KINDS OF WRATH
Those who are genuine Christians have been justified by the blood of the Lord Jesus Christ. This verse promises that they will be *"saved from wrath."* This means all kinds of *"wrath,"* not only the wrath of Hell and everlasting fire, but also the wrath of God that will be poured out during the seven-year Tribulation period. This promises a Pre-Tribulation Rapture by the Lord Jesus Christ of all true Christians.

- Ephesians 5:6
"Let no man deceive you with vain words: for because of these things cometh the wrath of God upon the children of disobedience."

CAUSING GOD'S WRATH TO COME
Those who practice the many sins found in Ephesians 5:3-5 will cause the wrath of God to come upon them. This will include the everlasting fire of Hell.

- 1 Thessalonians 1:10
"And to wait for his Son from heaven, whom he raised from the dead, *even* Jesus, which delivered us from the wrath to come."
This is another clear verse for the Pre-Tribulation Rapture of all genuine Christians. They will never experience any of God's wrath during the Tribulation's seven years of wrath, or the wrath of an eternal Hell-fire.

- Revelation 6:16
"And said to the mountains and rocks, Fall on us, and hide us from the face of him that sitteth on the throne, and from the wrath of the Lamb:"

THE WRATH OF THE LAMB OF GOD
This sixth chapter of Revelation is near the very beginning of the seven-year Tribulation period. The judgements of the unsaved people then living will be so great that they will cry out for deliverance from the wrath of the Lamb, the Lord Jesus Christ. He came the first time to save all those who truly trust Him. He will come back the second time to judge those who have rejected Him.

1 Thessalonians 5:10

"Who died for us, that, whether we wake or sleep, we should live together with him."

CHRIST'S DEATH FOR THE SINS OF THE WHOLE WORLD

This verse gives us the purpose of the death of the Lord Jesus Christ. I believe the "*us*" refers not only for the genuine Christians at Thessalonica, but also for every man, woman, and child who ever lived upon this earth. His death was unlimited in its scope. It encompassed the whole world that God "*so loved.*" (John 3:16)

It is interesting to see what the Greek Word is for the preposition "*for.*" There are two Greek Words that are used in the Greek New Testament for this preposition. One Word is ANTI which means "*in place of, or as a substitute for.*" The other Greek Word used here is HUPER. This Word means not only "*in place of, or as a substitute for,*" but adds the additional meaning of "*for the benefit of.*"

CHRIST THE SUBSTITUTE FOR THE SINS OF THE WORLD

When this verse states that the Lord Jesus Christ "*died for us,*" I believe the "*us*" refers to all of us who are human beings. He was not only the Substitute for the sins of entire world, but also He provided the benefits of salvation, redemption, and eternal life for those who truly trust and receive Him as their Saviour.

CHRIST DIED FOR EVERYONE'S SINS

The "*for us*" means that Christ died for every person in the world. Those who are genuine Christians, will live together with Him for all eternity. "For us" includes the true Christians who are alive when He returns in the Rapture, as well as those who have died beforehand.

Verses Where Christ Died For All People

- **Romans 5:6**
  "For when we were yet without strength, in due time Christ died for the ungodly."

I believe this refers to all the ungodly people in the world, not just a certain tiny group of those hyper-Calvinists who call themselves "*the elect.*"

- **Romans 5:8**
"But God commendeth his love toward us, in that, while we were yet sinners, Christ died for us."
Again, I believe the *"us"* is the *"us"* of all human beings who are, in God's eyes, *"sinners."*
- **Romans 8:32**
"He that spared not his own Son, but delivered him up for us all, how shall he not with him also freely give us all things?"

CHRIST WAS DELIVERED UP TO DIE FOR ALL
I believe the phrase, *"Delivered Him up for us all,"* is a reference to everyone in the world. If those for whom He died are *"with Him"*--that is, are genuine Christians--He will give them all things.

- **1 Corinthians 5:7**
"Purge out therefore the old leaven, that ye may be a new lump, as ye are unleavened. For even Christ our passover is sacrificed for us:"

THE VITAL WORDS, "FOR US" MISSING IN SOME BIBLES
In the Gnostic Critical Greek Text which underlies modern Bible versions, the words, *"for us"* (referring to all of us humans who ever lived) are not to be found. The reason for this is that the Gnostics of Alexandria, Egypt, did not believe in the vicarious, substitutionary sacrifice of the Lord Jesus Christ for the sins of the world. They believed Him to be just a human being who was lost and needed to be saved Himself. They, therefore, could not believe He died *"for"* anyone as their Substitute.

OMISSIONS IN THE ASV, NASV, NIV, RSV, ESV++
These Greek Words are not found translated in any of the modern translations in any language of the world that are founded on this false Gnostic Critical Greek Text. You won't find them in such English versions as the ASV, NASV, NIV, RSV, NRSV, ESV, or any others. The truth is that He--that is, Christ our Passover--died for the sins of the whole world. I have written a tract entitled *"CHRIST OUR PASSOVER–SACRIFICED FOR US"* (BFT #129 @ $5/$2.00 + S&H).

- **1 Corinthians 15:3**
"For I delivered unto you first of all that which I also received, how that Christ died for our sins according to the scriptures;"

Once again, I believe, when this verse states that *"Christ died for our sins,"* it includes the sins of all the people who ever lived or will ever live in the future.
- **2 Corinthians 5:15**
"And *that* he died for all, that they which live should not henceforth live unto themselves, but unto him which died for them, and rose again."

"DIED FOR ALL" MEANS ALL PEOPLE
The words, *"died for all,"* I believe refer to all the people who have ever lived in this world. The Lord Jesus Christ died for all of them. That does not mean that all for whom He died are saved. Every person in the world must individually receive this gift by genuine faith in the Saviour for them to be redeemed. But the price for their redemption has been paid. It is a gift that must be received before it can be appropriated.

- **2 Corinthians 5:21**
"For he hath made him *to be* sin for us, who knew no sin; that we might be made the righteousness of God in him."

God the Father made the Lord Jesus Christ, God the Son, to be *"sin for us."* Again, I believe this is the *"us"* of every person in the world who has ever been born. It is true that every person who exercises true faith in the Lord Jesus Christ is given a righteous standing before God through the Saviour's dying for them on the cross.

- **Ephesians 5:2**
"And walk in love, as Christ also hath loved us, and hath given himself for us an offering and a sacrifice to God for a sweetsmelling savour."

CHRIST'S SACRIFICE WAS FOR EVERYONE
The Lord Jesus Christ gave Himself at the cross as an offering and sacrifice for every *"us"* of the entire world.

- **Titus 2:14**
"Who gave himself for us, that he might redeem us from all iniquity, and purify unto himself a peculiar people, zealous of good works."

The Lord Jesus Christ gave Himself for *"us"* human beings in order that He might purify those who truly trust in Him as a special and holy people.

- **1 John 3:16**
"Hereby perceive we the love *of God*, because he laid down his life for us: and we ought to lay down *our* lives for the brethren."

The Lord Jesus Christ laid down His life on the cross for "*us*" human beings so that after genuinely coming to Him in faith and trust, they might, if need be, lay down their lives for other true Christians.

Where True Christians Will Live With The Lord Jesus Christ Forever

1 Thessalonians 5:10 states that those who are genuine Christians, for whom the Lord Jesus Christ died, will live together with Him in Heaven.

- **John 14:3**

"And if I go and prepare a place for you, I will come again, and receive you unto myself; that where I am, *there* ye may be also."

The Lord Jesus Christ told his apostles, in this verse, that those who are true Christians would go to be with Him in Heaven's **place** that He would be preparing for them.

- **John 17:24**

"Father, I will that they also, whom thou hast given me, be with me where I am; that they may behold my glory, which thou hast given me: for thou lovedst me before the foundation of the world."

PRAYER THAT TRUE CHRISTIANS WILL GO TO HEAVEN

This is clear teaching that the Lord Jesus Christ prayed to God the Father that every genuine Christian might be with Him in Heaven to behold His glory.

- **Romans 8:17**

"And if children, then heirs; heirs of God, and joint-heirs with Christ; if so be that we suffer with *him*, that we may be also glorified together."

This speaks that true Christians, who are heirs of God as well as being joint-heirs with the Lord Jesus Christ, will be glorified. This glorification will take place when they are in Heaven.

- **Philippians 1:23**

"For I am in a strait betwixt two, having a desire to depart, and to be with Christ; which is far better:"

TRUE CHRISTIANS GO TO HEAVEN AT DEATH

Paul said he was in a tight place for making a decision. He had a desire to depart and be with the Lord Jesus Christ in Heaven. This shows two things:

(1) upon death Paul would go immediately to Heaven; and

(2) there is no purgatory or immediate state after death for the genuine Christian. It is an immediate transportation of

> the genuine Christian's spirit and soul straight to Heaven to be with the Lord Jesus Christ.

1 Thessalonians 5:11

"Wherefore comfort yourselves together, and edify one another, even as also ye do."

> **CHRISTIANS SHOULD COMFORT ONE ANOTHER**
> Because the genuine Christians will be taken out of this world by the Lord Jesus Christ before the Tribulation, and will be together with Him for all eternity to come, they should comfort one another. They should also continue to edify and encourage one another in the things of the Christian faith as taught in the Bible.

Verses About Comfort

- 2 Corinthians 1:4

"Who comforteth us in all our tribulation, that we may be able to comfort them which are in any trouble, by the comfort wherewith we ourselves are comforted of God."

God comforts genuine Christians in their tribulation so that they can learn how to comfort others.

- 1 Thessalonians 4:18

"Wherefore comfort one another with these words."

The preceding verses speak about the Rapture of all true Christians to Heaven before any part of the Tribulation where they will be with the Lord Jesus Christ forever. These truths should bring comfort to those genuine Christians who hear them.

- 1 Thessalonians 5:14

"Now we exhort you, brethren, warn them that are unruly, comfort the feebleminded, support the weak, be patient toward all *men*."

Genuine Christians are to comfort those who are "*feebleminded*" or in some way mentally incapacitated or challenged.

Verses About Edifying

As far as edifying, not only are true Christians to comfort one another, but they are also to build one another up in the things of the Lord.

> **THE MEANING OF THE GREEK WORD, "OIKODOMEO"**
> The Greek Word for "*edify*" is OIKODOMEO. Some of the meanings of this Word are:
> "*1) to build a house, erect a building; 1a) to build (up from the foundation); 1b) to restore by building, to rebuild, repair; 2) metaph. 2a) to found, establish; 2b) to promote growth in Christian wisdom, affection, grace, virtue, holiness, blessedness; 2c) to grow in wisdom and piety.*"

- **Romans 14:19**

"Let us therefore follow after the things which make for peace, and things wherewith one may edify another."

True Christians should do things that edify one another. This can be done by holding firmly to and telling others about the Words of God in an accurate Bible such as the King James Bible in English.

- **2 Corinthians 12:19**

"Again, think ye that we excuse ourselves unto you? we speak before God in Christ: but *we do* all things, dearly beloved, for your edifying."

Though the Apostle Paul had many critics in Corinth and in other places, he wrote his letters to the church at Corinth for their edification and growth in the ways of the Lord.

- **Ephesians 4:12**

"For the perfecting of the saints, for the work of the ministry, for the edifying of the body of Christ:"

> **THE WORDS OF GOD EDIFY TRUE CHRISTIANS**
> That's what the Words of God are to do for those genuine Christians who read and study them. They are to edify and build them up in the faith.

- **Ephesians 4:29**

"Let no corrupt communication proceed out of your mouth, but that which is good to the use of edifying, that it may minister grace unto the hearers."

> **CUT OUT FILTHY AND CORRUPT SPEECH**
> "*Corrupt communication*" would includes filthy talk of all kinds whether it comes from newspapers, magazines, television, Internet, or other sources. For true Christians,

such talk should not be uttered. Instead, words that minister grace and help should be spoken.

1 Thessalonians 5:12

"And we beseech you, brethren, to know them which labour among you, and are over you in the Lord, and admonish you;"

Paul is speaking of genuine Christians at Thessalonica. They are admonished to know those who labor among them. This would refer to the pastors-bishops-elders who *"labor"* among them in the various churches in Thessalonica.

THE MEANING OF THE GREEK WORD, "KOPIAO"

The Greek Word for *"labor"* is KOPIAO. Some of the meanings of this Word are:

"1) to grow weary, tired, exhausted (with toil or burdens or grief); 2) to labour with wearisome effort, to toil; 2a) of bodily labour."

Serving the Lord Jesus Christ in the ministry is indeed labor for those pastors-bishops-elders who have been called to this service.

Verses About Laboring For The Lord

- **Romans 16:12**

"Salute Tryphena and Tryphosa, who labour in the Lord. Salute the beloved Persis, which laboured much in the Lord."

Here are three true Christian workers who labored much in the Lord.

1 Timothy 5:17

"Let the elders that rule well be counted worthy of double honour, especially they who labour in the word and doctrine."

NEED FOR CLEAR PREACHING OF GOD'S WORDS

The pastors-bishops-elders should labor in preaching the Word of God and the doctrines found therein. That is not an easy task, but it is a vital task. The future Biblical positions of each local church are at stake.

Verses About Admonishing

These church leaders are to admonish those who are in their churches.

THE MEANING OF THE GREEK WORD, "NOUTHETEO"

The Greek Word for *"admonish"* is NOUTHETEO. Some of the meanings of that Word are:

"1) to admonish, warn, exhort"

This type of admonishing takes courage on the part of those who admonish and warn. Many in the churches like to hear only things that are positive and pleasant. But warning must be a part of all true Christian ministers.

- **Romans 15:14**

"And I myself also am persuaded of you, my brethren, that ye also are full of goodness, filled with all knowledge, able also to admonish one another."

FULL BIBLE KNOWLEDGE-THEN ADMONITION

Admonition and warning must be preceded by a sound knowledge of the Words of God. Otherwise, the admonition might not be Biblical.

- **Ephesians 6:4**

"And, ye fathers, provoke not your children to wrath: but bring them up in the nurture and admonition of the Lord."

The Greek Word behind *"nurture"* implies corporal discipline on the child if he needs it and when he needs it.

THE MEANING OF THE GREEK WORD, "PAIDEIA"

The Greek Word for *"nurture"* is PAIDEIA. Some of the meanings of this Word are:

"1. instruction (2Ti 3:16); 2. discipline, training (Eph 6:4); 3. punishment, chastisement for improving behavior (Heb 12:5, 7, 8, 11+)"

"*Admonition*" speaks of verbal guidance and warning as needed for the child. Both these things are important parts of raising young children.

- **Colossians 3:16**

"Let the word of Christ dwell in you richly in all wisdom; teaching and admonishing one another in psalms and hymns and spiritual songs, singing with grace in your hearts to the Lord."

If the Words of Christ dwell in genuine Christians and they know them well, they can admonish other true Christians as might be needed.

However, it must be pointed out that such admonition often leads to misunderstanding and trouble from the one being admonished.

1 Thessalonians 5:13

"And to esteem them very highly in love for their work's sake. And be at peace among yourselves."

Those pastors-bishops-elders and other teachers in local churches who labor faithfully in that capacity should be esteemed highly in love by those to whom the minister. Paul also told these genuine Christians at Thessalonica to be at peace among themselves. In a local church, this is a very difficult thing to accomplish because of the many personality conflicts that often are present. But that should be the goal, nonetheless.

Verses On Peace

- **1 Corinthians 14:33**

"For God is not *the author* of confusion, but of peace, as in all churches of the saints."

The God of the Bible is not the author of confusion, but of peace. He wants that to prevail in all of His genuine Christian churches.

- **2 Corinthians 13:11**

"Finally, brethren, farewell. Be perfect, be of good comfort, be of one mind, live in peace; and the God of love and peace shall be with you."

DIFFICULTY FOR PEACE IN TRUE CHRISTIAN CHURCHES
The command for true Christian churches to live in peace is a good one, but, sad to say, it is very difficult to put into practice in most of these churches. Invariably, there is warfare of some kind that is present, whether in the choir or in some other area.

- **Ephesians 4:3**

"Endeavouring to keep the unity of the Spirit in the bond of peace." This is a good endeavor in every genuine Christian church. Both unity and peace are needed.

- **1 Peter 3:11**

"Let him eschew evil, and do good; let him seek peace, and ensue it."

Peace is to be sought after even it might not always be found. If it can't be found, it should be pursued.

1 Thessalonians 5:14

"Now we exhort you, brethren, warn them that are unruly, comfort the feebleminded, support the weak, be patient toward all men."

PAUL'S FOUR EXHORTATIONS FOR TRUE CHRISTIANS
Paul exhorts these true Christians regarding four things. They are to:
(1) warn the unruly;
(2) comfort the feebleminded;
(3) support the weak; and
(4) be patient toward everyone.

Verses About Warning And Unruly

The first thing these brethren were to do was to warn them that are unruly. These apparently have no rules to live by. They are to be warned.

- **Psalms 19:11**

"Moreover by them is thy servant warned: *and* in keeping of them *there is* great reward."

By the Words of God the servants of God are warned. This is why His Words must be read, studied, and obeyed.

- **Ezekiel 3:17**

"Son of man, I have made thee a watchman unto the house of Israel: therefore hear the word at my mouth, and give them warning from me."

The prophet Ezekiel was to give his people warning from the Lord.

- **Ezekiel 33:7**

"So thou, O son of man, I have set thee a watchman unto the house of Israel; therefore thou shalt hear the word at my mouth, and warn them from me."

EZEKIEL AS A WARNING WATCHMEN FOR GOD
Ezekiel was to be a watchman to Israel. He was to hear God's Words and then warn them for Him. Pastors today should practice this as well.

- **Acts 20:31**

"Therefore watch, and remember, that by the space of three years I ceased not to warn every one night and day with tears."

Paul was a faithful servant of the Lord Jesus Christ. He reminded the pastors-bishops-elders from Ephesus that He had warned them about approaching evils and doctrinal errors for three years. This should be practiced today as well.

- **1 Corinthians 4:14**
"I write not these things to shame you, but as my beloved sons I warn *you.*"

Paul warned the true Christians in Corinth as he would his own sons. They needed this warning. Daughters need warning also.

- **Colossians 1:28**
"Whom we preach, warning every man, and teaching every man in all wisdom; that we may present every man perfect in Christ Jesus:"

Part of Paul's desire for genuine Christians to be mature in the Lord Jesus Christ was not only to teach them, but also to warn them concerning evil things and evil people.

- **Titus 1:6**
"If any be blameless, the husband of one wife, having faithful children not accused of riot or unruly."

PASTORS NEED TO HAVE FAITHFUL CHILDREN

This is one of the qualifications of New Testament pastors-bishops-elders. First, they must have children in their home. Second, these children must not be unruly, but they should be conformed to sound family rules.

- **Titus 1:10**
"For there are many unruly and vain talkers and deceivers, specially they of the circumcision:"

Pastor Titus, the pastor of the church of Crete, was told by Paul that there were many unruly and vain talkers on that little island.

- **James 3:8**
"But the tongue can no man tame; *it is* an unruly evil, full of deadly poison."

ONLY GOD'S POWER CAN TAME THE TONGUE

No man can tame the tongue. Only the Holy Spirit Who indwells and controls genuine Christians is able to tame their tongues.

Verses About Comforting

The second thing to do is to comfort the feebleminded.

> **THE MEANING OF "OLIGOPSUCHOS"**
> The Greek Word for "feebleminded" is OLIGOPSUCHOS. Some of the meanings for this Word are: *"discouraged, timid, or fainthearted (1Th 5:14+)"*

- **2 Corinthians 1:4**

"Who comforteth us in all our tribulation, that we may be able to comfort them which are in any trouble, by the comfort wherewith we ourselves are comforted of God."

God wants true Christians to bring comfort to others by the comfort He gives them. This would include those who might be discouraged, timid, or fainthearted.

- **2 Corinthians 2:6-7**

"Sufficient to such a man *is* this punishment, which *was inflicted* of many. So that contrariwise ye *ought* rather to forgive *him*, and comfort *him*, lest perhaps such a one should be swallowed up with overmuch sorrow."

Here is comfort which should be given by the genuine Christians at Corinth for the incestuous man who had repented of his sin, changed his lifestyle, and returned to the church. He was to be comforted rather than scorned.

Verses About Supporting The Weak

The third thing that Paul exhorted the true Christians at Thessalonica to do was to support the weak. Weak people need the help and support of those who are stronger.

- **Acts 20:35**

"I have shewed you all things, how that so labouring ye ought to support the weak, and to remember the words of the Lord Jesus, how he said, It is more blessed to give than to receive."

God wants all genuine Christians to help those who are weaker. They need a helping hand.

- **Romans 15:1**

"We then that are strong ought to bear the infirmities of the weak, and not to please ourselves."

ASSISTING THOSE WHO ARE WEAK IN THE FAITH
The true Christians who are weak in the faith have many infirmities because of their spiritual condition. Stronger Christians should assist these weak ones to get stronger in the Lord.

Comments About Being Patient
The fourth thing commanded in this verse is for genuine Christians to be patient toward all.

THE MEANING OF THE WORD, "MAKROTHUMEO"
The Greek Word for *"patient"* is MAKROTHUMEO. Some of the meanings of this Word are:

1) to be of a long spirit, not to lose heart; 1a) to persevere patiently and bravely in enduring misfortunes and troubles; 1b) to be patient in bearing the offenses and injuries of others; 1b1) to be mild and slow in avenging; 1b2) to be longsuffering, slow to anger, slow to punish"

Trench's Synonyms of the Greek New Testament gives an interesting meaning of this Greek Word. It comes from two words, MAKROS meaning *"long or far"* and THUMOS meaning *"hot or boiling like fire."* The result of the meaning of *"patience"* is for a person to live so that their boiling point or anger is still a long way away. This Word is usually translated *"longsuffering"* while another Word is usually used for *"patience."* Trench pointed out that patience normally refers to putting up with things and circumstances, while longsuffering refers to putting up with people.

1 Thessalonians 5:15
"See that none render evil for evil unto any man; but ever follow that which is good, both among yourselves, and to all men."

In this verse, Paul exhorts these genuine Christians at Thessalonica regarding two more things: They are (1) not to render evil for evil; and (2) to follow that which is good.

Verses About Evil
- **Romans 12:17**
"Recompense to no man evil for evil. Provide things honest in the sight of all men."

Paul told this same command to the true Christians at Rome. Don't give back evil to someone who gives you evil.
- **Romans 12:21**
"Be not overcome of evil, but overcome evil with good."

God does not want the genuine Christians to be overcome with evil, but to overcome evil with good. This is often difficult.
- **1 Peter 3:9**
"Not rendering evil for evil, or railing for railing: but contrariwise blessing; knowing that ye are thereunto called, that ye should inherit a blessing."

If evil comes to true Christians, they should not return evil back, but good.

Verses About Good

The second command found in this verse is to follow the good with everyone.
- **Romans 3:12**
"They are all gone out of the way, they are together become unprofitable; there is none that doeth good, no, not one."

No human being can do good as defined by God, regardless of what they might think is good. Goodness must be based on the Bible's standards.
- **Romans 7:18**
"For I know that in me (that is, in my flesh,) dwelleth no good thing: for to will is present with me; but *how* to perform that which is good I find not."

As far as God's standards are concerned, no good thing dwells in the flesh of any person.
- **Romans 7:21**
"I find then a law, that, when I would do good, evil is present with me."

Wherever good is, evil is also present with it. This is because of the sin that is in the world.
- **Romans 8:28**
"And we know that all things work together for good to them that love God, to them who are the called according to *his* purpose."

THINGS WORKING TOGETHER FOR GOOD

For the true Christians, all the things that come into their life, whether good or bad, work together for the good in the future plans of God for those people.

- **Romans 12:9**
"*Let* love be without dissimulation. Abhor that which is evil; cleave to that which is good."

God wants genuine Christians to hate evil and follow the good.

- **Romans 14:16**
"Let not then your good be evil spoken of:"
Sometimes this cannot happen, but wherever possible the good that true Christians do should not be criticized and made into an evil thing by others.
- **Romans 16:19**
"For your obedience is come abroad unto all *men*. I am glad therefore on your behalf: but yet I would have you wise unto that which is good, and simple concerning evil."
The only way that genuine Christians can be wise unto that which is good is to know what the Words of God teach regarding good. The Bible must be our standard for what's good and what's bad.
- **Galatians 4:18**
"But *it is* good to be zealously affected always in *a* good *thing*, and not only when I am present with you."
One of the things that is good is to be strongly affected in a good thing.
- **Galatians 6:10**
"As we have therefore opportunity, let us do good unto all *men*, especially unto them who are of the household of faith."
True Christians should seek to do good to everyone especially to other genuine Christians.
- **Ephesians 2:10**
"For we are his workmanship, created in Christ Jesus unto good works, which God hath before ordained that we should walk in them."

GOOD WORKS SHOULD FOLLOW SALVATION
After genuine Christians have been saved by true faith in the Lord Jesus Christ, God expects them to follow good works.

1 Thessalonians 5:16

"Rejoice evermore."

CONTINUAL REJOICING FOR TRUE CHRISTIANS
This command for genuine Christians is in the Greek present tense. As such, it means that they are to continue to rejoice, no matter what the circumstances might be.

Verses About Joy And Rejoicing
- **Psalms 5:11**
"But let all those that put their trust in thee rejoice: let them ever shout for joy, because thou defendest them: let them also that love thy name be joyful in thee."

In this verse David uses a form of the word, *"joy,"* three times. It is for those who have trusted in the Lord and that love His Name. They are to shout because of this joy God has given them.
- **Psalms 13:5**

"But I have trusted in thy mercy; my heart shall rejoice in thy salvation."

Here, <u>David is rejoicing in God's salvation. True Christians should do the same.</u>   **Philippians 3:1**

"Finally, my brethren, rejoice in the Lord. To write the same things to you, to me indeed *is* not grievous, but for you *it is* safe."

Genuine Christians are commanded to rejoice in the Lord Jesus Christ and in all that He has done for them in redeeming their souls.
- **Philippians 3:3**

"For we are the circumcision, which worship God in the spirit, and rejoice in Christ Jesus, and have no confidence in the flesh."

<u>Paul rejoices in Christ Jesus and has no confidence in his flesh.</u>
- **Philippians 4:4**

"Rejoice in the Lord alway: *and* again I say, Rejoice."

Paul was writing this from the prison in Rome. Despite his poor conditions of being confined in prison, he urged the true Christians in Philippi to follow his example and to rejoice in the Lord Jesus Christ, regardless of their own circumstances.
- **1 Peter 1:5-6**

"Who are kept by the power of God through faith unto salvation ready to be revealed in the last time. Wherein ye greatly rejoice, though now for a season, if need be, ye are in heaviness through manifold temptations:"

REJOICING EVEN IN MANIFOLD TESTINGS

Even though the genuine Christians to whom Peter was writing were in manifold temptations and in heaviness, they were to greatly rejoice because of their salvation.

- **1 Peter 1:8**

"Whom having not seen, ye love; in whom, though now ye see *him* not, yet believing, ye rejoice with joy unspeakable and full of glory:

TRUE CHRISTIANS REJOICE WITH UNSPEAKABLE JOY

Though these true Christians had never seen the Lord Jesus Christ as Peter had, because of their faith in Him, they were to rejoice with unspeakable and glorious joy.

1 Thessalonians 5:17

"Pray without ceasing."

Paul continues to tell the Thessalonian church what to do for their Saviour. In this verse it involves continuous prayer.

Verses About Prayer

- **Acts 12:5**

"Peter therefore was kept in prison: but prayer was made without ceasing of the church unto God for him."

Prayer was made without ceasing for Peter who was in prison. James had already been killed by the Roman government. God answered that prayer and by a series of miracles Peter was released from prison and certain death (Acts 12:1-17).

- **Romans 1:9**

"For God is my witness, whom I serve with my spirit in the gospel of his Son, that without ceasing I make mention of you always in my prayers;"

Paul intercedes in prayer continually for the true Christians at Rome.

- **1 Thessalonians 1:2-3**

"We give thanks to God always for you all, making mention of you in our prayers; Remembering without ceasing your work of faith, and labour of love, and patience of hope in our Lord Jesus Christ, in the sight of God and our Father;"

Paul remembers without ceasing the genuine Christians at Thessalonica for their work of faith, labour of love, and patience of hope in their Saviour.

- **1 Thessalonians 2:13**

"For this cause also thank we God without ceasing, because, when ye received the word of God which ye heard of us, ye received *it* not *as* the word of men, but as it is in truth, the word of God, which effectually worketh also in you that believe."

Paul thanked God continually because these genuine Christians at Thessalonica received the Words of God as coming from Him rather than from men.

- **2 Timothy 1:3**

"I thank God, whom I serve from *my* forefathers with pure conscience, that without ceasing I have remembrance of thee in my prayers night and day;"

Paul did not forget Pastor Timothy in his continual prayers as he ministered to the true Christians at Ephesus.

1 Thessalonians 5:18

"In every thing give thanks: for this is the will of God in Christ Jesus concerning you."

Here is another command from Paul to the genuine Christians in the church at Thessalonica. It concerns the giving of thanks as being the will of God in Christ Jesus.

Verses About Being Thankful

- **Psalms 79:13**

"So we thy people and sheep of thy pasture will give thee thanks for ever: we will shew forth thy praise to all generations."

The psalmist was thankful forever because he was one of the sheep of God's pasture.

- **John 6:11**

"And Jesus took the loaves; and when he had given thanks, he distributed to the disciples, and the disciples to them that were set down; and likewise of the fishes as much as they would."

THANKFULNESS BEFORE EATING

Before the Lord Jesus Christ performed the miracle of the feeding of the five thousand men plus women and children, He gave thanks to God the Father in prayer.

- **1 Corinthians 15:57**

"But thanks *be* to God, which giveth us the victory through our Lord Jesus Christ."

Paul was thankful to God for the victory He alone can give true Christians because of their genuine faith in the Lord Jesus Christ.

- **2 Corinthians 2:14**

"Now thanks *be* unto God, which always causeth us to triumph in Christ, and maketh manifest the savour of his knowledge by us in every place."

Genuine Christians should be thankful to God for causing them to triumph in Christ and instructing them how to manifest the Lord Jesus Christ wherever they might go.

- **2 Corinthians 9:15**

"Thanks *be* unto God for his unspeakable gift."

Paul was thankful to God for the unspeakable gift of salvation through His Son, the Lord Jesus Christ.

- **Ephesians 1:16**

"Cease not to give thanks for you, making mention of you in my prayers;"

When Paul was in a Roman dungeon, he continued to give thanks for the true Christians he knew at Ephesus as he prayed for them.
- **Ephesians 5:20**
"Giving thanks always for all things unto God and the Father in the name of our Lord Jesus Christ;"

RULES FOR TRUE CHRISTIANS' THANKSGIVING
This verse tells genuine Christians about their thanksgiving.
(1) It should be for all things;
(2) It should be to God the Father; and
(3) It should be in the Name of the Lord Jesus Christ.

- **Colossians 3:17**
"And whatsoever ye do in word or deed, *do* all in the name of the Lord Jesus, giving thanks to God and the Father by him."
True Christians should be very careful what they do either in word or in deed. It should be done in the name of the Lord Jesus Christ and it should be done with thankfulness to the Father by the Son.
- **Hebrews 13:15**
"By him therefore let us offer the sacrifice of praise to God continually, that is, the fruit of *our* lips giving thanks to his name."

THE SACRIFICE OF PRAISE TO GOD
The sacrifice in the New Testament here is not by blood offerings of animals, but it is rather the sacrifice of praise by genuine Christians giving thanks to God's Name.

---

1 Thessalonians 5:19
"Quench not the Spirit."
In this command, Paul tells the true Christians to stop quenching the Holy Spirit Who indwells them.

THE MEANING OF THE GREEK WORD, "SBENNUMI"
The Greek Word for *"quench"* is SBENNUMI. Some of the meanings of this Word are:
"1) to extinguish, quench; 1a) of fire or things on fire; 1a1) to be quenched, to go out; 1b) metaph. to quench, to suppress, stifle; 1b1) of divine influence."

Since this prohibition uses this Greek verb is in the presence tense, the meaning is to stop an action already in progress. Dr. Lewis Sperry Chafer, founder of Dallas Theological Seminary (and my professor at

Dallas Seminary for the four years of 1948-1952), commented on this in his book, *He that is Spiritual.*

THREE RULES FOR THE HOLY SPIRIT'S FILLING

Dr. Chafer said there are three qualifications for being filled with or controlled by the Spirit of God. Two are negatives and one is positive:

(1) quench not the Spirit,

(2) grieve not the Spirit, and

(3) walk in the Spirit.

These are the three prerequisites for the filling of God the Holy Spirit in the genuine Christian's life. Genuine Christians grieve the Holy Spirit by permitting known and unconfessed sin in their lives. They fail to walk in the Spirit when their flesh prevails in their lives.

Dr. Chafer explained the quenching the Holy Spirit was saying "no" to the will of God. When true Christians say "no" to the will of God, it is **not** simply saying to the Lord *"Lord, you first of all tell me what your will is and I'll make up my mind whether I'm going to do it."* That's not it.

WHAT QUENCHES THE SPIRIT'S MINISTRY?

In order not to quench the Holy Spirit, they must say: *"Whatever thou will have me to do, Lord, whatever it is, I will do it."*

Verses About Quenching

- **2 Samuel 21:17**

"But Abishai the son of Zeruiah succoured him, and smote the Philistine, and killed him. Then the men of David sware unto him, saying, Thou shalt go no more out with us to battle, that thou quench not the light of Israel."

God's light should not be quenched or extinguished.

- **Song of Solomon 8:7a**

"Many waters cannot quench love, neither can the floods drown it:" Nothing can extinguish or quench true love.

- **Jeremiah 4:4**

"Circumcise yourselves to the LORD, and take away the foreskins of your heart, ye men of Judah and inhabitants of Jerusalem: lest my fury come forth like fire, and burn that none can quench *it*, because of the evil of your doings."

In this case, it is fury's fire that cannot be quenched or extinguished.

- **Ephesians 6:16**
"Above all, taking the shield of faith, wherewith ye shall be able to quench all the fiery darts of the wicked."

FAITH'S SHIELD QUENCHES SATAN'S FIERY DARTS
In this instance, with the shield of faith, those who are genuine Christians can quench all of Satan's fiery darts if the shield of faith is used.

1 Thessalonians 5:20
"Despise not prophesyings."

PROPHECY CEASED WITH THE COMPLETED BIBLE
When Paul wrote this first letter of the New Testament, 1 Thessalonians, the gift of prophecy was still in the Church. It did not cease until the Bible was completed in 90 or 100 A.D.

Since this Greek verb for "*despise*" is in the Greek present tense, this prohibition means to stop an action already in progress. These genuine Christians in Thessalonica were despising prophesyings which at that time were being used of the Lord since the Bible had not yet been completed. Paul told them to stop it.

THE MEANING OF THE GREEK WORD, "EXOUTHENEO"
The Greek Word for "*despise*" is EXOUTHENEO. Some of the meanings for this Word are:
"*1) to make of no account, despise utterly*"

The gift of prophecy ceased after the completion of the Bible in 90 or 100 A.D. Look carefully at the following verses to see this.
- **1 Corinthians 13:8-11**
"Charity never faileth: but whether *there be* **prophecies, they shall fail**; whether *there be* tongues, they shall cease; whether *there be* knowledge, it shall vanish away. For we know in part, and **we prophesy in part**. But **when that which is perfect is come**, then **that which is in part shall be done away**. When I was a child, I spake as a child, I understood as a child, I thought as a child: but **when I became a man, I put away childish things.**"

THE COMPLETED BIBLE=NO MORE SIGN GIFTS
The termination of these and other sign gifts was "*when that which is perfect is come.*" The Pentecostals and Charismatics wrongly teach that "*that which is perfect*" refers

to the coming of the Lord Jesus Christ in the Rapture of the Church. If this were true, the Greek for it would read HO TELEIOS which is in the masculine gender. But this verse 8 reads TO TELEION which is in the neuter gender. It refers to TO BIBLION and to the perfect or complete Scripture as it was in 90 or 100 A.D. After that time, these three sign gifts as well as other sign gifts *"failed," "ceased,"* and *"vanished away."* They were no longer needed by the Lord because His final and complete revelation had been completed.

1 Thessalonians 5:21

"Prove all things; hold fast that which is good."

There are two commands that Paul gave to the true Christians in Thessalonica. (1) They were to prove, and (2) they were to hold fast. The first command was for them to *"prove all things."*

MEANING OF THE GREEK WORD, "DOKIMAZO"

The Greek Word for "prove" is DOKIMAZO. Some of the meanings of this Greek Word are:

"1) to test, examine, prove, scrutinise (to see whether a thing is genuine or not), as metals; 2) to recognise as genuine after examination, to approve, deem worthy"

Since this Greek verb is in the Greek present tense, it means that this examination, scrutiny, and testing out is to be a continuous action without any let up.

That's what true Christians must do concerning all things that surround them both in their churches and in the world in general. They must test them out to see if they are genuine and true. The name of our church is "The Bible for Today Baptist Church." I began the Bible For Today many years ago in Newton, Massachusetts. I have always used the Bible and applied it to the issues and problems of "today."

In our church morning services, I have a section at the beginning entitled "CURRENT COMMENTS FOR CONCERNED CHRISTIANS." I seek to inform our church of what's going on in both the religious world and the secular world. Many of the facts regarding these matters are not mentioned truthfully in the public media of either books, newspapers, radio, television, or the Internet. It is one of the duties of pastors-bishops-elders to be "WATCHMEN." Paul commanded Pastor Timothy at the church in Ephesus, for example: **"watch thou in all things**, . . ." (2 Timothy 4:5) The only way true Christians can *"prove"* and *"scrutinize"* and *"examine"* all things is to know truthfully about these things that need examination and scrutiny. This is especially needful when so many falsehoods abound in the present-day news media.

Verses On Proving
- **Deuteronomy 8:2**

"And thou shalt remember all the way which the LORD thy God led thee these forty years in the wilderness, to humble thee, *and* to prove thee, to know what *was* in thine heart, whether thou wouldest keep his commandments, or no."

> **ISRAEL FAILED GOD IN THE WILDERNESS**
> God led the Israelites for forty years in the wilderness to prove and test them whether or not they would keep His commands. They failed His test!

- **Psalms 26:2**

"Examine me, O LORD, and prove me; try my reins and my heart." David welcomed God's testing of his innermost being.

- **Daniel 1:12**

"Prove thy servants, I beseech thee, ten days; and let them give us pulse to eat, and water to drink."

Daniel wanted to be tested by eating only vegetables and drinking only water rather than the unclean meat of the king. He passed that test. Daniel and his three friends were more healthy and stronger than any of the others.

- **2 Corinthians 13:5**

"Examine yourselves, whether ye be in the faith; prove your own selves. Know ye not your own selves, how that Jesus Christ is in you, except ye be reprobates?"

All people were to test their own hearts to be sure they were genuine Christians.

Verses On Holding Fast

In addition to proving and testing things out, true Christians are also to "*hold fast*" to good things as measured by the Bible.

- **2 Timothy 1:13**

"Hold fast the form of sound words, which thou hast heard of me, in faith and love which is in Christ Jesus."

Paul told Pastor Timothy to hold fast to the sound Words of the Bible that He knew. Instead of the drifting away from sound words, true Christians should hold fast to their King James Bible and its underlying Hebrew, Aramaic, and Greek Words.

- **Hebrews 4:14**

"Seeing then that we have a great high priest, that is passed into the heavens, Jesus the Son of God, let us hold fast *our* profession."

Because genuine Christians have the Lord Jesus Christ as their great High Priest, they should hold fast to their Biblical faith.
- **Revelation 3:3**
"Remember therefore how thou hast received and heard, and hold fast, and repent. If therefore thou shalt not watch, I will come on thee as a thief, and thou shalt not know what hour I will come upon thee."

This church in Revelation was commanded by the Lord Jesus Christ to hold fast the true doctrines of the Christian faith.
- **Hebrews 10:23**
"Let us hold fast the profession of *our* faith without wavering; (for he *is* faithful that promised;)"

TRUE CHRISTIANS SHOULD HOLD FAST THEIR FAITH!
There should be no drifting or wavering on the part of genuine Christians regarding their Biblical faith because the Lord Jesus Christ is faithful Who promised to assist them. He does not lie.

1 Thessalonians 5:22
"Abstain from all appearance of evil."
True Christians are ordered here to completely refrain from all things that even appear to be evil. This verb is in the Greek present tense which implies a continuous and uninterrupted action. There should be no question of what evil is. It is defined in many places of the Bible. But here, the order is to abstain from even the *"appearance"* of evil–not evil, but all appearance of evil. You say "what's the difference?" Well, evil is actually evil, but appearance is what looks evil.

THE MEANING OF THE GREEK WORD, "EIDOS"
The Greek Word for *"appearance"* is EIDOS. Some of the meanings of this Word are:
"1) the external or outward appearance, form figure, shape; 2) form, kind"

ABSTAIN FROM THE APPEARANCE OF EVIL
What genuine Christians might be thinking, saying, or doing may not be evil but if it looks like it, if it gives the appearance of evil, they should to abstain from it.

Many Christians, whether men or women, don't seem to care how things look. If they go into a liquor store or a bar, for example, even if they do not drink any liquor, it might give the appearance that they're drinking and might end up being drunk. That would be the appearance of evil. There are many things that give the appearance of evil.

Many years ago, someone told me about a woman who used to work for a man in an office in his house. She would work in the day time and stay in his house sometimes until 8 or 10 p.m. Both of them were professing Christians. I wonder what the neighbors might have thought? They weren't married to each other. Though I am sure nothing untoward or evil went on in that house with these two people, yet, is this not an illustration of an appearance of evil? God tells true Christians that they are to continuously abstain, not only from evil, but from everything that might give the appearance of evil.

Verses On Abstaining From Things
- **Acts 15:29**

"That ye abstain from meats offered to idols, and from blood, and from things strangled, and from fornication: from which if ye keep yourselves, ye shall do well. Fare ye well."

Only these four things were brought over from the Old Testament to be applied to genuine Christians in the New Testament rather than for them to be forced to obey the entire Mosaic law. One of them was to abstain from meats offered to idols.
- **1 Thessalonians 4:3**

"For this is the will of God, *even* your sanctification, that ye should abstain from fornication:"

This command to abstain from fornication for true Christians, and for all others, is constantly being violated by both these groups. The rule for sexual activity today seems to be that anything goes and anything is all right. God and His Bible has a completely different standard of sexual purity. God wants His children to be sanctified in their sexual lives.
- **1 Peter 2:11**

"Dearly beloved, I beseech *you* as strangers and pilgrims, abstain from fleshly lusts, which war against the soul;"

LEAVE FLESHLY LUSTS THAT WAR AGAINST THE SOUL

God wants those who are genuine Christians to abstain from all sorts of fleshly lusts which war against their souls. Once again, this standard is, sad to say, often disregarded by Christians and unsaved people alike.

Verses On Appearances
- **1 Samuel 16:7**

"But the LORD said unto Samuel, Look not on his countenance, or on the height of his stature; because I have refused him: for *the*

LORD seeth not as man seeth; for man looketh on the outward appearance, but the LORD looketh on the heart."

It is so true that people can only look on outward appearances, but the God of the Bible can look right down into their heart and know their every whim, desire, and inclination.

- **John 7:24**

"Judge not according to the appearance, but judge righteous judgment."

TRUE CHRISTIANS SHOULD JUDGE RIGHTEOUSLY

This does not teach true Christians that they are not to judge and weigh things out. It teaches them to be sure that their judgments are righteous and true rather than merely based upon appearances and externals.

- **2 Corinthians 5:12**

"For we commend not ourselves again unto you, but give you occasion to glory on our behalf, that ye may have somewhat to *answer* them which glory in appearance, and not in heart."

This verse points out that there are those people—and there are many of them today—who glory in external appearances rather than things coming from the heart.

- **2 Corinthians 10:7**

"Do ye look on things after the outward appearance? If any man trust to himself that he is Christ's, let him of himself think this again, that, as he *is* Christ's, even so *are* we Christ's."

DON'T LOOK ON OUTWARD APPEARANCES

Genuine Christians are cautioned here not to look at things based on outward appearances alone. This can lead them astray.

---

1 Thessalonians 5:23

"And the very God of peace sanctify you wholly; and I pray God your whole spirit and soul and body be preserved blameless unto the coming of our Lord Jesus Christ."

GOD WANTS SANCTITY OF SPIRIT, SOUL, AND BODY

God is given the title here of being the *"God of peace"* Who is able to sanctify and set apart genuine Christians wholly in every part of their threefold personality—their whole spirit, soul, and body. God wants them wholly holy even today.

Verses Using The Word, Wholly
- **Numbers 32:12**
"Save Caleb the son of Jephunneh the Kenezite, and Joshua the son of Nun: for they have wholly followed the LORD."
Caleb and Joshua were the only two of the twelve spies who wholly followed the LORD Jehovah.
- **Acts 17:16**
"Now while Paul waited for them at Athens, his spirit was stirred in him, when he saw the city wholly given to idolatry."
Paul found Athens given wholly to the worship of false gods.
- **1 Timothy 4:15**
"Meditate upon these things; give thyself wholly to them; that thy profiting may appear to all."
Paul ordered Pastor Timothy to give himself wholly to the Words of the Living God without drifting away from them in any detail!

Verses On Being Blameless
- **1 Corinthians 1:8**
"Who shall also confirm you unto the end, *that ye may be* blameless in the day of our Lord Jesus Christ."
True Christians will one day be absolutely blameless when their Lord Jesus Christ transforms their bodies like unto His own at His appearing.
- **Philippians 2:15**
"That ye may be blameless and harmless, the sons of God, without rebuke, in the midst of a crooked and perverse nation, among whom ye shine as lights in the world;"
Paul, speaking from a Roman prison, showed clearly that the genuine Christians should live lives that were to be blameless and harmless in the midst of a crooked and perverse country. So should they be today.
- **1 Timothy 3:2**
"A bishop then must be blameless, the husband of one wife, vigilant, sober, of good behaviour, given to hospitality, apt to teach;"

BLAMELESSNESS, A STANDARD FOR PASTOR-LEADERS
One of the many qualifications and standards for New Testament true Christian pastors-bishops-elders was that they be blameless. It does not mean sinless perfection, but it implies that they have no serious charges against them that can be clearly substantiated. From the meaning of this word, false charges are not in view here.

- **1 Timothy 3:10**
"And let these also first be proved; then let them use the office of a deacon, being *found* blameless."

This section of 1 Timothy is giving the standard for genuine Christian deacons also to be blameless before being elected to that office.
- **Titus 1:6**
"If any be blameless, the husband of one wife, having faithful children not accused of riot or unruly."

Once again, this context speaks of the pre-qualifications of true Christians who were to be candidates for the office of deacon. They must be blameless.
- **2 Peter 3:14**
"Wherefore, beloved, seeing that ye look for such things, be diligent that ye may be found of him in peace, without spot, and blameless."

Though people often bring charges against genuine Christians, they should not be true, but false. God wants them to be good testimonies for the Lord Jesus Christ, their Saviour.

1 Thessalonians 5:24
"Faithful is he that calleth you, who also will do it."

GOD IS FAITHFUL IN ALL OF HIS PROMISES
The God of the Bible offers salvation to those who genuinely trust in His Son. These genuine believers are regenerated, saved, and born-again because of His promises. He is faithful in all that He has promised in His Bible Words. He always does what He says He will do.

Verses On God's Faithfulness
- **Lamentations 3:22-23**
"*It is of* the LORD'S mercies that we are not consumed, because his compassions fail not. *They are* new every morning: great *is* thy faithfulness."

God's faithfulness is not only certain, but it is great in every aspect of it.
- **Daniel 6:4**
"Then the presidents and princes sought to find occasion against Daniel concerning the kingdom; but they could find none occasion nor fault; forasmuch as he *was* faithful, neither was there any error or fault found in him."

Daniel was a faithful servant. The rulers of Babylon could find no error or fault against him.
- **Luke 16:10**
"He that is faithful in that which is least is faithful also in much: and he that is unjust in the least is unjust also in much."

God is faithful in both the least things and the great things. Genuine Christians should be faithful in these areas as well.

- 1 Corinthians 1:9

"God *is* faithful, by whom ye were called unto the fellowship of his Son Jesus Christ our Lord."

There is nothing that changes the Lord. He is faithful to us, as He has promised in His Words.

- 1 Corinthians 4:2

"Moreover it is required in stewards, that a man be found faithful."

STEWARDS MUST BE FAITHFUL IN THEIR STEWARDSHIP

If true Christians are doing something for someone else, they must be faithful in what they do since they are stewards for another person.

- 1 Corinthians 4:17

"For this cause have I sent unto you Timotheus, who is my beloved son, and faithful in the Lord, who shall bring you into remembrance of my ways which be in Christ, as I teach every where in every church."

Pastor Timothy was a faithful servant of the Lord Jesus Christ. Genuine Christians today should be faithful to their Master as well.

- 1 Corinthians 10:13

"There hath no temptation taken you but such as is common to man: but God *is* faithful, who will not suffer you to be tempted above that ye are able; but will with the temptation also make a way to escape, that ye may be able to bear *it*."

GOD IS ALWAYS FAITHFUL TO GENUINE CHRISTIANS

No matter what might be the calamities that confront true Christians today, their God is still faithful who will not allow more than they can bear. With the troubles, He will make His way to escape so that they will be able to put up with them.

- 2 Thessalonians 3:3

"But the Lord is faithful, who shall stablish you, and keep *you* from evil."

The Lord Jesus Christ was faithful to the genuine Christians at Thessalonica and He will be faithful to true Christians today. He will establish them and keep them from all evil.

- 1 Timothy 1:15

"This *is* a faithful saying, and worthy of all acceptation, that Christ Jesus came into the world to save sinners; of whom I am chief."

CHRIST DIED TO OFFER SALVATION TO ALL PEOPLE

This saying is faithful. Notice that it says clearly that the Lord Jesus Christ came into this world to save sinners, not just

> some sinners, or only those who are some kind of "elect" as the hyper-Calvinists teach. He came to save all the sinners who put their true faith and trust in Him as their Saviour.

- **Hebrews 10:23**

"Let us hold fast the profession of *our* faith without wavering; (for he *is* faithful that promised;)"

Genuine Christians should hold fast to their doctrines of the faith since God holds fast to everything He has promised in the Bible.

- **1 John 1:9**

"If we confess our sins, he is faithful and just to forgive us *our* sins, and to cleanse us from all unrighteousness."

> **AGREEING WITH GOD ON SIN BRINGS RESTORATION**
> True Christians should confess their sins. The Greek Word for *"confess"* is HOMOLOGEO. This means *"to say the same thing"* about the sins of thought, word, or deed that God says and therefore to agree with Him that it is sin. Then, and only then, after genuine confession of sin, God is faithful to forgive them their sins and cleanse them from all their unrighteousness.

- **Revelation 1:5**

"And from Jesus Christ, *who is* the faithful witness, *and* the first begotten of the dead, and the prince of the kings of the earth. Unto him that loved us, and washed us from our sins in his own blood,"

In this verse, the Lord Jesus Christ is called a faithful witness. He tells no lies. He told it like it was when on earth, and He tells the truth at the Father's right hand.

God's Faithfulness In His Promise of Plenary, Verbal Preservation Of The Bible's Original Hebrew, Aramaic, And Greek Words.

Notice that the following three identical verses from three of the Gospels teach very clearly God's promised faithfulness in preserving His original Hebrew, Aramaic, and Greek Words.

- **Matthew 24:35**

"Heaven and earth shall pass away, but my words shall not pass away."

- **Mark 13:31**

"Heaven and earth shall pass away: but my words shall not pass away."

- Luke 21:33
"Heaven and earth shall pass away: but my words shall not pass away."

> **THE GREEK WORDS, "OU ME" MEAN "NEVER, NEVER"**
> The Greek Word for *"not"* in all three of these above verses is OU ME. This is the strongest Greek negative in that language. It means *"never, never, and never."*
> When the Lord Jesus Christ mentioned *"my words,"* what did He mean? In the verses below, He taught His disciples that every Greek Word of the New Testament originated with Him. He then gave His Words to God the Holy Spirit Who, in turn, gave them to the human writers. By extension, I believe the Lord Jesus Christ is the Author of all of the Old Testament Hebrew and Aramaic Words as well. He is the LOGOS or Divine Revelator in both the Old and the New Testaments.

- John 16:12-14
"I have yet many things to say unto you, but ye cannot bear them now. Howbeit when he, the Spirit of truth, is come, he will guide you into all truth: for **he shall not speak of himself; but whatsoever he shall hear, *that* shall he speak**: and he will shew you things to come. He shall glorify me: for **he shall receive of mine, and shall shew *it* unto you**."

- Matthew 5:18
"For verily I say unto you, **Till heaven and earth pass**, one jot or one tittle shall in no wise pass from the law, till all be fulfilled."
In this verse, the Lord Jesus Christ revealed both the **duration** and the **details** of God's faithfulness in preserving His Words.

The Duration Of God's Faithful Bible Preservation

The **duration** of God's faithful promise to verbally preserve the Hebrew, Aramaic, and Greek Words is found in the first part of this verse in the words, *"till heaven and earth pass."* Since this has not yet taken place, the promise of things not passing from the law will likewise not occur. The word, *"law"* can be understood as the entire Words of God as in the Psalms when it states:

"The ***law of the LORD*** is perfect, converting the soul: ***the testimony of the LORD*** is sure, making wise the simple." (Psalms 19:7)
"ALEPH. Blessed are the undefiled in the way, who walk in ***the law of the LORD***."(Psalms 119:1)

Though this refers to the Old Testament Hebrew and Aramaic Words of God, it could also extend to the New Testament Greek Words as well.

The Details Of God's Faithful Bible Preservation

The **details** of this faithful promise are found in the words "jot" and "tittle." The "*jot*" (IOTA) is the Hebrew YODH which is the smallest letter in the Hebrew alphabet. The "*tittle*" (KERAIA) is a tiny vowel marking like a period or a little dot. The Lord Jesus Christ is promising to preserve even the smallest letter and the smallest part of the smallest letter of the Old Testament and, by extension, the smallest part of the New Testament as well.

It is indeed sad that many of the once so-called "fundamental" churches and institutions such as Bob Jones University do not believe in the verbal plenary preservation of the Hebrew, Aramaic, and Greek Words of the Bible. The head of the Hebrew department at BJU is on record as saying, for example, that there are many "*scribal errors*" in the Hebrew/Aramaic Old Testament, thereby denying this verbal plenary preservation promised by the Lord Jesus Christ in the above verses of the New Testament. I believe these promised verbal and plenary Hebrew, Aramaic, and Greek Words are the Words from which our King James Bible was faithfully and accurately translated.

1 Thessalonians 5:25

"Brethren, pray for us."

This is Paul's request for the genuine Christians in Thessalonica to intercede for him in prayer. It is in the Greek present tense which implies a continuous procedure.

Verses About Requesting Prayer

- **Colossians 1:9**

"For this cause we also, since the day we heard *it*, do not cease to pray for you, and to desire that ye might be filled with the knowledge of his will in all wisdom and spiritual understanding;"
Even though he was in a Roman prison, Paul interceded without ceasing for those true Christians in the church at Colosse.

- **2 Thessalonians 1:11**

"Wherefore also we pray always for you, that our God would count you worthy of *this* calling, and fulfil all the good pleasure of *his* goodness, and the work of faith with power:"
For those genuine Christians in Thessalonica, Paul prayed always, naming his requests for them.

- **2 Thessalonians 3:1**

"Finally, brethren, pray for us, that the word of the Lord may have *free* course, and be glorified, even as *it is* with you:"

In this verse, Paul requested the genuine Christians at Thessalonica to intercede and pray for him. He, and those with him, needed prayer as much as they did.
- **Hebrews 13:18**
"Pray for us: for we trust we have a good conscience, in all things willing to live honestly."
Paul asked the true Hebrew Christians to pray on his behalf as well.

1 Thessalonians 5:26

"Greet all the brethren with an holy kiss."

This is was something that was practiced in the early church. They greeted one another with a kiss on the cheek without any sexual connotations involved with this practice. There are five other verses in the New Testament on this subject.
- **Acts 20:37**
"And they all wept sore, and fell on Paul's neck, and kissed him,
- **Romans 16:16**
"Salute one another with an **holy kiss**. The churches of Christ salute you"
- **1 Corinthians 16:20**
"All the brethren greet you. Greet ye one another with an holy kiss."
- **2 Corinthians 13:12**
"Greet one another with an holy kiss."
- **1 Peter 5:14**
"Greet ye one another with a kiss of charity. Peace *be* with you all that are in Christ Jesus. Amen."

Thoughts About The Word, Kiss

1. Notice that in four of the six uses of the word, "*kiss*," it is to be a "*holy kiss*" This sets it apart from the kisses of passion with sexual connotations that occur in our culture today.

2. It was a form of greeting either of meeting with or departing from persons.

3. It was to be used only with "*brethren*" or genuine Christian people.

4. It was given on the cheek rather than on the lips as most often today.

5. The meaning of the Greek Word for "***kiss***" is important.

> **THE MEANING OF THE GREEK WORD, "PHILEMA"**
> The Greek Word for *"kiss"* is PHILEMA. It comes from two Greek Words, PHILOS and -MA. Some of the meanings of that Greek Word are:
> *"1) a kiss; 2) the kiss with which, as <u>a sign of fraternal affection</u>, Christians were accustomed to welcome or dismiss their companions in the faith."*

The first part of the word (PHIL-) comes from PHILOS which means *"love, affection, or friendship."* The Greek suffix (-MA) means *"the result of something."* In the early church, this was their custom kissing true Christians on the cheek as a result of their love, affection, and friendship. <u>Our Christian custom today when we meet and leave each other is to shake hands or to say hello and good bye. Unfriendly people sometimes refuse to extend a friendly handshake.</u> I have been on the receiving end in church on one occasion, sad to say.

Some denominations or local churches continue the practice of the early church, though, on occasion, the *"kiss"* is not a *"holy kiss"* as the Bible mentions in this verse. That's what that word means even though most Bible-believing churches don't necessarily practice that in their churches today. The early church did it properly.

Some of the Charismatic churches practice a form of this today. The trouble is many of the people in these churches do not stop with kissing on the cheek. They kiss on the mouth. Some churches stopped this practice because of that. Some of the people hug one another. The charismatic movement is doing this.

I remember one time I was in a church, in this area of New Jersey and one of the charismatic ladies came up to me and said 'Are you going to hug me?' and I said I would not. She was very hurt. That was her style. We don't have that style. A holy kiss as a result of love. Friendly greeting, shake hands, speaking one to another and encouraging one another.

1 Thessalonians 5:27

"I charge you by the Lord that this epistle be read unto all the holy brethren."

The reading of the Words of God is very important. It should be from the proper copies of the original Hebrew, Aramaic, and Greek manuscripts. It should also be accurately translated from those proper preserved Words. This is the case in English with the King James Bible, but not with any of the other modern English translations. This is also true of Dr. Humberto Gomez's Reina-Valera-Gomez Spanish translation. It is also true of Dr. D. S. Jung's Korean translation.

Verses On Reading And Heeding God's Words

- **Exodus 24:7**

"And he took the book of the covenant, and read in the audience of the people: and they said, All that the LORD hath said will we do, and be obedient."

Moses read to Israel from God's Words from the Mosaic Covenant. The Israelites said they would do what the LORD said, but they lied.

- **Deuteronomy 17:19**

"And it shall be with him, and he shall read therein all the days of his life: that he may learn to fear the LORD his God, to keep all the words of this law and these statutes, to do them:"

ISRAEL'S KINGS--COPY AND READ GOD'S WORDS

The kings of Israel were to write a copy of God's Old Testament Law and read it all the days of their lives. The kings failed to keep this commandment. As a result, most of them led their people into apostasy and wickedness.

- **Nehemiah 8:8**

"So they read in the book in the law of God distinctly, and gave the sense, and caused *them* to understand the reading."

READING AND UNDERSTANDING GOD'S WORDS

In Nehemiah's day, after Israel had returned to their own land from their seventy years of in Babylon, Ezra not only read God's Words to the people, but he also gave the sense of these Words so that the people could understand their meaning. Many only understood the language of Babylon which was slightly different from the Hebrew Old Testament. This is one reason why I use verse by verse expository preaching in our church so that those who listen might clearly understand the meaning of God's Words and obey them.

- **Nehemiah 8:18**

"Also day by day, from the first day unto the last day, he read in the book of the law of God. And they kept the feast seven days; and on the eighth day *was* a solemn assembly, according unto the manner."

Ezra read in God's Words each day throughout the entire seven days of this feast.

- **Nehemiah 9:3**

"And they stood up in their place, and read in the book of the law of the LORD their God *one* fourth part of the day; and *another* fourth part they confessed, and worshipped the LORD their God."

In the first part of the feast, the people read in God's Words daily one fourth of the day each of the eight days. Since a day is twenty-four hours, one fourth of a day would be six full hours.

How Reading Isaiah Brought The Ethiopian Eunuch To The Lord

The verses that follow tell the story of the important treasurer of Candace, queen of Ethiopia, and how he became a Christian through genuine faith in the Lord Jesus Christ while reading Isaiah.

- **Acts 8:27-32**

"And he arose and went: and, behold, a man of Ethiopia, an eunuch of great authority under Candace queen of the Ethiopians, who had the charge of all her treasure, and had come to Jerusalem for to worship, Was returning, and sitting in his chariot read Esaias the prophet. Then the Spirit said unto Philip, Go near, and join thyself to this chariot. And Philip ran thither to *him*, and heard him read the prophet Esaias, and said, Understandest thou what thou readest? And he said, How can I, except some man should guide me? And he desired Philip that he would come up and sit with him. The place of the scripture which he read was this, He was led as a sheep to the slaughter; and like a lamb dumb before his shearer, so opened he not his mouth:"

He was reading the Words of God from the book of Isaiah.

- **Acts 8:34-35**

"And the eunuch answered Philip, and said, I pray thee, of whom speaketh the prophet this? of himself, or of some other man? Then Philip opened his mouth, and began at the same scripture, and preached unto him Jesus."

PHILIP LED A TREASURER TO CHRIST FROM ISAIAH 53

Philip was told by the Lord to go down south of Jerusalem to the desert of Gaza. There he met an Ethiopian eunuch of great authority who served under Candace, the Queen of Ethiopia. He was in charge of all her treasure. He was returning from a feast in Jerusalem. The Holy Spirit told Philip to run to this man's chariot. Philip obeyed. This man was reading in the book of Isaiah Chapter 53, but didn't understand the meaning of this Chapter. Philip told him that Isaiah was speaking about the Lord Jesus Christ who died for his sins and for all the sins of the world. Philip then led this man to salvation by true faith in the Saviour. When they came to water, Philip baptized him by immersion as the man had requested.

> This conversion to the Lord Jesus Christ came because this man was reading God's Words in the Old Testament and wanted someone to explain to him their meaning. Bible reading is very important.

- **Colossians 4:16**
"And when this epistle is read among you, cause that it be read also in the church of the Laodiceans; and that ye likewise read the *epistle* from Laodicea."

Paul was in a Roman prison when he wrote to the true Christians in Colosse. He assumed that his letter to them would be read to them. He also wanted them to read this letter to the church at Laodicea. He then asked them to read the letter he wrote to Laodicea. Reading and then heeding the Words of God was vital to the Apostle Paul. It should also be vital to all genuine Christians today. It is very sad that so few true Christians are faithful in reading the sixty-six Books of God's Words in order to grow thereby.

- **2 Timothy 2:15**
"Study to shew thyself approved unto God, a workman that needeth not to be ashamed, rightly dividing the word of truth."

Though the word, *"read,"* doesn't appear in this verse, it is implied. If genuine Christians *"study"* God's Words, they must first read them. They should not be ashamed, but should rightly divide the Words of truth. I believe this to be by means of understanding the various Biblical dispensations. Many true Christians do not rightly divide God's Words, and therefore have all kinds of erroneous interpretations of them. These false interpretations are numerous indeed.

1 Thessalonians 5:28

"The grace of our Lord Jesus Christ be with you. Amen."

It was Paul's wish that the free grace of the Lord Jesus Christ might continue to be with them and strengthen them. In these five chapters, Paul told those genuine Christians in Thessalonica many important things in order that they, (as well as genuine Christians today) might know and perform them.

> **GRACE IS GETTING SOMETHING WE DON'T DESERVE**
> The grace of the Lord Jesus Christ is giving them something that they do not deserve. He loves to give it to them any way, even if undeserving. They should praise and thank Him for His marvelous and infinite grace throughout all the days of their lives. True Christians today should do likewise.

2 Thessalonians Chapter One

The Background Of 2 Thessalonians
This book was written by Paul around 54 A.D. shortly after he wrote 1 Thessalonians. Perhaps he wrote it after he received a report on the reception of his first letter to the true Christians at Thessalonica.

Verses That Mention Thessalonica
Here are the six verses in the New Testament that mention Thessalonica.
- **Acts 17:1**
"Now when they passed through Amphipolis and Apollonia, they came to Thessalonica, where was a synagogue of the Jews."
In this verse, we see that there was a synagogue of the Jews in the city of Thessalonica.
- **Acts 17:11**
"These were more noble than those in Thessalonica, in that they received the word with all readiness of mind, and searched the scriptures daily, whether those things were so."

BEREANS–SEARCHING THE SCRIPTURES DAILY
Paul was speaking about the genuine Christians who lived in Berea. They were the ones who were *"more noble"* than those in Thessalonica because of the way they received the Words of God *"with all readiness of mind, and searched the scriptures daily."*

- **Acts 17:13**
"But when the Jews of Thessalonica had knowledge that the word of God was preached of Paul at Berea, they came thither also, and stirred up the people."
The Thessalonian Jews hated that Paul preached the gospel to those at Berea. So they went to Berea and *"stirred up the people."*

- Acts 27:2

"And entering into a ship of Adramyttium, we launched, meaning to sail by the coasts of Asia; one Aristarchus, a Macedonian of Thessalonica, being with us."

Aristarchus, who was with Paul when he was shipwrecked, was from Thessalonica.

- Philippians 4:16

"For even in Thessalonica ye sent once and again unto my necessity."

THE PHILIPPIANS GAVE PAUL SOME GIFTS
The true Christians in Philippi gave Paul some of their funds on several occasions to help him with his needs.

- 2 Timothy 4:10

"For Demas hath forsaken me, having loved this present world, and is departed unto Thessalonica; Crescens to Galatia, Titus unto Dalmatia."

Demas, who forsook Paul during the last few weeks of his second Roman imprisonment, went to the city of Thessalonica. He loved this present world more than Paul, the Lord's servant.

2 Thessalonians 1:1

"Paul, and Silvanus, and Timotheus, unto the church of the Thessalonians in God our Father and the Lord Jesus Christ:"

Silas and Timothy joined Paul in greeting the genuine Christians in Thessalonica. These Christians, who make up the church of the Thessalonians, were in God and in the Lord Jesus Christ. This is true because they were redeemed by true faith in the Lord Jesus Christ Who died for their sins. Since some people might not know who God the Father and God the Son are, here are a few of their attributes.

Divine Attributes Of God The Father

Here are some of the characteristics of God the Father that explain Him to those who do not know anything about the God of the Bible.

a. **God the Father Is A Spirit.** As such, He cannot be seen or touched.

b. **God the Father Is Omniscient.** That means that He knows everything about every person and everything else in the universe. Nothing can be hidden from Him.

c. **God the Father Is Omnipotent.** As such, He is all powerful. There is nothing that He can't do, except doing

something contrary to His will. He cannot fail in any of His endeavors.
d. **God the Father Is Omnipresent.** That means <u>He is everywhere present</u>. Because of His omnipresence, He is everywhere at the same time all around this world and all around His universe.
e. **God the Father Is The Creator.** Despite the errors of the scientific and apostate religious community, <u>He created all things</u> on the earth and in the heavens.
f. **God the Father Is Holy.** <u>Holiness is at the very center of God's nature</u>, being surrounded by His love, truth, grace, mercy, justice, judgment and many other of His attributes.
g. **God the Father Sent His Son To Save Sinners.** He sent Him from Heaven to earth so that <u>those who genuinely trust Him might have everlasting life</u>.
h. **God the Father will Send To Hell Those Who Reject His Son.** <u>He wants everyone in the world to truly accept His Son as their Saviour.</u> If this does not happen, He will send them to the Lake of Fire for all eternity to come.

Divine Attributes Of God The Son

Here are some of the Divine attributes of God the Son that might explain Him to those who do not know anything about the Lord Jesus Christ.
a. **God the Son Was Miraculously Born Of A Virgin.** As such, <u>He had no human father</u>, but God the Holy Spirit conceived Him in Mary who was a virgin.
b. **God the Son Was Both Perfect God And Perfect Man.** This was because of the miracle of His virgin birth. Many have denied the virgin birth of Christ. They say 'we don't have to believe that to be saved.' They do. <u>Unless He were the God-Man (THEANTHROPOS), He could not be anyone's Saviour and Redeemer.</u>
c. **God the Son Is Omniscient.** Like God the Father, <u>He knows everything about everything</u>. He can read the hearts and minds of all the people of the earth.
d. **God the Son Is Omnipotent.** <u>He is all-powerful</u>, As such, He could heal diseases and perform many other kinds of miracles.
e. **God the Son Is Omnipresent.** <u>He is present everywhere</u>.

f. **God the Son Is Sinless.** This is why He could take the sins of the entire world upon Himself.
g. **God the Son performed miracles.** All kinds of miracles were performed by the Lord Jesus Christ. He raised the dead. He made the blind to see. He opened the ears of the deaf. He healed leprosy, and did many other miracles as God the Son.
h. **God the Son Shed His Blood As Payment For The Sins Of The World.** This included everyone who has ever been born, not just a small group of the "elect" has some erroneously teach.
i. **God the Son rose bodily from the grave after three days and three nights.** His resurrection was not merely spiritual as many false "Christian" churches believe. It was bodily. Matthew 28:6 declares: *"He is not here: for he is risen, as he said. Come, see the place where the Lord lay."*
j. **God the Son Ascended Bodily Into Heaven.** Forty days after His bodily resurrection, He ascended bodily into Heaven.
k. **God the Son Will Return In The Air For All His Saved Ones.** That is called the Rapture, spoken of in 1 Thessalonians and in other places in the New Testament.
l. **After The Seven Year Tribulation, God the Son will return to earth To Reign For One Thousand Years.** This is called the Millennium. Peace will finally prevail throughout the world.
m. **God the Son Commanded The True Christians To Preach The Gospel To Every Creature.** The Biblical gospel message is to be proclaimed throughout the world so that whosoever is willing might truly come to the Saviour and receive Him as their own.
n. **God the Son Is The Great High Priest In Heaven For Those Who Are True Christians.** As the genuine Christian's Great High Priest, He cares for them and represents them.
o. **God the Son Is Interceding For Those He Has Saved.** One of the ministries of the Lord Jesus Christ as the true Christians' Great High Priest is for Him to intercede and pray for them. He is their Advocate or Lawyer to ward off the attacks of Satan against them.
p. **God the Son Is Seated At The Right Hand Of God The Father.** This is the place of honor that God the

Father has given His Son Who died on the cross for the sins of the world and in Whom God the Father is well pleased.

These genuine Christians in the church at Thessalonica were joined to both God the Father (with all of His attributes) and to God the Son (with all of His attributes). That union is a precious and eternal union.

2 Thessalonians 1:2

"Grace unto you, and peace, from God our Father and the Lord Jesus Christ."

GREEK (CHARIS) AND HEBREW (SHALOM) GREETINGS

Paul greeted the true Christians at Thessalonica with two different words. *"Grace"* (CHARIS) is the greeting for the Greek Gentiles. It means getting something you don't deserve. It means unmerited favor from God. *"Peace"* is EIRENE in Greek, but in Hebrew it is SHALOM. That is the usual greeting for the Jews. With these words of greeting both the Greeks and the Hebrews are greeted by Paul. This twofold greeting is extended both from God the Father and from God the Son, the Lord Jesus Christ. Both have been mentioned the first verse.

Verses On Grace

- **Genesis 6:7-8**

"And the LORD said, I will destroy man whom I have created from the face of the earth; both man, and beast, and the creeping thing, and the fowls of the air; for it repenteth me that I have made them. But Noah found grace in the eyes of the LORD."

Though the entire world of his day was evil and ready to be destroyed, Noah found grace in the eyes of God and was delivered from the judgment of the flood.

- **John 1:14**

"And the Word was made flesh, and dwelt among us, (and we beheld his glory, the glory as of the only begotten of the Father,) full of grace and truth."

THE LORD JESUS CHRIST--FULL OF GRACE AND TRUTH

The Lord Jesus Christ was full of truth, but also full of grace as He dwelt here on earth among men for around thirty-three years.

- **John 1:17**

"For the law was given by Moses, *but* grace and truth came by Jesus Christ."

> **LAW AND GRACE CONTRASTED**
> This is a contrast between the law of Moses, which was a system of works, and the ministry of the Lord Jesus Christ, which was a ministry of grace and truth.

- Acts 15:11

"But we believe that through the grace of the Lord Jesus Christ we shall be saved, even as they."

> **BOTH JEWS AND GENTILES CAN BE SAVED BY FAITH**
> Paul and Barnabas stated that the Gentiles who truly believed on the Lord Jesus Christ would be just as saved by God's grace as the Jews who did the same. Good works cannot save a person. This can be only accomplished by God's grace and the merits of His Son, the Lord Jesus Christ.

- Romans 3:24

"Being justified freely by his grace through the redemption that is in Christ Jesus:"

"Freely" means without any payment at all. The redemptive payment was by the sacrificial death of the Lord Jesus Christ at Calvary which can only be received by genuine faith in Him.

- 2 Corinthians 8:9

"For ye know the grace of our Lord Jesus Christ, that, though he was rich, yet for your sakes he became poor, that ye through his poverty might be rich."

> **CHRIST BECAME POOR–TRUE CHRISTIANS MADE RICH**
> Only by the grace of the Lord Jesus Christ--Who came from Heaven to die on the cross to save those who truly trust in Him--can any who are poor in spirit be made rich in Him.

- Ephesians 1:7

"In whom we have redemption through his blood, the forgiveness of sins, according to the riches of his grace;"

Only by the riches of the grace of the Lord Jesus Christ can genuine Christians have redemption and forgiveness. The Gnostic Critical Greek Texts of Vatican ("B") and Sinai ("Aleph") wrongly omit *"through His blood."* This is because they downplayed the necessity of the shedding of the Lord Jesus Christ's blood to bring this redemption and forgiveness.

- Ephesians 2:8-10

"For by grace are ye saved through faith; and that not of yourselves: *it is* the gift of God: Not of works, lest any man should boast. For we are his workmanship, created in Christ Jesus unto good works, which God hath before ordained that we should walk in them."

TRUE FAITH WITHOUT WORKS BRINGS SALVATION
It's God's grace that gave salvation and it's by true faith that Christians can receive it. It is not by any works that we could do. After genuine Christians are born-again and saved, they are to do works that please the Lord.

- **Titus 2:11-12**

"For the grace of God that bringeth salvation hath appeared to all men, Teaching us that, denying ungodliness and worldly lusts, we should live soberly, righteously, and godly, in this present world;"
It is only by God's grace that salvation was made possible for lost and dying sinners. Those who truly trust the Lord Jesus Christ as their Saviour will be saved.

Verses On Peace

- **Romans 5:1**

"Therefore being justified by faith, we have peace with God through our Lord Jesus Christ:"
The only way a person can have peace with the Bible's God is by being justified by genuine faith in the Lord Jesus Who is God.

- **Philippians 4:6-7**

"Be careful for nothing; but in every thing by prayer and supplication with thanksgiving let your requests be made known unto God. And the peace of God, which passeth all understanding, shall keep your hearts and minds through Christ Jesus."
This verse talks about the peace "*of*" God. The preceding verse talked about peace "*with*" God. The peace of God surpasses all our understanding. It is able to keep the hearts and minds of true Christians through the Lord Jesus Christ, even in very trying circumstances.

2 Thessalonians 1:3

"We are bound to thank God always for you, brethren, as it is meet, because that your faith groweth exceedingly, and the charity of every one of you all toward each other aboundeth;"

COMMENDED FOR BIBLE KNOWLEDGE AND LOVE
Paul is writing to genuine Christians. He calls them "*brethren*" because they are true members of God's family. He is determined to give continuous thanks for them for two main reasons.

> (1) Their knowledge of the doctrines of the faith is growing exceedingly, and
> (2) their love toward one another is abounding. I wish that true Christians today would have similar qualities so people could thank God for them because of it.

Verses On Faith

Here are some verses that emphasize the importance of holding to sound doctrines and teachings of the "faith" which are found in the Bible.

- **Acts 14:22**

"Confirming the souls of the disciples, *and* exhorting them to continue in the faith, and that we must through much tribulation enter into the kingdom of God."

With the Greek article, *"the faith"* indicates the entire body of doctrine and theology of the Christian faith. Every Genuine Christian should continue in this by the diligent study of God's Words.

- **Acts 16:5**

"And so were the churches established in the faith, and increased in number daily."

Again, *"faith"* is with the Greek article, thus referring to doctrines and teachings of the Bible. These true Christians were established and founded in this vital area without any drift or changes.

- **2 Corinthians 10:15**

"Not boasting of things without *our* measure, *that is*, of other men's labours; but having hope, when your faith is increased, that we shall be enlarged by you according to our rule abundantly,"

Paul was not a boaster of other's men's labours. Since there is a Greek article with *"faith,"* it refers to their understanding of the doctrines and teachings of the Bible.

- **Colossians 1:22-23**

"In the body of his flesh through death, to present you holy and unblameable and unreproveable in his sight: If ye continue in the faith grounded and settled, and *be* not moved away from the hope of the gospel, which ye have heard, *and* which was preached to every creature which is under heaven; whereof I Paul am made a minister;"

Writing from prison, Paul wrote this letter to the Colossians. Paul wanted the genuine Christians at Colosse to *"continue"* in the body of doctrine found in the Bible. They should be grounded and settled in their Bible doctrines and theology with strong convictions.

- **Colossians 2:5**
"For though I be absent in the flesh, yet am I with you in the spirit, joying and beholding your order, and the stedfastness of your faith in Christ."
These true Christians were told to be steadfast in their Biblical doctrines. There should be no turning back or fluctuating from the Bible's truths.
- **Colossians 2:7**
"Rooted and built up in him, and stablished in the faith, as ye have been taught, abounding therein with thanksgiving."
Again, with the Greek article (HE), *"faith"* is referring to the doctrines of the faith and beliefs as found in the Bible. These genuine Christians should be established, grounded, and abounding in these teachings with thanksgiving as they were taught by Paul
- **1 Thessalonians 3:2**
"And sent Timotheus, our brother, and minister of God, and our fellowlabourer in the gospel of Christ, to establish you, and to comfort you concerning your faith:"
Why did Timothy go? Why did Paul send him to Thessalonica? Number one, to establish the genuine Christians there and found them on concrete rather than on sand in regard to their Bible doctrines and beliefs. The Greek article is used again with *"faith."*
- **1 Thessalonians 3:10**
"Night and day praying exceedingly that we might see your face, and might perfect that which is lacking in your faith?"
That was Paul's prayer. He wanted to mature and perfect that which was lacking in their understanding of the doctrines of the faith and Bible teachings.
- **Titus 1:13**
"This witness is true. Wherefore rebuke them sharply, that they may be sound in the faith;"

UNBIBLICAL TEACHERS MUST BE REBUKED SHARPLY
False and unBiblical teachers are to be rebuked sharply. The Greek article is again used here with *"faith,"* meaning the doctrines of Bible. Soundness in the doctrines and theology of the Bible is of paramount importance for true Christians today as well as in Paul's day.

Verses On Love

The second thing Paul thanked God for concerning the genuine Christians at Thessalonica was for their abounding love for one another. It is difficult sometimes to have love and charity towards fellow believers. God was able to give them this love through the power of the Holy Spirit.

- **2 Corinthians 2:4**

"For out of much affliction and anguish of heart I wrote unto you with many tears; not that ye should be grieved, but that ye might know the love which I have more abundantly unto you."

PAUL EXPLAINED HIS NEED FOR TOUGH LOVE

This is the second letter to the true Christians at Corinth. Paul scolded them in his first letter because they had permitted an incestuous man in their fellowship. A member of their church had sex with his own mother-in-law. In that letter, Paul was very harsh with the church. They finally removed this man from the church, but he was restored after confessing his sin, repenting, and getting back into fellowship with the Lord Jesus Christ. Paul reminded the church that it was out of his abundant love he wrote his first letter. His purpose was to restore the church to fellowship with the Lord and obedience to Him. Judgment for that sin had to precede Paul's abounding love.

- **2 Corinthians 12:15**

"And I will very gladly spend and be spent for you; though the more abundantly I love you, the less I be loved."

Though Paul loved the Corinthians abundantly, they didn't love him. Many times this is true with true Christians today. The reasons for this are varied. It is strange, but true.

- **1 Thessalonians 3:12**

"And the Lord make you to increase and abound in love one toward another, and toward all *men*, even as we *do* toward you:"

LOVE ONE ANOTHER AS PAUL LOVED THEM

Paul loved them and he wanted their love to abound to genuine Christians and toward all others as well.

- **1 Peter 1:22**

"Seeing ye have purified your souls in obeying the truth through the Spirit unto unfeigned love of the brethren, *see that ye* love one another with a pure heart fervently:"

True Christian love should be with a pure heart and fervent.

2 Thessalonians 1:4

"So that we ourselves glory in you in the churches of God for your patience and faith in all your persecutions and tribulations that ye endure:"

PATIENCE AND FAITH AND ENDURING PERSECUTIONS
Paul was pleased with the church at Thessalonica for two things especially. First, they had patience and faith, which all true Christians need. Second, they endured persecutions and tribulations because of their faith.

Verses On Patience

- **Romans 5:3**

"And not only *so*, but we glory in tribulations also: knowing that tribulation worketh patience;"

That's something that is difficult to do unless true Christians have the Spirit of God controlling them. That's the only way they can glory in persecutions and tribulations [THLIPSIS]. These tribulations bring forth patience provided that genuine Christians are willing to learn from them.

- **Romans 15:4**

"For whatsoever things were written aforetime were written for our learning, that we through patience and comfort of the scriptures might have hope."

Though all of the Scriptures of the Old Testament were not written **to** true Christians today, they were written **for** their learning. They give them patience and comfort that brings forth hope.

- **2 Corinthians 6:4**

"But in all *things* approving ourselves as the ministers of God, in much patience, in afflictions, in necessities, in distresses,"

GENUINE CHRISTIANS NEED MUCH PATIENCE
The first thing that genuine Christians should be approving themselves in, as God's ministers, is much patience. That is not an easy feat. It can only be accomplished if they are walking daily with the Lord Jesus Christ in obedience to God's Words.

- **Hebrews 12:1**

"Wherefore seeing we also are compassed about with so great a cloud of witnesses, let us lay aside every weight, and the sin which doth so easily beset *us*, and let us run with patience the race that is set before us,"

The cloud of witnesses refers to the many heroes of the faith from the Old Testament who are mentioned in Hebrews chapter 11. True Christians are exhorted to run their race with patience just like the Old Testament believers did. Everyone's race is different. They must run the race that is before them, looking unto the Lord Jesus Christ to help them in that race.

- James 5:10

"Take, my brethren, the prophets, who have spoken in the name of the Lord, for an example of suffering affliction, and of patience."

O. T. PROPHETS ARE EXAMPLES OF SUFFERING

The Old Testament prophets were examples of suffering and also of patience. This includes Isaiah, Jeremiah, Ezekiel, Daniel, and all the others.

- James 5:11

"Behold, we count them happy which endure. Ye have heard of the patience of Job, and have seen the end of the Lord; that the Lord is very pitiful, and of tender mercy."

JOB, A MAN OF GREAT PATIENCE

In this verse, Job is singled out as a man of patience. His calamities were the result of Satan's testings. He was not perfect, but God commended him for his patience in the many things that he suffered.

- Revelation 1:9

"I John, who also am your brother, and companion in tribulation, and in the kingdom and patience of Jesus Christ, was in the isle that is called Patmos, for the word of God, and for the testimony of Jesus Christ."

THE APOSTLE JOHN WAS PATIENT ON PATMOS ISLAND

The apostle John was exiled to the isle of Patmos because of his testimony for the Lord Jesus Christ. Yet, in all of the hardships in that island, he had the patience given to him from the Lord Jesus Christ.

2 Thessalonians 1:5

"Which is a manifest token of the righteous judgment of God, that ye may be counted worthy of the kingdom of God, for which ye also suffer:"

All of these torments and persecutions are "*a manifest token of the righteous judgment of God.*" God and his judgment is always righteous.

People don't think so, but it is true because God's Words in the Bible say it is so. Both God and His judgments are righteous no matter what people might think about them.

Verses On Judgment

God was about ready to judge Sodom and Gomorrah and wipe them off the face of the earth because of their sins of Sodomy and other evils. God told Abraham about it. Abraham then gave God an objection.

- **Genesis 18:25**

"That be far from thee to do after this manner, to slay the righteous with the wicked: and that the righteous should be as the wicked, that be far from thee: Shall not the Judge of all the earth do right?"

Abraham didn't want this judgment to come to his nephew, Lot. The Lord explained to Abraham that He **always** does right. He allowed "*just*" Lot (2 Peter 2:7), his wife, and his two daughters to escape the judgment of Sodom and Gomorrah. Lot's wife escaped the city, but she looked back and was slain by the Lord because of it.

- **Deuteronomy 32:4**

"*He is* the Rock, his work *is* perfect: for all his ways *are* judgment: a God of truth and without iniquity, just and right *is* he."

God is righteous and just. His judgments are always just.

- **Job 8:3**

"Doth God pervert judgment? or doth the Almighty pervert justice?"

No, He does not. He never twists or perverts either judgment or justice. God is always right in His judgments regardless of how perverted many things are in the world.

- **Job 34:12**

"Yea, surely God will not do wickedly, neither will the Almighty pervert judgment."

God never does any wickedness, nor does he pervert judgment.

- **Psalms 9:8**

"And he shall judge the world in righteousness, he shall minister judgment to the people in uprightness."

GOD'S JUDGMENTS ARE ALWAYS RIGHTEOUS

God's righteous judgments are for both the genuine Christians at the Judgment Seat of Christ (1 Corinthians 3:9-15) and for the unsaved people at the Great White Throne Judgment (Revelation 20:11)

- **Jeremiah 4:2**

"And thou shalt swear, The LORD liveth, in truth, in judgment, and in righteousness; and the nations shall bless themselves in him, and in him shall they glory."

> **GOD IS PERFECT IN RIGHTEOUSNESS AND HOLINESS**
> The God of the Bible is perfect and complete in His righteousness and holiness. There is no sin or evil in Him at all. The Lord Jesus Christ had no sin of any kind in Him until He took the sins of the whole world in His own body on the cross of Calvary.

- Jeremiah 9:24

"But let him that glorieth glory in this, that he understandeth and knoweth me, that I am the LORD which exercise lovingkindness, judgment, and righteousness, in the earth: for in these *things* I delight, saith the LORD."

Our God always exercises and delights in judgment and righteousness.

- John 5:22

"For the Father judgeth no man, but hath committed all judgment unto the Son:"

> **THE LORD JESUS CHRIST IS THE JUDGE OF ALL**
> The Son, the Lord Jesus Christ, will also judge righteously like God the Father. All judgment of people will be by the Son of God, the Lord Jesus Christ. This will be both at the Judgment Seat of Christ for true Christians and at the Great White Throne for all the lost people of the world.

- John 5:30

"I can of mine own self do nothing: as I hear, I judge: and my judgment is just; because I seek not mine own will, but the will of the Father which hath sent me."

The judgment of the Lord Jesus Christ is and will always be absolutely just and righteous.

- John 7:24

"Judge not according to the appearance, but judge righteous judgment."

> **CHRISTIANS SHOULD JUDGE RIGHTEOUS JUDGMENT**
> Genuine Christians should not judge on outward appearances, but should judge righteously based on all the facts. The Lord Jesus Christ commanded Christians to judge righteous judgment, though some disagree with the Lord Jesus Christ Himself and do not think they should judge at all. They are wrong and against the Bible in this.

- **Romans 2:5**
"But after thy hardness and impenitent heart treasurest up unto thyself wrath against the day of wrath and revelation of the righteous judgment of God;"

THE RIGHTEOUS JUDGMENT OF GOD
God's judgments are always righteous, even though people do not always understand them. The Judgment Seat of Christ where true Christians are judged will be perfectly righteous. The Great White Throne Judgment where all the unsaved will appear is also a perfectly righteous judgment.

- **2 Corinthians 5:10**
"For we must all appear before the judgment seat of Christ; that every one may receive the things *done* in *his* body, according to that he hath done, whether *it be* good or bad."

This is a summary of what will happen in the righteous judgment by the Lord Jesus Christ at the Judgment Seat of Christ.

- **Hebrews 9:27**
"And as it is appointed unto men once to die, but after this the judgment:"

THE JUDGMENT SEAT OF CHRIST
After physical death both genuine Christians and the unsaved will face a righteous judgment by the Lord Jesus Christ. The true Christians will appear before the Judgment Seat of Christ in righteous judgment. The unsaved and lost people will appear before the Great White Throne in righteous judgment.

- **Revelation 20:11**
"And I saw a great white throne, and him that sat on it, from whose face the earth and the heaven fled away; and there was found no place for them."

This is the righteous judgment of the unsaved and lost–both men and women. These people will be consigned by the Lord Jesus Christ to the Lake of Fire which is Hell.

- **Revelation 20:12**
"And I saw the dead, small and great, stand before God; and the books were opened: and another book was opened, which is *the book* of life: and the dead were judged out of those things which were written in the books, according to their works."

As the Lord Jesus Christ said, Sodom and Gomorrah will have it easier in the judgment than those people to whom He ministered when He was on this earth who rejected Him.

"Verily I say unto you, It shall be more tolerable for the land of Sodom and Gomorrha in the day of judgment, than for that city." (Matthew 10:15)
This indicates there will be degrees of punishment for the lost, though they will all be in Hell. Just like there will be degrees of blessings for the genuine Christians at the Judgment Seat of Christ. Some will have rewards in Heaven, and others will not.

2 Thessalonians 1:6

"Seeing it is a righteous thing with God to recompense tribulation to them that trouble you;"

God is a Righteous Judge. He will recompense and pay back those people who are persecuting and troubling the true Christians in Thessalonica.

God's judgment of Pharaoh, the king of Egypt, is an example of His righteous judgment. After God judged Pharaoh and the people of Egypt, with ten different plagues, He led the Israelites out of Egyptian bondage. 600,000 men of Israel, plus women and children, were freed by God's recompensing tribulation to those who had troubled them.

God righteous judgment against Haman in the book of Esther is another example of His recompense to this leader who troubled and wanted to kill His people, Israel. Because of his evil, Haman was hanged on the gallows he made for Mordecai.

Verses On God's Recompensing

Here are some verses that show how God recompenses those who trouble his people.

- **Psalms 35:1**
  "Plead *my cause*, O LORD, with them that strive with me: fight against them that fight against me."

David asked the LORD to plead his cause and recompense those who were his enemies.

- **Isaiah 35:4**
  "Say to them *that are* of a fearful heart, Be strong, fear not: behold, your God will come *with* vengeance, *even* God *with* a recompence; he will come and save you."

Here is God's promise to recompense and judge.

- **Isaiah 59:18**
  "According to *their* deeds, accordingly he will repay, fury to his adversaries, recompence to his enemies; to the islands he will repay recompence."

So God is going to render fair and righteous recompense to His enemies.

- **Isaiah 66:6**
"A voice of noise from the city, a voice from the temple, a voice of the LORD that rendereth recompence to his enemies."
God paid back and recompensed His enemies in the Old Testament and will do it in the New Testament as well.
- **Romans 1:27**
"And likewise also the men, leaving the natural use of the woman, burned in their lust one toward another; men with men working that which is unseemly, and receiving in themselves that recompence of their error which was meet."

GOD RECOMPENSES FOR AND JUDGES ALL SIN
Regardless of the legalization of the sin and corruption of homosexuality, God's Word is clear here that this is sin and contains His recompense for their error which is fitting.

- **Romans 1:26**
"For this cause God gave them up unto vile affections: for even their women did change the natural use into that which is against nature:"
This verse takes up the sin of women homosexuals or lesbians. They also die younger than many of non-Lesbian women. God's Word is very clear against this wicked sin. Because our country and culture has thrown out the Bible, the sin of male and female Sodomy has become accepted and acceptable. Sodom and Gomorrah conditions are alive and well in the United Sates of America, and in the world in general.
Here is a LINK that discusses mortality rates of same sex men and women couples that you might want to look into:
http://www.ncbi.nlm.nih.gov/pmc/articles/PMC2636618/
- **Hebrews 2:2-3**
"For if the word spoken by angels was stedfast, and every transgression and disobedience received a just recompence of reward; How shall we escape, if we neglect so great salvation; which at the first began to be spoken by the Lord, and was confirmed unto us by them that heard *him*;"

GOD JUDGED SODOM, GOMORRAH, AND THE WORLD
If God fulfilled His judgment of the angels, and the world with Noah and the world with Sodom and Gomorrah, how shall anyone escape if they neglect so great of salvation? This Biblical salvation is only found in truly receiving the Lord Jesus Christ as Saviour and Redeemer.

2 Thessalonians 1:7

"And to you who are troubled rest with us, when the Lord Jesus shall be revealed from heaven with his mighty angels,"

> **THE SECOND PHASE OF CHRIST'S RETURN**
> Paul is speaking here of the Lord Jesus Christ being *"revealed from Heaven with His mighty angels."* Paul is referring to the second phase of the Lord Jesus Christ's second coming. It is when He comes with His mighty angels to earth to set up His millennial kingdom for 1,000 years.

In this verse, the Rapture of all the true Christians has already taken place, as well as the seven-year Tribulation period. After this Tribulation period, Satan will cause all the nations of the earth to assemble around Jerusalem to destroy it and all the Jews who inhabit it. The Lord Jesus Christ, at the second phase of His coming, will destroy these Satanic warriors and prevent their plan of Jerusalem's and the Jews' destruction.

Verses On The Wicked

- Psalms 37:7

"Rest in the LORD, and wait patiently for him: fret not thyself because of him who prospereth in his way, because of the man who bringeth wicked devices to pass."

The wicked bring wicked devices to pass. The genuine Christian is not to be concerned about these wicked people.

- Isaiah 57:20

"But the wicked *are* like the troubled sea, when it cannot rest, whose waters cast up mire and dirt."

There is no rest to the wicked. They are like the troubled waves of the sea.

- Isaiah 48:22

"There is no peace, saith the LORD, unto the wicked."

There is no peace to the wicked people who are not true Christians. Genuine Christians can find rest even in troublesome times.

Verses On The Rest Found In Christ

- Matthew 11:28-30

"Come unto me, all *ye* that labour and are heavy laden, and I will give you rest. Take my yoke upon you, and learn of me; for I am meek and lowly in heart: and ye shall find rest unto your souls. For my yoke *is* easy, and my burden is light."

CHRIST INVITES ALL TO COME UNTO HIM
All people are invited by the Lord Jesus Christ to come unto Him, take His yoke upon them, learn of Him, and find His rest.

- **Mark 6:31**
"And he said unto them, Come ye yourselves apart into a desert place, and rest a while: for there were many coming and going, and they had no leisure so much as to eat."

PHYSICAL REST IS NECESSARY FOR SERVICE
The disciples were told by the Lord Jesus Christ that they needed some physical rest in the desert where there was peace and quietness.

- **Acts 9:31**
"Then had the churches rest throughout all Judaea and Galilee and Samaria, and were edified; and walking in the fear of the Lord, and in the comfort of the Holy Ghost, were multiplied."

At this time the churches that once had turmoil now had rest of soul and were edified by the Lord.

- **Hebrews 4:3**
"For we which have believed do enter into rest, as he said, As I have sworn in my wrath, if they shall enter into my rest: although the works were finished from the foundation of the world."

The true Christian who has been redeemed by the Lord Jesus Christ has been promised His rest.

- **Revelation 14:10-11**
"The same shall drink of the wine of the wrath of God, which is poured out without mixture into the cup of his indignation; and he shall be tormented with fire and brimstone in the presence of the holy angels, and in the presence of the Lamb: And the smoke of their torment ascendeth up for ever and ever: and they have no rest day nor night, who worship the beast and his image, and whosoever receiveth the mark of his name."

THE EVERLASTING TORMENT OF HELL'S FIRES
In the fires of everlasting Hell, there is no rest for those who have rejected the grace and everlasting life obtained from genuine trust in the Lord Jesus Christ as their Saviour.

- **Revelation 14:13**
"And I heard a voice from heaven saying unto me, Write, Blessed *are* the dead which die in the Lord from henceforth: yea, saith the

Spirit, that they may rest from their labours; and their works do follow them."

Those true Christians who die in the Lord will have perfect rest in Heaven for all eternity to come.

Verses On Judgment And The Battle Of Armageddon

When the Lord Jesus Christ returns to earth after the seven-year Tribulation period, He will judge those who are warring against His people and Jerusalem at the Battle of Armageddon. It will be a ferocious and furious scene.

- **Revelation 19:11**

"And I saw heaven opened, and behold a white horse; and he that sat upon him *was* called Faithful and True, and in righteousness he doth judge and make war."

CHRIST WILL WIN THE BATTLE OF ARMAGEDDON

The Lord Jesus Christ is the One on the white horse Who will judge and make war with the armies of Satan at the Battle of Armageddon.

- **Revelation 19:12**

"His eyes *were* as a flame of fire, and on his head *were* many crowns; and he had a name written, that no man knew, but he himself."

The Lord Jesus Christ is described here as He returns to this earth before the Millennium begins.

- **Revelation 19:13**

"And he *was* clothed with a vesture dipped in blood: and his name is called The Word of God."

His vesture and His Name are described in this verse.

- **Revelation 19:14**

"And the armies *which were* in heaven followed him upon white horses, clothed in fine linen, white and clean."

RESURRECTED CHRISTIANS WILL BE AT CHRIST'S SIDE

Those armies who follow the Lord Jesus Christ in this battle of Armageddon are the genuine Christians in their resurrected bodies. They will be on white horses, clothed in white and clean garments.

- **Revelation 19:15**

"And out of his mouth goeth a sharp sword, that with it he should smite the nations: and he shall rule them with a rod of iron: and he treadeth the winepress of the fierceness and wrath of Almighty God."

CHRIST WILL SET UP HIS 1,000-YEAR REIGN
The Lord Jesus Christ will smite these nations with His sharp sword and then set up His 1,000-year Millennium where he will rule as with a rod of iron.

- **Revelation 19:16**

"And he hath on *his* vesture and on his thigh a name written, KING OF KINGS, AND LORD OF LORDS."

This is a further description of the Lord Jesus Christ and His Name as KING OF KINGS AND LORD OF LORDS.

- **Revelation 19:17**

"And I saw an angel standing in the sun; and he cried with a loud voice, saying to all the fowls that fly in the midst of heaven, Come and gather yourselves together unto the supper of the great God;"

BIRDS WILL HAVE A SUPPER AFTER ARMAGEDDON
The fowls of the air will be invited to the supper of the great God. They will eat the dead bodies of those who will be slain at the Battle of Armageddon.

- **Revelation 19:18**

"That ye may eat the flesh of kings, and the flesh of captains, and the flesh of mighty men, and the flesh of horses, and of them that sit on them, and the flesh of all *men, both* free and bond, both small and great."

Multitudes—bond and free, small and great--will die and their bodies will be eaten by the hungry fowls of the air in this battle.

- **Revelation 19:19**

"And I saw the beast, and the kings of the earth, and their armies, gathered together to make war against him that sat on the horse, and against his army."

Satan and his kings and armies will be making war here against the Lord Jesus Christ and His army.

- **Revelation 19:20**

"And the beast was taken, and with him the false prophet that wrought miracles before him, with which he deceived them that had received the mark of the beast, and them that worshipped his image. These both were cast alive into a lake of fire burning with brimstone."

RELIGIOUS AND POLITICAL BEASTS CAST INTO HELL
Both the political beast and the religious beast are taken here and cast alive into Hell which is described as a lake of fire burning with brimstone.

- **Revelation 19:21**
"And the remnant were slain with the sword of him that sat upon the horse, which *sword* proceeded out of his mouth: and all the fowls were filled with their flesh."
At this battle of Armageddon Satan and all his armies will be slain by the Lord Jesus Christ. Their bodies will be meat for the fowls of the air.

2 Thessalonians 1:8
"In flaming fire taking vengeance on them that know not God, and that obey not the gospel of our Lord Jesus Christ:"

THE SECOND PHASE OF CHRIST'S RETURN
This verse describes the second phrase of the coming of the Lord Jesus Christ. He will come in flaming fire to take vengeance on those who are lost and who have not obeyed the gospel of the Lord Jesus Christ. This flaming fire is just as literal as the fires in Hell are literal.

Rick Warren won't speak about the literal fire in Hell. In fact, Billy Graham, in the 1950s, proclaimed very clearly that he did not believe there was literal fire in Hell. Others who are new evangelicals agree with Billy Graham on this serious Biblical error.

CHRIST WILL RETURN TO EARTH IN FLAMING FIRE
One day the Lord Jesus Christ will return to this earth in the second phase of His return. It will not be as the gentle Saviour to offer salvation to those who truly believe on Him. On the contrary, it will be for judgment. It will be in flaming fire to take vengeance on Satan and his followers.

Verses On God's Vengeance
- **Deuteronomy 32:41**
"If I whet my glittering sword, and mine hand take hold on judgment; I will render vengeance to mine enemies, and will reward them that hate me."
God will render righteous vengeance on all His enemies.
- **Deuteronomy 32:43**
"Rejoice, O ye nations, *with* his people: for he will avenge the blood of his servants, and will render vengeance to his adversaries, and will be merciful unto his land, *and* to his people."
God will render vengeance on His adversaries. Though it might be postponed, it will come. He's not on our time schedule.

- **Jeremiah 46:10**
"For this *is* the day of the Lord GOD of hosts, a day of vengeance, that he may avenge him of his adversaries: and the sword shall devour, and it shall be satiate and made drunk with their blood: for the Lord GOD of hosts hath a sacrifice in the north country by the river Euphrates."

God is a God of love, but He's also a God of righteousness. As such, he must judge sin. This will take place in the day of the Lord. That's when God himself will take vengeance on the adversaries.

- **Romans 3:5**
"But if our unrighteousness commend the righteousness of God, what shall we say? *Is* God unrighteous who taketh vengeance? (I speak as a man)"

God is not unrighteous when He takes vengeance. He's doing it in a righteous path because the people he judges deserve that righteous judgment.

- **Romans 12:19**
"Dearly beloved, avenge not yourselves, but *rather* give place unto wrath: for it is written, Vengeance *is* mine; I will repay, saith the Lord."

The Lord Jesus Christ must be in charge of vengeance, not the genuine Christians.

- **Jude 1:7**
"Even as Sodom and Gomorrha, and the cities about them in like manner, giving themselves over to fornication, and going after strange flesh, are set forth for an example, suffering the vengeance of eternal fire."

MANY U.S.A. CITIES ARE SODOMITE CITIES

These were two Sodomite cities of ancient times. Like these two cities, many of the cities of the United States have become Sodomite cities. The Supreme Court has decreed that it is all right to have homosexual marriages—men with men and women with women. This ungodly Sodomy is strongly condemned in the both Old and the New Testaments of the Bible. If God strongly judged and eradicated Sodom and Gomorrah for their Sodomite and other wicked practices, when is He going to judge the United States of America in like manner? God brought fire and brimstone on them and saved only four people from the overthrow.

2 Thessalonians 1:9

"Who shall be punished with everlasting destruction from the presence of the Lord, and from the glory of his power;"

THE EVERLASTING PUNISHMENT OF THE UNSAVED

Paul is talking about people who have never genuinely received the Lord Jesus Christ as their Saviour. God promises in this verse everlasting destruction from God's presence and glorious power. This involves the everlasting and literal fires of Hell. This is something you will not hear from many modern preachers. They don't speak about the everlasting fires of Hell. They just talk about nice things in order to bring in the crowds. But the Bible speaks of the everlasting fire in Hell.

- Revelation 19:20

"And the beast was taken, and with him the false prophet that wrought miracles before him, with which he deceived them that had received the mark of the beast, and them that worshipped his image. These both were cast alive into a lake of fire burning with brimstone."

This will be the fate of the false prophet and the political beast of the end times.

- Revelation 20:10

"And the devil that deceived them was cast into the lake of fire and brimstone, where the beast and the false prophet *are*, and shall be tormented day and night for ever and ever."

This Lake of Fire is real. It torments forever and ever. Notice, after 1,000 years, the political beast and false prophet are still there, alive, and in torment. They are not burned up and put out of existence, but are still in conscious torment in the everlasting fires of Hell.

TEACHING NO LITERAL HELL IS HERESY!

Those who teach that either there is no literal Hell with fire, or that Hell is not everlasting are teaching heresy.

- Revelation 20:11-14

"And I saw a great white throne, and him that sat on it, from whose face the earth and the heaven fled away; and there was found no place for them. And I saw the dead, small and great, stand before God; and the books were opened: and another book was opened, which is *the book* of life: and the dead were judged out of those

things which were written in the books, according to their works. And the sea gave up the dead which were in it; and death and hell delivered up the dead which were in them: and they were judged every man according to their works. And death and hell were cast into the lake of fire. This is the second death."
Those who have rejected the Lord Jesus Christ as their Saviour, and are therefore unsaved, will suffer what the Bible calls "*the second death.*" This puts these who are not genuine Christians into the eternal and conscious suffering in the literal fire of Hell.

People who follow Dave Hunt's perverted view that the everlasting fire of Hell is not literal fire, are believing a heretical view of the Lake of Fire or Hell. Billy Graham, in the 1950's, also taught this perversion of there not being any real fire in the Lake of Fire.

Verses On Everlasting, Literal Fire In Hell
- **Matthew 18:8**

"Wherefore if thy hand or thy foot offend thee, cut them off, and cast *them* from thee: it is better for thee to enter into life halt or maimed, rather than having two hands or two feet to be cast into everlasting fire."

HELL AND ETERNAL LIFE ARE BOTH EVERLASTING

Just as eternal life is everlasting life, so everlasting fire is eternal and real fire. There is no such thing as the Roman Catholic purgatory. Those who die go either to Heaven or to the fires of Hell.

- **Matthew 25:41**

"Then shall he say also unto them on the left hand, Depart from me, ye cursed, into everlasting fire, prepared for the devil and his angels:"
The fires of Hell were prepared for the Devil and his angels. Those who follow him rather than the Lord Jesus Christ go to the Devil's place for all eternity.

- **Matthew 25:46**

"And these shall go away into everlasting punishment: but the righteous into life eternal."
Hell is everlasting punishment. It has no end.

- **Mark 9:43**

"And if thy hand offend thee, cut it off: it is better for thee to enter into life maimed, than having two hands to go into hell, into the fire that never shall be quenched:"
This plain talk by the Lord Jesus Christ lets us draw two conclusions:
(1) Hell has literal fire.
(2) It is eternal fire that never shall be quenched.

- Jude 1:6

"And the angels which kept not their first estate, but left their own habitation, he hath reserved in everlasting chains under darkness unto the judgment of the great day."

The chains of Hell are everlasting chains. It is never ending.

- Jude 1:7

"Even as Sodom and Gomorrah, and the cities about them in like manner, giving themselves over to fornication, and going after strange flesh, are set forth for an example, suffering the vengeance of eternal fire."

Here again, Hell has literal fire and it is *"eternal fire."* Just as eternal life is eternal, so the second death in Hell is eternal fire.

2 Thessalonians 1:10

"When he shall come to be glorified in his saints, and to be admired in all them that believe (because our testimony among you was believed) in that day."

CHRIST'S RETURN TO EARTH IN GLORY

This speaks of the return of the Lord Jesus Christ. He will return in two phases. The first phase is the Rapture where He will transform all the genuine Christians who have died and who are still living at the time with glorified and resurrected bodies taking them into the clouds of Heaven. The Lord Jesus Christ will be glorified in His saints and admired in all of these true Christians.

After the Rapture of all genuine Christians, the entire world will experience seven years of Tribulation. It is called Daniel's Seventieth Week and the Time of Jacob's Trouble. At the end of this Tribulation period, Satan will cause thousands to come to the Jerusalem area to fight against its inhabitants. That Battle of Armageddon and its warriors will be put down by the Lord Jesus Christ with His glorified saints following Him. Many of these saints became true Christians because Paul's testimony in his many New Testament books was believed.

After this decisive battle, the Lord Jesus Christ will set up His thousand year reign and rule. During this Millennium, all the changes spoken of in the Old Testament will come pass, including longevity of people, the taming of wild and poisonous animals, topographical changes of the earth, and many other features.

Verses On Genuine Christians Being With the Lord Jesus Christ When He Comes

- **John 17:24**

"Father, I will that they also, whom thou hast given me, be with me where I am; that they may behold my glory, which thou hast given me: for thou lovedst me before the foundation of the world."

TRUE CHRISTIANS–WITH CHRIST IN GLORY

In His high priestly prayer, the Lord Jesus Christ prayed for those who trust Him to be with Him to behold His glory. That will be fulfilled for all those true Christians who will be with Him in Heaven.

- **1 Thessalonians 2:19**

"For what *is* our hope, or joy, or crown of rejoicing? *Are* not even ye in the presence of our Lord Jesus Christ at his coming?"

All genuine Christians will be with the Lord Jesus Christ at His coming in the Rapture.

- **1 Thessalonians 3:13**

"To the end he may stablish your hearts unblameable in holiness before God, even our Father, at the coming of our Lord Jesus Christ with all his saints."

CHRIST RETURNS WITH HIS SAINTS BY HIS SIDE

This verse speaks also of the coming of the Lord Jesus Christ. In this case it is *"with all His saints."* It is after the Rapture and at the end of the Battle of Armageddon. At that battle, He will come back *"with"* His saints by His side.

- **2 Thessalonians 2:8**

"And then shall that Wicked be revealed, whom the Lord shall consume with the spirit of his mouth, and shall destroy with the brightness of his coming:"

This will take place at the second phase of the coming of the Lord Jesus Christ. It will be at the end of the seven years of Tribulation at the Battle of Armageddon. The Wicked one, including Satan and all of his cohorts, will all be destroyed with the brightness of the coming of the Lord Jesus Christ.

- **2 Peter 3:12**

"Looking for and hasting unto the coming of the day of God, wherein the heavens being on fire shall be dissolved, and the elements shall melt with fervent heat?"

THE SECOND PHASE OF CHRIST'S COMING
This refers to the second phase of the coming of the Lord Jesus Christ. It will take place after the seven years of Tribulation before the 1,000-year millennial reign of the Lord Jesus Christ upon this earth. It will bring about a new heavens and a new earth during the Millennium.

2 Thessalonians 1:11
"Wherefore also we pray always for you, that our God would count you worthy of this calling, and fulfil all the good pleasure of his goodness, and the work of faith with power:"

CHRISTIANS SHOULD BE WORTHY OF GOD'S CALLING
Paul was an intercessor for the genuine Christians in Thessalonica. He prayed that God would count them worthy of His calling them to be true Christians and their accepting this call. Paul also wanted them to fulfill the good pleasure of God's goodness to them. He hoped that they would have faith which was powerful and pleasing to God.

Verses On Being Worthy
There are many different references in the Bible to worthiness--which means profitability. Not that genuine Christians are worthy in themselves, but as they follow the Lord Jesus Christ, according to God's Words and as the Holy Spirit leads them, they are worthy. Paul wanted them to be worthy of God's Heavenly calling.
- **Genesis 32:10**
"I am not worthy of the least of all the mercies, and of all the truth, which thou hast shewed unto thy servant; for with my staff I passed over this Jordan; and now I am become two bands."
Jacob was very humble. He realized that he was not worthy of all that God had done for him. That humility and worthiness should be possessed of every truly born-again Christian.

ONLY GOD'S GRACE CAN BRING REDEMPTION
It is only by the grace of God and the redemption of the Lord Jesus Christ that genuine Christians are worthy in His sight. They cannot boast of their own worthiness, but only of the One Who made them worthy by His salvation.

- **John 14:6**

"Jesus saith unto him, I am the way, the truth, and the life: no man cometh unto the Father, but by me."

Only when people come in true faith to the Lord Jesus Christ as their Saviour can they be worthy of coming to God the Father and to His Heaven.

- **Psalms 18:3**

"I will call upon the LORD, *who is worthy* to be praised: so shall I be saved from mine enemies."

The Lord alone is worthy. He is worthy to be praised. We are to count Him as worthy and praise His Name.

- **Mark 1:7**

"And preached, saying, There cometh one mightier than I after me, the latchet of whose shoes I am not worthy to stoop down and unloose."

JOHN THE BAPTIST KNEW HE WAS UNWORTHY

When John the Baptist realized the worthiness of the Lord Jesus Christ, he was humbled. He knew he was not worthy even to loose the shoes of the Lord Jesus Christ.

- **Luke 7:4**

"And when they came to Jesus, they besought him instantly, saying, That he was worthy for whom he should do this:"

The man that needed a miracle was said to be worthy. Perhaps on the standards of men, he might have been worthy, but not based on God's standards. No man or woman is worthy in God's sight.

- **Luke 7:6**

"Then Jesus went with them. And when he was now not far from the house, the centurion sent friends to him, saying unto him, Lord, trouble not thyself: for I am not worthy that thou shouldest enter under my roof:"

The Centurion, who was the commander of one hundred Roman soldiers, knew that he was not worthy of the Lord Jesus Christ.

- **Luke 15:21**

"And the son said unto him, Father, I have sinned against heaven, and in thy sight, and am no more worthy to be called thy son."

THE PRODIGAL SON RETURNED TO HIS FATHER

This is the man's son who went astray. He was a prodigal son who took half of all his father's inheritance and wasted it. When he was hungry, he ate unclean food given to the hogs. When he came to himself, this prodigal son repented of his sins. He knew that his father's servants were better off then he was. He finally decided to return to his home and to his father whom he had left.

When he met his father, this is when he said:
"*Father, I have sinned against heaven and in thy sight, and am no more worthy to be called thy son.*" (Luke 15:21b)
Even though unworthy, his father forgave him and welcomed him back home.

- **Acts 5:41**

"And they departed from the presence of the council, rejoicing that they were counted worthy to suffer shame for his name."
This happened after these Christian disciples were heavily beaten with rods. They at least knew they were worthy to suffer shame for the Name of the Lord Jesus Christ. The apostles were commanded by the authorities not to preach or speak in the name of the Lord Jesus Christ. They obeyed God rather than men and continued to reach others and speak in Christ's Name (Acts 5:29b).

So-called "hate speech" has been enforced in Canada and is threatened to be in force here in the U.S.A.–especially after the Supreme Court's decision approving Sodomite marriages. When we call homosexuality by its right name as a blatant sin against our holy God, we might be penalized by some in our present government. But we must speak God's truths no matter what man's rules and laws are that are contrary to those truths, whatever the cost and penalty.

- **Ephesians 4:1**

"I therefore, the prisoner of the Lord, beseech you that ye walk worthy of the vocation wherewith ye are called,"

WALKING WORTHY BY FOLLOWING GOD'S WORDS

Genuine Christians are to walk worthy of their Heavenly calling. This can only be done in the power of God the Holy Spirit Who indwells them and by closely following God's Words.

- **1 Thessalonians 2:12**

"That ye would walk worthy of God, who hath called you unto his kingdom and glory."
Here, the true Christians are requested to walk worthy of their God Who called them.

- **James 2:7**

"Do not they blaspheme that worthy name by the which ye are called?"

CHRIST'S NAME IS WORTHY THOUGH BLASPHEMED
The Name of the Lord Jesus Christ is worthy, though blasphemed by the unsaved and non-Christian world around us.

- **Revelation 3:4**
"Thou hast a few names even in Sardis which have not defiled their garments; and they shall walk with me in white: for they are worthy."

The Lord Jesus Christ said of these in Sardis who were genuine Christians, that in Heaven they would walk with Him in white, because they would then be worthy. At that time, they will have their glorified bodies.

- **Revelation 4:11**
"Thou art worthy, O Lord, to receive glory and honour and power: for thou hast created all things, and for thy pleasure they are and were created."

Here is another testimony of the worthiness of the Lord Jesus Christ.

- **Revelation 5:12**
"Saying with a loud voice, Worthy is the Lamb that was slain to receive power, and riches, and wisdom, and strength, and honour, and glory, and blessing."

This song will be sung during the Tribulation period. It will say, "*Worthy is the Lamb that was slain.*"

2 Thessalonians 1:12
"That the name of our Lord Jesus Christ may be glorified in you, and ye in him, according to the grace of our God and the Lord Jesus Christ."

CHRIST'S NAME MUST BE GLORIFIED NOT CURSED
Paul's prayer in this verse was that the Name of our Lord Jesus Christ might be glorified in them. He wanted to have them give His Name top honor rather than be used in swearing or cursing. Only God's grace can perform this in the Genuine Christian.

Verses On Glorifying God
- **Psalms 86:12**
"I will praise thee, O Lord my God, with all my heart: and I will glorify thy name for evermore."

True Christians must praise and glorify the name of the Lord Jesus Christ in every way possible.

- **Matthew 5:16**

"Let your light so shine before men, that they may see your good works, and glorify your Father which is in heaven."

LIGHT SHOULD SHINE IN CHRISTIANS' LIVES
When the light of genuine Christians is shining in their lives, the result is their Heavenly Father is glorified.

- **John 15:8**

"Herein is my Father glorified, that ye bear much fruit; so shall ye be my disciples."

When true born-again Christians bear fruit in their lives, God their Father is glorified.

- **John 16:14**

"He shall glorify me: for he shall receive of mine, and shall shew *it* unto you."

This refers to God the Holy Spirit Who will glorify the Lord Jesus Christ rather than Himself. This explains how the Words of the Bible were given by the Lord Jesus Christ through the Holy Spirit to the human writers. The Pentecostals and Charismatics have it all wrong. They think the Holy Spirit of God is glorifying Himself. The Holy Spirit was the conduit by which the Words of the Lord Jesus Christ were conveyed to the Bible writers.

- **Acts 3:13**

"The God of Abraham, and of Isaac, and of Jacob, the God of our fathers, hath glorified his Son Jesus; whom ye delivered up, and denied him in the presence of Pilate, when he was determined to let *him* go."

God the Father glorified His Son, the Lord Jesus Christ even though the godless Jews had Him crucified by the Roman government.

- **Romans 15:6**

"That ye may with one mind *and* one mouth glorify God, even the Father of our Lord Jesus Christ."

UNITED TO GLORIFY GOD AND CHRIST
The genuine Christians at Rome were not to be divided, but united so that with one mind and one mouth they might glorify God, the Father of the Lord Jesus Christ.

- **1 Corinthians 6:19-20**

"What? know ye not that your body is the temple of the Holy Ghost *which is* in you, which ye have of God, and ye are not your own? For ye are bought with a price: therefore glorify God in your body, and in your spirit, which are God's."

True born-again Christians have been bought with the price of the blood of the Lord Jesus Christ. They are not their own because of this. They are owned by God Himself. They should therefore glorify Him in their body and their spirit.
- **1 Peter 4:14**
"If ye be reproached for the name of Christ, happy *are ye*; for the spirit of glory and of God resteth upon you: on their part he is evil spoken of, but on your part he is glorified."

The Apostle Peter knew that the people to whom he was writing had undergone many difficulties and persecutions. True Christians are also often reproached for the Name of the Lord Jesus Christ. They should be happy even during such reproaches. They should not cease from glorifying their Saviour.

2 Thessalonians Chapter Two

2 Thessalonians 2:1

"Now we beseech you, brethren, by the coming of our Lord Jesus Christ, and by our gathering together unto him,"

The "*gathering together unto him*" is the Rapture of the Church. In effect, Paul said: "I want you to be crystal clear, the Lord Jesus Christ is going to return in the Rapture of all genuine Christians before any part of the seven years of Tribulation." Whether at the Rapture--if the true Christians are still living--or at their death, God has promised that they will go to Heaven to be with Him for all eternity.

Verses On The Coming of Christ
To Take True Christians To Heaven

- John 14:2-3

"In my Father's house are many mansions: if *it were* not *so*, I would have told you. I go to prepare a place for you. And if I go and prepare a place for you, I will come again, and receive you unto myself; that where I am, *there* ye may be also."

The Lord Jesus Christ told His disciples that He was preparing a place for them to be with Him in His Father's House in Heaven.

- John 17:24

"Father, I will that they also, whom thou hast given me, be with me where I am; that they may behold my glory, which thou hast given me: for thou lovedst me before the foundation of the world."

> **TRUE CHRISTIANS WILL BE WITH CHRIST FOREVER**
> In His High Priestly prayer, the Lord Jesus Christ prayed that all the genuine Christians might be with Him where He is in Heaven to behold His glory. That will come to pass.

- 2 Corinthians 5:6

"Therefore *we are* always confident, knowing that, whilst we are at home in the body, we are absent from the Lord:"

The clear implication here (which is stated in the next verse), is when true Christians are absent from their body in death, they will be present with the Lord Jesus Christ in Heaven.
- **2 Corinthians 5:7-8**

"(For we walk by faith, not by sight:) We are confident, *I say*, and willing rather to be absent from the body, and to be present with the Lord."

ABSENT FROM THE BODY, PRESENT WITH THE LORD
Genuine Christians will be present with the Lord Jesus Christ in Heaven, when they are absent from their bodies.

- **Philippians 1:23**

"For I am in a strait betwixt two, having a desire to depart, and to be with Christ; which is far better:"

Paul was in a Roman prison. He had a desire to depart to be with the Lord Jesus Christ in Heaven, but knew it was more needful for them for his further ministry to them.

- **1 Thessalonians 4:15**

"For this we say unto you by the word of the Lord, that we which are alive *and* remain unto the coming of the Lord shall not prevent them which are asleep."

This is a statement regarding the Rapture of all true Christians before the Tribulation period. Those who died and are buried will rise first, then the living will be taken up to meet the Lord Jesus Christ in the air.

- **1 Thessalonians 4:16-17**

"For the Lord himself shall descend from heaven with a shout, with the voice of the archangel, and with the trump of God: and the dead in Christ shall rise first: Then we which are alive *and* remain shall be caught up together with them in the clouds, to meet the Lord in the air: and so shall we ever be with the Lord."

THE MEANING OF "RAPTURE"
This verse provides the details for the preceding verse. The word "*caught up*" is HARPAZO. The Latin is RAPERE from which we get the word, "rapture."

- **1 Corinthians 15:49**

"And as we have borne the image of the earthy, we shall also bear the image of the heavenly."

This speaks of genuine Christians and their receiving their new bodies.

- **1 Corinthians 15:50-54**

"Now this I say, brethren, that flesh and blood cannot inherit the kingdom of God; neither doth corruption inherit incorruption. Behold, I shew you a mystery; We shall not all sleep, but we shall

all be changed, In a moment, in the twinkling of an eye, at the last trump: for the trumpet shall sound, and the dead shall be raised incorruptible, and we shall be changed. For this corruptible must put on incorruption, and this mortal *must* put on immortality. So when this corruptible shall have put on incorruption, and this mortal shall have put on immortality, then shall be brought to pass the saying that is written, Death is swallowed up in victory."

In these verses, Paul gives a detailed description of God's transformation of true Christians before taking them to Heaven.

- **Philippians 3:20-21**

"For our conversation is in heaven; from whence also we look for the Saviour, the Lord Jesus Christ: Who shall change our vile body, that it may be fashioned like unto his glorious body, according to the working whereby he is able even to subdue all things unto himself."

VILE BODIES TRANSFORMED TO GLORIFIED BODIES
God will change the vile bodies of genuine Christians into bodies like unto that glorified body of the Lord Jesus Christ. They will dwell with Him forever in Heaven.

- **1 John 3:2**

"Beloved, now are we the sons of God, and it doth not yet appear what we shall be: but we know that, when he shall appear, we shall be like him; for we shall see him as he is."

TRUE CHRISTIANS' BODIES MADE LIKE CHRIST'S BODY
When the Lord Jesus Christ appears in the clouds at the Rapture of all true Christians, they shall be made like Him. They shall dwell with Him in Heaven for all eternity to come.

- **1 Corinthians 1:7**

"So that ye come behind in no gift; waiting for the coming of our Lord Jesus Christ:"

The genuine Christians in Corinth were waiting for the coming of the Lord Jesus Christ to take them to Heaven.

- **1 Corinthians 15:23**

"But every man in his own order: Christ the firstfruits; afterward they that are Christ's at his coming."

This refers to the first phase of the return of the Lord Jesus Christ at the Rapture of all true Christians to take them to Heaven.

- **1 Thessalonians 2:19**

"For what *is* our hope, or joy, or crown of rejoicing? *Are* not even ye in the presence of our Lord Jesus Christ at his coming?"

This also speaks of the Rapture of all genuine Christians to take them to Heaven.
- **1 Thessalonians 4:15**
"For this we say unto you by the word of the Lord, that we which are alive *and* remain unto the coming of the Lord shall not prevent them which are asleep."

DEAD IN CHRIST FIRST, THEN THOSE WHO ARE ALIVE
Those true Christians who have died will be raptured first. Afterward, those who are still alive at the coming of the Lord Jesus Christ will be caught up to Heaven.

- **1 Thessalonians 5:23**
"And the very God of peace sanctify you wholly; and *I pray God* your whole spirit and soul and body be preserved blameless unto the coming of our Lord Jesus Christ."

This coming refers to the Rapture of all genuine Christians who will be caught up to Heaven for all eternity to come.
- **James 5:7**
"Be patient therefore, brethren, unto the coming of the Lord. Behold, the husbandman waiteth for the precious fruit of the earth, and hath long patience for it, until he receive the early and latter rain."

PATIENCE WHILE AWAITING CHRIST'S COMING
True Christians must be patient while awaiting the coming of the Lord Jesus Christ to take them to Heaven.

- **James 5:8**
"Be ye also patient; stablish your hearts: for the coming of the Lord draweth nigh."

If the coming of the Lord Jesus Christ was nigh in the time of James, just think how much closer it is today.
- **1 John 2:28**
"And now, little children, abide in him; that, when he shall appear, we may have confidence, and not be ashamed before him at his coming."

LIVING UNASHAMED LIVES FOR THE RAPTURE
Genuine Christians should live their lives so as not to be ashamed when the Lord Jesus Christ returns in the Rapture.

2 Thessalonians 2:2

"That ye be not soon shaken in mind, or be troubled, neither by spirit, nor by word, nor by letter as from us, as that the day of Christ is at hand."

There is a textual and an interpretational difference of opinion in this verse.

The false Gnostic Critical Greek Text reads "*the day of the Lord.*" The true Traditional Received Greek Text reads as the King James Bible, "*the day of Christ.*"

It is entirely possible that this phrase, "*the day of Christ,*" could refer to "*the day of the Lord*" since the first part of His Name is "**Lord**" (Jesus Christ). If it is understood in this way, it would refer to the 2nd phase of His coming when He established His 1,000-year Millennial reign. This would be preceded by the seven-year Tribulation ending with the Battle of Armageddon.

On the other hand, if "*the day of Christ*" is interpreted as in Philippians 1:10 and 2:16, it would refer to the first phase of the coming of the Lord Jesus Christ in the air, or the Rapture as in the two verses which I cite below. Certainly this would fit in with the preceding verse 2:1 which is a definite reference to the "*gathering together unto*" the Lord Jesus Christ of all genuine Christians in the Rapture.

- **Philippians 1:10**

"That ye may approve things that are excellent; that ye may be sincere and without offence till **the day of Christ;**"
This reference is usually taken to refer to the Rapture of all true Christians before the Tribulation period.

- **Philippians 2:16**

"Holding forth the word of life; that I may rejoice in **the day of Christ**, that I have not run in vain, neither laboured in vain."
This reference is also usually taken to refer to the Rapture of all genuine Christians before the Tribulation period.

If this is the proper interpretation, let me explain how it would make sense.

2 Thessalonians 2:3

"Let no man deceive you by any means: for that day shall not come, except there come a falling away first, and that man of sin be revealed, the son of perdition;"

> **AORIST TENSE=DON'T EVEN BEGIN TO BE DECEIVED**
> The clause, *"let no man deceive you,"* is in Greek aorist tense. It is a prohibition. Being in that Greek tense, it means to don't even begin to be deceived by anyone.

Paul did not want the true Christians in Thessalonica to even begin to deception of any kind. I have given some verses on deception below.

You'll notice that *"that day shall not come"* is in italics and has been added by the KJB translators to bring out the sense. If these words refer to the Rapture of the genuine Christians to meet the Lord Jesus Christ in the air, there must be a clear sense of the meaning of the Greek Word translated in our King James Bible as *"falling away."*

The Greek Word used for this term is APOSTASIA. It comes from two Greek Words, APO ("from" or "away") and STASIA which is from the verb HISTEMI ("to stand," "to put," or "to place.") The meaning of APOSTASIA can be understood as a "standing away," a "placing away," or a *"departure."*

The LOGOS Greek Bible Program uses the English words for APOSTASIA, APOSTASION, or APOSTATES as follows:

(1) *"abandonment"*;
(2) *"divorce"*; or
(3) *"desert."*

> **APOSTASIA--STANDING AWAY OR DEPARTING**
> If a person *"stands away,"* they might leave. If a person *"abandons"* a place, they *"depart"* from that place. If a person *"divorces"* a person, they *"depart"* from that person. If a person *"deserts"* a person or a place, they *"depart"* from that person or that place. I believe this to be a sound and correct interpretation of the Greek Word, APOSTASIA.

What is crystal clear from all the elements of both the Old Testament and the New Testament regarding future prophetic events, the following chronology is clear:

(1) the Lord Jesus Christ will return to remove and snatch away every genuine Christian in the Rapture before any part of the seven-year Tribulation takes place.

(2) There will then be seven years of Tribulation on this earth called "Daniel's 70th Week" or "the Time of Jacob's Trouble."
(3) During this seven-year Tribulation, the "man of sin" (the Antichrist) will be revealed.
(4) This Tribulation will end at the Battle of Armageddon where all the nations of the earth will gather together round Jerusalem to capture it and the Jews who are defending it.

CHRIST'S VICTORY AT ARMAGEDDON'S BATTLE
This battle will end when the Lord Jesus Christ comes down from Heaven in the second phase of His second coming, sets His feet on the Mount of Olives, and defeats all His enemies.

Verses On Deception
- **Jeremiah 29:8**

"For thus saith the LORD of hosts, the God of Israel; Let not your prophets and your diviners, that *be* in the midst of you, deceive you, neither hearken to your dreams which ye cause to be dreamed."

MANY PREACHERS ARE DECEIVING PEOPLE
We have prophets and preachers today that are deceiving people, right and left. God does not want this to happen any time or anywhere.

- **Matthew 24:4**

"And Jesus answered and said unto them, Take heed that no man deceive you."
The Lord Jesus Christ warned about deceivers who would come. Deception is with us today just as it was in His day.

- **Matthew 24:5**

"For many shall come in my name, saying, I am Christ; and shall deceive many."
The Saviour warned the people of His day that some would even come claiming to be "Christ" in order to deceive many.

- **Matthew 24:11**

"And many false prophets shall rise, and shall deceive many."
Certainly this prophecy of the Lord Jesus Christ has been fulfilled today as in the early church. There are many modernistic, apostate false prophets in our day.

- **Matthew 24:24**

"For there shall arise false Christs, and false prophets, and shall shew great signs and wonders; insomuch that, if *it were* possible, they shall deceive the very elect."

Signs and miracles are great methods of deception today. They are as false as those who perform them. Genuine Christians must compare everything with the doctrines of the Bible.
- Luke 21:8

"And he said, Take heed that ye be not deceived: for many shall come in my name, saying, I am *Christ*; and the time draweth near: go ye not therefore after them."

In the news recently, there was a man saying he was Jesus. He's married to a girl named Mary Magdalene. No one should be fooled by this phony deceiver.
- Romans 16:17-18

"Now I beseech you, brethren, mark them which cause divisions and offences contrary to the doctrine which ye have learned; and avoid them. For they that are such serve not our Lord Jesus Christ, but their own belly; and by good words and fair speeches deceive the hearts of the simple."

AVOID THOSE WHO PREACH FALSE DOCTRINE
Those who teach and preach doctrines contrary to the Bible should be avoided. They deceive people with "fair speeches" and "good," lying words.

- 2 Timothy 3:13

"But evil men and seducers shall wax worse and worse, deceiving, and being deceived."

SEDUCERS AND DECEIVERS WILL INCREASE
We are living in times when this verse is being fulfilled as it was fulfilled in the early church. These evil men and seducers are getting worse and worse, not better. Not only do they deceive others, but are deceived themselves.

- Titus 1:10-11

"For there are many unruly and vain talkers and deceivers, specially they of the circumcision: Whose mouths must be stopped, who subvert whole houses, teaching things which they ought not, for filthy lucre's sake."

Paul wrote to Pastor Timothy that there were many Jewish deceivers who subverted whole houses in order to get filthy money.
- 2 John 1:7

'For many deceivers are entered into the world, who confess not that Jesus Christ is come in the flesh. This is a deceiver and an antichrist."

> **DECEIVERS DENY CHRIST'S INCARNATION AND DEITY**
> The definition in this verse of a deceiver and an antichrist is one that denies the incarnation of the Lord Jesus Christ. This would be the name of teachers and students at most of the apostate so-called "Christian" colleges and seminaries around the world. One of the cardinal false doctrines of these schools is to deny the virgin birth and the Divine incarnation of the Lord Jesus Christ, the Son of God.

The next verse describes some of the traits and actions of the "*man of sin*" and the "*son of perdition.*"

2 Thessalonians 2:4

"Who opposeth and exalteth himself above all that is called God, or that is worshipped; so that he as God sitteth in the temple of God, shewing himself that he is God."

We do not know who this Antichrist is or will be. Many people have named those they believe to be the Antichrist. I noted on the Internet recently that many have been named as the Antichrist during the years that have passed--including Barack Hussein Obama. Time alone will tell who he will be. The genuine Christians will be raptured out of this world before the Tribulation period when he will be revealed.

> **DESCRIPTION OF THE MAN OF SIN**
> This verse gives some description of the "*man of sin,*" the "*son of perdition,*" including the Antichrist himself.
> (1) <u>First of all, he opposes things</u>. This is the present Greek tense which implies a continuous opposition. That is present tense, continuous action–continues to oppose.
> (2) Second, being in the Greek present tense, <u>he continuously exalts himself above all that is called God or that is worshipped</u>.
> (3) <u>He sits in the temple of God as God Himself.</u>   (4) <u>He believes and pretends that he himself is God.</u>

Verses From Daniel About The Antichrist

Daniel chapter 11 adds some other things to this description here in 2 Thessalonians. <u>Notice these details</u>:
- **Daniel 11:36**
"And the king shall do according to his will; and he shall exalt himself, and magnify himself above every god, and shall speak

marvellous things against the God of gods, and shall prosper till the indignation be accomplished: for that that is determined shall be done."

THE ANTICHRIST'S SELFISHNESS
This Antichrist will do as his own will, exalting himself above every god. He will also speak against the true God.

- Daniel 11:37

"Neither shall he regard the God of his fathers, nor the desire of women, nor regard any god: for he shall magnify himself above all."

WILL THE ANTICHRIST BE PRO-HOMOSEXUAL?
The Antichrist will not care about the true God of his fathers. He doesn't care about the desire of women, but will probably stand for homosexual marriages–man with man or woman with woman.

- Daniel 11:38

"But in his estate shall he honour the God of forces: and a god whom his fathers knew not shall he honour with gold, and silver, and with precious stones, and pleasant things."

THE ANTICHRIST'S GOD OF FORCES
The Antichrist will believe in the God of forces--not in the God of the Bible. He'll give all kinds of money for this false god. It reminds me of the idolatry of the church of Rome. Some have believed in the past that a Roman Catholic Pope will be the Antichrist. There is no way of knowing who he will be exactly.

- Daniel 11:39

"Thus shall he do in the most strong holds with a strange god, whom he shall acknowledge *and* increase with glory: and he shall cause them to rule over many, and shall divide the land for gain."

THE ANTICHRIST'S STRANGE GOD
The Antichrist will acknowledge and glorify a strange god. He will also divide land for the money it will bring him.

- Daniel 11:40

"And at the time of the end shall the king of the south push at him: and the king of the north shall come against him like a whirlwind, with chariots, and with horsemen, and with many ships; and he shall enter into the countries, and shall overflow and pass over."
Both the king of the south and the king of the north shall come against the Antichrist to defeat him, if possible.

- **Daniel 11:41**
"He shall enter also into the glorious land, and many *countries* shall be overthrown: but these shall escape out of his hand, *even* Edom, and Moab, and the chief of the children of Ammon."

> **THE ANTICHRIST'S OVERTHROWING COUNTRIES**
> The Antichrist shall enter into the area of Jerusalem and will overthrow many countries with the exception of Edom, Moab, and Ammon.

- **Daniel 11:42**
"He shall stretch forth his hand also upon the countries: and the land of Egypt shall not escape."

> **THE ANTICHRIST'S CAPTURE OF EGYPT**
> The Antichrist will capture Egypt as well.

- **Daniel 11:43**
"But he shall have power over the treasures of gold and of silver, and over all the precious things of Egypt: and the Libyans and the Ethiopians *shall be* at his steps."

> **THE ANTICHRIST'S INTERNATIONAL BANKING**
> Apparently, the Antichrist may be in charge of some part of the international banking of his day.

- **Daniel 11:44**
"But tidings out of the east and out of the north shall trouble him: therefore he shall go forth with great fury to destroy, and utterly to make away many."

> **THE ANTICHRIST'S GREAT FURY**
> Because of news from the east and north, the Antichrist will go forth with great fury and destroy many.

- **Daniel 11:45**
"And he shall plant the tabernacles of his palace between the seas in the glorious holy mountain; yet he shall come to his end, and none shall help him."

> **THE ANTICHRIST DESTROYED AT ARMAGEDDON**
> The Antichrist will come to his end and eventually will be destroyed by the Lord Jesus Christ at the battle of Armageddon.

2 Thessalonians 2:5

"Remember ye not, that, when I was yet with you, I told you these things?"

Paul reminded the true Christians at Thessalonica that he told them about the Antichrist when he was there with them. He was faithful in telling them what would one day come to pass.

2 Thessalonians 2:6

"And now ye know what withholdeth that he might be revealed in his time."

THE MEANING OF THE GREEK WORD, "KATECHO"

The word, "*withholdeth*," is from the Greek Word, KATECHO. Some of the meanings of this Word are: κατέχω *(katechō)*: *1. prevent, hinder, restrain, keep from (Ro 1:18); 2. continue belief, implying appropriate action (1Co 11:2; 15:2); 3. possess, have, own (2Co 6:10; Jn 5:4); 4. control, restrain continuously (Lk 4:42); 5. occupy, be in a place (Lk 14:9)*

In this context, meanings #1 and #4 would probably be accurate. It refers to "*preventing, hindering, restraining, or controlling*" something.

Who is the reference to "*what withholdeth?*" It's a reference to God the Holy Spirit. The Greek article, TO, used with the noun, "*the Withholder*" is neuter. It refers to the Word for the Holy Spirit which is also a neuter Word in Greek. One of the ministries of the Holy Spirit is to restrain the evil around us. The Holy Spirit indwells the genuine Christians and restrains much of the evil that otherwise would manifest itself. When the Holy Spirit is gone, at the Rapture of the true Christians, the Antichrist will be revealed, and the restraint of the Holy Spirit will be removed.

- **Psalms 76:10**

"Surely the wrath of man shall praise thee: the remainder of wrath shalt thou restrain."

2 Thessalonians 2:7

"For the mystery of iniquity doth already work: only he who now letteth will let, until he be taken out of the way."

THE RESTRAINING WORK OF THE HOLY SPIRIT

As mentioned before, God the Holy Spirit hinders or restrains much (but not all) of the evil in our world. When He will be *"taken out of the way"* at the Rapture of genuine Christians, His ministry of restraining will be removed also.

2 Thessalonians 2:8

"And then shall that Wicked be revealed, whom the Lord shall consume with the spirit of his mouth, and shall destroy with the brightness of his coming:"

The following extended verses from Zechariah 14:1-15 and Revelation 19:11-21 describe the destruction of the Antichrist after he is revealed after the Rapture of all the true Christians.

THE SECOND PHASE OF CHRIST'S RETURN

Both of these passages describe the second phase of the coming of the Lord Jesus Christ when He will come back to earth with His glorified Christians to battle the Antichrist and his followers at the Battle of Armageddon.

CHRIST'S MILLENNIAL REIGN SET UP

After the defeat of the Antichrist and his armies, the Lord Jesus Christ will set up his thousand year reign on this earth. It will be the long awaited and prophesied Millennium.

- Zechariah 14:1-15

¹Behold, the day of the LORD cometh, and thy spoil shall be divided in the midst of thee.

²For I will gather all nations against Jerusalem to battle; and the city shall be taken, and the houses rifled, and the women ravished; and half of the city shall go forth into captivity, and the residue of the people shall not be cut off from the city.

³Then shall the LORD go forth, and fight against those nations, as when he fought in the day of battle.

⁴And his feet shall stand in that day upon the mount of Olives, which is before Jerusalem on the east, and the mount of Olives shall cleave in the midst thereof toward the east and toward the west,

and there shall be a very great valley; and half of the mountain shall remove toward the north, and half of it toward the south.

⁵And ye shall flee to the valley of the mountains; for the valley of the mountains shall reach unto Azal: yea, ye shall flee, like as ye fled from before the earthquake in the days of Uzziah king of Judah: and the LORD my God shall come, *and* all the saints with thee.

⁶And it shall come to pass in that day, *that* the light shall not be clear, *nor* dark:

⁷But it shall be one day which shall be known to the LORD, not day, nor night: but it shall come to pass, *that* at evening time it shall be light.

⁸And it shall be in that day, *that* living waters shall go out from Jerusalem; half of them toward the former sea, and half of them toward the hinder sea: in summer and in winter shall it be.

⁹And the LORD shall be king over all the earth: in that day shall there be one LORD, and his name one.

¹⁰All the land shall be turned as a plain from Geba to Rimmon south of Jerusalem: and it shall be lifted up, and inhabited in her place, from Benjamin's gate unto the place of the first gate, unto the corner gate, and from the tower of Hananeel unto the king's winepresses.

¹¹And *men* shall dwell in it, and there shall be no more utter destruction; but Jerusalem shall be safely inhabited.

¹²And this shall be the plague wherewith the LORD will smite all the people that have fought against Jerusalem; Their flesh shall consume away while they stand upon their feet, and their eyes shall consume away in their holes, and their tongue shall consume away in their mouth.

¹³And it shall come to pass in that day, *that* a great tumult from the LORD shall be among them; and they shall lay hold every one on the hand of his neighbour, and his hand shall rise up against the hand of his neighbour.

¹⁴And Judah also shall fight at Jerusalem; and the wealth of all the heathen round about shall be gathered together, gold, and silver, and apparel, in great abundance.

¹⁵And so shall be the plague of the horse, of the mule, of the camel, and of the ass, and of all the beasts that shall be in these tents, as this plague.

- **Revelation 19:11-21**

¹¹And I saw heaven opened, and behold a white horse; and he that sat upon him *was* called Faithful and True, and in righteousness he doth judge and make war.

¹² His eyes *were* as a flame of fire, and on his head *were* many crowns; and he had a name written, that no man knew, but he himself.
¹³ And he *was* clothed with a vesture dipped in blood: and his name is called The Word of God.
¹⁴ And the armies *which* were in heaven followed him upon white horses, clothed in fine linen, white and clean.
¹⁵ And out of his mouth goeth a sharp sword, that with it he should smite the nations: and he shall rule them with a rod of iron: and he treadeth the winepress of the fierceness and wrath of Almighty God.
¹⁶ And he hath on *his* vesture and on his thigh a name written, KING OF KINGS, AND LORD OF LORDS.
¹⁷ And I saw an angel standing in the sun; and he cried with a loud voice, saying to all the fowls that fly in the midst of heaven, Come and gather yourselves together unto the supper of the great God;
¹⁸ That ye may eat the flesh of kings, and the flesh of captains, and the flesh of mighty men, and the flesh of horses, and of them that sit on them, and the flesh of all *men, both* free and bond, both small and great.
¹⁹ And I saw the beast, and the kings of the earth, and their armies, gathered together to make war against him that sat on the horse, and against his army.
²⁰ And the beast was taken, and with him the false prophet that wrought miracles before him, with which he deceived them that had received the mark of the beast, and them that worshipped his image. These both were cast alive into a lake of fire burning with brimstone.
²¹ And the remnant were slain with the sword of him that sat upon the horse, which *sword* proceeded out of his mouth: and all the fowls were filled with their flesh.

2 Thessalonians 2:9

"Even him, whose coming is after the working of Satan with all power and signs and lying wonders,"

ANTICHRIST REVEALED AFTER THE RAPTURE

After the Rapture of all the genuine Christians, the Antichrist will be revealed. He will be hidden for the first half of the seven-year Tribulation, but will reveal himself at the

> beginning of the last three and one half years. His working will be after Satan's power, signs, and lying wonders.

Verses About Satan

The Antichrist will be motivated by Satan.
- **1 Chronicles 21:1**

"And Satan stood up against Israel, and provoked David to number Israel."

Satan wrongly influenced David to number Israel, even though God had told him not to do this.
- **Job 1:6**

"Now there was a day when the sons of God came to present themselves before the LORD, and Satan came also among them."

Before his fall, Satan was an exalted angel who had access to the presence of the LORD. He still has access today.
- **Matthew 4:10**

"Then saith Jesus unto him, Get thee hence, Satan: for it is written, Thou shalt worship the Lord thy God, and him only shalt thou serve."

The Lord Jesus Christ reproved Satan for his suggestion that he should worship him. Worship only God.
- **Matthew 16:23**

"But he turned, and said unto Peter, Get thee behind me, Satan: thou art an offence unto me: for thou savourest not the things that be of God, but those that be of men."

PETER WAS INFLUENCED BY SATAN

Peter was one of the leading apostles of the Lord Jesus Christ, but he was adversely influenced by Satan. His answer to the Lord Jesus Christ was so wrong in this instance that the Lord, in responding to Peter, addressed Satan who had influenced his wrong answer.

- **Mark 4:15**

"And these are they by the way side, where the word is sown; but when they have heard, Satan cometh immediately, and taketh away the word that was sown in their hearts."

If the Words of God fall on the way side, Satan takes away that seed out of the hearts of those who received it by the way side.
- **Luke 22:3**

"Then entered Satan into Judas surnamed Iscariot, being of the number of the twelve."

SATAN ENTERED INTO JUDAS ISCARIOT

Satan, though not all-powerful, is able to enter the bodies of unsaved people like Judas Iscariot. The Antichrist will also be able to pose like a disciple of the Lord Jesus Christ, like Judas did in order to fool many people.

- **Acts 26:18**
"To open their eyes, *and* to turn *them* from darkness to light, and *from* the power of Satan unto God, that they may receive forgiveness of sins, and inheritance among them which are sanctified by faith that is in me."

PAUL'S MISSION WAS TO PREACH THE GOSPEL

When the Lord Jesus Christ saved Paul, his mission was to preach the gospel which would turn sinners from the power of Satan unto God. This shows that non-Christians are under the power of Satan before they are born-again and saved. Satan is their spiritual father.

- **1 Corinthians 7:5**
"Defraud ye not one the other, except *it be* with consent for a time, that ye may give yourselves to fasting and prayer; and come together again, that Satan tempt you not for your incontinency."

SATAN'S TEMPTATION IN MARRIAGE

When husbands and wives refuse one another sexual intimacy without proper reasons and for too long a time, Satan is able to tempt either the husband or the wife or both of them because of this disobedience to this verse.

- **2 Corinthians 2:11**
"Lest Satan should get an advantage of us: for we are not ignorant of his devices."

Satan has many devices or strategies that he uses to take advantage of genuine Christians. Paul knew about these Satanic devices.

- **2 Corinthians 11:14**
"And no marvel; for Satan himself is transformed into an angel of light."

One of the Satanic tricks that the Antichrist will possess is the ability to appear like an angel of light when, in fact, he is an angel of darkness. This is how he will disguise himself for the first three and one half years of the Tribulation. He will appear as good and light, but in reality he is evil and darkness. Everyone will think he is wonderful! Probably all the news media of the day will write articles praising the Antichrist.

- **1 Thessalonians 2:18**
'Wherefore we would have come unto you, even I Paul, once and again; but Satan hindered us."
Paul mentioned that Satan hindered him from going to the true Christians in Thessalonica. Satan and the Antichrist are able to hinder God's people from doing God's work.
- **1 Timothy 5:15**
"For some are already turned aside after Satan."
Professing Christians, but not possessing Christians, apparently can be turned aside to go after Satan when they are so persuaded.
- **Revelation 2:24**
"But unto you I say, and unto the rest in Thyatira, as many as have not this doctrine, and which have not known the depths of Satan, as they speak; I will put upon you none other burden."
This verse speaks of the fact that Satan has many deep things or depths of his methods and influences. He is wise, but not all-wise as the God of the Bible. True Christians should be aware of and avoid all Satanic teachings, whether deep or shallow.
- **Revelation 12:9**
"And the great dragon was cast out, that old serpent, called the Devil, and Satan, which deceiveth the whole world: he was cast out into the earth, and his angels were cast out with him."
Satan and his angels have been cast out on to the earth. He is a deceiver who deceives the whole world.
- **Revelation 20:2**
"And he laid hold on the dragon, that old serpent, which is the Devil, and Satan, and bound him a thousand years,"
- **Revelation 20:7**
"And when the thousand years are expired, Satan shall be loosed out of his prison,"

SATAN WILL BE BOUND 1,000 YEARS, THEN LOOSED
During the entire Millennium, God will bind Satan in prison. At the end of the Millennium, he will be loosed to deceive people once again.

Verses About False Christs, Signs, And Wonders
- **Matthew 24:24**
"For there shall arise false Christs, and false prophets, and shall shew great signs and wonders; insomuch that, if *it were* possible, they shall deceive the very elect."
The signs and wonders by these false Christs and false prophets will be lying and deceiving signs.

- **Mark 13:22**
  "For false Christs and false prophets shall rise, and shall shew signs and wonders, to seduce, if *it were* possible, even the elect."

As in the previous verse cited above, Satanic miracles, which appear as true signs and wonders, will deceive many in the future, even as the present signs and wonders of Charismatics and Pentecostals are deceiving many today.

- **John 4:48**
  "Then said Jesus unto him, Except ye see signs and wonders, ye will not believe."

The Lord Jesus Christ rebuked the unbelieving Jews of his day for insisting on signs and wonders.

- **Acts 2:43**
  "And fear came upon every soul: and many wonders and signs were done by the apostles."

MIRACLE WORKERS ONLY IN THE EARLY CHURCH

These were proper signs and miracles in the early church. These miracles were in the plan of God, but have ceased since the Bible has been completed in 90 or 100 A.D.

- **Acts 4:30**
  "By stretching forth thine hand to heal; and that signs and wonders may be done by the name of thy holy child Jesus."

THE APOSTLES WERE GIVEN SPECIAL SIGN GIFTS

The apostles were given proper, special sign gifts and miracles. However, the Antichrist will perform false and fake signs, and false and fake miracles.

- **Acts 5:12**
  "And by the hands of the apostles were many signs and wonders wrought among the people; (and they were all with one accord in Solomon's porch."

These were proper signs and wonders, but those by the Antichrist will be false and deceitful.

- **Hebrews 2:3-4**
  "How shall we escape, if we neglect so great salvation; which at the first began to be spoken by the Lord, and was confirmed unto us by them that heard *him*; God also bearing *them* witness, both with signs and wonders, and with divers miracles, and gifts of the Holy Ghost, according to his own will?"

In the New Testament, special miracles were the stamp of God's approval on the apostles and the Lord Jesus Christ.

- **Revelation 13:13**

"And he doeth great wonders, so that he maketh fire come down from heaven on the earth in the sight of men,"

This Antichrist's false power, motivated and empowered by Satan, will deceive many.

2 Thessalonians 2:10

"And with all deceivableness of unrighteousness in them that perish; because they received not the love of the truth, that they might be saved."

THE ANTICHRIST USES TOTAL DECEPTION

This powerful Antichrist will operate with total deceivableness and unrighteousness to those who are lost and bound for Hell. The reason they will perish in Hell is because they refused to receive the love of the truth and the Lord Jesus Christ that they might become genuine Christians. The Antichrist will so deceive people that Bible truth will be scoffed at and thrown out the window. The Antichrist will not want anybody to become true Christians. People will perish in Hell because of the deceptiveness of Satan.

Verses About Deceit

- **Psalms 10:7**

"His mouth is full of cursing and deceit and fraud: under his tongue *is* mischief and vanity."

This is speaking of the wicked. His mouth is full of deceit.

- **Proverbs 12:20**

"Deceit *is* in the heart of them that imagine evil: but to the counsellors of peace *is* joy."

Those who imagine evil have deceit down in their heart.

- **Proverbs 26:24**

"He that hateth dissembleth with his lips, and layeth up deceit within him;"

Those with lying lips lay up deceit inside themselves.

- **Romans 16:18**

"For they that are such serve not our Lord Jesus Christ, but their own belly; and by good words and fair speeches deceive the hearts of the simple."

- **Ephesians 4:14**

"That we *henceforth* be no more children, tossed to and fro, and carried about with every wind of doctrine, by the sleight of men, *and* cunning craftiness, whereby they lie in wait to deceive;"

These deceivers use cunning craftiness. They lie in wait to deceive.
- **Revelation 20:3**
"And cast him into the bottomless pit, and shut him up, and set a seal upon him, that he should deceive the nations no more, till the thousand years should be fulfilled: and after that he must be loosed a little season."
The Antichrist and Satan, himself, major in deceiving the nations. This will come to a stop in this verse.
- **Revelation 20:8**
"And shall go out to deceive the nations which are in the four quarters of the earth, Gog and Magog, to gather them together to battle: the number of whom *is* as the sand of the sea."

SATAN'S DECEPTION FOR BATTLING THE LORD
Satan and the Antichrist will deceive the nations to come again to battle the Lord Jesus Christ.

Verses About Perishing Without Christ
- **John 3:16**
"For God so loved the world, that he gave his only begotten Son, that whosoever believeth in him should not perish, but have everlasting life."

TRUE CHRISTIANS WILL NOT PERISH IN HELL
In this verse, God promises those people, who truly believe on the Lord Jesus Christ as their Saviour--Who died for their sins--will not perish in Hell. That's a great promise!

- **John 10:28**
"And I give unto them eternal life; and they shall never perish, neither shall any *man* pluck them out of my hand."
This is another promise from the Lord Jesus Christ Himself that those who have eternal life will never perish in Hell.
- **1 Corinthians 1:18**
"For the preaching of the cross is to them that perish foolishness; but unto us which are saved it is the power of God."
Those who will perish in Hell think the preaching of the cross of the Lord Jesus Christ and what He did there was foolishness. To the saved, it is the power of God. What a contrast!
- **2 Peter 3:9**
"The Lord is not slack concerning his promise, as some men count slackness; but is longsuffering to us-ward, not willing that any should perish, but that all should come to repentance."

> **SALVATION MUST BE A VOLUNTARY CHOICE**
> Though the Lord is not willing that any person perish in Hell, He doesn't force them to accept His Son as their Saviour. He wants every person to change their minds about the Lord Jesus Christ and sincerely trust Him as their Saviour.

2 Thessalonians 2:11

"And for this cause God shall send them strong delusion, that they should believe a lie:"

The Antichrist's deception will be so persuasive that unbelievers and non-Christians will believe his lies. It will be a strong delusion.

THE MEANING OF THE GREEK WORD, "PLANE"

The Greek Word for *"delusion"* is PLANE. Some of the meanings of that Word are:

"1) a wandering, a straying about; 1a) one led astray from the right way, roams hither and thither; 2) metaph; 2a) mental straying; 2a1) error, wrong opinion relative to morals or religion; 2b) error which shows itself in action, a wrong mode of acting; 2c) error, that which leads into error, deceit or fraud."

Verses About Lies, Lying, And Liars

- **Numbers 23:19**

"God *is* not a man, that he should lie; neither the son of man, that he should repent: hath he said, and shall he not do *it*? or hath he spoken, and shall he not make it good?"

The Devil and his Antichrist are liars. God is not a liar. He deals only in the truth at all times.

- **Psalms 40:4**

"Blessed *is* that man that maketh the LORD his trust, and respecteth not the proud, nor such as turn aside to lies."

We can not abide lies. The Antichrist is a master of lies, as Satan is.

- **Psalms 116:11**

"I said in my haste, All men *are* liars."

MANY SO-CALLED "SCHOLARS" LIE

That's so true. One of our Dean Burgon Society speakers said several years ago, "Scholars lie." Yes, they are part of the *"men"* whom God calls *"liars."*

- **Proverbs 14:5**

"A faithful witness will not lie: but a false witness will utter lies."

FAITHFUL WITNESSES DO NOT LIE

Lying does not proceed from faithful witnesses, only from those who are false.

- **Proverbs 30:6**

"Add thou not unto his words, lest he reprove thee, and thou be found a liar."

NEW BIBLE VERSIONS ARE BASED ON LYING TEXTS

The modern Bible versions, which are based on the New Testament Gnostic Critical Greek Text, have added many words that should not be added at all. God reproves all of them in this verse. God calls them liars.

- **John 8:44**

"Ye are of *your* father the devil, and the lusts of your father ye will do. He was a murderer from the beginning, and abode not in the truth, because there is no truth in him. When he speaketh a lie, he speaketh of his own: for he is a liar, and the father of it."

Satan is a liar as well as a murderer. He is also the father of lies. True Christians must flee all falsehoods of Satan.

- **Romans 1:25**

"Who changed the truth of God into a lie, and worshipped and served the creature more than the Creator, who is blessed for ever. Amen."

The heathen nations changed God's truth into a lie. They worshipped their idols rather than the Creator.

- **Colossians 3:9**

"Lie not one to another, seeing that ye have put off the old man with his deeds;"

COLOSSIAN CHRISTIANS WERE TO STOP LYING

Paul wrote from Roman prison to the true Christians in Colosse to stop lying to one another. That's a work of the flesh.

- **1 Timothy 4:2**

"Speaking lies in hypocrisy; having their conscience seared with a hot iron;"

This verse speaks of those with a broken conscience who speak hypocritical lies. This same spirit is with us today.

- **Titus 1:2**

"In hope of eternal life, which God, that cannot lie, promised before the world began;"

God the Father cannot lie. He tells only the truth. The Lord Jesus Christ is the truth and cannot lie either.
- **Hebrews 6:18**
"That by two immutable things, in which *it was* impossible for God to lie, we might have a strong consolation, who have fled for refuge to lay hold upon the hope set before us:"

It is certainly impossible for the God of the Bible to lie in any matter whatsoever!
- **1 John 1:6**
"If we say that we have fellowship with him, and walk in darkness, we lie, and do not the truth:"

WALKING IN SPIRITUAL DARKNESS, NOT LIGHT
Some genuine Christians say they are walking in fellowship with the Lord Jesus Christ, but are walking in spiritual darkness. If this is the case, God tells them that they are liars.

- **1 John 2:4**
"He that saith, I know him, and keepeth not his commandments, is a liar, and the truth is not in him."

If professing Christians say they know the Lord Jesus Christ as their Saviour and yet don't keep His commandments, God calls them liars.

2 Thessalonians 2:12
"That they all might be damned who believed not the truth, but had pleasure in unrighteousness."

THE ANTICHRIST BRINGS IN STRONG DELUSION
The reason that the Antichrist will send people strong delusion to believe a lie is that they might be damned and sent to Hell because they didn't receive the Lord Jesus Christ, Who is the Truth, as their Saviour. On the contrary, they will have pleasure in that which is evil and wicked. This action will be motivated by the Antichrist himself.

Verses About Condemnation And Damnation
- **Matthew 23:33**
"*Ye* serpents, *ye* generation of vipers, how can ye escape the damnation of hell?"

The Antichrist will influence and cause people to go into the damnation of Hell.

- **John 3:17-18**
"For God sent not his Son into the world to condemn the world; but that the world through him might be saved. He that believeth on him is not condemned: but he that believeth not is condemned already, because he hath not believed in the name of the only begotten Son of God."

ESCAPING HELL THROUGH GENUINE FAITH IN CHRIST
The only way that people can escape the damnation and condemnation of Hell is by accepting the plan of God. That plan is for people to sincerely trust His Son Who died on the cross for their sins. Faith in Him brings eternal life. Not trusting Him brings eternal condemnation in Hell.

- **John 5:24**
"Verily, verily, I say unto you, He that heareth my word, and believeth on him that sent me, hath everlasting life, and shall not come into condemnation; but is passed from death unto life."
Hearing the Lord Jesus Christ and trusting in the Father Who sent him brings everlasting life and delivers from condemnation and damnation.

- **Romans 8:1**
"There is therefore now no condemnation to them which are in Christ Jesus, who walk not after the flesh, but after the Spirit.
People who are *"in Christ Jesus"* and are saved will suffer no condemnation or judgment in the Lake of Fire, but have eternal life.

Verses On Loving Unrighteous Pleasures

- **Proverbs 21:17**
"He that loveth pleasure *shall be* a poor man: he that loveth wine and oil shall not be rich."
Pleasure, whether it's drugs, gambling, or whatever it might be costs money. The love of it will bring poverty. One man that I heard about spent from $30,000 to $60,000 on his adultery with a woman of the street. He ended up a very poor man.

- **Luke 8:14**
"And that which fell among thorns are they, which, when they have heard, go forth, and are choked with cares and riches and pleasures of *this* life, and bring no fruit to perfection."
As this parable from the Lord Jesus Christ says, the pleasures of this life choke out the Words of God.

- **Romans 1:32**
"Who knowing the judgment of God, that they which commit such things are worthy of death, not only do the same, but have pleasure in them that do them."

Sinners not only do sinful things, but have pleasure in others who are doing these evil things as well.
- 2 Timothy 3:1-5

"This know also, that in the last days perilous times shall come. For men shall be lovers of their own selves, covetous, boasters, proud, blasphemers, disobedient to parents, unthankful, unholy, Without natural affection, trucebreakers, false accusers, incontinent, fierce, despisers of those that are good, Traitors, heady, highminded, lovers of pleasures more than lovers of God; Having a form of godliness, but denying the power thereof: from such turn away."

THE LAST DAYS WILL BRING PERILOUS TIMES

In the last days especially, these perilous times shall come. One of the signs of these times is that people will be "*lovers of pleasures more than lovers of God.*"

- Titus 3:3

"For we ourselves also were sometimes foolish, disobedient, deceived, serving divers lusts and pleasures, living in malice and envy, hateful, *and* hating one another."

Before these people were saved, they served different lusts and pleasures.
- Hebrews 11:25

"Choosing rather to suffer affliction with the people of God, than to enjoy the pleasures of sin for a season;"

Moses chose to suffer with God's people rather than to enjoy the pleasures of Egyptian sin for a season.

2 Thessalonians 2:13

"But we are bound to give thanks alway to God for you, brethren beloved of the Lord, because God hath from the beginning chosen you to salvation through sanctification of the Spirit and belief of the truth:"

CORPORATE ELECTION EXPLAINED BRIEFLY

Paul was thankful for the true Thessalonian Christians. God chose them to salvation. I believe the word "*chosen*" talks about God's corporate election whereby he chose the Church as a corporate body from before the foundation of the world. When someone genuinely accepts the Lord Jesus Christ as their Saviour, they become part of that chosen, corporate group called the Church. It is the group that is chosen as a corporate entity. Though others differ on election, this is my understanding of what the Bible means by it.

Verses On Chosen, Election, And Sanctification
- **Ephesians 1:4**
"According as he hath chosen us in him before the foundation of the world, that we should be holy and without blame before him in love:"
Why did He choose the true Christians? He wants them to be holy and without blame before Him.
- **1 Corinthians 1:30**
"But of him are ye in Christ Jesus, who of God is made unto us wisdom, and righteousness, and sanctification, and redemption:"
A person who is truly saved has perfect positional sanctification before God on His books in Heaven.
- **Romans 8:33**
"Who shall lay any thing to the charge of God's elect? *It is* God that justifieth."

THE TRUE CHURCH WHICH IS CHRIST'S BODY
Paul is speaking of those who are this elect or chosen group, the Church which is His body.

- **1 Thessalonians 1:4**
"Knowing, brethren beloved, your election of God."
This speaks of the same thing for all genuine Christians. They are in an elect group or body called the true Church.
- **Titus 1:1**
"Paul, a servant of God, and an apostle of Jesus Christ, according to the faith of God's elect, and the acknowledging of the truth which is after godliness;"

"GOD'S ELECT" ARE ALL TRULY SAVED PEOPLE
Once people have genuine faith in the Lord Jesus Christ and are saved, they are called *"God's elect."* This refers to all who are in that elect or chosen Body, the Church.

- **1 Peter 1:2**
"Elect according to the foreknowledge of God the Father, through sanctification of the Spirit, unto obedience and sprinkling of the blood of Jesus Christ: Grace unto you, and peace, be multiplied."
God wants true Christians who are a part of this elect or chosen Body to be set apart unto Him.
- **2 Peter 1:10**
"Wherefore the rather, brethren, give diligence to make your calling and election sure: for if ye do these things, ye shall never fall:"
Peter wants his readers to be sure they are genuine Christians who, as such, are part of the previously chosen group called the Church.

2 Thessalonians 2:14

"Whereunto he called you by our gospel, to the obtaining of the glory of our Lord Jesus Christ."

PEOPLE ARE SAVED BY BELIEVING CHRIST'S GOSPEL
God called people to be true Christians by means of the gospel of the Lord Jesus Christ.

Verses On God's Calling

- **Romans 8:28**
"And we know that all things work together for good to them that love God, to them who are the called according to *his* purpose."

All genuine Christians who have trusted the Lord Jesus Christ as their Saviour and were thus called by God according to His purpose.

- **1 Corinthians 1:1**
"Paul, called *to be* an apostle of Jesus Christ through the will of God, and Sosthenes *our* brother,"

In this verse, we see that God, according to His will, called Paul to be an apostle of the Lord Jesus Christ.

- **1 Corinthians 1:26**
"For ye see your calling, brethren, how that not many wise men after the flesh, not many mighty, not many noble, *are called*:"

God does not call many who are wise, mighty, or noble.

- **1 Thessalonians 2:12**
"That ye would walk worthy of God, who hath called you unto his kingdom and glory."

God wants every true Christian who has accepted God's call to walk worthy of God.

- **2 Thessalonians 1:11**
"Wherefore also we pray always for you, that our God would count you worthy of *this* calling, and fulfil all the good pleasure of *his* goodness, and the work of faith with power:"

God wants the genuine Christians whom He has called to walk worthy of that calling.

- **2 Timothy 1:9**
"Who hath saved us, and called *us* with an holy calling, not according to our works, but according to his own purpose and grace, which was given us in Christ Jesus before the world began,"

The calling to salvation of every true Christian, who genuinely trusts the Lord Jesus Christ, is a holy calling. It is not a result of any of their good works. Rather, it is by God's purpose and grace.

2 Thessalonians 2:15

"Therefore, brethren, stand fast, and hold the traditions which ye have been taught, whether by word, or our epistle."

TRUE CHRISTIANS SHOULD STAND FAST IN CHRIST
Because of their salvation by trusting the Lord Jesus Christ, every true Christian has been ordered to "stand fast" and continue to hold the traditions taught either by the words of the apostles, or by the Words found in their epistles.

THE MEANING OF THE GREEK WORD, "STEKO"
The Greek Word for *"stand fast"* is STEKO. Some of the meanings for that Greek Word are:

"1) to stand firm; 2) to persevere, to persist; 3) to keep one's standing"

THE MEANING OF THE GREEK WORD, "KRATEO"
The Greek Word for *"hold"* is KRATEO. Some of the meanings of that Greek Word are:

"1) to have power, be powerful; 1a) to be chief, be master of, to rule; 2) to get possession of; 2a) to become master of, to obtain; 2b) to take hold of; 2c) to take hold of, take, seize; 2c1) to lay hands on one in order to get him into one's power; 3) to hold; 3a) to hold in the hand; 3b) to hold fast, i.e. not discard or let go; 3b1) to keep carefully and faithfully; 3c) to continue to hold, to retain; 3c1) of death continuing to hold one; 3c2) to hold in check, restrain."

Because of all the false teachings of the coming Antichrist, Paul is telling these genuine Christians (and by application all the genuine Christians alive today) to stand fast and hold the teachings of the Bible rather than any other teachings contrary to the Bible.

This is why it is vital to stand fast and hold to the Traditional Hebrew, Aramaic, and Greek Words that underlie our King James Bible and not depart from any of them.

THE KJB--THE ONLY FAITHFUL ENGLISH TRANSLATION
The King James Bible is the only faithful translation of those Words in the English language. Therefore, true

> Christians should stand fast and hold to the King James Bible as well.

Verses On Standing Fast Or Holding Fast

- **1 Corinthians 16:13**

"Watch ye, stand fast in the faith, quit you like men, be strong." When the Greek Word for "*faith*" (PISTIS) has the article, "*the*," (HE), it refers to the body of doctrine or teachings of the Bible. Genuine Christians should not be wishy-washy about the doctrines and teachings of the Bible.

- **Galatians 5:1**

  "Stand fast therefore in the liberty wherewith Christ hath made us free, and be not entangled again with the yoke of bondage."

Standing fast in Christian liberty for true Christians is vitally important. The Galatians were bothered by those who wanted to mix New Testament teachings with the law of Moses.

- **Philippians 1:27**

  "Only let your conversation be as it becometh the gospel of Christ: that whether I come and see you, or else be absent, I may hear of your affairs, that ye stand fast in one spirit, with one mind striving together for the faith of the gospel;"

Paul wanted the genuine Christians in Philippi to stand fast in one unified spirit in line with the teachings of God's Words.

- **Philippians 4:1**

  "Therefore, my brethren dearly beloved and longed for, my joy and crown, so stand fast in the Lord, *my* dearly beloved."

Stand fast in the Lord for all of His doctrines and teachings.

- **Matthew 6:24**

  "No man can serve two masters: for either he will hate the one, and love the other; or else he will hold to the one, and despise the other. Ye cannot serve God and mammon."

True Christians should hold to their God and His Words, not to worldly pursuits and pleasures.

- **1 Thessalonians 5:21**

  "Prove all things; hold fast that which is good."

Genuine Christians must hold fast things that are good as defined in God's Words.

- **2 Timothy 1:13**

  "Hold fast the form of sound words, which thou hast heard of me, in faith and love which is in Christ Jesus."

Paul told Pastor Timothy to hold fast the sound Words of the Bible before all those who attended his church in Ephesus.

Verses On Bible Traditions
- **Matthew 15:6**
"And honour not his father or his mother, *he shall be free*. Thus have ye made the commandment of God of none effect by your tradition."

> **THE WORDS OF GOD–ABOVE HUMAN TRADITIONS**
> The Lord Jesus Christ exposed the Pharisees about their error of exalting their human traditions above the Words of God.

- **Mark 7:8**
"For laying aside the commandment of God, ye hold the tradition of men, *as* the washing of pots and cups: and many other such like things ye do."

This tradition of men caused the Pharisees to lay aside God's Words and holy traditions.

- **Galatians 1:14**
"And profited in the Jews' religion above many my equals in mine own nation, being more exceedingly zealous of the traditions of my fathers."

Before Paul became a true Christian, he was very zealous in following the false traditions of Judaism, many of which conflicted even with the Old Testament teachings. That was sad indeed.

- **Colossians 2:8**
"Beware lest any man spoil you through philosophy and vain deceit, after the tradition of men, after the rudiments of the world, and not after Christ."

Paul cautioned the genuine Christians at Colosse to beware of being spoiled human philosophy, deceit, and tradition.

- **2 Thessalonians 3:6**
"Now we command you, brethren, in the name of our Lord Jesus Christ, that ye withdraw yourselves from every brother that walketh disorderly, and not after the tradition which he received of us."

> **SEPARATE FROM DISORDERLY CHRISTIANS**
> Though many true Christians do not practice this command of God's Words, it is crystal clear. They should separate from other true Christians who are living disorderly lives rather than following the traditions of the Bible.

- **1 Peter 1:18**
"Forasmuch as ye know that ye were not redeemed with corruptible things, *as* silver and gold, from your vain conversation *received* by tradition from your fathers;"

The genuine Christians that Peter was writing to had been redeemed by the blood of the Lord Jesus Christ and separated from the unscriptural traditions of their fathers.

2 Thessalonians 2:16

"Now our Lord Jesus Christ himself, and God, even our Father, which hath loved us, and hath given us everlasting consolation and good hope through grace,"

God the Son and God the Father have given true Christians everlasting consolation through Their grace.

THE MEANING OF THE GREEK WORD, "PARAKLESIS"

The Greek Word for *"consolation"* is PARAKLESIS. Some of the meanings of this Greek Word are:

"1) a calling near, summons, (esp. for help); 2) importation, supplication, entreaty; exhortation, admonition, encouragement; 4) consolation, comfort, solace; that which affords comfort or refreshment; 4a) thus of the Messianic salvation (so the Rabbis call the Messiah the consoler, the comforter); 5) persuasive discourse, stirring address; 5a) instructive, admonitory, conciliatory, powerful hortatory discourse."

Verses On Consolation

- **Romans 15:5**

"Now the God of patience and consolation grant you to be likeminded one toward another according to Christ Jesus:"

The *"God of consolation"* is one of the names of our Lord. One that gives genuine Christians solace and comfort.

- **2 Corinthians 1:5**

"For as the sufferings of Christ abound in us, so our consolation also aboundeth by Christ."

CHRIST GIVES CONSOLATION IN SUFFERINGS

Even though true Christians undergo sufferings, the Lord Jesus Christ gives them consolation in the midst of their sufferings.

- **Hebrews 6:18**
"That by two immutable things, in which *it was* impossible for God to lie, we might have a strong consolation, who have fled for refuge to lay hold upon the hope set before us:"
Strong consolation and hope are promised to genuine Christians who have fled to the Lord Jesus Christ for refuge from trouble.

Verses On Hope
- **Romans 5:2**
'By whom also we have access by faith into this grace wherein we stand, and rejoice in hope of the glory of God.'
The glory of God in Heaven is the hope of all true Christians. In this they rejoice.
- **Romans 15:4**
"For whatsoever things were written aforetime were written for our learning, that we through patience and comfort of the scriptures might have hope."

GOD ALWAYS FULFILLS HIS PROMISES
God's faithfulness to fulfill His promises in the Old Testament gives hope to true Christians today that He will fulfill His New Testament promises as well.

- **Romans 15:13**
"Now the God of hope fill you with all joy and peace in believing, that ye may abound in hope, through the power of the Holy Ghost."
One of the titles of the God of the Bible is "*The God of Hope*." That should cause all genuine Christians to have hope in Him and in His Words.
- **1 Corinthians 15:19**
"If in this life only we have hope in Christ, we are of all men most miserable."

AFTER TRUE CHRISTIANS' PERSECUTION–HEAVEN
Without the hope of Heaven for the true Christians, the life of persecution and troubles on earth would be miserable. But they have the hope of eternal glory in Heaven when they leave this earth.

- **Ephesians 1:18**
"The eyes of your understanding being enlightened; that ye may know what is the hope of his calling, and what the riches of the glory of his inheritance in the saints,"
The hope of God's calling in the Lord Jesus Christ is Heaven for all eternity to come.

- **Colossians 1:5**
"For the hope which is laid up for you in heaven, whereof ye heard before in the word of the truth of the gospel;"

> **REAL HOPE IS IN THE BIBLE'S HEAVEN**
> The hope for genuine Christians is laid up in the Bible's Heaven. That is real hope.

- **Colossians 1:27**
"To whom God would make known what *is* the riches of the glory of this mystery among the Gentiles; which is Christ in you, the hope of glory:
This verse, and others, teach us that the Lord Jesus Christ indwells every true Christian. That indwelling is the hope of glory in Heaven one day for all of them.

- **Titus 1:2**
"In hope of eternal life, which God, that cannot lie, promised before the world began;"
For genuine Christians, there is a future hope of eternal life in Heaven with God the Father and the Lord Jesus Christ.

- **Titus 2:13**
"Looking for that blessed hope, and the glorious appearing of the great God and our Saviour Jesus Christ;"
I believe this blessed hope refers to the Pre-Tribulation Rapture of all true Christians by the Lord Jesus Christ Himself. He will take them all to Heaven before any part of the Tribulation begins.

- **Titus 3:7**
"That being justified by his grace, we should be made heirs according to the hope of eternal life."
Eternal life for all genuine Christians is called hope. It's eternal. It's future, but it's guaranteed for all of them.

2 Thessalonians 2:17

"Comfort your hearts, and stablish you in every good word and work."

Continuing from verse 16, Paul is asking the Lord Jesus Christ and God the Father to comfort the hearts of these true Christians at Thessalonica, and also to establish them in every good word and work.

THE MEANING OF THE GREEK WORD, "STERIZO"

The Greek Word for *"stablish"* is STERIZO. Some of the meanings of that Greek Word are:

"1) to make stable, place firmly, set fast, fix; 2) to strengthen, make firm; 3) to render constant, confirm, one's mind."

Verses On Comfort

- **John 11:19**

"And many of the Jews came to Martha and Mary, to comfort them concerning their brother."

The Jews came to Mary and Martha to comfort them in the death of their brother, Lazarus.

- **2 Corinthians 1:3**

"Blessed *be* God, even the Father of our Lord Jesus Christ, the Father of mercies, and the God of all comfort;"

As the God of all comfort, the Father is the most important One to give the genuine Christians comfort.

- **2 Corinthians 1:4**

"Who comforteth us in all our tribulation, that we may be able to comfort them which are in any trouble, by the comfort wherewith we ourselves are comforted of God."

God the Father is able to comfort true Christians.

- **Colossians 4:8**

"Whom I have sent unto you for the same purpose, that he might know your estate, and comfort your hearts;"

Paul was going to send Tychicus to comfort the hearts of the genuine Christians in Colosse.

- **1 Thessalonians 3:2**

"And sent Timotheus, our brother, and minister of God, and our fellowlabourer in the gospel of Christ, to establish you, and to comfort you concerning your faith:"

In this verse, Paul sent Timothy to comfort the true Christians at Thessalonica.

- **1 Thessalonians 4:18**

"Wherefore comfort one another with these words."

The message of the Rapture of all genuine Christians with their transformed and glorified bodies bringing comfort to those who are listening.

Verses On Being Established And Being Firm

- **Romans 16:25**

"Now to him that is of power to stablish you according to my gospel, and the preaching of Jesus Christ, according to the revelation of the mystery, which was kept secret since the world began,"

God is able to establish true Christians by His gospel and true preaching about the Lord Jesus Christ.

- **1 Thessalonians 3:13**

"To the end he may stablish your hearts unblameable in holiness before God, even our Father, at the coming of our Lord Jesus Christ with all his saints."

God wants genuine Christians to be established and fixed in holiness before Him.

- **2 Thessalonians 3:3**

"But the Lord is faithful, who shall stablish you, and keep *you* from evil."

The Lord was faithful to establish true Christians in Thessalonica and keep them from evil. He is also faithful for true Christians today.

- **James 5:8**

"Be ye also patient; stablish your hearts: for the coming of the Lord draweth nigh."

Genuine Christians should establish and fix their hearts to live for Him.

- **1 Peter 5:10**

"But the God of all grace, who hath called us unto his eternal glory by Christ Jesus, after that ye have suffered a while, make you perfect, stablish, strengthen, settle *you*."

<u>After suffering, God wants true Christians to be established, strengthened, and settled.</u>

2 Thessalonians Chapter Three

2 Thessalonians 3:1

"Finally, brethren, pray for us, that the word of the Lord may have free course, and be glorified, even as it is with you:"

PRAYER FOR GOD'S WORDS TO BE GLORIFIED

Paul requested prayer from the genuine Christians in Thessalonica. Notice the subject of his prayer. He wanted the Word of the Lord to have free course and be glorified as those true Christians in Thessalonica had glorified It. For this to happen, people must have the accurate and proper *"Word of the Lord."*

This is why our Bible For Today ministries and the Dean Burgon Society have stressed so forcefully and clearly that there must be the correct Bible foundations as in the accurate and proper Hebrew, Aramaic, and Greek Words on which the King James Bible is based.

THE PROPER ORIGINAL HEBREW AND GREEK WORDS

These accurate and proper original language Words are as follows:

(1) For the Old Testament Hebrew and Aramaic Words, the source should be the Masoretic Text and the Words underlying the King James Bible.

(2) For the New Testament Greek Words, the source should be the Traditional Received Words underlying the King James Bible and not the Gnostic Critical Greek Text underlying the modern versions in most of the languages of the world. That false Gnostic text has over 8,000 differences from the Traditional Received Text. In these 8,000 Gnostic Critical Greek Text differences, there are 356 doctrinal passages which give false doctrines and theology.

> **THE MEANING OF THE GREEK WORD, "TRECHO"**
> The Greek Word for *"free course"* is TRECHO. Some of the meanings of that Greek Word are:
> *"1. run, implying speed or haste (Lk 15:20; Heb 12:1; Rev 9:9; Mt 28:9; Ac 19:28); 2. try to do, strive, give effort (Ro 9:16); 3. progress in one's behavior or conduct (Gal 5:7); 4. τρέχει (logos trechei),* <u>message spread</u> *(2Th 3:1+)"*

That's why we pray to God that our Internet may continue to be uncontrolled and uncensored by either the United Nations or our United States government. Both groups have been trying to do this for many months and years now. The Words of God and other truths should be able to be shared around the entire world.

Verses On The Word Of The Lord
- Psalms 18:30

"*As for* God, his way *is* perfect: the word of the LORD is tried: he *is* a buckler to all those that trust in him."

> **GOD'S WORDS HAVE BEEN OFTEN TRIED AND TESTED**
> God's Words have been tried and tested through many centuries. We can trust the perfection in the Hebrew, Aramaic, and Greek Words underlying our King James Bible.

- Psalms 33:4

"For the word of the LORD *is* right; and all his works *are done* in truth."

<u>The Words of the Lord are right and truth. No lies are there.</u>
- Acts 8:25

"And they, when they had testified and preached the word of the Lord, returned to Jerusalem, and preached the gospel in many villages of the Samaritans."

That's what I seek to preach faithfully in our Bible For Today Baptist Church in all of our services–the Words of the Lord, in a verse by verse manner.

- Acts 13:49

"And the word of the Lord was published throughout all the region."

It is a wonderful thing to be able to publish the Words of the Lord all over the world through the Internet which is, as of this writing, still free and uncontrolled either by the UN or by the U. S. government. Each month we have from 2,000 to 3,000 downloads of our messages from 60 to 70 foreign countries and all 50 of our States. Before various countries

(like China, for instance) took control of the Internet, we used to have 10,000 downloads and one time we had 20,000. This has been made possible by the knowledge and skill of Pastor Daniel Waite, our youngest son who assists in the Bible For Today ministries.
* **Acts 15:35**
"Paul also and Barnabas continued in Antioch, teaching and preaching the word of the Lord, with many others also."
These two apostles both taught and preached the Words of the Lord along with others. Both methods are needed in an unlearned and sleepy world. Though this is done in our church, it is absent in many, many churches.
* **Acts 15:36**
"And some days after Paul said unto Barnabas, Let us go again and visit our brethren in every city where we have preached the word of the Lord, *and see* how they do."
After preaching the Words of the Lord, Paul and Barnabas followed up that preaching to see how the people were doing in the faith.
* **1 Peter 1:25**
"But the word of the Lord endureth for ever. And this is the word which by the gospel is preached unto you."

THE BIBLE TEACHES ITS OWN PRESERVATION

We believe the Bible clearly teaches its own endurance and preservation. The Lord Jesus Christ promised that His Words would never, never pass away (Matthew 24:35; Mark 13:31; Luke 21:33). These are the preserved Words of the original Hebrew, Aramaic, and Greek which underlie the King James Bible.

2 Thessalonians 3:2

"And that we may be delivered from unreasonable and wicked men: for all men have not faith."

REQUEST FOR DELIVERANCE FROM WICKED PEOPLE

Paul wanted the genuine Christians in Thessalonica to pray for him to be delivered from unreasonable and wicked men. All do not have *"the faith"* [HE PISTIS]. With the Greek article this word means *"the doctrines and teachings of the faith"* as found in the Bible.

As in Paul's day, so in our day, if we stand for the faith and doctrines of the Bible, wicked and unreasonable people (including in current days, U. S. government) will be against us. The DHS

(Department of Homeland Security) recently included *"evangelical Christians"* in their 70 or so list of people they consider to be "potential terrorists." This included those who are for the U. S. Constitution, and against abortion and many other things. It would include those who are against lesbianism, homosexuality, and Sodomite marriages as well.

Verses On Deliverance
- **Romans 8:21**

"Because the creature itself also shall be delivered from the bondage of corruption into the glorious liberty of the children of God."

ANIMALS WILL BE DELIVERED FROM THEIR BONDAGE

During the Millennial reign of the Lord Jesus Christ on this earth (after the Tribulation period) all the animals who were changed after Noah's flood will be delivered from the bondage and curse God placed upon them after the fall of Adam.

- **Romans 11:26**

"And so all Israel shall be saved: as it is written, There shall come out of Sion the Deliverer, and shall turn away ungodliness from Jacob:"

ISRAEL WILL ALSO BE DELIVERED FROM BONDAGE

One day, the Deliverer, the Lord Jesus Christ will deliver Israel out of their present bondage. This will take place at the second phase of His return after the Tribulation period when He set up His thousand year millennial reign.

- **Romans 15:31**

"That I may be delivered from them that do not believe in Judaea; and that my service which *I have* for Jerusalem may be accepted of the saints;"

Paul sought prayer for his deliverance from the unbelieving Jews of Judaea. They wanted to kill him.

- **2 Corinthians 1:10**

"Who delivered us from so great a death, and doth deliver: in whom we trust that he will yet deliver *us*;"

THREE TENSES OF GOD'S SALVATION

Here are the three tenses of God's salvation for genuine Christians—past, present, and future.

(1) past deliverance—from the penalty of sin;

(2) present deliverance—from the power of sin; and

(3) future deliverance—from the presence of sin.

- **Galatians 1:4**
"Who gave himself for our sins, that he might deliver us from this present evil world, according to the will of God and our Father:"
The Lord Jesus Christ gave Himself by dying at Calvary for the sins of the entire world so that those who receive Him as Saviour might be delivered from this present evil world.
- **Colossians 1:13**
"Who hath delivered us from the power of darkness, and hath translated *us* into the kingdom of his dear Son:"
Genuine Christians have been delivered by true faith in the Lord Jesus Christ from the power of darkness and translated into His kingdom.
- **1 Thessalonians 1:10**
"And to wait for his Son from heaven, whom he raised from the dead, *even* Jesus, which delivered us from the wrath to come."
Genuine Christians have been delivered by the Lord Jesus Christ from the everlasting wrath of the Lake of Fire in Hell.
- **2 Timothy 3:11**
"Persecutions, afflictions, which came unto me at Antioch, at Iconium, at Lystra; what persecutions I endured: but out of *them* all the Lord delivered me."
God delivered Paul from all these persecutions and afflictions which he endured. He is a delivering God.
- **2 Timothy 4:17**
"Notwithstanding the Lord stood with me, and strengthened me; that by me the preaching might be fully known, and *that* all the Gentiles might hear: and I was delivered out of the mouth of the lion."
God delivered Paul *"out of the mouth of the lion."* It is not clear whether this *"lion"* is Satan, as in 1 Peter 5:8:
"*Be sober, be vigilant; because your adversary the devil, as a roaring lion, walketh about, seeking whom he may devour:*"
Or it might mean deliverance from the lions of the arena where many Christians were placed to be killed as the Roman crowds watched. It is unclear what is meant here.
- **2 Timothy 4:18**
"And the Lord shall deliver me from every evil work, and will preserve *me* unto his heavenly kingdom: to whom *be* glory for ever and ever. Amen."

2 TIMOTHY WAS PAUL'S LAST LETTER BEFORE DEATH
This was Paul's last letter. Even though he was beheaded by the Roman government, God delivered him from every evil

work and preserved him for His Heavenly kingdom. Rome could not remove Paul's eternal salvation from him, no matter how they killed him.

- Hebrews 2:15

"And deliver them who through fear of death were all their lifetime subject to bondage."

The Lord Jesus Christ is able to deliver all genuine Christians from Satanic bondage and from fear of death.

- 2 Peter 2:9

"The Lord knoweth how to deliver the godly out of temptations, and to reserve the unjust unto the day of judgment to be punished:"

God can deliver true Christians out of temptations if they let Him.

2 Thessalonians 3:3

"But the Lord is faithful, who shall stablish you, and keep you from evil."

GOD'S PROMISE TO KEEP FROM EVIL

The Lord is always faithful. It is certainly possible for genuine Christians to be unfaithful to Him, but He is always faithful to them. God wants to do two things for them. He wants to *"stablish"* them and He wants to *"keep"* them from evil.

THE MEANING OF THE GREEK WORD, "STERIZO"

The Greek Word for *"stablish"* is STERIZO. Some of the meanings of this Word are:

"1) to make stable, place firmly, set fast, fix;
2) to strengthen, make firm;
to render constant, confirm, one's mind."

True Christians who are not established these days will become weak and wobbly in their doctrines and lifestyle.

The Greek Word for *"keep"* is PHULASSO. Some of the meanings of that Greek Word are:

"1) to guard; 1a) to watch, keep watch; 1b) to guard or watch, have an eye upon: lest he escape; 1c) to guard a person (or thing) that he may remain safe; 1c1) lest he suffer violence, be despoiled, etc. to protect; 1c2) to protect one from a person or thing; 1c3) to keep from being snatched away, preserve safe and unimpaired; 1c4) to guard

from being lost or perishing; 1c5) to guard one's self from a thing; 1d) to guard i.e. care for, take care not to violate; 1d1) to observe; 2) to observe for one's self something to escape; 2a) to avoid, shun flee from; 2b) to guard for one's self (i.e. for one's safety's sake) so as not to violate, i.e. to keep, observe (the precepts of the Mosaic law):
God wants all of His genuine Christians to be kept preserved safe from any evil that surrounds them in this world.

Verses On Stablish
- **Romans 16:25**
"Now to him that is of power to stablish you according to my gospel, and the preaching of Jesus Christ, according to the revelation of the mystery, which was kept secret since the world began,"

God's power to establish His true Christians is miraculous. They must walk closely with Him, following His words so that He can accomplish this stability.
- **1 Thessalonians 3:13**
"To the end he may stablish your hearts unblameable in holiness before God, even our Father, at the coming of our Lord Jesus Christ with all his saints."

HEARTS ESTABLISHED IN HOLINESS NEEDED
This verse points out the need for the hearts of genuine Christians to be established in holiness. God wants to do this.

- **2 Thessalonians 2:17**
"Comfort your hearts, and stablish you in every good word and work."

This is Paul's prayer that both the Lord Jesus Christ and God the Father might not only comfort the hearts of the true Christians in Thessalonica, but also establish them in their good words and works.
- **James 5:8**
"Be ye also patient; stablish your hearts: for the coming of the Lord draweth nigh."

This is a wish from James that genuine Christians' hearts might be established, because the return of the Lord Jesus Christ might come at any moment.
- **1 Peter 5:10**
"But the God of all grace, who hath called us unto his eternal glory by Christ Jesus, after that ye have suffered a while, make you perfect, stablish, strengthen, settle *you*."

> **NO DRIFTING FROM THE WORDS IN GOD'S BIBLE**
> Peter's prayer concerning his true Christian readers is that God would establish, strengthen, and settle them. They were not to wander or drift from God's Words revealed in the Bible.

Verses On Keep

- **Philippians 4:7**

"And the peace of God, which passeth all understanding, shall keep your hearts and minds through Christ Jesus."

God's surpassing peace can keep both the hearts and the minds of genuine Christians.

- **1 Timothy 6:20**

"O Timothy, keep that which is committed to thy trust, avoiding profane *and* vain babblings, and oppositions of science falsely so called:"

Paul told Pastor Timothy to keep the doctrines and teachings that were committed to him by Paul without wavering in any way. He was especially urged to resist the errors of false science.

- **2 Timothy 1:12**

"For the which cause I also suffer these things: nevertheless I am not ashamed: for I know whom I have believed, and am persuaded that he is able to keep that which I have committed unto him against that day."

God was able to keep the people Paul ministered to who genuinely trusted the Lord Jesus Christ as their Saviour.

- **Jude 1:24**

"Now unto him that is able to keep you from falling, and to present *you* faultless before the presence of his glory with exceeding joy,"

> **TRUE CHRISTIANS CANNOT LOSE THEIR SALVATION**
> This is another verse that teaches eternal security for the true Christians. God is able to keep them from losing their salvation.

2 Thessalonians 3:4

"And we have confidence in the Lord touching you, that ye both do and will do the things which we command you."

Paul has continual confidence in the Lord that what the genuine Christians in Thessalonica are doing, and will continue to do God's command given to them through Paul.

THE MEANING OF THE GREEK WORD, "PEITHO"

The Greek Word for *"confidence"* is PEITHO. Some of the meanings of this Greek Word are:

"1) persuade; 1a) to persuade, i.e. to induce one by words to believe; 1b) to make friends of, to win one's favour, gain one's good will, or to seek to win one, strive to please one; 1c) to tranquillise; 1d) to persuade unto i.e. move or induce one to persuasion to do something; 2) be persuaded; 2a) to be persuaded, to suffer one's self to be persuaded; to be induced to believe: to have faith: in a thing; 2a1) to believe; 2a2) <u>to be persuaded of a thing concerning a person</u>; 2b) to listen to, obey, yield to, comply with; 3) to trust, have confidence, be confident."

Verses On Confidence

- **Psalms 65:5**

"*By* terrible things in righteousness wilt thou answer us, O God of our salvation; *who art* the confidence of all the ends of the earth, and of them that are afar off *upon* the sea:"

God Himself is the confidence of all people, but specially of genuine Christians.   **Psalms 118:9**

"*It is* better to trust in the LORD than to put confidence in princes." Princes, presidents, mayors, and all other governmental leaders often do not merit confidence from true Christians. They must trust the Lord instead.

- **Isaiah 30:15**

"For thus saith the Lord GOD, the Holy One of Israel; In returning and rest shall ye be saved; in quietness and in confidence shall be your strength: and ye would not."

Israel refused to put their confidence in the Lord GOD.

- **Proverbs 25:19**

"Confidence in an unfaithful man in time of trouble *is like* a broken tooth, and a foot out of joint."

These are two examples of putting confidence in unfaithful people. It is a very foolish practice, yet followed by many.

- **Acts 28:31**

"Preaching the kingdom of God, and teaching those things which concern the Lord Jesus Christ, with all confidence, no man forbidding him."

> **PAUL'S BEING JAILED DIDN'T SILENCE HIS PREACHING**
> Even though Paul was then a prisoner of Rome, he continued preaching and teaching the doctrines of the Lord Jesus Christ with all confidence. Captivity didn't silence him in any way.

- Ephesians 3:12

"In whom we have boldness and access with confidence by the faith of him."

This is speaking of the Lord Jesus Christ in Whom genuine Christians have access and can have perfect confidence.

- Philippians 3:3

"For we are the circumcision, which worship God in the spirit, and rejoice in Christ Jesus, and have no confidence in the flesh."

> **THERE SHOULD BE NO CONFIDENCE IN THE FLESH**
> True Christians (and everyone else) should agree with Paul and have no confidence whatsoever in their flesh.

- 1 John 2:28

"And now, little children, abide in him; that, when he shall appear, we may have confidence, and not be ashamed before him at his coming."

Genuine Christians must abide closely in the Lord Jesus Christ so they might have confidence in Him at His coming in the Rapture.

2 Thessalonians 3:5

"**And the Lord direct your hearts into the love of God, and into the patient waiting for Christ.**"

Paul wanted these true Christians in Thessalonica to have the Lord direct their hearts both into love for God and waiting patiently for the return of the Lord Jesus Christ in the Rapture.

> **THE MEANING OF THE GREEK WORD, "KATEUTHUNO"**
> The Greek Word for *"direct"* is KATEUTHUNO. Some of the meanings of this Greek Word are:
> "*1) to make straight, guide, direct; 1a) of the removal of the hindrances to coming to one*"

Verses On Direction

- Proverbs 3:6

"In all thy ways acknowledge him, and he shall direct thy paths."

THE LORD WANTS TO DIRECT THE CHRISTIAN'S PATHS
If genuine Christians acknowledge the Lord and His Words, He has promised to direct their paths.

- Jeremiah 10:23

"O LORD, I know that the way of man *is* not in himself: *it is* not in man that walketh to direct his steps."

True Christians, who want to walk in God's steps, won't know the way unless they follow His directions in His Words.

Verses On Waiting For Christ's Coming
- 1 Corinthians 1:7

"So that ye come behind in no gift; waiting for the coming of our Lord Jesus Christ:"

While possessing many spiritual gifts, the genuine Christians at Corinth were waiting for the coming of the Lord Jesus Christ

- Hebrews 10:37

"For yet a little while, and he that shall come will come, and will not tarry."

EVERY TRUE CHRISTIAN WILL BE RAPTURED OUT
The return of the Lord Jesus Christ in the Rapture--to take every true Christian out of this world and into Heaven--has been assuredly promised by the Lord. The *"little while"* has now been over 2,000 years, but He will one day come and will not tarry.

2 Thessalonians 3:6

"Now we command you, brethren, in the name of our Lord Jesus Christ, that ye withdraw yourselves from every brother that walketh disorderly, and not after the tradition which he received of us."

SEPARATION FROM DISORDERLY CHRISTIANS
This is a very important and vital verse that demands genuine Christians separate from other Christians who are living in disobedience to the Words of God. This is called a *"disorderly"* walk.

This has been called "secondary separation," because it calls for separation from true Christians. This includes religious leaders especially, though not exclusively. It is a part of Biblical separation.

It is in contrast to what is called "primary separation" which is separation from non-Christians who are living their lives in disobedience to the Words of God. This include unsaved religious leaders especially, though not exclusively. It is also a part of Biblical separation.

SEPARATION IS A COMMAND, NOT A SUGGESTION

By the command in this verse, God wants genuine Biblical Christians to withdraw themselves and separate from true Christians who are disobedient to the Bible and therefore walking disorderly. Notice, this is not merely a "suggestion." It's a *"command"*!

There is an organization that majors in not-separating from apostasy and apostates. It is called the National Association of Evangelicals (NAE). It is a master compromising organization. I went to their meetings for five or ten years, took notes, and reported on all their various compromises. They are a disorderly group from which genuine Christians should withdraw, in obedience to this verse.

THE MEANING OF THE GREEK WORD, "STELLO"

The Greek Word for *"withdraw"* is STELLO. It is in the Greek present tense which depicts a continuous and unending action. Some of the meanings of this Word are:

"1) to set, place, set in order, arrange; 1a) to fit out, to prepare, equip; 1b) to prepare one's self, to fit out for one's self; 1c) to fit out for one's own use; 1d) to prepare one's self, to fit out for one's self; 1e) to fit out for one's own use; 1e1) arranging, providing for this, etc.; 2) to bring together, contract, shorten; 2a) to diminish, check, cause to cease; 2b) to cease to exist; 2c) to remove one's self, withdraw one's self, to depart; 2d) to abstain from familiar intercourse with one."

If true Christians are not walking after the traditions and teachings given them by Paul in the Bible (as well as other Bible teachings), this withdrawal, in any close and personal relationship, must take place. These are not man's traditions such as taught by the Roman Catholic Church or other church groups. They are Bible teachings, even if they disagree with man's teachings.

Verses On Withdrawal From The Disorderly
- 2 Thessalonians 2:15

"Therefore, brethren, stand fast, and hold the traditions which ye have been taught, whether by word, or our epistle."

Genuine Christians are to hold fast to the Bible's teachings and not be disorderly.
- **Matthew 18:15-17**
"Moreover if thy brother shall trespass against thee, go and tell him his fault between thee and him alone: if he shall hear thee, thou hast gained thy brother. But if he will not hear *thee, then* take with thee one or two more, that in the mouth of two or three witnesses every word may be established. And if he shall neglect to hear them, tell *it* unto the church: but if he neglect to hear the church, let him be unto thee as an heathen man and a publican."

AN ILLUSTRATION OF DISORDERLINESS

This principle is stated clearly in these verses in Matthew. If a *"brother"* (which would imply a true Christian) commits some unrepentant trespass that he or she does not make right, he should be treated as walking disorderly. Genuine Christians should withdraw from and treat him just like the heathen, even though he is a true Christian.

- **1 Corinthians 5:6**
"Your glorying *is* not good. Know ye not that a little leaven leaveneth the whole lump?"

In this instance, the Corinthian church had within it a man who had sexual relations with his father's wife--possibly his stepmother. The church did not withdraw from him, as they should have, until he repented of that disorderly walk. He was like *"a little leaven"* that could leaven the entire *"lump"* of the church.

- **1 Corinthians 5:7**
"Purge out therefore the old leaven, that ye may be a new lump, as ye are unleavened. For even Christ our passover is sacrificed for us:"

Paul commanded that this Corinthian church should purge out, and withdraw themselves, from this incestuous man who was walking disorderly and in sin.

- **1 Corinthians 5:8-11**
"Therefore let us keep the feast, not with old leaven, neither with the leaven of malice and wickedness; but with the unleavened *bread* of sincerity and truth. I wrote unto you in an epistle not to company with fornicators: Yet not altogether with the fornicators of this world, or with the covetous, or extortioners, or with idolaters; for then must ye needs go out of the world. But now I have written unto you not to keep company, if any man that is called a brother be a fornicator, or covetous, or an idolater, or a railer, or a drunkard, or an extortioner; with such an one no not to eat."

In these verses, Paul illustrated what to do with a disorderly person, even though he was a true Christian. Don't even eat with him or any other genuine Christian who is walking disorderly such as a railer, drunkard, or extortioner. Don't even eat with them.

Eventually, this man who was walking disorderly repented and made it right with everyone in the church. Then they brought him back into the church.

2 Thessalonians 3:7

"For yourselves know how ye ought to follow us: for we behaved not ourselves disorderly among you;"

PAUL DID NOT WALK DISORDERLY

Paul set a good example of not walking in a disorderly manner when he was among them. Paul was one of those faithful preachers who preached the Word and taught throughout all the different churches where he went. True Christians should follow this example and not behave themselves in a disorderly manner.

Verses On Disorderliness

- Hebrews 13:7

"Remember them which have the rule over you, who have spoken unto you the word of God: whose faith follow, considering the end of *their* conversation."

Genuine Christian leaders should be standards of orderliness.

- 2 Thessalonians 3:11

"For we hear that there are some which walk among you disorderly, working not at all, but are busybodies."

One of the disorderly actions of these true Christians was refusing to do any labor. Instead, they were busybodies.

THE MEANING OF THE GREEK WORD, "ATAKTEO"

The Greek Word for *"disorderly"* is ATAKTEO. Some of the meanings of this Greek Word are:

"1) disorderly, out of ranks (often so of soldiers); 2) irregular, inordinate, immoderate pleasures; 3) deviating from the prescribed order or rule."

When my father and mother sent me to a summer camp from age nine through about fifteen years old, we had to work on getting our camp emblem or letter. One of the things we had to pass was *"tactics."* These were a number of "marching commands" which are followed in the U. S.

Army or Marine Corps. These commands, if followed, kept the entire group in order.

FURTHER MEANING OF THE GREEK WORD, "ATAKTEO"

The Greek Word, ATAKTEO, comes from "A" meaning "*no*" or "*not*" and TAKTEO meaning "*in order.*" If troops were marching ATAKTEO, there would be chaos rather than order.

2 Thessalonians 3:8

"Neither did we eat any man's bread for nought; but wrought with labour and travail night and day, that we might not be chargeable to any of you:"

THE MEANING OF THE GREEK WORD, "KOPOS"

Paul worked and labored night and day. The Greek Word for "work" is KOPOS. Some of the meanings of that Greek Word are:

"*1) a beating; 2) a beating of the breast with grief, sorrow; 3) labour; 3a) trouble; 3a1) to cause one trouble, make work for him; 3b) intense labour united with trouble and toil.*"

THE MEANING OF THE GREEK WORD, "MOCHTHOS"

The Greek Word for "*travail*" is MOCHTHOS. Some of the meanings of this Greek Word are:

"*1) a hard and difficult labour, toil, travail, hardship, distress*"

Because of his personal hard labor and travail, Paul was not on any bread lines. He didn't have others provide him with food or other needs. He worked night and day so he wouldn't be chargeable to any of the true Christians in Thessalonica.

Verses On Paul's Teachings
On Supporting True Christian Workers

- 1 Corinthians 4:12

"And labour, working with our own hands: being reviled, we bless; being persecuted, we suffer it:"

Paul labored making tents. This was a very stressful occupation in addition to his preaching and teaching ministries.

- 1 Corinthians 9:6

"Or I only and Barnabas, have not we power to forbear working?"

> **PAUL WORKED WHEN HE COULD HAVE HAD SUPPORT**
> According to this verse, and others in 1 Corinthians 9, Paul was able to cease his working and have the churches support him as they do present pastors, evangelists and missionaries. But he did not want it to be applied to himself. He wanted it to be applied for future genuine Christian workers, but not for himself. He did not want to stumble anyone in this matter.

- 1 Corinthians 9:11

"If we have sown unto you spiritual things, *is it* a great thing if we shall reap your carnal things?"

Paul encourages future servants of the Lord to receive gifts and offerings for ministering spiritual things.

- 1 Corinthians 9:12

"If others be partakers of *this* power over you, *are* not we rather? Nevertheless we have not used this power; but suffer all things, lest we should hinder the gospel of Christ."

Paul could have been wholly supported by people to whom he ministered, but did not do it so as not to hinder the gospel of the Lord Jesus Christ.

2 Thessalonians 3:9

"Not because we have not power, but to make ourselves an ensample unto you to follow us."

> **THE MEANING OF THE GREEK WORD, "TUPOS"**
> Paul was clear that he could have been supported by people's gifts, but he wanted to be a good example. The Greek Word for *"ensample"* (or *"example"*) is TUPOS. Some of the meanings of this Greek Word are:
>
> *"1) the mark of a stroke or blow, print; 2) a figure formed by a blow or impression; 2a) of a figure or image; 2b) of the image of the gods; 3) form; 3a) the teaching which embodies the sum and substance of religion and represents it to the mind, manner of writing, the contents and form of a letter; 4) an example; 4a) in the technical sense, the pattern in conformity to which a thing must be made; 4b) in an ethical sense, a dissuasive example, a pattern of warning; 4b1) of ruinous events which serve as*

> *admonitions or warnings to others; 4c) an example to be imitated; 4c1) of men worthy of imitation; 4d) in a doctrinal sense; 4d1) of a type i.e. a person or thing prefiguring a future (Messianic) person or thing."*

When something is put in the sand and an impression is made, it makes a pattern. Ladies who sew have patterns that they follow.

Like Paul, genuine Christians should live exemplary lives. Although not perfect, their lives should be a good example and pattern to follow.

Verses On Ensamples Or Examples

- **1 Corinthians 10:11**

"Now all these things happened unto them for ensamples: and they are written for our admonition, upon whom the ends of the world are come."

THE OLD TESTAMENT IS FOR OUR LEARNING
Paul is speaking of the people who lived in the Old Testament times. Their lives give to true Christians both good and bad examples. They should be able to learn to follow the good and flee from the bad.

- **Philippians 3:17**

"Brethren, be followers together of me, and mark them which walk so as ye have us for an ensample."

Paul was an example-man. He was one that people could follow as he followed the Lord Jesus Christ and God's Words. He told them to mark out and notice the walk of people which were not good examples. They were not to follow them.

- **1 Thessalonians 1:7**

"So that ye were ensamples to all that believe in Macedonia and Achaia."

THESSALONIAN CHRISTIANS WERE GOOD EXAMPLES
The genuine Christians at Thessalonica were good examples to all other true Christians in the regions of Macedonia and Achaia because of their walk in the paths of the Words of God.

- **1 Peter 5:3**

"Neither as being lords over *God's* heritage, but being ensamples to the flock."

> **PASTORS MUST BE GOOD EXAMPLES**
> In this context, the Apostle Peter was speaking to each and every one of the pastors-bishops-elders. One of their qualifications was that they were to be good examples to the flock over which God had given them the oversight. They were not be lords and dictators over their people.

- **2 Peter 2:6**
"And turning the cities of Sodom and Gomorrah into ashes condemned *them* with an overthrow, making *them* an ensample unto those that after should live ungodly;"

The destruction of Sodom and Gomorrah--because of their unrepentant sinfulness--was an example which was not to be followed. It was a bad example of how people should live. True Christians should be able to learn from both the good examples (which they should follow) and the bad examples (which they should not follow.)

Verses On Being Obedient To The Lord

- **2 Timothy 2:19**
"Nevertheless the foundation of God standeth sure, having this seal, The Lord knoweth them that are his. And, Let every one that nameth the name of Christ depart from iniquity."

Genuine Christians, who name the name of the Lord Jesus Christ, are ordered to depart from sin of any kind. They must walk after God the Holy Spirit Who indwells them and not after their flesh which leads to sin.

- **Galatians 5:16**
"*This* I say then, Walk in the Spirit, and ye shall not fulfil the lust of the flesh."

The only way for true Christians not to fulfill the lusts of their flesh is to walk in dependence upon and in the power of the Holy Spirit Who indwells them.

- **Galatians 5:17**
"For the flesh lusteth against the Spirit, and the Spirit against the flesh: and these are contrary the one to the other: so that ye cannot do the things that ye would."

> **CONSTANT BATTLE BETWEEN THE FLESH AND SPIRIT**
> Paul is very clear here as well as in Romans 7, that there is a constant battle in genuine Christians between their flesh and God the Holy Spirit Who indwells them. Because of this battle, they cannot do the things that they really want to do when overpowered by their flesh.

2 Thessalonians 3:10

"For even when we were with you, this we commanded you, that if any would not work, neither should he eat."

Paul reminds the true Christians at Thessalonica that he gave them a command about working and eating when he was with them. *"If any would not work, neither should he eat."* What is the meaning of *"would not"*?

THE MEANING OF THE GREEK WORD, "THELO"

The Greek Word for *"would"* is THELO. Some of the meanings of that Greek Word are:

"1) <u>to will</u>, have in mind, intend; 1a) to be resolved or determined, to purpose; 1b) to desire, to wish; 1c) to love; 1c1) <u>to like to do a thing</u>, be fond of doing; 1d) to take delight in, have pleasure,"

This word is in the Greek present tense and means someone who is continuously and perpetually not willing to work. It does not mean that he or she might be disabled and NOT ABLE to work. It implies that the person is able to work, but unwilling to work. The Greek Word for *"work"* is also in the present tense which indicates continuous working day by day rather than just one time.

THE MEANING OF THE GREEK WORD, "ESTHIO"

The Greek Word for *"eat"* is ESTHIO. Some of the meanings of this Greek Word are:

"1) to eat; 2) to eat (consume) a thing; 2a) to take food, <u>eat a meal</u>; 3) metaph. to devour, consume."

This Greek Word is also in the present tense. It implies a continuous eating on a regular basis, not just one time.

The meaning is quite clear, in view of the wording of this clause. <u>Any genuine Christian in the church at Thessalonica (and, by implication, in any church, either then or now) who is perfectly able to work, but is continuously not willing to do so, should not be given food on a regular and continuous basis.</u>

If this rule for true Christians were followed by non-Christians and others, there would be fewer millions of people receiving food stamps as many are today. It's not a question of their being sick or incapacitated. It applies to those who are able-bodied and able to work, but refuse to do so. It would seem that after a while, those in this situation would get hungry and begin to work again.

Verses On Working And Labor

- **Genesis 5:29**

"And he called his name Noah, saying, This *same* shall comfort us concerning our work and toil of our hands, because of the ground which the LORD hath cursed."

The "ground" was "cursed" because of Adam's sin. Noah means "comfort." God comforted Noah who had to work in the cursed ground due to Adam's sin. It was no longer as easy to farm as it had been before the curse. It now took much labor.

- **Exodus 20:9**

"Six days shalt thou labour, and do all thy work:"

One of the ten commandments God gave to Israel was that they were to labor for six out of the seven days each week.

- **Matthew 21:28-29**

"But what think ye? A *certain* man had two sons; and he came to the first, and said, Son, go work to day in my vineyard. He answered and said, I will not: but afterward he repented, and went."

The son who worked was honored, even if he said he wouldn't work at first.

- **1 Corinthians 4:11-12**

"Even unto this present hour we both hunger, and thirst, and are naked, and are buffeted, and have no certain dwelling place; And labour, working with our own hands: being reviled, we bless; being persecuted, we suffer it:"

PAUL WAS AN EXAMPLE OF LABORERS WHO WORK

Paul labored, working with his own hands, even though he could have been supported fully by the churches. He was not afraid to work, as an example of laborers that are working.

- **1 Corinthians 9:6**

"Or I only and Barnabas, have not we power to forbear working?"

Paul and Barnabas had the ability and authority not to work, but they worked anyway so as not to offend.

- **1 Corinthians 9:7**

"Who goeth a warfare any time at his own charges? who planteth a vineyard, and eateth not of the fruit thereof? or who feedeth a flock, and eateth not of the milk of the flock?"

> **EXAMPLES OF SOLDIERS, FARMERS, AND SHEPHERDS**
> Paul was showing that genuine Christian workers, such as he, could receive support. He gives three illustrations of this principle:
> (1) soldiers receive pay for fighting;
> (2) farmers eat of the produce they have raised; and
> (3) shepherds drink the milk of the flock they care for.

- **Philippians 2:29-30**

"Receive him therefore in the Lord with all gladness; and hold such in reputation:Because for the work of Christ he was nigh unto death, not regarding his life, to supply your lack of service toward me."

Paul is speaking here of Epaphroditus (verse 25). He worked night and day for the cause of the Lord Jesus Christ. Because of this hard labor, he was near death.

- **1 Thessalonians 4:11**

"And that ye study to be quiet, and to do your own business, and to work with your own hands, as we commanded you;"

Paul wanted the true Christians in Thessalonica to work with their own hands.

- **Nehemiah 4:21**

"So we laboured in the work: and half of them held the spears from the rising of the morning till the stars appeared."

Nehemiah's people who returned to Jerusalem after 70 years of captivity in Babylon worked all day in rebuilding the wall that had been broken down.

- **Psalms 104:23**

"Man goeth forth unto his work and to his labour until the evening."

This would mean from morning until the evening.

- **Psalms 128:2**

"For thou shalt eat the labour of thine hands: happy *shalt* thou *be*, and *it shall be* well with thee."

This speaks of people eating because of their own hard labor.

- **Proverbs 10:16**

"The labour of the righteous *tendeth* to life: the fruit of the wicked to sin."

God commends the labor of the righteous.

- **Proverbs 13:11**

"Wealth *gotten* by vanity shall be diminished: but he that gathereth by labour shall increase."

Again, God commends working and labor.

- **Proverbs 14:23**
"In all labour there is profit: but the talk of the lips *tendeth* only to penury."
Labor is much more profitable than talking with the lips.
- **Proverbs 21:25**
"The desire of the slothful killeth him; for his hands refuse to labour."

GOD OPPOSES LAZY AND SLOTHFUL PEOPLE
God is against slothful and lazy people who don't work.

- **Ecclesiastes 5:12**
"The sleep of a labouring man *is* sweet, whether he eat little or much: but the abundance of the rich will not suffer him to sleep."
God is in favor of the laboring man.
- **Matthew 9:37**
"Then saith he unto his disciples, The harvest truly *is* plenteous, but the labourers *are* few;"
The Lord Jesus Christ was looking for laborers who would preach His gospel to the ends of the earth.
- **Matthew 9:38**
"Pray ye therefore the Lord of the harvest, that he will send forth labourers into his harvest."
Prayer was to be made for laborers for God's harvest.
- **Matthew 20:2**
"And when he had agreed with the labourers for a penny a day, he sent them into his vineyard."
In this verse, the workers were called laborers.
- **Matthew 20:3**
"And he went out about the third hour, and saw others standing idle in the marketplace,"
Some of these people were idle rather than working.
- **Matthew 20:4**
"And said unto them; Go ye also into the vineyard, and whatsoever is right I will give you. And they went their way."
These laborers were paid in a proper fashion by the owner.
- **Luke 10:7**
"And in the same house remain, eating and drinking such things as they give: for the labourer is worthy of his hire. Go not from house to house."
Those who labor deserve to get proper remuneration for their work.

- **Acts 20:35**
"I have shewed you all things, how that so labouring ye ought to support the weak, and to remember the words of the Lord Jesus, how he said, It is more blessed to give than to receive."
It is honorable to labor and support those who are weak and unable to labor.
- **Romans 16:6**
"Greet Mary, who bestowed much labour on us."
Mary labored greatly in helping Paul.
- **Romans 16:12**
"Salute Tryphena and Tryphosa, who labour in the Lord. Salute the beloved Persis, which laboured much in the Lord."
The first two women labored in the Lord, but Persis labored much more than them.
- **2 Corinthians 6:5**
"In stripes, in imprisonments, in tumults, in labours, in watchings, in fastings;"
Among Paul's many circumstances that happened unto him, he lists labors. He worked hard at tent-making.
- **2 Corinthians 11:23**
"Are they ministers of Christ? (I speak as a fool) I *am* more; in labours more abundant, in stripes above measure, in prisons more frequent, in deaths oft."
Paul had more labors than any of his enemies.
- **Ephesians 4:28**
"Let him that stole steal no more: but rather let him labour, working with *his* hands the thing which is good, that he may have to give to him that needeth."

THIEVES SHOULD STOP STEALING AND SHOULD WORK
The thieves were told to stop their stealing and labor with their hands to give to those who had need.

- **Philippians 2:25**
"Yet I supposed it necessary to send to you Epaphroditus, my brother, and companion in labour, and fellowsoldier, but your messenger, and he that ministered to my wants."
Epaphroditus was Paul's companion as he labored for the Lord.
- **Philippians 4:3**
"And I intreat thee also, true yokefellow, help those women which laboured with me in the gospel, with Clement also, and *with* other my fellowlabourers, whose names *are* in the book of life."
In this verse, it mentions that even some women labored with him in the gospel of the Lord Jesus Christ.

- **1 Thessalonians 2:9**
"For ye remember, brethren, our labour and travail: for labouring night and day, because we would not be chargeable unto any of you, we preached unto you the gospel of God."

PAUL LABORED NIGHT AND DAY
Paul was an excellent example of laboring night and day so as not to be chargeable to anyone.

- **2 Thessalonians 3:8**
"Neither did we eat any man's bread for nought; but wrought with labour and travail night and day, that we might not be chargeable to any of you:"

Paul didn't want anyone's bread without charge, but he worked hard day and night so he could take care of himself without assistance from anyone.

- **1 Timothy 5:17**
"Let the elders that rule well be counted worthy of double honour, especially they who labour in the word and doctrine."

The pastors-bishops-elders who labored in the Words of God and who labor today in the Words of God should be honored doubly.

- **1 Timothy 5:18**
"For the scripture saith, Thou shalt not muzzle the ox that treadeth out the corn. And, The labourer *is* worthy of his reward."

Those who labor and work deserve to be paid for that labor.

- **2 Timothy 2:6**
"The husbandman that laboureth must be first partaker of the fruits."

A farmer who plants his garden should be able to eat some of the fruits of that garden.

Verses On Slothfulness

Sloths are a very slow-moving creatures. You can hardly see them move. They move very gradually.

- **Proverbs 12:24**
"The hand of the diligent shall bear rule: but the slothful shall be under tribute."

The non-working, slothful person will be under the control of others.

- **Proverbs 19:15**
"Slothfulness casteth into a deep sleep; and an idle soul shall suffer hunger."

In this verse, Paul's position is maintained. Slothful and lazy, non-working people in the Old Testament Bible period would hunger.

2 Thessalonians 3:11

"For we hear that there are some which walk among you disorderly, working not at all, but are busybodies."

> **IT IS DISORDERLY NOT TO WORK**
> One of the actions that is considered *"disorderly"* is the refusal to work on the part of genuine Christians. Without working they have time on their hands, and they become busybodies.

> **THE MEANING OF THE GREEK WORD, "ATAKTOS"**
> As mentioned above, the Greek Word for *"disorderly"* is ATAKTOS. Some of the meanings of this Greek Word are:
> > *"1) disorderly, <u>out of ranks</u> (often so of soldiers); 2) irregular, inordinate, immoderate pleasures; 3) <u>deviating from the prescribed order or rule.</u>"*

This is Paul's name for those true Christians who refuse to work and turn into busybodies.

> **THE MEANING OF THE GREEK WORD, "PERIERGAZOMAI"**
> The Greek Word for *"busybodies"* PERIERGAZOMAI. Some of the meanings of this Greek Word are:
> > *"1) to bustle about uselessly, to busy one's self about trifling, needless, useless matters; 1a) used apparently of a <u>person officiously inquisitive about other's affairs.</u>"*

God doesn't like these kinds of disorderly genuine Christians. They should get to work and stop their disorderliness.

2 Thessalonians 3:12

"Now them that are such we command and exhort by our Lord Jesus Christ, that with quietness they work, and eat their own bread."

Paul commands these disorderly, idle, busybody, true Christians to get back to work for their own bread rather than taking it from others. The Greek verb *"command"* is in the Greek present tense indicating that Paul is constantly and continuously commanded them to get back to work.

> **THE MEANING OF THE GREEK WORD, "HESUCHIA"**
> The Greek Word for *"quietness"* is HESUCHIA. Some of the meanings of this Greek Word are:
> *"1) quietness; 1a) description of the life of one who stays at home doing his own work, and <u>does not officiously meddle with the affairs of others</u>; 2) silence."*

Paul wanted them to get to work immediately!

2 Thessalonians 3:13

"But ye, brethren, be not weary in well doing."

On the other hand, Paul addresses the genuine Christians about *"well doing."* This includes working rather than loafing and being slothful as some were.

> **THE MEANING OF THE GREEK WORD, "EKKAKEO"**
> The Greek Word for the verb *"be not weary"* is EKKAKEO. Some of the meanings of this Greek Word are:
> *"1) to be utterly spiritless, to be wearied out, exhausted"*

This Greek Word is in the Greek aorist tense. <u>As a prohibition in the Greek aorist tense, it means don't even begin an action.</u> Paul does not want any of these true Christians even to begin to be weary in well doing. This includes working rather than loafing.

Verses On Weariness

- **Proverbs 3:11**

"My son, despise not the chastening of the LORD; neither be weary of his correction:"

Genuine Christians should take this to heart. <u>They should not be weary when God corrects them for their wrong thoughts or actions.</u>

- **Ecclesiastes 12:12**

"And further, by these, my son, be admonished: of making many books *there is* no end; and much study *is* a weariness of the flesh."

Much study, for those who have done it, makes one very weary and tired out.

- **Isaiah 40:30**

"Even the youths shall faint and be weary, and the young men shall utterly fall:"

<u>Youths can be weary, not just older people.</u>

- Isaiah 40:31
"But they that wait upon the LORD shall renew *their* strength; they shall mount up with wings as eagles; they shall run, and not be weary; *and* they shall walk, and not faint."

WAITING ON THE LORD RENEWS STRENGTH

When true Christians wait upon the Lord, they shall not be weary or faint, even though they run or walk around. That's quite a promise. I often quote this verse when visiting people who are in hospital beds.

- John 4:6
"Now Jacob's well was there. Jesus therefore, being wearied with *his* journey, sat thus on the well: *and* it was about the sixth hour."

CHRIST (WAS & IS) PERFECT GOD AND PERFECT MAN

Though the Lord Jesus Christ was perfect God, He was also Perfect Man. As such, He knew the feeling of being weary so He could sympathize with and understand what humans go through.

- 2 Corinthians 11:27
"In weariness and painfulness, in watchings often, in hunger and thirst, in fastings often, in cold and nakedness."

Paul knew from his own experiences what weariness felt like. He had plenty of it. Imagine his three missionary journeys which involved much walking and weariness. Also, remember the painfulness of his various imprisonments in dirty jail conditions.

- Galatians 6:9
"And let us not be weary in well doing: for in due season we shall reap, if we faint not."

Genuine Christians are exhorted not to be weary in doing what is good and Biblical. One day, they will reap their rewards for following this exhortation.

- Hebrews 12:3
"For consider him that endured such contradiction of sinners against himself, lest ye be wearied and faint in your minds."

When true Christians realize what the Lord Jesus Christ endured for them, they should not be wearied nor faint in their minds.

2 Thessalonians 3:14

"And if any man obey not our word by this epistle, note that man, and have no company with him, that he may be ashamed."

SEPARATION FROM DISOBEDIENT CHRISTIANS

This is a verse that commands genuine Christians to be separated from true Christians who are disobedient. There should be no company with these, so that they might be ashamed.

THE MEANING OF THE GREEK WORD, "SEMEIOO"

The Greek Word for *"note"* is SEMEIOO. Some of the meanings of this Greek Word are:

*"1) to mark, to note, distinguish by marking;
2) to mark or note for one's self"*

Since this Greek verb is in the Greek present tense, it means that genuine Christians should continuously distinguish and *note* true Christians who are disobedient to the Words of God in some way or another. This is why, as a pastor, I seek to *note* and expose those who are genuine Christians, but a part of the disobedient "new evangelical" beliefs and practices such as practiced in the National Association of Evangelicals (NAE) and in many other groups and organizations. This included, in Paul's day, those Christians who were capable of working, but did not work.

Many people get upset when pastors name the names and expose those who are walking contrary to some of the commands of the Bible. It would be impossible to *"note"* or distinguish someone without naming them. This is why I name and note many who are either pagans, religious apostates, or true Christians who are disobedient in important doctrines taught clearly in the Bible.

MEANING OF THE GREEK WORD, "SUNANAMIGNUMI"

The Greek Word for *"have no company"* is SUNANAMIGNUMI. Some of the meanings of this Greek Word are:

"1) to mix up together; 2) to keep company with, be intimate with one"

Since this is a prohibition and the Greek verb is in the Greek present tense, it means to stop an action already in progress. Apparently, the genuine Christians at Thessalonica were continuing to have close fellowship with other true Christians who were disobedient to some of the Words of God as found in the Bible. Paul commanded them to cease from such fellowship. Genuine Christians today should obey this command as well.

Verses On Noting And Separating From The Disobedient

- **Romans 16:17-18**

"Now I beseech you, brethren, mark them which cause divisions and offences contrary to the doctrine which ye have learned; and avoid them. For they that are such serve not our Lord Jesus Christ, but their own belly; and by good words and fair speeches deceive the hearts of the simple."

The genuine Christians in Rome were to "note" and mark those who caused divisions contrary to the doctrines of the Bible.

- **1 Corinthians 1:10-13**

"Now I beseech you, brethren, by the name of our Lord Jesus Christ, that ye all speak the same thing, and *that* there be no divisions among you; but *that* ye be perfectly joined together in the same mind and in the same judgment. For it hath been declared unto me of you, my brethren, by them *which are of the house* of Chloe, that there are contentions among you. Now this I say, that every one of you saith, I am of Paul; and I of Apollos; and I of Cephas; and I of Christ. Is Christ divided? was Paul crucified for you? or were ye baptized in the name of Paul?"

Paul described and noted those who were dividing the church at Corinth.

- **Ephesians 5:11**

"And have no fellowship with the unfruitful works of darkness, but rather reprove *them*."

THE MEANING OF THE GREEK WORD, "ELENCHO"

The Greek Word for *"reprove"* is ELENCHO. Some of the meanings of this Greek Word are:

"ἐλέγχω (elegchō): vb.; rebuke, expose; refute, show one's fault, implying that there is a convincing of that fault (Mt 18:15; Jn 3:20; 16:8; Eph 5:11; 1Ti 5:20; 2Ti 4:2; Tit 1:9; Heb 12:5; Jas 2:9; Jude 15; Rev 3:19; Jn 8:9; Jude 22, 23)"

The true Christians in Ephesus were commanded by Paul to reprove, expose, and bring to light the unfruitful works of darkness. This should be done today as well by all genuine Christians.

- **1 Timothy 5:19-21**

"Against an elder receive not an accusation, but before two or three witnesses. Them that sin rebuke before all, that others also may fear. I charge *thee* before God, and the Lord Jesus Christ, and the elect angels, that thou observe these things without preferring one before another, doing nothing by partiality."

When some believe that a pastor-bishop-elder has committed some sin or impropriety, he is not to be exposed by an accusation unless two or three honest witnesses bring such before the church. When found guilty, he is to be rebuked before all whether he is a big preacher with a big church, or a little preacher with a little church.

Pastors who had committed adultery--whose churches were a part of the General Association of Regular Baptist Churches--used to be exposed in the *Baptist Bulletin*. This was done when Dr. R. T. Ketcham was leading that group, but they don't do it any more.

- **2 Timothy 1:15**

"This thou knowest, that all they which are in Asia be turned away from me; of whom are Phygellus and Hermogenes."

Paul gives these examples, noting disobedient men who turned away from him and the truth. They were named Phygellus and Hermogenes.

- **2 Timothy 3:8**

"Now as Jannes and Jambres withstood Moses, so do these also resist the truth: men of corrupt minds, reprobate concerning the faith."

Once again, Paul named and exposed. This time it was the magicians Jannes and Jambres who withstood Moses.

- **2 Timothy 4:14-15**

"Alexander the coppersmith did me much evil: the Lord reward him according to his works: Of whom be thou ware also; for he hath greatly withstood our words."

Paul noted, named, and exposed Alexander who did him much evil.

- **2 Timothy 2:17-18**

"And their word will eat as doth a canker: of whom is Hymenaeus and Philetus; Who concerning the truth have erred, saying that the resurrection is past already; and overthrow the faith of some. "

He also noted and exposed Hymenaeus and Philetus. They greatly erred, saying that the resurrection was past. They had overthrown the faith of some.

- **2 Timothy 4:10**

"For Demas hath forsaken me, having loved this present world, and is departed unto Thessalonica; Crescens to Galatia, Titus unto Dalmatia."

Paul noted and exposed Demas who had left him and gone back into the worldly life.
- **Titus 1:9-13**
"Holding fast the faithful word as he hath been taught, that he may be able by sound doctrine both to exhort and to convince the gainsayers. For there are many unruly and vain talkers and deceivers, specially they of the circumcision: Whose mouths must be stopped, who subvert whole houses, teaching things which they ought not, for filthy lucre's sake. One of themselves, *even* a prophet of their own, said, The Cretians *are* alway liars, evil beasts, slow bellies. This witness is true. Wherefore rebuke them sharply, that they may be sound in the faith;"

Paul quoted a prophet's statement to Titus who was the pastor of the church at Crete. He told him to rebuke these liars sharply so that they might be sound in the faith.
- **3 John 1:9-10**
"I wrote unto the church: but Diotrephes, who loveth to have the preeminence among them, receiveth us not. Wherefore, if I come, I will remember his deeds which he doeth, prating against us with malicious words: and not content therewith, neither doth he himself receive the brethren, and forbiddeth them that would, and casteth *them* out of the church."

THE CHURCH BOSS DIOTREPHES THEN AND NOW

The Apostle John noted and exposed Diotrephes who loved to have the preeminence among those in that church. He wanted to rule the church. There are similar people in Bible-believing churches today. I experienced a few Diotrephes-type of people when I pastored my first church in Newton, Massachusetts, in the 1960's.

- **1 Corinthians 5:9-11**
"I wrote unto you in an epistle not to company with fornicators: Yet not altogether with the fornicators of this world, or with the covetous, or extortioners, or with idolaters; for then must ye needs go out of the world. But now I have written unto you not to keep company, if any man that is called a brother be a fornicator, or covetous, or an idolater, or a railer, or a drunkard, or an extortioner; with such an one no not to eat."

AVOID CLOSE FELLOWSHIP WITH THE WORLDLY

If genuine Christians separate from all the world, they would have to stay out of the world. They are to separate from

> close fellowship and relationships with the disorderly and disobedient, even though they might be true Christians.

- **2 Thessalonians 3:6**

"Now we command you, brethren, in the name of our Lord Jesus Christ, that ye withdraw yourselves from every brother that walketh disorderly, and not after the tradition which he received of us."

> **WITHDRAW FROM DISORDERLY CHRISTIANS**
> This is Paul's further command to withdraw from every true Christian who is walking in a disorderly manner in violation of the Bible's standards.

2 Thessalonians 3:15

"Yet count him not as an enemy, but admonish him as a brother."

This involves a genuine Christian who has gone astray from the Bible's teachings in some way. Such a one is not to be treated by other true Christians as an enemy, they should admonish him as a brother in Christ.

> **THE MEANING OF THE GREEK WORD, "NOTHETEO"**
> The Greek Word *"admonish"* is NOUTHETEO. Some of the meanings of that Greek Word are:
> *"1) to admonish, warn, exhort"*

Verses On Admonition

- **Ecclesiastes 4:13**

"Better *is* a poor and a wise child than an old and foolish king, who will no more be admonished."

Wisdom at whatever age is to be valued more than a person of high stature who refuses to be admonished.

- **Jeremiah 42:19**

"The LORD hath said concerning you, O ye remnant of Judah; Go ye not into Egypt: know certainly that I have admonished you this day."

The prophet Jeremiah admonished Judah not to return into Egypt.

- **Acts 27:9-10**

"Now when much time was spent, and when sailing was now dangerous, because the fast was now already past, Paul admonished *them*, And said unto them, Sirs, I perceive that this voyage will be with hurt and much damage, not only of the lading and ship, but also of our lives."

Paul was a Roman prisoner on a ship sailing on the Mediterranean Sea. He admonished and warned them about the great storm that was about to come upon that ship.
- **Romans 15:14**
"And I myself also am persuaded of you, my brethren, that ye also are full of goodness, filled with all knowledge, able also to admonish one another."

ADMONISH BASED ON THE TEACHINGS THE BIBLE
Born-again, true Christians are able, in a proper manner, to admonish their fellow true Christians provided they are filled with the knowledge of the teachings of the Bible.

- **1 Corinthians 10:11**
"Now all these things happened unto them for ensamples: and they are written for our admonition, upon whom the ends of the world are come."

The things that happened in the Old Testament were written for the admonition and warning of the genuine Christians of all ages. Though the Old Testament was written **to** the nation of Israel, it was written **for** the the church as well.

- **Ephesians 6:4**
"And, ye fathers, provoke not your children to wrath: but bring them up in the nurture and admonition of the Lord."

THE MEANING OF THE GREEK WORD, "PAIDEIA"
The Greek Word for "*nurture*" is PAIDEIA. Some of the meanings of that Greek Word are:

"*παιδεία (paideia), ἡ (hē): n.fem.; 1. instruction (2Ti 3:16); 2. discipline, training (Eph 6:4); 3. punishment, chastisement for improving behavior (Heb 12:5, 7, 8, 11+)*"

This word, "*nurture,*" speaks of the discipline of a parent's children, including spanking them as needed and as the Bible instructs in the verses below and many others.

"*He that spareth his rod hateth his son: but he that loveth him chasteneth him betimes.*" (Proverbs 13:24)
"*Chasten thy son while there is hope, and let not thy soul spare for his crying.*" (Proverbs 19:18)

THE MEANING OF THE GREEK WORD, "NOUTHESIA"
The Greek Word for "*admonition*" here is NOUTHESIA. Some of the meanings of that Greek Word are:

> "νουθεσία (nouthesia), ας (as), ἡ (hē): n.fem.; 1. teaching, **instruction** (1Co 10:11; Tit 3:10+); 2. warning, admonition (Eph 6:4+)"

This speaks of the instructing and talking with the children so that they can understand why they are being corrected.
- **Colossians 3:16**
"Let the word of Christ dwell in you richly in all wisdom; teaching and admonishing one another in psalms and hymns and spiritual songs, singing with grace in your hearts to the Lord."

SINGING IS ONE MEANS OF ADMONISHING
Only if the Words of God are dwelling in genuine Christians richly in all wisdom will they be able to admonish other genuine Christians. According to this verse, singing is one way of admonishing.

- **1 Thessalonians 5:12**
"And we beseech you, brethren, to know them which labour among you, and are over you in the Lord, and admonish you;"
The ones who labored among these true Christians at Thessalonica admonished them to walk with the Lord Jesus Christ.
- **Titus 3:10**
"A man that is an heretick after the first and second admonition reject;"
According to this verse, a person who is a heretic and believes some serious false doctrine, should be given two admonitions or warnings only. If he refuses to go back to Biblical truth, he is to be rejected.

2 Thessalonians 3:16
"Now the Lord of peace himself give you peace always by all means. The Lord be with you all."

One of the titles of the Lord Jesus Christ is that He is the "*Lord of peace.*" Paul wishes that He would grant the genuine Christians in Thessalonica His peace.

Verses On Peace
- **Psalms 4:8**
"I will both lay me down in peace, and sleep: for thou, LORD, only makest me dwell in safety."
David trusted in the God of the Bible Who gave him peace.

- **Isaiah 9:6**

"For unto us a child is born, unto us a son is given: and the government shall be upon his shoulder: and his name shall be called Wonderful, Counsellor, The mighty God, The everlasting Father, The Prince of Peace."

One of the titles of the Lord Jesus Christ is *"The Prince of Peace."*

- **Isaiah 9:7**

"Of the increase of *his* government and peace *there shall be* no end, upon the throne of David, and upon his kingdom, to order it, and to establish it with judgment and with justice from henceforth even for ever. The zeal of the LORD of hosts will perform this."

This will take place during the millennial reign of the Lord Jesus Christ when He returns to this earth.

- **Isaiah 26:3**

"Thou wilt keep *him* in perfect peace, *whose* mind *is* stayed *on thee*: because he trusteth in thee."

This is a wonderful promise of God. It is possible only with a mind that is stayed on Him.

- **Isaiah 48:22**

"There is no peace, saith the LORD, unto the wicked."

Unless people are genuine Christians, they have no real peace.

- **Mark 4:39**

"And he arose, and rebuked the wind, and said unto the sea, Peace, be still. And the wind ceased, and there was a great calm."

The Lord Jesus Christ, as Perfect God, had the power to stop the boisterous sea.

- **Luke 2:14**

"Glory to God in the highest, and on earth peace, good will toward men."

The only time that this verse about peace will be fulfilled is when the Lord Jesus Christ reigns on earth during the Millennium.

- **John 14:27**

"Peace I leave with you, my peace I give unto you: not as the world giveth, give I unto you. Let not your heart be troubled, neither let it be afraid."

This is the inner peace that the Lord Jesus Christ alone can give to those who trust Him as their Saviour.

- **John 16:33**

"These things I have spoken unto you, that in me ye might have peace. In the world ye shall have tribulation: but be of good cheer; I have overcome the world."

The world knows nothing about the peace that the Lord Jesus Christ can give those who have received Him as their Redeemer.

- **John 20:19**
"Then the same day at evening, being the first *day* of the week, when the doors were shut where the disciples were assembled for fear of the Jews, came Jesus and stood in the midst, and saith unto them, Peace be unto you."

After His crucifixion for the sins of the entire world, and His bodily resurrection from the dead, the Lord Jesus Christ greeted the doubting apostles with the words, *"Peace be unto you."*

- **Romans 5:1**
"Therefore being justified by faith, we have peace with God through our Lord Jesus Christ:"

JUSTIFIED BY TRUE FAITH IN CHRIST ALONE
Being justified by genuine faith in the Lord Jesus Christ is the only way anyone on earth can have genuine and eternal peace with the God of the Bible.

- **Romans 15:13**
"Now the God of hope fill you with all joy and peace in believing, that ye may abound in hope, through the power of the Holy Ghost."

There is true joy and peace in the Lord by genuinely believing in the Lord Jesus Christ for salvation.

- **Galatians 5:22-23**
"But the fruit of the Spirit is love, joy, peace, longsuffering, gentleness, goodness, faith, meekness, temperance: against which there is no law"

One of the nine characteristics possible for genuine Christians who are filled with the Holy Spirit is God's peace.

- **Philippians 4:6-7**
"Be careful for nothing; but in every thing by prayer and supplication with thanksgiving let your requests be made known unto God. And the peace of God, which passeth all understanding, shall keep your hearts and minds through Christ Jesus."

Through true Christians' prayer and supplication, God will give them what He calls *"the peace of God."*

- **Colossians 1:20**
"And, having made peace through the blood of his cross, by him to reconcile all things unto himself; by him, *I say*, whether *they be* things in earth, or things in heaven."

PEACE WITH GOD ONLY THROUGH CHRIST
The only way any human being can get peace is through the shed blood of the Lord Jesus Christ Who died for the sins of the whole world.

---

2 Thessalonians 3:17

"The salutation of Paul with mine own hand, which is the token in every epistle: so I write."
- 1 Corinthians 16:21
"The salutation of *me* Paul with mine own hand."
This shows Paul wrote and signed this letter himself.
- Colossians 4:18
"The salutation by the hand of me Paul. Remember my bonds. Grace *be* with you. Amen."
Paul wrote and signed Colossians as well.

2 Thessalonians 3:18

"The grace of our Lord Jesus Christ be with you all. Amen."
The grace of the Lord Jesus Christ is the possession of all genuine Christians.

THE MEANING OF THE GREEK WORD, "CHARIS"

The Greek Word for "grace" is CHARIS. Some of the meanings of that Greek Word are:

"1) grace; 1a) that which affords joy, pleasure, delight, sweetness, charm, loveliness: grace of speech; 2) good will, loving-kindness, favour' 2a) of the merciful kindness by which God, exerting his holy influence upon souls, turns them to Christ, keeps, strengthens, increases them in Christian faith, knowledge, affection, and kindles them to the exercise of the Christian virtues; 3) what is due to grace; 3a) the spiritual condition of one governed by the power of divine grace; 3b) the token or proof of grace, benefit; 3b1) a gift of grace; 3b2) benefit, bounty; 4) thanks, (for benefits, services, favours), recompense, reward."

TRUE CHRISTIANS ARE RECIPIENTS OF GOD'S GRACE

Those who are true Christians who have been saved eternally by genuine faith in the Lord Jesus Christ are the recipients of God's grace. It is getting from God something that they do not deserve.

Verses On God's Grace

- **Genesis 6:8**

"But Noah found grace in the eyes of the LORD."
Just he and seven other people were spared from the universal flood upon the earth.

- **John 1:14**

"And the Word was made flesh, and dwelt among us, (and we beheld his glory, the glory as of the only begotten of the Father,) full of grace and truth."

The Lord Jesus Christ was full of grace in all of His activities while on earth.

- **John 1:17**

"For the law was given by Moses, *but* grace and truth came by Jesus Christ."

The Lord Jesus Christ brought grace and truth which was not in existence during the law of Moses in the same magnitude.

- **Acts 15:11**

"But we believe that through the grace of the Lord Jesus Christ we shall be saved, even as they."

Both true believing Gentiles as well as Jews will be saved by God's grace.

- **Acts 20:32**

"And now, brethren, I commend you to God, and to the word of his grace, which is able to build you up, and to give you an inheritance among all them which are sanctified."

The *"Word of His grace"* is a name for the Bible. It is the only Thing that is able to build up genuine Christians in the faith.

- **Romans 3:24**

"Being justified freely by his grace through the redemption that is in Christ Jesus:"

WORKS CANNOT BRING SALVATION WITH GOD

God can only declare sinners justified by His grace. Their works, however commendable, will not prevail.

- **1 Corinthians 15:10**

"But by the grace of God I am what I am: and his grace which *was* bestowed upon me was not in vain; but I laboured more abundantly than they all: yet not I, but the grace of God which was with me."

Paul, though a self-righteous Pharisee, was very evil. He imprisoned and witnessed the murderer of true Christians. But God, in His matchless grace, saved Paul's soul by his true trust in His Son and transformed his life.

- **2 Corinthians 8:9**
"For ye know the grace of our Lord Jesus Christ, that, though he was rich, yet for your sakes he became poor, that ye through his poverty might be rich."

CHRIST'S POVERTY CAN MAKE PEOPLE RICH

The Lord Jesus Christ showed His grace in giving mankind something they did not deserve. He descended from Heaven and willingly died on the cross for the sins of the entire world so that those who truly trust in Him as their Saviour might have everlasting life. Genuine Christians are made rich by His poverty in coming to earth to save them.

- **2 Corinthians 12:8-9**
"For this thing I besought the Lord thrice, that it might depart from me. And he said unto me, My grace is sufficient for thee: for my strength is made perfect in weakness. Most gladly therefore will I rather glory in my infirmities, that the power of Christ may rest upon me."

PAUL'S THORN IN THE FLESH

For his thorn in the flesh, Paul besought the Lord three times. God did not remove the thorn, but he said that His grace would be sufficient for him. Paul was satisfied with God's answer. He learned that God's grace was made perfect through his weakness.

- **Ephesians 2:8-9**
"For by grace are ye saved through faith; and that not of yourselves: *it is* the gift of God: Not of works, lest any man should boast."
It is only by the grace of God that true Christians are saved. It is not by any works that they may have do or have done.

- **2 Corinthians 13:14**
"The grace of the Lord Jesus Christ, and the love of God, and the communion of the Holy Ghost, *be* with you all. Amen."
Paul wished the grace of the Lord Jesus Christ on all the genuine Christians in Corinth.

- **Galatians 6:18**
"Brethren, the grace of our Lord Jesus Christ *be* with your spirit. Amen."

PAUL CLOSES HIS LETTERS WITH "GRACE"

As you can see by the following books and verses, Paul wanted the grace of the Lord Jesus Christ to be with all the true Christians. This was true for the Galatians, the Ephesians, the Colossians, the Thessalonians, for Timothy, for Titus, for Philemon, and for the Hebrews.

- Ephesians 6:24

"Grace *be* with all them that love our Lord Jesus Christ in sincerity. Amen."

- Philippians 4:23

"The grace of our Lord Jesus Christ *be* with you all. Amen."

- Colossians 4:18

"The salutation by the hand of me Paul. Remember my bonds. Grace *be* with you. Amen."

- 1 Thessalonians 5:28

"The grace of our Lord Jesus Christ *be* with you. Amen."

- 2 Thessalonians 3:18

"The grace of our Lord Jesus Christ *be* with you all. Amen."

- 1 Timothy 6:21

"Which some professing have erred concerning the faith. Grace *be* with thee. Amen."

- 2 Timothy 4:22

"The Lord Jesus Christ *be* with thy spirit. Grace *be* with you. Amen."

- Titus 3:15

"All that are with me salute thee. Greet them that love us in the faith. Grace *be* with you all. Amen."

- Philemon 1:25

"The grace of our Lord Jesus Christ *be* with your spirit. Amen."

- Hebrews 13:25

"Grace *be* with you all. Amen."

THE MEANING OF THE GREEK WORD, "AMEN"

The last word in 2 Thessalonians 3:18 is "Amen." Here is a background and definition of this Greek Word AMEN.

"The word "amen" is a most remarkable word. It was transliterated directly from the Hebrew into the Greek of the

> *New Testament, then into Latin and into English and many other languages, so that it is practically a universal word. It has been called the best known word in human speech. The word is directly related -- in fact, almost identical--to the Hebrew word for "believe" (aman), or faithful. Thus, it came to mean "sure" or "truly," an expression of absolute trust and confidence"*

Paul wrote this small little letter of Second Thessalonians to urge the genuine Christians there to be obedient to the Lord Jesus Christ in separating from true Christians who were disobedient to the Words of God. They were to be separated unto the Lord Jesus Christ, and His will and way in their lives, so that they might bear fruit and live for Him faithfully.

Index of Words and Phrases

1 Thessalonians Chapter Five................................ iv
1 Thessalonians Chapter Four................................ iv
1 Thessalonians Chapter One................................. iv
1 Thessalonians Chapter Three............................... iv
1 Thessalonians Chapter Two................................. iv
2 Thessalonians Chapter One................................. iv
2 Thessalonians Chapter Three............................... iv
2 Thessalonians Chapter Two................................. iv
3½ YEARS OF PHONY ANTICHRIST PEACE.................. 135
A FALSE CHARGE OF STEALING FUNDS..................... 119
A GREAT MULTITUDE WERE SAVED........................ 3
ABOUNDING IN HOPE THROUGH GOD'S SPIRIT............. 18
About the Author.. iv
abstain............ 97, 100, 101, 109, 112, 140, 143, 144, 169, 170, 260
ACCOUNTABILITY OF THOSE WHO WATCH FOR SOULS...... 143
Acknowledgments... ii, iv
admonish...................................... 153, 154, 278, 279
adultery............... 31, 35, 48, 100, 102, 103, 107, 110, 238, 276
afflictions.................. 10, 21-23, 32, 67-70, 140, 142, 192, 253
AFTER SALVATION GOD CAN SANCTIFY..................... 106
After The Seven Year Tribulation, God the Son will return........ 186
aged women... 92, 112
agree................... 47, 68, 86, 113, 114, 175, 196, 203, 257, 260
AGREEING WITH GOD ON SIN BRINGS RESTORATION....... 175
aim and burden.. iii
alcohol... 140, 144
all... i, iii, 1, 3-16, 18-36, 38-44, 48-53, 55-58, 60-63, 66-71, 73-94, 96, 98-102, 105-131, 134-138, 140-142, 144, 146-170, 172-181, 183-212, 215-235, 237-248, 250-261, 263-269, 271, 273, 275-286
ALL ARE TO FLEE THE LUSTS OF YOUTH.................. 109
all people........... 22, 60, 86, 119, 148, 149, 168, 174, 199, 257
always fulfills.. 245
amen................... 10, 32, 83, 178, 181, 236, 253, 282, 284, 285
AN ILLUSTRATION OF DISORDERLINESS.................. 260
animals...................... 8, 44, 100, 103, 164, 207, 252
Antichrist.35, 137, 138, 220, 222-226, 228-230, 232, 233, 235, 237, 242
ANTICHRIST REVEALED AFTER THE RAPTURE.............. 228
Antioch................................ 5, 9, 26, 32, 57, 251, 253
any moment... 126, 255

aorist tense.. 219, 272
apostasia... 220
APOSTASIA--STANDING AWAY OR DEPARTING.............. 220
apostasy. 61, 142, 179, 259
apostles... 5, 10, 18, 24-26, 42, 46, 57, 62, 98, 134, 150, 210, 229, 231, 232, 241, 251, 281
appearance..................................... 100, 169-171, 195
APPOINTED TO AFFLICTIONS........................ 22, 67, 68
Armageddon.. 89, 92, 124, 136, 200-202, 207, 208, 219, 220, 225, 226
armor... 73
arrogant.. 27
ascended bodily.. 25, 186
ASSISTING THOSE WHO ARE WEAK IN THE FAITH.......... 158
assurance.. 15, 18, 19, 116
ASV.. 149
AT THE RAPTURE, ALL CHRISTIANS ARE WITH CHRIST....... 63
atakteo... 262
atheteo... 112
Author... iv, 23, 155, 175
avoid....................... 102, 103, 221, 222, 231, 254, 275, 277
avoid fornication....................................... 102, 103
AVOID THOSE WHO PREACH FALSE DOCTRINE............. 222
background............................... 1, 2, 27, 183, 285
banking.. 224
battle.... 89, 92, 124, 129, 135-137, 165, 200-202, 207, 208, 219, 220, 225-227, 233, 265
beasts.. 202, 227, 276
BEFORE SALVATION LIVES ARE UNCLEAN................ 110
Behaving Holily... 47
Behaving Justly... 47
Behaving Unblameably................................... 47
behavior..................... 92, 112, 124, 154, 250, 279
Berea....................................... 1, 3, 4, 60, 183
BEREANS-SEARCHING THE SCRIPTURES DAILY............ 183
beware... 37, 243
BEWARE OF FALSE TEACHERS AND PREACHERS............ 37
BFT #4137... i
BFT Phone: 856-854-4452................................. i
Bible condemns sodomy................................. 108
Bible doctrines..................... 66, 72, 77, 78, 81, 82, 190
Bible For Today....................... i-iii, 25, 35, 62, 167, 249, 250
Bible For Today Baptist Church.............. i, iii, 25, 35, 167, 250
BIBLE FOR TODAY PRESS................................. i

Bible knowledge.. 189
Bible preservation.. 176
Bible versions.................................... 35, 149, 235
BIBLE "SAINTS" ARE GENUINE CHRISTIANS............... 103
Bible's Doctrines... 72
Biblical doctrine....................................... 50, 89
BIBLICAL RIGHTEOUSNESS BRINGS ASSURANCE.......... 116
birds.. 202
BIRDS WILL HAVE A SUPPER AFTER ARMAGEDDON......... 202
blameless...................... 47, 93, 106, 140, 157, 171, 172, 218
blaspheme... 52, 210
blessings... 122, 197
bodies..... 19, 28, 68, 91-93, 102, 104-107, 110-112, 124, 129, 172, 201,
               202, 207, 211, 216, 217, 229, 247, 261, 263, 271
bodies transformed..................................... 93, 217
BODIES UNTO SANCTIFICATION AND HONOR............... 105
BODIES YIELDED TO HOLINESS............................ 111
bodily......................... 25, 29, 111, 123, 153, 185, 186, 281
bodily resurrection............................... 29, 186, 281
Body of Christ...................................... 10, 14, 152
bondage............................... 32, 197, 242, 252, 253
born of a virgin... 185
boss... 277
bound... 7, 18, 38, 58, 61, 86, 91, 95, 114, 167, 189, 191, 192, 231, 232,
               239, 244, 245, 281
breastplate... 144, 145
builder.. 33
calling.......... 36, 128, 129, 134, 177, 208, 210, 240, 241, 244, 245
cannot lose their salvation................................. 256
Canter.. iii
capture of Egypt... 224
CAST OFF THE WORKS OF DARKNESS..................... 141
CAUSING GOD'S WRATH TO COME....................... 147
Chafer... 165
Chapter Five.. iv, 133
Chapter Four.. iv, 95
Chapter One.. iv, 1, 183
Chapter Three..................................... iv, 65, 66, 249
Chapter Two.. iv, 33, 215
character... 39, 47
charis... 4, 186, 282
chosen.................. 5, 7, 14, 15, 47, 97, 104, 138, 139, 239, 240
Christ alone.. 122, 281

CHRIST BECAME POOR–TRUE CHRISTIANS MADE RICH..... 188
Christ died. 8, 123, 124, 148-150, 174
Christ died for all.................................. 123, 148, 149
CHRIST DIED FOR EVERYONE'S SINS...................... 148
CHRIST GAVE US AN EXAMPLE OF SUFFERING. 25
CHRIST GIVES CONSOLATION IN SUFFERINGS.............. 244
CHRIST INVITES ALL TO COME UNTO HIM................. 199
CHRIST IS GOD'S UNSPEAKABLE GIFT...................... 79
CHRIST THE SUBSTITUTE FOR THE SINS OF THE WORLD.... 148
CHRIST WAS DELIVERED UP TO DIE FOR ALL............... 148
CHRIST WILL RETURN TO EARTH IN FLAMING FIRE. 203
CHRIST WILL SET UP HIS 1,000-YEAR REIGN................ 201
Christian love................................. 86, 87, 112-114, 192
CHRISTIAN LOVE FOR OTHER TRUE CHRISTIANS........... 113
CHRISTIANS MUST WALK WORTHY OF THE LORD. 52
CHRISTIANS PROMISED TRIBULATION..................... 71
CHRISTIANS SHOULD COMFORT ONE ANOTHER........... 151
Christians' future... 62
Christians' walk.. 95
CHRISTIANS--APPOINTED TO AFFLICTIONS. 68
Christian's paths.. 258
Christ's Body. 14, 217, 239
Christ's coming. 92, 208, 218, 258
Christ's death.. 147
CHRIST'S GOSPEL--THE POWER OF GOD TO SALVATION...... 17
Christ's incarnation...................................... 222
CHRIST'S MILLENNIAL REIGN SET UP..................... 226
Christ's Name.. 210, 211
CHRIST'S POVERTY CAN MAKE PEOPLE RICH............... 284
Christ's return. 89, 93, 136, 199, 203, 206, 226
CHRIST'S RETURN TO EARTH IN GLORY.................... 206
CHRIST'S RETURN WITH ALL HIS SAINTS................... 89
Christ's sacrifice... 150
CHRIST'S SACRIFICE WAS FOR EVERYONE.................. 150
church boss... 277
Church Phone: 856-854-4747. i
clean. 36, 106, 110, 124, 168, 201, 210, 228
clear preaching... 153
Collingswood. .... i, iii
Collingswood, New Jersey. .... i, iii
Colossian.. 7, 83, 236
comfort. 12, 36, 49, 50, 54, 65-68, 71, 74-77, 82, 90, 118, 131, 151, 152,
155-157, 190, 192, 200, 244-247, 255, 266, 267

COMFORT OF TRUE CHRISTIANS GOING TO HEAVEN.. 131
comfort one another. 50, 67, 68, 75, 131, 151, 152, 247
coming of Christ.. . . . . 94, 124, 215
command. . 26, 50, 51, 72, 79, 86, 100, 116-118, 130, 141, 155, 159, 161,
     163, 164, 167, 170, 243, 256, 259, 266, 272, 274, 277
COMMENDED FOR BIBLE KNOWLEDGE AND LOVE.. 189
Comments About Being Patient.. 158
Communism.. 121
complaining. 118
condemnation. 95, 237
confidence.. . . . . 37, 94, 116, 161, 218, 256, 257
Congregation. ii
consolation.. . . . . 36, 236, 244, 245
CONSTANT BATTLE BETWEEN THE FLESH AND SPIRIT. 265
contend.. . . . . 35, 81, 82
contend for Bible Doctrines. 82
CONTINUAL REJOICING FOR TRUE CHRISTIANS. 161
CONTROLLED BY THE SPIRIT FOR GOD'S POWER. 18
corporate election. 14, 239
CORPORATE ELECTION EXPLAINED BRIEFLY. 239
correct.. . . . . 56, 220, 249
CORRECT TRANSLATIONS ARE ESSENTIAL. 56
covet. 123
covetousness.. . . . . 7, 37, 39-41, 101-103, 110, 111
COVETOUSNESS–THE ITCH FOR MORE.. 41
Creator. 100, 184, 236
crop.. 14
crown.. . . . . 61, 62, 93, 207, 217, 242
CUT OUT FILTHY AND CORRUPT SPEECH.. 153
damnation. 237
Daniel. 22, 25, 31, 137, 138, 168, 173, 193, 223-225, 250
darkness. 31, 45, 91, 96, 105, 135, 136, 138, 139, 141, 143, 144, 206,
     229, 230, 236, 253, 275
David.. . . . . 74, 75, 98, 128, 145, 161, 165, 168, 197, 228, 229, 280
day of the Lord.. . . . . 134-138, 203, 219, 226
dead in Christ.. . . . . 63, 93, 126, 127, 216, 218
death. 7, 10, 16, 21, 23, 29, 30, 32, 45, 47, 63, 68, 74, 75, 88, 103,
     111, 113, 121, 123-125, 128, 147, 148, 151, 162, 187, 190, 196,
     205, 206, 215-217, 237, 238, 241, 247, 252, 253, 267
deceit.. . . . . 17, 36, 37, 41, 101, 233, 235, 243
deceive.. . . . . 71, 147, 219, 221, 222, 231-233, 275
deceiver.. . . . . 221, 222, 231
deceivers.. . . . . 157, 221, 222, 233, 276

DECEIVERS DENY CHRIST'S INCARNATION AND DEITY...... 222
deceiving people.. 221
deception. 220, 221, 232-234
Defined King James Bible.. iv
Deity. 4, 222
deliverance. 30-32, 68, 147, 251-253
DELIVERANCE FROM THIS PRESENT EVIL WORLD........... 31
delivered...... ii, 15, 29-32, 35, 45, 69, 81, 99, 146-149, 187, 205, 212, 251-253
DELIVERED FROM HELL & THE TRIBULATION............... 30
DELIVERED FROM SATAN'S BONDAGE. 32
DELIVERED FROM THIS WICKED WORLD.. 99
DELIVERED FROM WORLD DARKNESS & FROM HELL. 31
DESCRIPTION OF THE MAN OF SIN.. 223
Details Of God's Faithful Bible Preservation. 176
Devil. 32, 61, 70, 72, 73, 128, 145, 205, 206, 231, 235, 253
die. 9, 45, 62, 122, 124, 148, 188, 196, 198, 200, 202, 206
die for all.. 148
DIFFICULTY FOR PEACE IN TRUE CHRISTIAN CHURCHES. .. 155
Diotrephes. 277
disagreement. 35
discipleship.. .... 86, 113
dishonor. 104, 107, 110
disobedient............................... 238, 259, 274-277, 286
disobeyed. 26
disorderly. 243, 259-262, 271, 272, 277
Divine attributes. 184, 185
Divine Attributes Of God The Father. 184
Divine Attributes Of God The Son.. 185
DO HONEST THINGS NOT EVIL THINGS. 120
doctrine.. 27, 28, 35, 49, 50, 55, 66, 74, 81, 89, 121, 134, 153, 189, 190, 221, 222, 230, 233, 242, 270, 275, 276, 280
doctrines... 6, 49, 66, 67, 72-78, 81, 82, 86, 88, 90, 113, 114, 123, 153, 168, 174, 189-191, 221, 222, 242, 249, 251, 254, 255, 257, 274, 275
DOING GOD'S WILL FROM THE HEART. 99
dokimazo.. .... 38, 167
don't even begin.. .... 219, 272
DON'T GIVE THE DEVIL ANY ROOM. 73
DON'T RECEIVE GOD'S WORDS ON STONY GROUND......... 21
DON'T WALK AS THE HEATHEN WALK. 96
Dr. Chafer.. 165
drift. 67, 72, 78, 189, 255
drifting. 72, 77, 78, 90, 168, 169, 172, 255

drifting badly. 78
duration. 176
Duration Of God's Faithful Bible Preservation. 176
edify.. 105, 151, 152
educated. 27
Egypt. 22, 28, 69, 85, 149, 197, 224, 278
eidos. 169
EIGHT CHARACTERISTICS OF SATAN. 61
ekkakeo... 272
elders. 5, 25, 52, 59, 140, 142, 153, 155-157, 167, 172, 265, 270
elect. 14, 50, 148, 221, 231, 239, 240, 275
election. 14, 239, 240
elencho. 275
eleventh in a series. iii
ensamples................................... 24, 25, 264, 278
epistles. 16, 241
epithumia. 107
error.. .... 36, 75, 108, 127, 173, 198, 203, 234, 235, 243
escape. 137, 174, 194, 198, 224, 232, 237, 254
escaping. 146, 237
ESCAPING THE WRATH OF GOD AND HELL. 146
establish. 48, 65, 66, 89, 90, 112, 117, 152, 174, 190, 246-248, 255, 280
established. . 66, 67, 89-91, 118, 189, 190, 219, 247, 248, 254, 255, 260
ESTABLISHED IN GOOD WORDS AND WORKS. 118
established in the Faith. 66, 90, 189
esthio... 266
ESV. 149
eternal glory. 21, 67, 91, 245, 248, 255
eternal life. 15, 19, 20, 79, 148, 206, 234, 236, 237, 246
ETERNAL LIFE CAN NEVER BE WITHDRAWN. 15
everlasting. 31, 38, 44, 83, 86, 91, 129, 130, 146, 147, 185, 200,
204-206, 233, 237, 244, 253, 280, 284
everlasting punishment. 204, 206
everlasting torment. 200
EVERY CHRISTIAN SHOULD BE HOLY. 47
everyone. . . . 15, 51, 63, 73, 122, 138, 148, 150, 156, 159, 160, 185, 230,
257, 261
evil. . . . 19, 31, 32, 34, 35, 37, 41, 43, 54, 57, 61, 66, 74, 90, 91, 98-101,
103, 106, 107, 111, 117, 119, 120, 123, 135, 155-157, 159, 160, 165, 169,
174, 187, 195, 197, 213, 222, 225, 226, 230, 233, 237, 238,
248, 252-254, 276, 284
example. 6, 19, 22, 24, 25, 70, 86, 103, 161, 167, 169, 176, 193, 197,
204, 206, 261, 263-265, 267, 270

examples.................... 24, 114, 193, 257, 264, 265, 267, 276
EXAMPLES OF SOLDIERS, FARMERS, AND SHEPHERDS. 267
Exhortation Not In Guile. 37
exoutheneo... 166
EZEKIEL AS A WARNING WATCHMEN FOR GOD............. 156
e-mail: BFT@BibleForToday.org. i
faith without works.. 188
faithful....... 5, 13, 27, 34, 55, 59, 62, 66, 90, 100, 124, 134, 140, 156,
    157, 169, 172-176, 181, 201, 225, 227, 235, 242, 248, 254, 261,
    276, 286
faithful Bible preservation. 176
faithful children.. 157, 172
faithful English translation. 242
faithful witness... 175, 235
FAITHFUL WITNESSES DO NOT LIE. 235
FAITH'S SHIELD QUENCHES SATAN'S FIERY DARTS......... 166
false doctrine... 222, 280
false teachers.. 37, 38, 135
farmer... 14, 271
farmers.. 267
FAX: 856-854-2464. i
fellowlabourer.. 65, 90, 190, 247
fiery darts.. 165, 166
fire...... 9, 31, 60, 61, 103, 107, 124, 146, 147, 158, 164, 165, 185, 196,
    200-206, 208, 228, 232, 237, 253
firm............. 43, 66, 74, 78, 83, 89, 90, 142, 241, 246, 247, 254
fivefold indictment. 58, 59
flattering words... 39, 40
flattery... 39, 40, 107
FLATTERY SOUNDS SWEET, BUT IS REALLY SOUR........... 40
flee...................... 73, 102, 109, 146, 227, 235, 254, 264
flesh and spirit... 91, 111, 265
fleshly lusts.. 100, 109, 170
following... ii, iii, 17, 19-21, 45, 113, 142, 166, 175, 207, 210, 220, 226,
    243, 255, 273, 285
following Christ.. 20
FOLLOWING CHRIST AND HIS WORDS. 20
following the Bible.. 21
FOLLOWING THE LORD BY FOLLOWING THE BIBLE.......... 21
following the Lord Jesus Christ............................ 20
for us........... 7, 21, 24, 34, 69, 75, 120, 124, 147-150, 177, 249, 260
Foreword... iii, iv
fornication. 7, 35, 97, 100-103, 110, 111, 170, 204, 206

FORNICATION NOT REPENTED OF. 102
fruit. . 8, 14, 23, 80, 91, 94, 119, 164, 212, 218, 238, 267, 268, 281, 286
fruits of the Holy Spirit. 80
FULL BIBLE KNOWLEDGE–THEN ADMONITION. 154
fullness of joy. 80
FULLNESS OF JOY IN GOD'S PRESENCE.. 80
fury. 165, 197, 225
FUTURE deliverance–from the presence of sin. 31, 252
future wrath. 146
Galatia. 2, 11, 18, 23, 29, 31, 34, 80, 87, 96, 98, 102, 108, 110, 160, 184, 242, 243, 252, 265, 273, 276, 281, 284, 285
gaps. 90
generation gaps. 90
GENERATION GAPS ARE NOT NECESSARY. 90
gentle. 42, 43, 203
GENUINE CHRISTIANS NEED GOD'S COMFORT. 67
GENUINE CHRISTIANS NEED MUCH PATIENCE. 94, 193
genuine faith.. 6, 9, 10, 38, 71, 76, 97, 106, 114, 122, 139, 144-146, 149, 163, 180, 187, 188, 237, 240, 281, 283
GENUINE FAITH AS A HELMET OF PROTECTION. 145
Gertrude Grace.. 130
gift. 33, 66, 79, 90, 92, 149, 163, 164, 166, 188, 217, 258, 283, 284
glorified bodies.. .... 68, 211, 217, 247
glorify God. 21, 120, 212
GOD ALWAYS FULFILLS HIS PROMISES.. 245
GOD CAN DIRECT US WHEN WE'RE MOVING.. 85
GOD CAN ESTABLISH TRUE CHRISTIANS. 66, 90
God corrects. 51, 272
GOD CORRECTS AS FATHERS SHOULD. 51
GOD DELIVERED ISRAEL FROM AFFLICTIONS. 69
God is always faithful. 174
GOD IS FAITHFUL IN ALL OF HIS PROMISES. 173
God is not willing. 60
GOD IS NOT WILLING THAT ANY PERISH IN HELL.. 60
GOD IS SINLESS AND HOLY. 111
GOD JUDGED SODOM, GOMORRAH AND THE WORLD. 198
GOD KILLED 23,000 BECAUSE OF FORNICATION. 102
GOD KNOW EVERYTHING ABOUT US. 46
god of forces. 223
GOD OPPOSES LAZY AND SLOTHFUL PEOPLE. 268
God tests. 39
GOD TESTS HEARTS. 39
God the Father. 2, 4, 7, 8, 52, 78, 79, 84, 97, 122, 125, 127, 129, 133,

.... 149, 150, 163, 164, 184-187, 195, 209, 212, 236, 240, 244, 246, 247, 255
God the Father Is A Spirit.................................... 184
God the Father Is Holy.. 185
God the Father Is Omnipotent................................. 184
God the Father Is Omnipresent................................ 184
God the Father Is Omniscient................................. 184
God the Father Is The Creator................................ 184
God the Father Sent His Son To Save Sinners.................. 185
God the Father will Send To Hell Those Who Reject His Son...... 185
God the Son........................... 4, 84, 133, 149, 184-187, 244
God the Son Ascended Bodily Into Heaven..................... 186
God the Son Commanded The True Christians To Preach.......... 186
God the Son Is Interceding For Those He Has Saved............. 186
God the Son Is Omnipotent.................................... 185
God the Son Is Omnipresent................................... 185
God the Son Is Omniscient.................................... 185
God the Son Is Seated At The Right Hand Of God The Father..... 186
God the Son Is Sinless.. 185
God the Son Is The Great High Priest In Heaven................ 186
God the Son performed miracles............................... 185
God the Son rose bodily from the grave....................... 185
God the Son Shed His Blood As Payment For The Sins........... 185
God the Son Was Both Perfect God And Perfect Man............. 185
God the Son Was Miraculously Born Of A Virgin................ 185
God the Son Will Return In The Air For All His Saved Ones...... 186
GOD WANTS NON-HYPOCRITICAL LOVE....................... 88
GOD WANTS SANCTITY OF SPIRIT, SOUL, AND BODY......... 171
godly life... 46
GOD'S BLESSINGS WITHOUT SORROW...................... 122
God's comfort... 67
God's epistles... 16
God's grace............ 9, 15, 16, 33, 37, 187, 188, 209, 211, 283, 284
GOD'S JUDGMENTS ARE ALWAYS RIGHTEOUS........... 195, 196
God's power............................. 18, 27, 49, 139, 157, 255
GOD'S PROMISE TO KEEP FROM EVIL....................... 254
GOD'S RIGHTEOUSNESS IS LIKE A BREASTPLATE............ 145
GOD'S ROD AND STAFF COMFORTED DAVID................. 74
God's salvation....................................... 145, 161, 252
God's strength.. 82
GOD'S STRENGTH MADE PERFECT IN OUR WEAKNESS....... 82
GOD'S WHOLE ARMOR DEFEATS SATAN'S TRICKS............ 73
God's will............................... 7, 28, 82, 83, 98-100

GOD'S WILL IS PERFECT, THOUGH OFTEN DIFFICULT........ 28
God's Words......... iii, 16, 21, 26, 27, 49, 53, 72, 83, 85, 91, 96, 105, 117, 139, 179-181, 189, 193, 194, 208, 210, 242, 243, 249, 250, 255, 264
GOD'S WORDS HAVE BEEN OFTEN TRIED AND TESTED...... 250
GOD'S WORDS MUST BE STUDIED AND BELIEVED........... 105
GOD'S WORDS SANCTIFY.................................. 105
Gomorrah........................... 194, 196, 198, 204, 206, 265
GOOD WORK TO GLORIFY CHRIST. 10
good works............ 83, 96, 118, 120, 150, 160, 187, 188, 211, 241
GOOD WORKS SHOULD FOLLOW SALVATION........... 96, 160
grace and truth.. 187, 283
GRACE IS GETTING SOMETHING WE DON'T DESERVE....... 181
great fury... 225
Great High Priest................................... 168, 186
great patience... 193
gregoreuo... 141
guidance... 84, 154
guile.. 36, 37
hagiasmos... 100
hard labor.................................... 45, 262, 267, 268
harpazo... 133, 216
heart. 19, 29, 30, 37, 39-41, 44, 48, 53, 55, 60, 69, 75, 88, 91, 99-101, 107, 109, 111, 113, 116, 119, 123, 125, 137, 143, 158, 161, 165, 168, 170, 171, 191, 192, 196, 197, 199, 211, 233, 272, 281
hearts... 19, 37-39, 41, 48, 56, 66, 67, 85, 89, 90, 92, 94, 99, 107, 108, 110, 112, 118, 119, 123, 137-139, 154, 168, 185, 189, 207, 218, 221, 229, 233, 246-248, 255, 258, 275, 279, 282
HEARTS ESTABLISHED IN HOLINESS NEEDED.............. 255
HEARTS ESTABLISHED UNBLAMEABLE. 89
heathen............... 27, 78, 96, 108, 110, 124, 146, 227, 236, 260
heathen world. 108, 110
Heaven. 12, 13, 21, 24, 25, 29-32, 57, 60, 62, 63, 69, 72, 79, 89, 93, 100, 114, 121-127, 129-131, 134, 136, 138, 139, 144, 146, 147, 150, 151, 176, 185, 186, 188, 190, 196, 197, 199-202, 205-207, 209-211, 215-218, 220, 227, 228, 232, 239, 245, 246, 253, 258, 282, 284
Heaven is forever................................. 125, 129, 130
HEAVEN IS FOREVER FOR TRUE CHRISTIANS.............. 125
Heavenly Home... 30
Heaven's glory... 69
Hebrew... 4, 35, 43, 46, 53, 56, 86, 87, 95, 99, 105, 113, 168, 175-177, 179, 186, 242, 249-251, 285, 286

Hell. 30, 31, 38, 60, 107, 146, 147, 185, 196, 197, 200, 202-206, 232-234, 237, 253
Hell's fires. 200
helmet. 55, 144, 145
heralds.. 46
HERALDS MUST HAVE PROPER BIBLE WORDS. 46
heresy. 15, 28, 72, 205
hesuchazo. 115
hesuchia. 272
High Priest. 168, 186
hindrances. 60, 84, 258
holily. 46, 47
holiness. . . 15, 48, 89, 91, 92, 100, 110-112, 152, 185, 195, 207, 247, 255
Holy Spirit. . . 15, 17-19, 21-23, 29, 32, 52, 69, 80, 87, 92, 95, 96, 104, 106, 108, 112, 133, 157, 164, 165, 175, 180, 185, 191, 208, 210, 212, 225, 226, 265, 281
homosexual. 35, 103, 104, 107, 108, 204, 223
homosexuality. 31, 100, 101, 103, 198, 210, 251
honest. 40, 114, 118-120, 159, 275
honor. 3, 52, 104, 105, 186, 211, 269
hope. . . . . iii, 8, 12-14, 18, 19, 49, 54, 61, 71, 75, 93, 121, 122, 131, 140, 144, 162, 190, 192, 207, 217, 236, 244-246, 279, 281
HOW TO AVOID FORNICATION. 103
human traditions. 243
husbands. 44, 105, 230
HUSBANDS TO LOVE THEIR WIVES AS THEMSELVES. 44
hyper-dispensationalists. 75
HYPER-DISPENSATIONALISTS ARE IN SERIOUS ERROR. 75
IF UNWILLING TO WORK, NO EATING. 118
IN THE NEW TESTAMENT, "PATIENCE". 12
INDEX. . . . . iii, iv, 287
Index of Words and Phrases. . . . . iv, 287
indictment. 58, 59
interceding. 186
international banking. 224
Internet. . . . . iii, 25, 53, 99, 153, 167, 222, 250
Internet by computer streaming. iii
IS THE LORD JESUS CHRIST YOUR BUILDER?. 33
Isaiah. 14, 18, 22, 30, 60, 116, 117, 135, 143, 145, 180, 181, 193, 197, 199, 257, 273, 280
Isaiah 53. 180

Israel. . . . 14, 28, 69, 70, 76, 85, 104, 128, 133, 134, 141, 156, 165, 168,
179, 197, 221, 228, 229, 252, 257, 267, 279
ISRAEL'S KINGS--COPY AND READ GOD'S WORDS. 179
IT IS DISORDERLY NOT TO WORK. 271
jailed. 5, 257
Jericho's walls. 128
JERICHO'S WALLS REALLY FELL DOWN FLAT. 128
Jew. 17, 58
Jews. . . . 1-5, 8, 23, 26, 34, 49, 56-59, 75, 183, 186, 187, 199, 212, 220,
231, 247, 252, 281, 283
Job. 14, 193, 194, 229
JOB, A MAN OF GREAT PATIENCE. 193
John MacArthur. 28
John the Baptist. 46, 48, 209
JOHN THE BAPTIST WAS JUST AND HOLY. 48
joy. 18, 19, 21-23, 61, 63, 67, 69, 71, 78, 80, 81, 89, 93, 98,
130, 143, 161, 162, 207, 217, 233, 242, 245, 256, 281, 282
JOY BY WALKING IN THE WORDS OF GOD. 81
JOY FROM GOD THE HOLY SPIRIT. 19, 22, 23
Judas. 5, 229
judge. 26, 51, 124, 147, 170, 171, 194-197, 200, 201, 203, 204, 227
judge of all. 194, 195
judge righteously. 171, 195
judges. 198, 204
judgment. . . . 9, 32, 58, 117, 124, 134, 170, 185, 187, 191, 194-198, 200,
203, 204, 206, 237, 238, 254, 275, 280
judgment seat of Christ. 9, 195-197
judgments. 171, 194-196
justified. 106, 146, 147, 187, 188, 246, 281, 283
JUSTIFIED BY TRUE FAITH IN CHRIST ALONE. 281
justly. 46, 47
katecho. 225
kateuthuno. 84, 258
King David. 75, 98
KING DAVID FOUND NO COMFORTERS. 75
King James Bible. . i, iv, 35, 46, 53, 83, 86, 99, 105, 113, 152, 168, 176,
179, 219, 220, 242, 249-251
kingdom of Heaven. 134
KJB. 220, 242
kopiao. 153
kopos. 45, 262
labor. 10-12, 34, 45, 72, 153, 155, 261, 262, 266-270
LABOR MOTIVATED BY LOVE. 10

laboring................ 10, 11, 45, 83, 99, 153, 268, 270
laboring in vain. 11
lacking.................................. 42, 81, 84, 114, 121, 190
Lamb of God... 147
last days. 94, 238
law......... ii, 23, 34, 35, 37, 47, 87, 101, 107, 159, 170, 176, 179, 180,
187, 191, 242, 254, 283
law and grace.. 187
LAW AND GRACE CONTRASTED......................... 187
lazy.. 117, 268, 271
leaders......... 16, 19, 103, 119, 120, 138, 142, 154, 172, 257, 259, 261
learning............................. 12, 49, 75, 131, 192, 245, 264
LEAVE FLESHLY LUSTS THAT WAR AGAINST THE SOUL. 170
liar... 89, 235, 236
lies....................................... 12, 40, 137, 175, 234-236, 250
light........... 21, 54, 56, 69, 73, 91, 96, 105, 107, 135, 138, 139, 141,
143, 165, 199, 211, 212, 227, 229, 230, 236, 275
LIGHT AFFLICTION VERSUS ETERNAL GLORY. 21
LIGHT SHOULD SHINE IN CHRISTIANS' LIVES. 212
LINK #1.. iii
LINK #2.. iii
lion.. 32, 73, 166, 253
literal fire. 203, 205, 206
literal Hell.. 205
lordship salvation. 28
LOST JEWS STIRRED UP THE PEOPLE. 4
LOVE FOR GOD BRINGS LOVE FOR TRUE CHRISTIANS........ 89
LOVE ONE ANOTHER AS PAUL LOVED THEM. 192
LOVING TRUE CHRISTIANS–A MARK OF DISCIPLESHIP....... 86
lust............................... 29, 96, 100, 107, 108, 198, 265
lusts.............. 29, 94, 99, 100, 107-110, 170, 188, 235, 238, 265
lying....................... 58, 76, 222, 228, 231, 233, 235, 236
lying texts.. 235
MacArthur, John... 28
MACARTHUR'S HERESY OF LORDSHIP SALVATION........... 28
makrothumeo... 158
man of sin... 219, 223
MANY PREACHERS ARE DECEIVING PEOPLE................ 221
MANY SO-CALLED "SCHOLARS" LIE. 235
MANY U.S.A. CITIES ARE SODOMITE CITIES.................. 204
MANY WERE SAVED AT BEREA............................... 3
Mark 16:9-20.. 16
marriage.. 102, 230

mature. 82-84, 91, 111, 156, 190
maturity. 82, 83
MATURITY AND GROWN-UPNESS NEEDED. 82
MEANING OF THE GREEK WORD, "ATAKTEO". 262
meek. 116, 199
MEEK AND QUIET SPIRITS NEEDED. 116
methusko. 143
Millennial. 89, 92, 136, 199, 208, 219, 226, 252, 280
Millennial reign. 92, 208, 219, 226, 252, 280
minister of God. 65, 90, 190, 247
miracle workers. 232
miracles. 162, 185, 202, 205, 221, 228, 231, 232
missing. 149
missing in some Bibles. 149
mochthos. 262
mortify. 111
MORTIFY ANY UNCLEANNESS. 111
mutual faith. 67, 75-77
NASV. 149
NEED FOR A PRE-TRIBULATION RAPTURE LIFESTYLE. 133
need for patience. 13
need to contend. 82
nephaleos. 140
nepho. 139, 140, 144
never perish. 15, 19, 20, 234
never, never. 16, 251
New Testament. 4, 8, 12, 20, 24, 29, 62, 80, 83, 95, 97, 112, 122,
      131, 140, 148, 157, 158, 164, 166, 170, 172, 175-177,
      183, 186, 198, 207, 220, 232, 235, 242, 245, 249, 285
night and day. 11, 45, 81, 142, 156, 163, 262, 267, 270
NIV. 149
No Cloke Of Covetousness. 40
no confidence in the flesh. 161, 257
NO DRIFTING FROM THE WORDS IN GOD'S BIBLE. 255
No Flattering Words. 39
NO FUTURE WRATH FOR TRUE CHRISTIANS. 146
NO LONGER IN DARKNESS. 138
no more sign gifts. 166
NO PROPHETIC EVENTS BEFORE THE RAPTURE. 134
NON-CHRISTIANS HAVE SORROWFUL HEARTS. 123
non-hypocritical love. 88
not drifting. 90
NOT LABORING IN VAIN. 11

not to preach. 26, 210
not to work. 267, 271
nourishment. 55
nouthesia. 279
noutheteo. 154, 278
O. T. PROPHETS ARE EXAMPLES OF SUFFERING. 193
obedient. 179, 265, 286
oikodomeo. 152
old age. 122
Old Testament. 8, 12, 13, 20, 22, 24, 52, 59, 70, 75, 97, 102,
107, 118, 129-131, 144, 170, 175, 176, 179, 181, 192, 193,
198, 207, 220, 243, 245, 249, 264, 271, 279
oligopsuchos. 157
omissions. 149
Omnipotent. 184, 185
Omnipresent. 184, 185
Omniscient. 46, 184, 185
ONE OF GOD'S TITLES--"THE GOD OF ALL COMFORT". 131
only faithful English translation. 242
ONLY GOD CAN ESTABLISH TRUE CHRISTIANS. 90
ONLY GOD'S GRACE CAN BRING REDEMPTION. 209
ONLY GOD'S POWER CAN TAME THE TONGUE. 157
ONLY THE LORD JESUS CHRIST IS WORTHY. 53
Order Blank Pages. iv
orders. . . . . i, iv, 26, 50, 97
orders disobeyed. 26
Orders: 1-800-John 10:9. i
orphans. 60
ou me. 16, 175
pagan world. 101, 107
paideia. 154, 279
paraklesis. 36, 244
PAST deliverance–from the penalty of sin. 31, 252
Pastor D. A. Waite, Th.D.,Ph.D. 1
pastors. 10, 17, 25, 37, 41, 48, 73, 134, 140, 142, 143, 153, 155-157,
167, 172, 263,
265, 270, 274, 276
PASTORS MUST BE GOOD EXAMPLES. 265
paths. 85, 258, 264
PATIENCE IS DIFFICULT BUT NECESSARY. 29
PATIENCE MUST MATURE AND FULLY GROWN. 83
patient. 12-14, 22, 29, 30, 43, 71, 85, 86, 94, 99, 152, 155, 156, 158,
193, 218, 248, 255, 258

patient waiting. 29, 30, 85, 258
Patient Waiting For God. 29
PATIENT WAITING FOR OUR HEAVENLY HOME. 30
Patmos island. 193
Patricia Canter. iii
Paul and Silas. 2, 3, 5, 34
PAUL AND SILAS WERE JAILED AT PHILIPPI. 5
PAUL DID NOT FORGET THE CHRISTIANS. 8
PAUL DID NOT USE A CLOKE OR A PRETEXT. 41
PAUL DID NOT USE GUILE. 37
PAUL DID NOT WALK DISORDERLY. 261
PAUL DIDN'T BURDEN PEOPLE. 42
PAUL DIDN'T WANT TO LABOR IN VAIN. 34
PAUL EXPLAINED HIS NEED FOR TOUGH LOVE. 191
PAUL LEFT THESSALONICA AND WENT TO BEREA. 3
PAUL LIVED A BLAMELESS LIFE. 47
PAUL LIVED A GODLY LIFE. 46
PAUL USED PERSUASIVE SPEAKING. 36
PAUL WANTED THE GUIDANCE OF THE LORD. 84
PAUL WANTED TO PLEASE GOD, NOT HIMSELF. 38
PAUL WAS CLEAN AND PURE FOR CHRIST. 36
PAUL WAS EDUCATED, BUT NOT ARROGANT. 27
PAUL WAS STONED AT ANTIOCH. 57
PAUL WAS THERE FOR THREE WEEKS. 2
PAUL WORKED WHEN HE COULD HAVE HAD SUPPORT. 263
PAUL–A JEW BY BIRTH, A CHRISTIAN BY NEW BIRTH. 58
PAUL'S AND TRUE CHRISTIANS' MUTUAL FAITH. 77
PAUL'S FOUR EXHORTATIONS FOR TRUE CHRISTIANS. 155
PAUL'S HARD WORK AT GALATIA. 11
PAUL'S LABOR NIGHT AND DAY. 11
PAUL'S LABOR OF FOR THE LORD JESUS CHRIST. 12
PAUL'S SAVIOUR STOOD WITH HIM NEAR DEATH. 32
PAUL'S THORN IN THE FLESH. 284
payment. 185, 187
payment for the sins. 185
peace. 4, 18, 23, 71, 80, 82, 83, 92, 93, 106, 109, 116, 120, 135,
137, 152, 155, 171, 172, 178, 186, 188, 189, 199, 200, 218,
233, 240, 245, 255, 280-282
PEACE IN THE MOUTH, BUT WAR IN THE HEART. 137
peace with God. 188, 281, 282
PEACE WITH GOD ONLY THROUGH CHRIST. 282
peitho. 256
PEOPLE ARE SAVED BY BELIEVING CHRIST'S GOSPEL. 240

perfect..... 10, 17, 25, 28, 67, 81-85, 91, 98, 99, 111, 121, 155, 156, 166, 176, 185, 190, 193-195, 200, 239, 248, 255, 257, 264, 273, 280, 281, 284
perfect God. 185, 273, 281
perfect Man. 84, 185, 273
PERFECTING WHAT IS LACKING. 81
perilous times. 238
perish.. .... 15, 19, 20, 27, 31, 60, 86, 107, 130, 232-234
persecution. 6, 21, 57, 58, 68, 70, 71, 245
persuasive speaking.. 36
PETER WAS INFLUENCED BY SATAN. 229
philema. 178
Philip. 20, 26, 180, 181
Philippi. 2, 5, 10, 19, 34, 53, 63, 82, 120, 125, 151, 161, 172, 184, 189, 216, 217, 219, 242, 255, 257, 264, 267, 270, 282, 285
phone.. i
PHYSICAL REST IS NECESSARY FOR SERVICE. 200
plane. 36, 234
please God. 38, 42, 58, 95, 97
pleasing God.. .... 38, 97
pleasures. 22, 70, 80, 130, 238, 242, 262, 271
poem. 130
poor. 34, 42, 161, 188, 238, 278, 284
porneia. 100, 103
poverty. 21, 69, 188, 238, 284
power of God. 17, 22, 27, 32, 61, 70, 87, 95, 96, 161, 210, 234
praise to God. 8, 80, 164
PRAY THAT RULERS BRING US PEACEABLE LIVES.. 116
PRAYER FOR GOD'S WORDS TO BE GLORIFIED.. 249
PRAYER THAT TRUE CHRISTIANS WILL GO TO HEAVEN..... 150
preach the gospel. 16-18, 25-27, 186, 230
preached these sermons. iii
preacher. 15, 26, 38, 46, 276
preachers. 16, 17, 37-40, 83, 204, 221, 261
preaching. 1, iii, 15, 17, 18, 22, 25-27, 32-34, 38-40, 43, 48, 49, 57, 66, 90, 134, 153, 179, 234, 247, 251, 253, 254, 257, 263
PREACHING IN WORD AND POWER. 15
Preaching Verse by Verse. 1
PRESENT deliverance–from the power of sin.. .... 31, 252
present tense. 27, 29, 95, 139, 161, 166, 167, 169, 177, 223, 259, 266, 272, 274
preservation. 35, 175, 176, 251
pretext. 40, 41

pre-tribulation rapture......... 126, 127, 130, 131, 133, 146, 147, 246
prodigal son. 210
promise. . 13, 30, 62, 94, 99, 125, 130, 175, 176, 197, 234, 254, 273, 280
promises. 13, 20, 30, 85, 91, 111, 137, 138, 147, 173, 204, 234, 245
proper Bible Words. 46
proper leaders. 19
prophecy. 56, 126, 138, 166, 221
prophetic events.. .... 134, 220
prophets. 10, 22, 58, 59, 70, 193, 221, 231
protection. 49, 145
provisions. 108
Pro-homosexual.. .... 103, 223
Publisher's Data.. iv
punishment. 154, 157, 197, 204, 206, 279
pure. 19, 36, 88, 109, 113, 120, 163, 192
purgatory. 62, 63, 125, 151, 206
PURGATORY IS FALSE--NOT IN THE BIBLE.. 63
quench.. 164-166
quiet.. .... 114-116, 120, 268
rapture.. ..... 29, 30, 50, 62, 63, 68, 86, 93, 94, 114, 115, 118, 121, 122,
              124, 126-131, 133, 134, 136, 144, 146-148, 151, 166, 186,
                                      199, 206, 207, 215-220, 226,
                                          228, 246, 247, 257, 258
raptured. 93, 129, 133, 136, 138, 218, 223, 258
READING AND UNDERSTANDING GOD'S WORDS............ 179
REAL HOPE IS IN THE BIBLE'S HEAVEN. 246
rebuked sharply. 191
RECOMMENDED BY GOD'S GRACE. 9
recompenses.. .... 197, 198
reconciliation. 55
redemption. 148, 149, 187, 188, 209, 239, 283
reign. 61, 92, 108, 112, 125, 126, 186, 201, 207, 208, 219, 226, 252, 280
reject. 112, 185, 280
reject his Son. 185
rejoice. 23, 34, 53, 54, 161, 162, 219, 245, 257
rejoicing. 26, 54, 61, 78, 80, 93, 161, 162, 207, 210, 217
REJOICING EVEN IN MANIFOLD TESTINGS. 162
RELIGIOUS AND POLITICAL BEASTS CAST INTO HELL. 202
REQUEST FOR DELIVERANCE FROM WICKED PEOPLE.. 251
rest. 17, 48, 82, 99, 115, 123, 199, 200, 230, 257, 284
restoration. 120, 175

return. 61, 86, 89, 93, 112, 126, 136, 141, 159, 186, 199, 203, 206, 210, 215, 217, 220, 226, 252, 255, 258, 278
return in the air. 186
return to earth. 186, 203, 206
rich.. . . . . 51, 122, 188, 238, 268, 284
right hand of God.. . . . . 127, 186
right Words of God. 53
righteous. 22, 55, 68, 91, 118, 150, 170, 171, 194-197, 203, 204, 206, 268, 284
righteous judgment. 170, 194-197, 204
righteousness. 18, 19, 55, 85, 91, 109-111, 116, 124, 134, 145, 149, 194, 195, 201, 203, 204, 227, 239, 256
roaring lion. 73, 253
rod and staff. 74
rose bodily. 123, 185
RSV. 149
rulers. 3, 57, 116, 173
running. 13, 115
RUNNING LIFE'S RACE WITH PATIENCE. 13
sacrifice. 8, 28, 80, 135, 137, 149, 150, 164, 203
saints. 7, 10, 13, 27, 35, 48, 77, 81, 87, 89, 92, 102, 110, 112, 113, 125, 152, 155, 206, 207, 227, 245, 247, 252, 255
SALVATION IS ONLY FOR THOSE WHO TRUST CHRIST.. 47
SALVATION MUST BE A VOLUNTARY CHOICE. 234
SALVATION MUST BE PERSONAL, NOT FAMILIAL. 35
Sanborn.. . . . . ii, 130
sanctification. 7, 97, 100, 104, 105, 170, 239, 240
SANCTIFIED IN SPIRIT, SOUL, AND BODY. 106
sanctify. 54, 55, 93, 105, 106, 171, 218
Satan. 60, 61, 72, 73, 105, 124, 138, 186, 199, 201-203, 207, 208, 228-233, 235, 253
SATAN ENTERED INTO JUDAS ISCARIOT. 229
SATAN IS A TEMPTER AND TESTER.. 73
SATAN WILL BE BOUND 1,000 YEARS. 61, 231
SATAN WILL BE BOUND 1,000 YEARS, THEN LOOSED. 231
SATAN'S TEMPTATION IN MARRIAGE. 230
save sinners. 174, 185
SAVED FROM ALL KINDS OF WRATH. 147
SAVING FAITH COMES FROM RECEIVING GOD'S WORDS. 16
sbennumi. 164
Scriptures. 1-3, 12, 21, 46, 49, 75, 131, 133, 149, 183, 192, 245
seated. 186

seated at the right hand. 186
second phase. 61, 92, 126, 199, 203, 208, 220, 226, 252
seducers. 222
SEDUCERS AND DECEIVERS WILL INCREASE. 222
selfishness... 223
semeioo.. 274
sent His Son. 185
separate...................... 18, 71, 91, 101, 106, 243, 259, 277
SEPARATE FROM CHRISTIAN FORNICATORS. 101
SEPARATE FROM DISORDERLY CHRISTIANS................ 243
SEPARATION FROM DISORDERLY CHRISTIANS. 259
serious error... 75
servants.......... 41, 43-45, 91, 99, 110, 111, 156, 168, 203, 210, 263
SERVANTS OF THE LORD MUST BE GENTLE. 43
SEVEN DOCTRINES WHERE PEOPLE DISAGREE. 113
SHALL NEVER PERISH--ASSURANCE FOREVER. 19
shalom... 186
sharing. 121
shed His Blood... 185
shepherds.. 267
shield.. 165, 166
sign gifts.. 166, 167, 232
signs................................... 221, 228, 231, 232, 238
signs and wonders.................................... 221, 231, 232
SINGING IS ONE MEANS OF ADMONISHING. 279
sinless. 92, 111, 172, 185
sinners.22, 38, 73, 108, 123, 135, 148, 174, 185, 188, 230, 238, 273, 283
SIX DIFFERENT VIEWS ABOUT THE RAPTURE. 126
sleep as death.. 123
slothful people. 268
Sodom......................... 103, 194, 196-198, 204, 206, 265
Sodomite.......................... 103, 104, 204, 210, 251
Sodomite cities...204
sodomy. 103, 108, 194, 198, 204
soldiers. 97, 209, 262, 267, 271
sorrow....................................... 45, 121-123, 157, 262
sorrowful hearts.. 123
sound......... 4, 9, 13, 27, 35, 40, 55, 71, 72, 81, 89, 127-129, 140, 154,
                 157, 168, 189, 191, 216, 220, 243, 276, 277
special sign gifts... 232
speech...................................... 17, 71, 153, 282, 286
spirit, soul, and body................................. 93, 106, 171
SPIRITUAL ADULTERY–LOOKING WITH LUST. 107

SPIRITUAL JOY AMIDST AFFLICTIONS.. 23
stablish. 48, 66, 67, 89-91, 94, 112, 118, 174, 207, 218, 246-248, 254, 255
stand fast.. . . . . 77, 78, 142, 241, 242, 260
STAND FAST IN BIBLE DOCTRINES. 77
standing. 35, 43, 99, 144, 150, 202, 220, 228, 242, 269
STANDING COMPLETE IN THE WILL OF GOD.. 99
steadfast. 6, 61, 77, 190
STEADFAST IN DOCTRINES–NOT DRIFTING. 77
steal. 136, 270
stealing. 118, 119, 270
steko. 78, 241
stello. 259
sterizo. 66, 89, 246, 254
stewards. 173
STEWARDS MUST BE FAITHFUL IN THEIR STEWARDSHIP. . . 173
stoned. 57
STONY GROUND SEED AND AFFLICTION. 69
stop. 28, 29, 41, 63, 87, 91, 110, 139, 164-166, 178, 233, 236, 270, 271, 274, 281
stop stealing. 270
strange god. 224
straying. 36, 54, 123, 234
STRAYING FROM THE FAITH BRINGS MANY SORROWS. 123
streaming. iii
streaming around the world.. iii
strength.. . . . . . . 17, 23, 30, 52, 59, 82, 116, 122, 148, 211, 257, 273, 284
strengthened.. . . . . 13, 32, 67, 89, 91, 248, 253
STRENGTHENED TO PATIENCE & HOPE. 13
strong delusion. 234, 237
studied and believed. 105
substitute. 148, 149
suffering. 22, 25, 26, 56, 70, 91, 99, 103, 193, 204-206, 248
SUFFERING FROM UNBELIEVING JEWS. 56
Table of Contents.. iv
TEACH ONLY BIBLICAL DOCTRINE. 50
TEACHING NO LITERAL HELL IS HERESY!. 205
tempter. 11, 72, 73
tested.. . . . . 73, 168, 250
testings. 162, 193
tests. 39
THANKFUL FOR THE THESSALONIAN BELIEVERS.. 6
thankfulness. 163, 164

THANKFULNESS BEFORE EATING.. 163
thanksgiving. 6, 79, 164, 189, 190, 282
THANKSGIVING FOR VICTORY IN CHRIST. 79
THANKSGIVING IN ALL CIRCUMSTANCES. 79
THE ANTICHRIST BREAKS HIS PROMISES. 138
THE ANTICHRIST DESTROYED AT ARMAGEDDON. 225
THE ANTICHRIST USES TOTAL DECEPTION. 232
THE ANTICHRIST'S CAPTURE OF EGYPT. 224
THE ANTICHRIST'S GOD OF FORCES. 223
THE ANTICHRIST'S GREAT FURY. 225
THE ANTICHRIST'S INTERNATIONAL BANKING. 224
THE ANTICHRIST'S SELFISHNESS. 223
THE ANTICHRIST'S STRANGE GOD. 224
THE APOSTLES REMOVED FROM SOME CITIES.. 57
The Background Of 1 Thessalonians. 1
The Background Of 2 Thessalonians.. 183
The Background Of The Church At Thessalonica. 2
THE BEHAVIOR OF THE AGED WOMEN. 112
THE BIBLE CONDEMNS SODOMY.. 108
THE BIBLE TEACHES ITS OWN PRESERVATION. 251
THE BIBLE–CHRIST'S LOVE LETTER TO US. 21
THE BIBLE'S GOD IS THE "GOD OF ALL COMFORT". 50
THE BODY OF CHRIST–CORPORATE ELECTION. 14
THE CHRISTIAN'S BREASTPLATE AND HELMET. 144
THE CHURCH HAD SAVED MEMBERS IN IT. 2
THE COMING OF CHRIST MUCH NEARER NOW. 94
THE COMMAND NOT TO PREACH THE GOSPEL. 26
THE COMPLETED BIBLE=NO MORE SIGN GIFTS.. 166
The Congregation. ii
THE DEITY OF THE LORD JESUS CHRIST. 4
THE DEVIL'S REAL CHARACTER–A ROARING LION. 73
the faith. 9, 35, 49, 61, 66, 67, 69-72, 74, 76-78, 81, 82, 90, 121,
123, 142, 152, 158, 168, 174, 178, 189-191, 193, 239,
242, 251, 257, 276, 277, 283, 285
THE FAITH REFERS TO THE BIBLE'S DOCTRINES. 72
THE FARMER'S PATIENCE FOR HIS CROP. 14
THE FRUIT OF THANKS TO GOD.. 8
THE GOSPEL IS GOD'S POWER. 27
THE GREEK WORDS, "OU ME" MEAN "NEVER, NEVER".. 175
THE HEART IS THE CENTER OF OUR BEING. 39
THE HINDRANCES OF SATAN. 60
THE HOLY SPIRIT WITHIN VESSELS OF CLAY. 104
THE IMPORTANCE OF BIBLE DOCTRINES. 81

THE JEWS' HATRED OF PAUL. 1
THE JUDGMENT SEAT OF CHRIST. 9, 195-197
THE KJB--THE ONLY FAITHFUL ENGLISH TRANSLATION. ... 242
THE LAST DAYS WILL BRING PERILOUS TIMES. 238
THE LORD JESUS CHRIST GAVE US AN EXAMPLE. 24
THE LORD JESUS CHRIST'S BODILY RESURRECTION. 29
THE LORD WANTS TO DIRECT THE CHRISTIAN'S PATHS. 258
THE MEANING OF THE GREEK WORD "METHUSKO". 143
THE MEANING OF THE GREEK WORD, "AMEN". 285
THE MEANING OF THE GREEK WORD, "ATAKTEO". 262
THE MEANING OF THE GREEK WORD, "ATHETEO". 112
THE MEANING OF THE GREEK WORD, "CHARIS". 282
THE MEANING OF THE GREEK WORD, "EIDOS". 169
THE MEANING OF THE GREEK WORD, "EPITHUMIA". 107
THE MEANING OF THE GREEK WORD, "GREGOREUO". 141
THE MEANING OF THE GREEK WORD, "HAGIASMOS". 100
THE MEANING OF THE GREEK WORD, "HESUCHIA". 272
THE MEANING OF THE GREEK WORD, "HUPERBAINO". 109
THE MEANING OF THE GREEK WORD, "KATECHO". 225
THE MEANING OF THE GREEK WORD, "KATEUTHUNO". 258
THE MEANING OF THE GREEK WORD, "KOPIAO". 153
THE MEANING OF THE GREEK WORD, "NEPHO". 139
THE MEANING OF THE GREEK WORD, "NOTHETEO". 278
THE MEANING OF THE GREEK WORD, "NOUTHETEO". 154
THE MEANING OF THE GREEK WORD, "OIKODOMEO". 152
THE MEANING OF THE GREEK WORD, "PAIDEIA". 154
THE MEANING OF THE GREEK WORD, "PARAKLESIS". 244
THE MEANING OF THE GREEK WORD, "PHILEMA". 178
THE MEANING OF THE GREEK WORD, "PLANE". 234
THE MEANING OF THE GREEK WORD, "PORNEIA". 100
THE MEANING OF THE GREEK WORD, "SBENNUMI". 164
THE MEANING OF THE GREEK WORD, "STEKO". 241
THE MEANING OF THE GREEK WORD, "STERIZO". 246, 254
THE MEANING OF THE GREEK WORD, "THELO". 266
THE MEANING OF THE GREEK WORD, "TRECHO". 250
THE MEANING OF THE GREEK WORD, "TUPOS". 263
THE MEANING OF "RAPTURE". 216
THE MEANING OF "WALK" TO PLEASE GOD. 95
The Need To Be As A Father. 51
The Need To Be Charged. 50
The Need To Be Comforted. 49
The Need To Be Exhorted.. 49
THE NEED TO BE GIVEN ORDERS. 50

THE NEED TO CONTEND FOR BIBLE DOCTRINES	82
THE NEED TO PERFECT WHAT IS LACKING	121
THE NEED TO STAND FAST IN THE LORD	78
THE NEED TO YIELD OUR BODIES TO GOD	91
THE OLD TESTAMENT IS FOR OUR LEARNING	264
THE OLD TESTAMENT TEACHES PATIENCE & HOPE	12
THE ONLY ONES WHO CAN PLEASE GOD	97
THE POWER BEHIND TRUE CHRISTIAN LOVE	87
THE POWER OF GOD THE HOLY SPIRIT	17, 87, 95, 96, 210
THE RAPTURE FOR TRUE CHRISTIANS AT ANY MOMENT	126
THE RAPTURE OF ALL TRUE CHRISTIANS	93, 126, 134, 136, 151, 216, 217, 219
THE RAPTURE PRECEDES THE DAY OF THE LORD	136
THE RAPTURE TRUMPET FOR ALL TRUE CHRISTIANS	129
THE RIGHT WORDS OF GOD ARE VITAL	53
THE RIGHTEOUS JUDGMENT OF GOD	194, 196
THE SACRIFICE OF PRAISE TO GOD	8, 80, 164
THE SECOND PHASE OF CHRIST'S COMING	208
THE SECOND PHASE OF CHRIST'S RETURN	199, 203, 226
THE SINS OF THE PAGAN WORLD	107
THE SORROWS OF OLD AGE	122
THE SOUL-WINNER'S CROWN	62
THE SPECIAL USES FOR TRUMPETS	129
THE THESSALONIAN CHURCH WAS SOUND	4
THE THESSALONIANS WERE DEAR TO PAUL	44
THE TRUE CHURCH WHICH IS CHRIST'S BODY	239
THE UNEXPECTED "DAY OF THE LORD"	136
THE VALIDITY OF MARK 16:9-20	16
THE VITAL WORDS, "FOR US" MISSING IN SOME BIBLES	149
THE WILL OF GOD–ABSTAIN FROM FORNICATION	97
THE WORDS OF GOD EDIFY TRUE CHRISTIANS	152
THE WORLD'S GREATEST LOVE	86
THE WRATH OF THE LAMB OF GOD	147
THEIR GENUINE FAITH WAS KNOWN WORLDWIDE	76
thelo	266
THESE SERVANTS LOVED THE THESSALONIANS	44
thief	134-138, 168
thief in the night	134-136
THINGS WORKING TOGETHER FOR GOOD	160
thorn in the flesh	17, 284
three characteristics	6, 36
THREE CHARACTERISTICS ABOUT TIMOTHY	6
three rules	165

three tenses... 30, 252
THREE TENSES OF GOD'S SALVATION....................... 252
throughout the world. 186
TIMOTHY BROUGHT GOOD NEWS ABOUT THEM............. 74
TIMOTHY INTRODUCED..................................... 65
Timothy Was A Brother In Christ. 65
Timothy Was A Fellowlabourer In The Gospel. 65
Timothy Was A Minister Of God............................... 65
Timothy Was To Establish Them In The Faith. 66
tongue..................................... 40, 107, 157, 227, 233
tough love... 191
traditions. 241, 243, 244, 260
translation. 53, 99, 105, 113, 179, 242
translations... 56, 149, 179
TREAT ELDERS AS YOU SHOULD TREAT FATHERS. 52
trecho. 250
tribulation.. 30, 49, 61, 68, 70, 71, 89, 121, 124-127, 130, 131, 133-139,
    146, 147, 151, 157, 186, 189, 192, 193, 197, 199, 200, 207,
    208, 211, 215, 216, 219, 220, 223, 228, 230, 246, 247, 252, 281
TRIBULATION CAN'T SEPARATE FROM CHRIST'S LOVE....... 71
tried... 57, 250
TRUE CHRISTIAN FAITH WAS SPREAD ABROAD............... 77
true Christian love...................... 86, 87, 112, 113, 192
TRUE CHRISTIANS ARE LIKE GOD'S EPISTLES. 16
TRUE CHRISTIANS CAN COMFORT ONE ANOTHER. 68, 75
TRUE CHRISTIANS CANNOT LOSE THEIR SALVATION. 256
TRUE CHRISTIANS REJOICE WITH UNSPEAKABLE JOY...... 162
TRUE CHRISTIANS SHOULD HOLD FAST THEIR FAITH!...... 169
TRUE CHRISTIANS SHOULD JUDGE RIGHTEOUSLY. 171
TRUE CHRISTIANS SHOULD STAND FAST IN CHRIST. 241
TRUE CHRISTIANS WILL NOT PERISH IN HELL. 234
TRUE CHRISTIANS' BODIES TRANSFORMED.................. 93
TRUE CHRISTIANS–WITH CHRIST IN GLORY................ 207
true church.. 14, 86, 106, 239
trumpet.. 127-129, 216
tupos... 263
TWO PHASES OF CHRIST'S COMING......................... 92
unashamed lives. 218
unbiblical government. 26
UNBIBLICAL GOVERNMENT ORDERS DISOBEYED............ 26
unbiblical teachers... 191
UNBIBLICAL TEACHERS MUST BE REBUKED SHARPLY...... 191
unblameable................. 47, 48, 89, 92, 112, 190, 207, 247, 255

uncleanness. 7, 36, 92, 102, 103, 107, 110, 111
UNITED TO GLORIFY GOD AND CHRIST. 212
unspeakable joy. 162
VARIOUS GROUPS ARE DRIFTING BADLY TODAY. 78
Verses About Affliction. 68
Verses About Being Thankful. 163
Verses About Comfort. 151
Verses About Comforting. 157
Verses About Condemnation And Damnation. 237
Verses About Deceit. 233
Verses About Edifying. 152
Verses About Evil. 159
Verses About Faith. 76
Verses About Good. 159
Verses About Joy And Rejoicing. 161
Verses About Laboring For The Lord. 153
Verses About Lies, Lying, And Liars. 235
Verses About Prayer. 162
Verses About Quenching. 165
Verses About Satan. 72, 228
Verses About Supporting The Weak. 158
Verses About Tribulation. 70
Verses About Warning And Unruly. 156
Verses From Daniel About The Antichrist. 223
Verses On Abstaining From Things. 170
Verses On Appearances. 170
Verses On Being Established. 66, 89, 247
Verses On Being Established In The Faith. 66
Verses On Being Gentle. 43
Verses On Being Honest. 118
Verses On Being Obedient To The Lord. 265
Verses On Being Quiet. 115
Verses On Characteristics Of The Bible. 53
Verses On Chosen, Election, And Sanctification. 239
Verses On Comfort. 67, 74, 247
Verses On Confidence. 256
Verses On Departing From Sin And Evil. 100
Verses On Doing Business. 116
Verses On Faith. 189
Verses On Flattery. 40
Verses On Following The Proper Leaders. 19
VERSES ON GOD'S GRACE. 283
Verses On God's Recompensing. 197

Verses On Grace. 187
Verses On Having Joy In God The Holy Spirit. 23
Verses On Holiness. 111
Verses On Hope. 245
Verses On Judgment. 194, 200
Verses On Loving Unrighteous Pleasures.. 238
Verses On NEPHO Or NEPHALEOS. 140
Verses On Not Sleeping. 141
Verses On Paul's Fivefold Indictment.. 59
Verses On Paul's Persecution.. 57
Verses On Peace.. .... 155, 188, 280
Verses On Pleasing God. 97
Verses On Sanctification.. 105
Verses On Sorrow. 122
Verses On Stablish.. 254
Verses On Thanks. 78
Verses On Thanksgiving. 6
Verses On The Breastplate. 144
Verses On The Christians' Walk.. 95
Verses On The Coming Of Christ To Judge. 124
Verses On The Coming Of The Lord. 92
Verses On The Day Of The Lord. 135
Verses On The Gospel And Faith In It. 16
Verses On The Gospel Preached. 17, 18
Verses On The Helmet. 145
Verses On The Meaning Of Sleep As Death. 123
Verses On The Rest Found In Christ.. 199
Verses On The Sin Of Fornication. 100
Verses On The Will Of God.. 98
Verses On The Word Of The Lord. 250
Verses On Things "Lacking". 84
Verses On True Christian Character Traits. 47
Verses On True Christian love. 86, 112
Verses On True Christians' Future In Heaven. 62
Verses On Uncleanness.. 110
Verses On Vessels. 104
Verses On Waiting For Christ's Coming. 258
Verses On Watching. 141
Verses On Weariness.. 272
Verses On Working And Labor. 266
Verses That Mention Thessalonica. 1, 183
Verses That Mention Thessalonica or The Thessalonians. 1
Verses Where Christ Died For All People. 148

vessel. 104-106
vessels of clay. 104
VESSELS OF HONOR OR DISHONOR. 104
VICTORY AT THE BATTLE OF ARMAGEDDON. 92, 136
victory in Christ. 79
views about the rapture. 126
virgin. 185, 222
vital. 44, 53, 149, 153, 181, 189, 242, 259
Waite. .... 1, i-iii, 1, 25, 250
waiting. 29, 30, 85, 86, 92, 93, 144, 217, 218, 258, 273
waiting for Christ. 85, 258
waiting on the Lord. 273
WAITING ON THE LORD RENEWS STRENGTH. 273
walk worthy. 52, 53, 210, 240, 241
walking. ... 6, 52, 81, 94, 96, 193, 200, 210, 236, 259-261, 273, 274, 277
WALKING IN SPIRITUAL DARKNESS, NOT LIGHT. 236
walking worthy. 52, 210
WALKING WORTHY BY FOLLOWING GOD'S WORDS. 210
war in the heart. 137
warfare. 50, 155, 267
warning. 83, 154, 156, 264, 279
watchmen. 33, 156
we don't deserve. 181
WE MUST WAR A GOOD WARFARE. 50
weak. 6, 124, 141, 152, 155, 156, 158, 254, 269
weariness. 272, 273
Website: www.BibleForToday.org. i
WHAT HAPPENS AT THE RAPTURE?. 127
WHEN FATHERS LEAVE, THE CHILDREN ARE ORPHANS. 60
wilderness. 121, 167, 168
will of God. 7, 13, 28, 30, 31, 82, 83, 85, 97-100, 163, 165, 170, 240, 252
with Christ forever. 215
With The Lord Jesus Christ. 30, 63, 89, 122-125, 129, 134, 151, 191,
193, 196, 207, 216, 236, 280
WITHDRAW FROM DISORDERLY CHRISTIANS. 277
withdrawal. 260
women. 2, 3, 6, 13, 16, 38, 43, 57, 92, 107, 112, 135, 163, 169,
196-198, 204, 223, 226, 269, 270
wonders. 111, 221, 228, 231, 232
Words of God. .... iii, 1, 2, 16, 21, 23, 26, 27, 43, 46, 53-56, 69,
70, 72, 75, 81, 90, 95, 105, 106, 112, 114, 134, 143, 152, 154,
156, 160, 163, 176, 179-181, 183, 229, 238, 243, 250, 259,
264, 270, 274, 279, 286

Words Of God Are Powerful. 55
Words Of God Are Right. 53
Words Of God Are Righteous. 55
Words Of God Are Something To Preach. 55
Words Of God Are The Sword Of The Spirit. 55
Words Of God Can Bring New Birth. 56
Words Of God Can Bring Rejoicing. 54
Words Of God Can Build Up. 55
Words Of God Can Cleanse. 53
Words Of God Can Comfort. 54
Words Of God Can Convince The Unbelievers. 55
Words Of God Can Give Accurate Prophecy. 56
Words Of God Can Give Faith. 55
Words Of God Can Give Growth. 56
Words Of God Can Give Hope. 54
Words Of God Can Give Nourishment. 55
Words Of God Can Give Reconciliation. 55
Words Of God Can Give Understanding. 54
Words Of God Can Keep From Evil Ways. 54
Words Of God Can Keep From Iniquity. 54
Words Of God Can Keep From Straying. 54
Words Of God Can Keep From Transgression. 54
Words Of God Can Light Our Feet And Path. 54
Words Of God Can Prevent From Sinning. 53
Words Of God Can Sanctify And Cleanse. 54
Words Of God Can Strengthen. 54
Words Of God Give The Gospel. 56
WORK QUIETLY WITHOUT COMPLAINING. 118
working together for good. 160
works. 9, 28, 83, 90, 96, 102, 110, 117, 118, 120, 136, 141,
           143, 144, 150, 160, 187, 188, 196, 200, 205, 211, 241,
           250, 255, 275, 276, 283, 284
WORKS AS A PROOF OF TRUE FAITH. 83
worldly. 188, 242, 276, 277
worthy. 26, 38, 45, 52, 53, 153, 174, 177, 194, 208-211, 238, 240,
           241, 264, 269, 270
wrath. 29-31, 59, 102, 108, 110, 127, 135, 146, 147, 154, 196, 200,
           201, 204, 226, 228, 253, 279
wrath of the Lamb. 147
yield. 56, 91, 110, 111, 256
"ASLEEP" HERE REFERS TO DEATH. 121
"DAY OF THE LORD" DURING TRIBULATION PERIOD. 134
"DIED FOR ALL" MEANS ALL PEOPLE. 149

About The Author

The author of this book, Dr. D. A. Waite, received a B.A. (Bachelor of Arts) in classical Greek and Latin from the University of Michigan in 1948, a Th.M. (Master of Theology), with high honors, in New Testament Greek Literature and Exegesis from Dallas Theological Seminary in 1952, an M.A. (Master of Arts) in Speech from Southern Methodist University in 1953, a Th.D. (Doctor of Theology), with honors, in Bible Exposition from Dallas Theological Seminary in 1955, and a Ph.D. in Speech from Purdue University in 1961. He held both New Jersey and Pennsylvania teacher certificates in Greek and Language Arts.

He has been a teacher in the areas of Greek, Hebrew, Bible, Speech, and English for over thirty-five years in ten schools, including one junior high, one senior high, four Bible institutes, two colleges, two universities, and one seminary. He served his country as a Navy Chaplain for five years on active duty; pastored three churches; was Chairman and Director of the Radio and Audio-Film Commission of the American Council of Christian Churches; since 1969, has been Founder, President, and Director of THE BIBLE FOR TODAY; since 1978, has been Founder and President of the DEAN BURGON SOCIETY; has produced over 700 other studies, books, cassettes, VHS's, CD's, or VCR's on various topics; and is often heard on a thirty-minute weekly radio program IN DEFENSE OF TRADITIONAL BIBLE TEXTS, on radio, shortwave, and streaming on the Internet at BibleForToday.org, 24/7/365 on the BROWN BOX.

Dr. and Mrs. Waite have been married since 1948; they have four sons, one daughter, and, at present, eight grandchildren, and fifteen great-grandchildren. Since October 4, 1998, he has been the Pastor of the Bible For Today Baptist Church in Collingswood, New Jersey. His sermons are heard both on radio and the Internet over www.BibleForToday.org on the BROWN BOX.

Order Blank (p. 1)

Name:_____
Address:_____
City & State:_____Zip:_____
Credit Card #:_____Expires:_____

Verse by Verse Preaching Books By Dr. D. A. Waite

[ ] Send *1 & 2 Thessalonians–Preaching Verse By Verse* By Pastor D. A. Waite, 327 pages ($15.00 + $8.00 S&H) fully indexed.
[ ] Send *Hebrews–Preaching Verse by Verse*, By Pastor D. A. Waite, 616 pages ($30.00 +$10.00 S&H) fully indexed.
[ ] Send *Revelation–Preaching Verse by Verse*, By Pastor D. A. Waite, 1032 pages ($50.00 + $10.00 S&H) fully indexed.
[ ] Send *1 Timothy--Preaching Verse by Verse*, by Pastor D. A. Waite, 288 pages, hardback ($11+$5 S&H) fully indexed.
[ ] Send *2 Timothy--Preaching Verse by Verse*, by Pastor D. A. Waite, 250 pages, hardback ($11+$5 S&H) fully indexed.
[ ] Send *Romans--Preaching Verse by Verse* by Pastor D. A. Waite 736 pp. Hardback ($25+$8 S&H) fully indexed
[ ] Send *Colossians & Philemon--Preaching Verse by Verse* by Pastor D. A. Waite ($12+$5 S&H) hardback, 240 pages.
[ ] Send *Philippians--Preaching Verse by Verse* by Pastor D. A. Waite ($10+$5 S&H) hardback, 176 pages. fully indexed.
[ ] Send *Ephesians--Preaching Verse by Verse* by Pastor D. A. Waite ($12+$5 S&H) hardback, 224 pages. fully indexed.
[ ] Send *Galatians--Preaching Verse By Verse* by Pastor D. A. Waite ($12+$5 S&H) hardback, 216 pages. fully indexed.
[ ] Send *1 Peter–Preaching Verse By Verse* by Pastor D. A. Waite ($10.00 + $5.00 S&H) hardback, 176 pages. fully indexed.

Other Books By Dr. D. A. Waite

[ ] Send *A Critical Answer to God's Word Preserved* by Pastor D. A. Waite, 192 pp. perfect bound ($11.00+$4.00 S&H)
[ ] Send *Defending the King James Bible* by DAW ($12+$5 S&H) A hardback book, indexed with study questions.
[ ] Send *BJU's Errors on Bible Preservation* by Dr. D. A. Waite, 110 pages, paperback ($8+$4 S&H) fully indexed

Send or Call Orders to:
THE BIBLE FOR TODAY
900 Park Ave., Collingswood, NJ 08108
Phone: 856-854-4452; FAX:--2464; Orders: 1-800 JOHN 10:9
E-Mail Orders: BFT@BibleForToday.org; Credit Cards OK

Order Blank (p. 2)

Name:_____
Address:_____
City & State:_____Zip:_____
Credit Card #:_____Expires:_____

Other Books By Dr. D. A. Waite (Continued)

[ ] Send *Fundamentalist Deception on Bible Preservation* by Dr. D. A. Waite, ($8+$4 S&H), paperback, fully indexed
[ ] Send *Fundamentalist MIS-INFORMATION on Bible Versions* by Dr. Waite ($7+$4 S&H) perfect bound, 136 pages
[ ] Send *Fundamentalist Distortions on Bible Versions* by Dr. Waite ($6+$3 S&H) A perfect bound book, 80 pages
[ ] Send *Fuzzy Facts From Fundamentalists* by Dr. D. A. Waite ($8.00 + $4.00) printed booklet
[ ] Send *Foes of the King James Bible Refuted* by DAW ($10 +$4 S&H) A perfect bound book, 164 pages in length.
[ ] Send *Central Seminary Refuted on Bible Versions* by Dr. Waite ($10+$4 S&H) A perfect bound book, 184 pages
[ ] Send *The Case for the King James Bible* by DAW ($7 +$3 S&H) A perfect bound book, 112 pages in length.
[ ] Send *Theological Heresies of Westcott and Hort* by Dr. D. A. Waite, ($7+$3 S&H) A printed booklet.
[ ] Send *Westcott's Denial of Resurrection*, Dr. Waite ($4+$3)
[ ] Send *Four Reasons for Defending KJB* by DAW ($3+$3)
[ ] Send *Holes in the Holman Christian Standard Bible* by Dr. Waite ($3+$2 S&H) A printed booklet, 40 pages
[ ] Send *Contemporary Eng. Version Exposed*, DAW ($3+$2)
[ ] Send *NIV Inclusive Language Exposed* by DAW ($5+$3)
[ ] Send *26 Hours of KJB Seminar* (4 videos) by DAW ($50.00)
[ ] Send *Making Marriage Melodious* by Pastor D. A. Waite ($7+$4 S&H), perfect bound, 112 pages.
[ ] Send *Burgon's Warnings on Revision* by DAW ($7+$4 S&H) A perfect bound book, 120 pages in length.
[ ] Send *The Superior Foundation of the KJB* By Dr. D. A. Waite ($10.00 + $7.00 S&H)

Send or Call Orders to:
THE BIBLE FOR TODAY
900 Park Ave., Collingswood, NJ 08108
Phone: 856-854-4452; FAX:--2464; Orders: 1-800 JOHN 10:9
E-Mail Orders: BFT@BibleForToday.org; Credit Cards OK

Order Blank (p. 3)

Name:_____
Address:_____
City & State:_____Zip:_____
Credit Card #:_____Expires:_____

Other Books By Dr. D. A. Waite (Continued)

[ ] Send *Biblical Separation–1,896 Bible Verses About It* by Dr. D. A. Waite ($14.00 + $7.00 S&H)
[ ] Send *Westcott & Hort's Greek Text & Theory Refuted by Burgon's Revision Revised--Summarized* by Dr. D. A. Waite ($7.00+$4 S&H), 120 pages, perfect bound.
[ ] Send *Dean Burgon's Confidence in KJB* by DAW ($3+$3)
[ ] Send *Vindicating Mark 16:9-20* by Dr. Waite ($3+$3S&H)
[ ] Send *Summary of Traditional Text* by Dr. Waite ($3 +$3)
[ ] Send *Summary of Causes of Corruption*, DAW ($3+$3)
[ ] Send *Summary of Inspiration* by Dr. Waite ($3+$3 S&H)
[ ] Send *Soulwinning's Versions-Perversions* By Dr. D. A. Waite ($6.00 + $5.00 S&H)

Books By Dean John William Burgon

[ ] Send *The Revision Revised* by Dean Burgon ($25 + $5 S&H) A hardback book, 640 pages in length.
[ ] Send *The Last 12 verses of Mark* by Dean Burgon ($15+$5 S&H) A hardback book 400 pages.
[ ] Send *The Traditional Text* hardback by Burgon ($16+$5 S&H) A hardback book, 384 pages in length.
[ ] Send *Causes of Corruption* by Burgon ($15+$5 S&H) A hardback book, 360 pages in length.
[ ] Send *Inspiration and Interpretation*, Dean Burgon ($25+$5 S&H) A hardback book, 610 pages in length.

Books By Dr. Jack Moorman

[ ] Send *Samuel P. Tregelles--The Man Who Made the Critical Text Acceptable to Bible Believers* by Dr. Moorman ($2+$1)
[ ] Send *8,000 Differences Between TR & CT* by Dr. Jack Moorman [$65 + $7.50 S&H] Over 500-large-pages of data [ ] Send *356 Doctrinal Errors in the NIV & Other Modern Versions*, 100-large-pages, $10.00+$6 S&H.

Send or Call Orders to:
THE BIBLE FOR TODAY
900 Park Ave., Collingswood, NJ 08108
Phone: 856-854-4452; FAX:--2464; Orders: 1-800 JOHN 10:9

Order Blank (p. 4)

Name:_____
Address:_____
City & State:_____Zip:_____
Credit Card #:_____Expires:_____

More Books By Dr. Jack Moorman

[ ] Send *The Doctrinal Heart of the Bible--Removed from Modern Versions* by Dr. Jack Moorman, VCR, $15 +$4 S&H
[ ] Send *Modern Bibles--The Dark Secret* by Dr. Jack Moorman, $5+$3 S&H
[ ] Send *The Manuscript Digest of the N.T.* (721 pp.) By Dr. Jack Moorman, copy-machine bound ($50+$7 S&H)
[ ] *Early Manuscripts, Church Fathers, & the Authorized Version* by Dr. Jack Moorman, $18+$5 S&H. Hardback
[ ] Send *Forever Settled--Bible Documents & History Survey* by Dr. Jack Moorman, $20+$5 S&H. Hardback book.
[ ] Send *When the KJB Departs from the So-Called "Majority Text"* by Dr. Jack Moorman, $16+$5 S&H
[ ] Send *Missing in Modern Bibles--Nestle-Aland/NIV Errors* by Dr. Jack Moorman, $8+$4 S&H

Books By Miscellaneous Authors

[ ] Send *Guide to Textual Criticism* by Edward Miller ($7+$4) Hardback book
[ ] Send *Scrivener's Greek New Testament Underlying the King James Bible*, hardback, ($14+$5 S&H)
[ ] Send *Scrivener's <u>Annotated</u> Greek New Testament*, by Dr. Frederick Scrivener: Hardback--($35+$5 S&H); Genuine Leather--($45+$5 S&H)
[ ] Send *Why Not the King James Bible?--An Answer to James White's KJVO Book* by Dr. K. D. DiVietro, $10+$5 S&H
[ ] Send Brochure #1: *"1000 Titles Defending the KJB/TR"* No Charge
[ ] Send *The LIE That Changed the Modern World* by Dr. H. D. Williams ($16+$5 S&H) Hardback book
[ ] Send *With Tears in My Heart* by Gertrude G. Sanborn. Hardback 414 pp. ($25+$5 S&H) 400 Christian Poems

Send or Call Orders to:
THE BIBLE FOR TODAY
900 Park Ave., Collingswood, NJ 08108
Phone: 856-854-4452; FAX:--2464; Orders: 1-800 JOHN 10:9

Order Blank (p. 5)

Name:_____
Address:_____
City & State:_____Zip:_____
Credit Card #:_____Expires:____

More Books By Miscellaneous Authors

[ ] Send *Able To Bear It* By Gertrude Sanborn ($14.00 + $7.00 S&H
[ ] Send *Visitation In Action* By Mr. R. O. Sanborn ($10.00 + $7.00 S&H)
[ ] Send *Daily Bible Blessings From Daily Bible Readings* By Yvonne Sanborn Waite ($30.00 + $10.00 S&H)
[ ] Send *Husband-Loving Lessons* By Yvonne Sanborn Waite ($25.00 + $8.00 S&H)
[ ] Send *Gnosticism–The Doctrinal Foundation of New Bibles* by J. Moser ($20.00 + $8.00 S&H)
[ ] Send *Dean Burgon's Defense of the Authorised Version* By Dr. David Bennett ($14.0 + 8.00 S&H)
[ ] Send *Drift in Baptist Missions, Churches & Schools* by Dr. David Bennett ($12.00 + $8.00 S&H)
[ ] Send *God's Marvelous Book* By Dr. David Bennett ($15.00 + $8.00 S&H)
[ ] Send *CCM Not The Problem–Only A Symptom* By Dr. David Bennett ($12.00 + $7.00 S&H)
[ ] Send *English Standard Bible (ESV) Deficiencies* By several authors ($7.00 + $4.00 S&H)
[ ] Send *Strong's Micro-Print Concordance* By the Sherbornes ($21.00 + $8.00 S&H)

Books by D. A. Waite, Jr.

[ ] Send *The Doctored New Testament* by D. A. Waite, Jr. ($25+$5 S&H) Greek MSS differences shown, hardback
[ ] Send *Readability of A.V. (KJB)* by D. A. Waite, Jr. ($6+$3)
[ ] Send *4,114 Definitions from the Defined King James Bible* by D. A. Waite, Jr. ($7.00+$4.00 S&H)

Send or Call Orders to:
THE BIBLE FOR TODAY
900 Park Ave., Collingswood, NJ 08108
Phone: 856-854-4452; FAX:--2464; Orders: 1-800 JOHN 10:9
E-Mail Orders: BFT@BibleForToday.org; Credit Cards OK

Order Blank (p. 6)

Name:_____
Address:_____
City & State:_____Zip:_____
Credit Card #:_____Expires:_____

Question And Answer Books By Dr. D. A. Waite

[ ] Send *The First 200 Questions Answered* By Dr. D. A. Waite ($15.00 + $7.00 S&H)

[ ] Send *The Second 200 Questions Answered* By Dr. D. A. Waite ($15.00 + $7.00 S&H)

[ ] Send *The Third 200 Questions Answered* By Dr. D. A. Waite ($15.00 + $7.00 S&H)

[ ] Send *The Fourth 200 Questions Answered* By Dr. D. A. Waite ($15.00 + $7.00 S&H)

[ ] Send *The Fifth 200 Questions Answered* By Dr. D. A. Waite ($15.00 + $7.00 S&H)

[ ] Send *The Sixth 200 Questions Answered* By Dr. D. A. Waite ($15.00 + $7.00 S&H)

Send or Call Orders to:
THE BIBLE FOR TODAY
900 Park Ave., Collingswood, NJ 08108
Phone: 856-854-4452; FAX:--2464; Orders: 1-800 JOHN 10:9
E-Mail Orders: BFT@BibleForToday.org; Credit Cards OK

The Defined King James Bible

Uncommon Words Defined Accurately

I. Deluxe Genuine Leather

◆Large Print--Black or Burgundy◆

1 for $44.00+$12.00 S&H

◆Case of 12 for◆

$34.00 each+$50.00 S&H

◆Medium Print--Black or Burgundy◆

1 for $39.00+$8.00 S&H

◆Case of 12 for◆

$29.00 each+$40.00 S&H

II. Deluxe Hardback Editions

1 for $22.00+12.00 S&H (Large Print)

◆Case of 12 for◆

$17.00 each+$40.00 S&H (Large Print)

1 for $19.50+$8.00 S&H (Medium Print)

◆Case of 12 for◆

$12.50 each+$30.00 S&H (Medium Print)

Order Phone:1-800-JOHN 10:9

Pastor D. A. Waite, Th.D., Ph.D.

The Lord Jesus Christ's Return

The Description Of The Two Phases Of His Return.
The first phase of the return of the Lord Jesus Christ is when He comes back in the air at the Rapture. The second phase of His return is when He comes back to earth to begin His thousand-year Millennial reign of peace.

The Time Of The Two Phases Of His Return.
The first phase of Christ's return in the air at the Rapture is imminent. It can occur at any time. There are no prophecies that must be fulfilled prior to it. The second phase of His return to earth for His thousand-year Millennial reign will be preceded by the Rapture followed by the seven-year Tribulation Period and the Battle of Armageddon.

The People Involved In Christ's Return.
The people who are genuinely saved Christians from the Day of Pentecost to the Rapture will take part in the first phase of the coming of the Lord Jesus Christ. They will receive their glorified bodies at that time. The people who survive the seven-year Tribulation and the Battle of Armageddon will take part in the peaceful thousand-year reign of the Lord Jesus Christ on the earth.

Living In The Light Of Christ's Return.
The genuine Christians who have been born-again by true faith in the Lord Jesus Christ as their Saviour should live every moment of their days in anticipation of meeting the Lord Jesus Christ in the air at His coming in the Rapture. They should *"abide in Him"* that *"when he shall appear"* they should *"not be ashamed before Him at His coming"* (1 John 2:28). They should be *"Looking for that blessed hope, and the glorious appearing of the great God and our Saviour Jesus Christ"* (Titus 2:13).

www.BibleForToday.org

BFT 4137   ISBN #978-1-56848-102-9

www.ingramcontent.com/pod-product-compliance
Lightning Source LLC
Chambersburg PA
CBHW051035160426
43193CB00010B/952